THE

BIG BASICS

BOOK OF

WINDOWS® 95

Second Edition

by Shelley O'Hara, Faithe Wempen,
Dan Bobola, and Ed Guilford

A Division of Macmillan Computer Publishing
A Prentice Hall Macmillan Company
201 West 103rd Street, Indianapolis, Indiana 46290 USA

International Standard Book Number: 07897-1222-9
Library of Congress Catalog Card Number: 97-65529

99 98 97   5 4

Interpretation of the printing code: the rightmost number of the first series of numbers is the year of the book's printing; the rightmost number of the second series of numbers is the number of the book's printing. For example, a printing code of 97-1 shows that the first printing of the book occurred in 1997.

Screen reproductions in this book were created by means of the program Collage Complete from Inner Media, Inc., Hollis, NH.

Printed in the United States of America

Publisher
Roland Elgey

Publishing Director
Lynn Zingraf

Marketing Manager
Barry Pruett

Editorial Services Director
Elizabeth Keaffaber

Managing Editor
Tom Hayes

Development Editors
John Gosney
Nancy Price Warner

Production Editor
Linda Seifert

Cover Designer
Dan Armstrong

Book Designer
Anne Dickerson

Indexer
Chris Wilcox

Production Team
Tammy Ahrens
Lissa Auciello-Brogan
Kathleen Caulfield
Jerry Cole
Michelle Croninger
Toi Davis
Dana Davis
Natalie Hollifield
Joy Dean Lee
Pete Lippincott
Kevin J. MacDonald
Candyce McCreary
Stephanie Mohler
Angel Perez
Linda Quigley
Karen Teo

➤ *Special thanks to Rick Brown, Don Funk, Curtis Knight, and Keith Underdahl for ensuring the technical accuracy of this book.*

Contents

Part 1 How to...

Use MultimediaPrograms   239

Get Your DOS Programs to Run   257

Communicate with Other Computers   275

Use the Microsoft Network and the Internet   307

Maintain Your System   337

Use Windows 95 on a Network   367

Part 2   Do It Yourself...

Get It Done with the Accessories   395

Use the Control Panel to Customize Windows 95   427

Perform Common Housekeeping Chores   471

Get the Most from Your Laptop with Windows 95   489

Part 3   Quick Fixes...

Questions and Answers   507

Part 4   Handy References

Introduction

Computers in general are supposed to make your life easier, and Windows 95 in particular was designed to make using a computer easier. But is it easy to use? By comparison, Windows 95 is much more attractive and much more intuitive than other operating systems. (The operating system is what you use to start the computer and run programs.) However, even with Windows 95, it's not easy for a new user to just sit down and start using the computer without some help.

Why This Book?

When you start using your computer, you may wish you had a book that would show you what to do—a visual guide like those hardware store books that show you how to build a deck or landscape your house. Well, here's the book for you. *The Big Basics Book of Windows 95, Second Edition* provides *Guided Tours* that show you which keys to press and which commands to select. By following the step-by-step, picture-by-picture presentations, you learn all the basics you need to know to run Windows 95.

Where's the Information I Need?

How you use this book is basically up to you. You can read the book from cover to cover to move through the tasks in a logical progression, you can jump around, or you can use the table of contents and the index to quickly find specific information. In addition, running heads at the top of each page show you which chapter you're in and which task you're on, so you can simply flip through the book to scan for a topic.

We've divided this book into four parts so you can quickly find the specific information you need:

- *Part 1: How to* covers all the skills that a new or casual Windows user needs. You learn how to start Windows, run and use Windows applications (programs), organize your disks and files, and use the popular accessories that come with Windows. Each task leads you step by step through the basics. To find out more about each task, read the accompanying explanation.

- *Part 2: Do It Yourself* shows you how to apply the skills you learned in Part 1 to create real projects. You'll learn how to create an attractive letterhead in WordPad, customize Windows, connect to one of the popular online services, and much more.

- *Part 3: Quick Fixes* provides quick answers to your questions and quick solutions to your problems. When an error message pops up in Windows, you'll be able to stare the problem down and get up and running in a snap. Quick Finder tables help you zero in on the solution that's right for you.

- *Part 4: Handy References* is a collection of reference information: keyboard shortcuts, comparison of Windows 3.1 and Windows 95, and more.

Conventions, Conventions, Conventions

This book was specially designed to make it easy to use. Each task has a title that tells you what you'll be doing. Immediately following the title is a *Guided Tour*, which shows you step by step how to perform the task. Each *Guided Tour* has additional text that tells you why you might want to perform the task and provides additional details on what to do. The following figure shows you the format of the book.

Running heads help you find what you want to learn.

Tips provide shortcuts or reference other useful information.

Additional information answers all your questions.

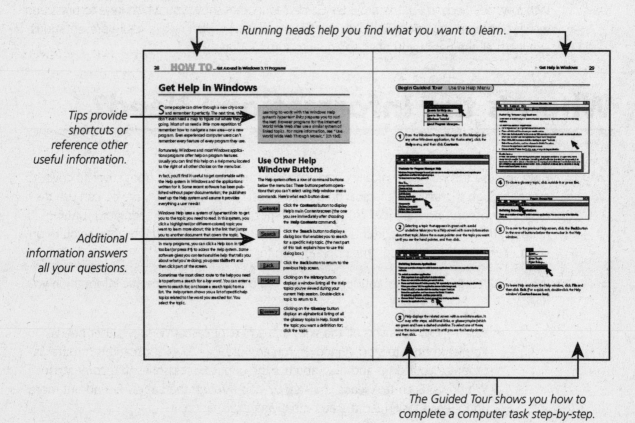

The Guided Tour shows you how to complete a computer task step-by-step.

The following special conventions were used to make the book easier to use:

Text you are supposed to type appears bold. For example, if the step says, type **win** and press **Enter**, type the command "win" and press the Enter key on your keyboard.

Keys you are supposed to press are bold, too, to make them easier to spot.

Key+Key combinations are used when you have to press two or more keys to enter a command. When you encounter one of these combinations, hold down the first key and press the second key.

Menu names and **commands** you need to choose are also bold. When you're told to open a menu and select a command, move the mouse pointer over it, and press and release the left mouse button.

Look for these sidebars for tips, hints, and shortcuts.

Trademarks

Terms suspected of being trademarks or service marks have been appropriately capitalized. Que Corporation cannot attest to the accuracy of this information. Use of a term in this book should not be regarded as affecting the validity of any trademark or service mark.

PART 1

How To...

When you want to learn how to do something in Windows 95, look in this part. This part covers the major features of Windows 95 and provides easy-to-follow illustrated steps for hundreds of tasks. You simply turn to the topic you want and follow the *Guided Tour*. For example, if you need to copy a file or install new fonts, you'll find everything you need to know in this part.

This part is broken down into the following sections:

What You Will Find in This Part

HOW TO...

Master Windows Basics

Ready to get started using Windows 95? Want to know what's new? Want to know what appears on the screen in Windows 95—and what you can do with those tools that do appear? Then this section is the right place to start.

In this section, you first learn how to install and start Windows. Then you learn some fundamental tasks that will help you not only in Windows, but in all Windows applications.

This section covers the following topics:

What You Will Find in This Section

Highlight of What's New

If you are new to Windows 95, you are lucky because the whole interface (what you see on-screen and how you use the program) has been designed to make it as easy to use as possible. Microsoft focused on the results of usability tests and designed the program so that a beginner could start Windows and get to work immediately. You can review this section if you are interested in the changes. Otherwise, just skip this task on what's new because everything will be new for you.

> If you are upgrading from Windows 3.1 to Windows 95, review Part 4 for a detailed table that compares the two versions of Windows.

If you use Windows 3.1 and are upgrading to Windows 95, you'll notice some significant changes (the most obvious being the drastically redesigned interface). But take heart. The changes are designed to make Windows easier to use. At first, you may wonder what happened to a certain feature or how you perform a certain task. However, once you master the basics of Windows 95 with the help of this book, you should find that you can do all the things you did in Windows 3.1—but more efficiently.

The following list summarizes the major areas in which Windows 95 differs from Windows 3.1, as well as where you can find additional information about the changes:

- The desktop (what you see when you start Windows) has been redesigned. For information on what appears on-screen, see "Understand the Desktop" on page 9.

- You now use the Start button to start a program instead of opening program groups and finding program icons. For help on starting programs, see "Start and Exit a Program" on page 42.

- Switching among programs is made simpler with the taskbar, which appears along the bottom of the screen. See "Switch Between Open Applications" on page 50.

- Because most users found Windows 3.1's File Manager difficult and cumbersome to understand, Microsoft left it out of Windows 95. Instead, you can use Windows Explorer (a redesigned file management program) or My Computer to manage the folders (called directories in Windows 3.1) and files on your computer. You also can use the new Find command to search for a particular file on your computer. These features are covered in the section "Manage Folders and Files" on page 67.

- You can use the Documents command on the Start menu to open a document and start a program.

- You are not limited to eight characters for a file name and three characters for an extension (a file naming convention often abbreviated 8.3). In Windows 95, you can use long file names— up to 255 characters. Also, Windows 95 includes its own version of DOS.

- Other features, such as Print Manager and Control Panel, have the same purpose in Windows 95 that they did in Windows 3.1, but they have been redesigned. For example, the Control Panel includes a hardware wizard that leads you step by step through the process of installing a new piece of equipment (see "Use the Control Panel to Customize Windows 95" on page 427. For information on printing, flip to "Print Your Documents" on page 149.

- Windows 95 supports Plug and Play technology, which enables you to plug in the new hardware component and start using it right away. Turn to "Maintain Your System" on page 337 for help installing new hardware.

- Instead of Write and Paintbrush, Windows 95 includes a similar word processing program called WordPad and a similar paint program called Paint. You can find sections on how to use WordPad and Paint in Part 1, and Part 2 includes some projects using these programs.

- Windows 95 includes new features for networking, managing communication, and hooking up to Microsoft's online service, Microsoft Network. There is a section for each of these topics in Part 1.

There are, of course, many other changes and enhancements, which are covered throughout the rest of this book.

Begin Guided Tour A Look at Windows New Features

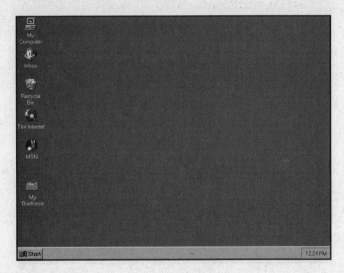

1 When you turn on the computer, Windows starts automatically, and you see the redesigned desktop.

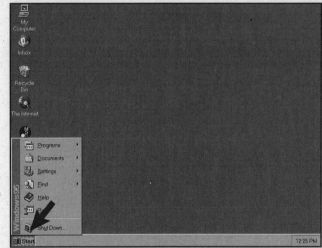

2 You use the Start button to start programs.

(continues)

Begin Guided Tour A Look at Windows New Features

(continued)

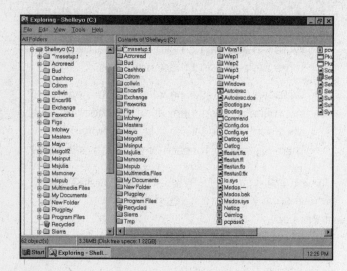

3 The Windows Explorer replaced File Manager. You can use Windows Explorer to manage the files and folders on your computer.

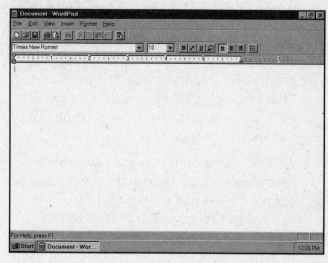

5 Windows 95 comes with a word processing program called WordPad. You can use this program to create simple documents.

4 You use the programs in the Control Panel to customize and set up your system.

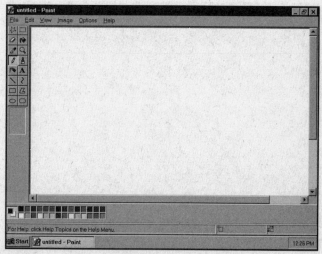

6 You can explore your artistic talents with the paint program, called Paint, included with Windows 95.

Start and Exit Windows

In previous versions of Windows, either you had to give a command to start Windows, or you had to set up your system so the command was given automatically each time you started the computer. This is not so with Windows 95. In this version, you simply turn on the computer, and Windows 95 starts automatically.

What else do you need to know about starting Windows? Consider the following ideas:

- If you turn on your computer and nothing happens, make sure you turned on both your monitor and your computer. Also, if you are using a power strip, make sure it is on and plugged in. If you are sure everything is turned on and still nothing happens, jump ahead to Part 3 "Quick Fixes" on page 505.

- If you are hooked up to a network, you may be prompted to log on to the network and type a password. Check with your system administrator for the proper steps to start Windows on your network.

- What you see on-screen depends on how you set up your desktop. In the next task, "Understand the Desktop" (page 9), I'll show you what you should see if you install Windows using the Typical option. For information on customizing the desktop, see the section "Use the Control panel to Customize Windows 95" on page 427.

- If you want, you can start a program each time you start Windows. To learn how to set up programs to start automatically, see "Set Up and Run Programs," page 39.

Shut Down Windows

It's not a good idea to just turn off the power switch when you are finished working in Windows. Why not? Well, before you turn off the computer, Windows needs to take care of some housekeeping tasks. Therefore, you should always use the Shut Down command when you are finished working on the computer and want to turn it off.

You also can use the Shut Down command to restart the computer. Sometimes a program makes changes to your overall system and requires that you exit and restart Windows. When that happens, you can use the Shut Down command to restart. Additionally, you can use the Shut Down command to restart the computer in MS-DOS mode. This option often is used to start MS-DOS programs (games in particular) that won't work in Windows. If you are running Windows 95 on a network, you may have the option to log on as a different user. See the section "Use Windows 95 on a Network" (page 367) for information on log on options.

You also may have a Suspend command that you can use to conserve power if you are using a portable computer.

Besides shutting down Windows using the proper command, you also should be sure to exit all programs properly before you exit Windows. First, save all documents that you are working on. Then exit all running programs (see "Start and Exit a Program" on page 42).

Begin Guided Tour   Start Windows

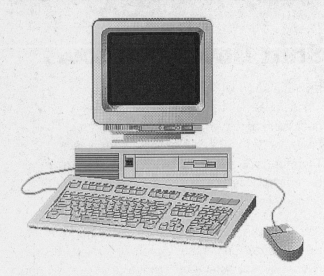

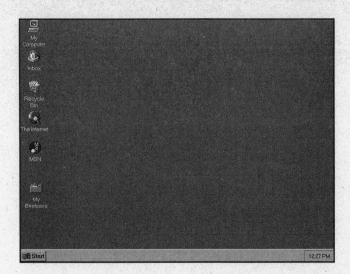

1 Turn on your computer and monitor.

2 Windows goes through its startup routine. You may see some commands and other information flash by on-screen. Eventually, the desktop appears.

Begin Guided Tour   Shut Down Windows

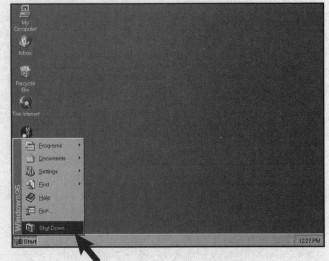

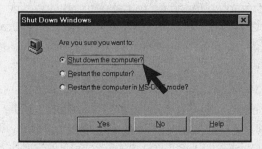

2 The Shut Down Windows dialog box appears, and asks you to confirm that you want to shut down Windows. Indicate whether you want to shut down the computer, restart the computer, or restart the computer in MS-DOS mode by clicking on the corresponding option button. Then click the **Yes** button.

1 Click on the **Start** button. The Start menu appears. Select the **Shut Down** command to shut down Windows.

Understand the Desktop

Just as you work on a desktop in your office or at home, you work on a desktop in Windows 95. And just as you have certain tools on your desktop (a stapler or scissors, for example), Windows 95 also has tools, called icons, on its desktop. Which tools you see depend on how your system is set up.

> You can customize the desktop to suit your needs and your way of working. See "Use the Control Panel to Customize Windows 95" on page 427 for information on some of the cosmetic changes you can make.

On the desktop, you'll see the following icons:

- **My Computer** Click on this icon to browse through the contents of your computer. Check out what's on disks in your floppy drive(s) or CD-ROM drive, or view the contents of your hard disk.

- **Network Neighborhood** If you are hooked up to a network, you will see this icon, with which you can browse through your network. For information on using a network, see "Use Windows 95 on a Network" on page 367.

- **Inbox** If you installed Microsoft Exchange when you installed Windows 95, your inbox appears on the desktop. See the section "Use Microsoft Exchange" (286) for help on using this icon.

- **Recycle Bin** Use this trash can to delete files, programs, and icons that you no longer need.

- **Online Services** Use this folder to set up subscriptions to online services such as America Online.

- **Internet** You may have an icon that provides access to the Internet.

- **Taskbar** At the bottom of the screen, you see the taskbar, which contains the Start button. You can use the Start button to start programs, get help, open documents, and more. The taskbar also displays a button for each program that is running; you can use the taskbar to switch quickly to any of the programs. Finally, the taskbar displays other information, such as the time.

You may also see other icons for programs you have added. For example, if you installed Microsoft Network, you'll see an icon for this program on your desktop.

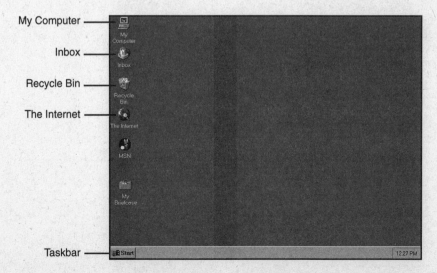

My Computer —
Inbox —
Recycle Bin —
The Internet —
Taskbar —

Begin Guided Tour   Understand the Desktop

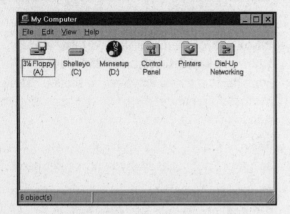

1 Use the My Computer icon to browse through the contents of your system.

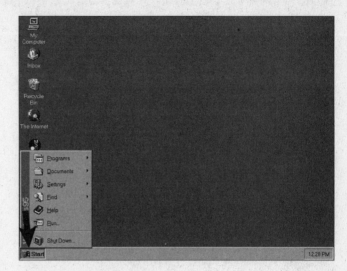

3 The Start button is where the action is in Windows 95. You use this button to start programs, open documents, get help, and customize Windows.

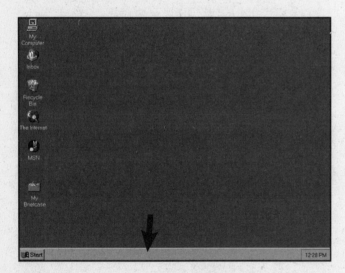

2 The taskbar includes the Start button and the time. The taskbar also displays a button for each program that is running, enabling you to quickly switch between programs.

Open and Close a Window

Windows gets its name from the on-screen areas, called windows, that appear when you use Windows. Everything you do in Windows is displayed in one of two types of windows: a *program window* or a *document window*. If you browse the contents of My Computer, the contents are displayed in a program window. If you start a program, that program is displayed in a program window. Once you've got a program window open, when you create a file (a memo, a letter, or a picture, for example), the program opens a document window. The name of the window appears in the top bar called the *title bar*.

It may be hard for a beginner to grasp the idea of a document window within a program window. When you are running a program and working in a document, you actually have two windows open: one for the program and one for the document. If you open a second document, you have two document windows, each of which has its own set of controls. If you close a document window, you close only the document; if you close the program window, you exit the program, and all documents are automatically closed.

While it may seem confusing to think of so many windows, you simply need to keep in mind that all windows work the same way: you open, close, move, resize, and scroll all windows the same way. That means once you learn the basics of working with windows, you can use those skills in any other program in Windows 95.

If you take a close look at the windows, you'll note that they all have the same controls. The following table describes those controls.

Icon	Name	Description
	Control menu icon	Click on this icon to display a drop-down menu of commands. You can use the commands to close, resize, move, and otherwise manipulate the window. Double-click this icon to close the window.
	Minimize button	Click on this button to reduce the window so it no longer appears on-screen. The window and program are still running, as indicated by a button on the taskbar. See the task "Change the Window Size" (page 13) for more information.
	Maximize button	Use this button to expand the window to fill the entire screen. See the task "Change the Window Size" (page 13) for more information.
	Restore button	When a window is maximized, you can use this button to restore the window to its previous size. See the task "Change the Window Size" (page 13) for more information.
	Close button	Use this button to close the window, as covered in the *Guided Tour*.

If you are used to using Windows 3.1, keep in mind that the Close button is now where the Maximize button used to be. This arrangement may take some getting used to.

This task covers opening and closing a window. See the other tasks in this section for help on some of the other changes you can make to a window—changing its size, moving it around on the desktop, arranging all open windows on-screen, and so on.

Begin Guided Tour   Open a Window

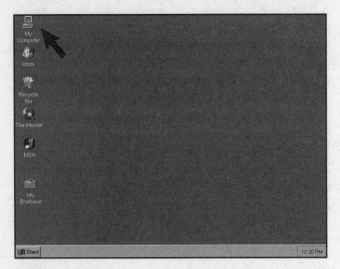

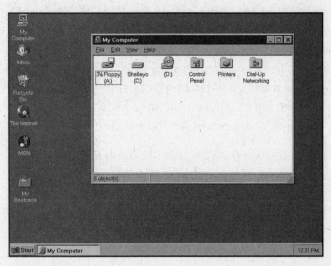

1 Double-click on the icon you want to open.

2 Windows opens a window and displays the contents of the icon. For example, if you double-click on the My Computer icon, you see the contents of your computer (shown here).

Begin Guided Tour   Close a Window

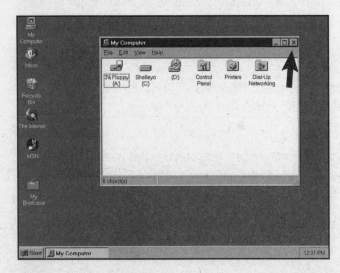

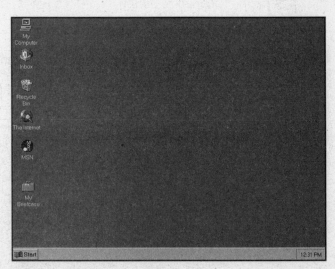

1 Click on the **Close** button.

2 Windows closes the window.

Change the Window Size

If you have ever had to clear off an area of your desk to make room to work on something else, you'll understand the concept of changing the size of one window to make room for another one you need to work in. Perhaps you have a small notebook and need to clear off a small area of your desk so you can work in the notebook. Or, perhaps you need to clear off your entire desk so you can spread out a blueprint. Similarly, in Windows 95, you can change the shape and size of your open windows so that they take up only a small part of the desktop or so that they fill the entire desktop.

There are two ways to change the size of the window. You can use the buttons in the upper-right corner of the window to minimize the window (reduce it to a taskbar button), maximize the window (make it fill the entire screen), or close the window. Or you can resize the window to any size you want by dragging one of its borders.

Keep the following things in mind when you are changing a window's size:

- When you maximize a window, it fills the entire screen and does not have any borders. Because the window is as big as it can get, you can't resize a maximized window by dragging its border.

- When you maximize a window, the Maximize button is replaced by the Restore button. You can click on the Restore button to restore the window to its previous size. A restored window has borders, which means you can resize it by dragging the border.

- When you minimize a window, you have not exited the program; you've shrunk it to a button on the taskbar. The program is still running.

Resizing Tips

You can resize the length of a window, the width of a window, or both by dragging the window's borders.

- To change the height of a window, position the pointer on the top or bottom border and drag to expand or shrink the window.

- To change the width, position the pointer on the left or right border and drag to resize.

- To resize the height and width of the window at the same time, place the mouse pointer on one of the corners of the border and drag to resize.

> When you have the mouse pointer correctly positioned on the window border, the pointer changes to a double-headed arrow (as shown in the *Guided Tour*).

Begin Guided Tour   Minimize a Window

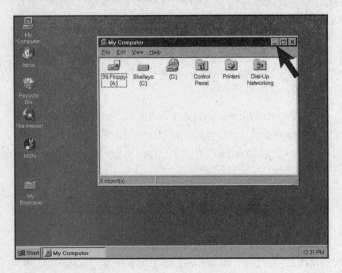

1 Click the **Minimize** button.

2 The window disappears, but its button remains on the taskbar. Click the window's taskbar button to reopen the window.

Begin Guided Tour   Maximize a Window

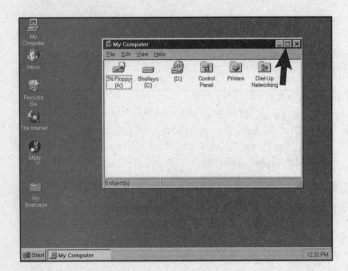

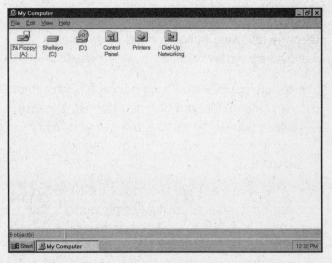

1 Click the Maximize button.

2 Windows enlarges the window so that it fills the entire screen.

Begin Guided Tour　Restore a Window

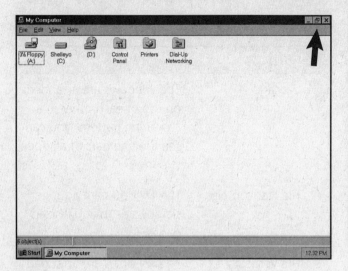

1 In the maximized window, click on the **Restore** button.

2 Windows resizes the window to its previous size and shape (before it was maximized).

Begin Guided Tour　Resize a Window

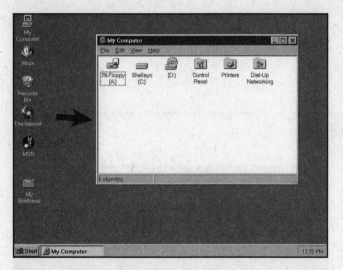

1 Position the mouse pointer on the border you want to change (if you're pointing at the top border, make sure the pointer is not on the title bar. If it's on the title bar, you move instead of resize the window).

2 Press and hold the left mouse button and drag to expand or shrink the width of the window. An outline appears to show you where the border will be. Release the mouse button when the window is the size you want.

Move and Arrange Windows

Think back again to your desk in your home or office. Is it covered with papers and other stuff? When you sit down to work, what's the first thing you do? Do you move things around and put the document(s) you want to work with on top? If you are working with several documents, don't you arrange them so that you can see everything you need?

When you sit down to work in Windows 95, you can do the same thing. That is, you can arrange the windows so you can see what you need. For example, suppose you are working on several documents at once. You need the financial figures from one document to complete a report that's in another document. You can arrange the document windows so you can see both.

You can arrange all open windows manually by dragging them to where you want them, or you can have Windows automatically arrange them for you. To manually move a window, you simply drag its title bar. If you want Windows to arrange them, you can choose from the following types of arrangements:

Option	Description
Cascade	The windows are arranged on top of each other in a cascading pattern; you can see the title bars of all open windows.
Tile Horizontally	The windows are arranged side by side in equal-sized panes.
Tile Vertically	The windows are arranged top to bottom in equal-sized panes.
Minimize All Windows	All windows are minimized to icons.

Begin Guided Tour Manually Move a Window

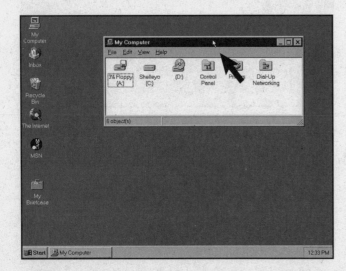

 Point to the title bar of the open window. Then press and hold the left mouse button and drag the window to a new location.

 The window moves with the mouse pointer as you drag.

Begin Guided Tour   Have Windows 95 Arrange Your Windows

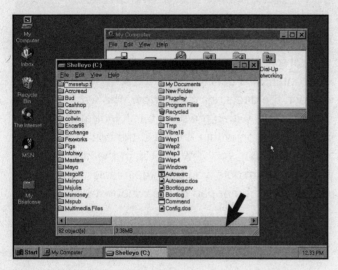

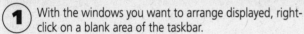

1 With the windows you want to arrange displayed, right-click on a blank area of the taskbar.

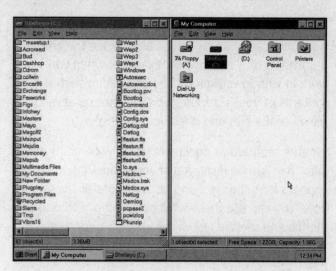

3 Windows arranges the windows accordingly. Here the windows are tiled vertically.

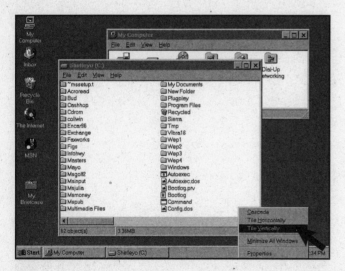

2 In the shortcut menu that appears, select the arrangement you want.

Scroll a Window

In some cases, you won't be able to see the entire contents of a window. For example, when you work in Windows Explorer and browse through the contents of your computer, you may not be able to see all of the files and directories at once.

When a program or document window contains more data than can be displayed in one window, scroll bars appear along the right and bottom sides of the window. You can use these scroll bars to move through the file and see the rest of the window's contents.

You can click below or above the scroll box to move the file or program up or down a screenful.

The scroll arrows appear at the top and bottom of the vertical scroll bar and at the left and right ends of the horizontal scroll bars. Click on the scroll arrows to move in the direction of the arrow. The scroll box is the gray area within the scroll bar. It indicates the relative position within the file: if the box is at the top of the scroll bar, you view the top of the file; if the box is in the middle, you view the middle. You can move to a different part of the window by dragging the scroll box.

Begin Guided Tour   Use the Scroll Bars

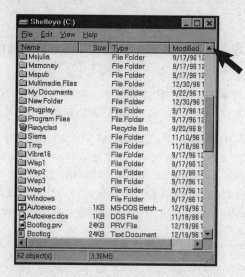

1 Click the **up scroll arrow** to scroll up through the window.

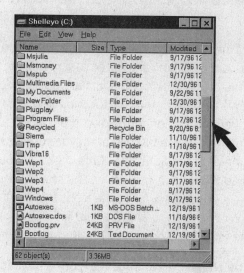

3 Drag the scroll box up or down to scroll the relative distance in that direction.

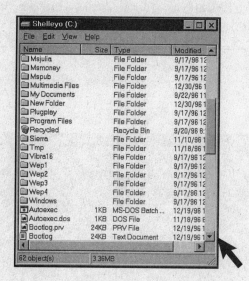

2 Click the **down scroll arrow** to scroll down through the window.

Arrange Icons

When you start Windows 95, the desktop icons are automatically placed in a row along the left edge of the desktop. But just as you can move windows around on the desktop, you also can move icons. Perhaps you prefer to keep them along the bottom, next to the taskbar, or maybe you like to have them on the right side of the desktop. You easily can drag the icons anywhere on the screen, or you can have Windows arrange the icons for you. If you want Windows 95 to arrange your icons, you can choose from the following automatic arrangements:

- **by Name**   To arrange the icons alphabetically by name.

- **by Type**   To arrange the icons by type (for example, by program first, and then by document).

- **by Size**   To arrange the icons in ascending order by size (smallest to largest).

- **by Date**   To arrange the icons in order by date of creation (most recent files listed first).

- **AutoArrange**   To keep the icons spaced evenly on a grid. The spacing intervals are set in the Display dialog box. See "Use the Control Panel to Customize Windows 95" on page 427 for information on changing the spacing interval.

If you move an icon and it flies back to its original location, you have turned on AutoArrange. To turn the feature off, right-click on the desktop and select AutoArrange (click on AutoArrange to remove the check mark).

Begin Guided Tour   Move an Icon

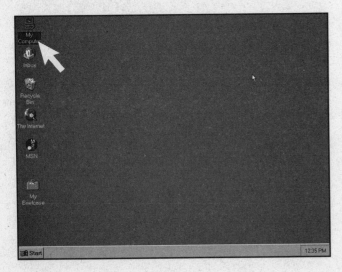

1 Position the pointer on the icon you want to move. Press and hold the left mouse button, and drag the icon to a new location.

2 The icon moves as you move your mouse. The icon appears as a ghosted image when you drag it.

Begin Guided Tour Have Windows 95 Arrange Your Icons

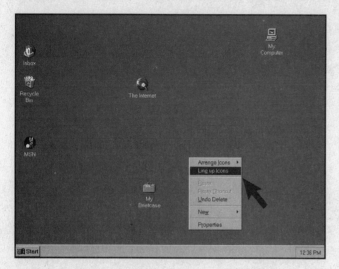

1 To simply line up the icons, select the **Line up Icons** command and skip the remaining steps.

3 Windows aligns the icons accordingly.

To rearrange icons automatically, right-click on a blank area on the desktop. A shortcut menu appears (as shown in following figure).

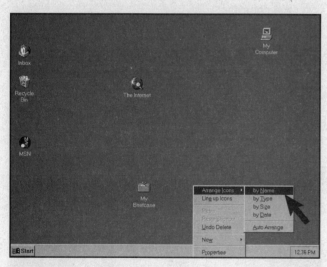

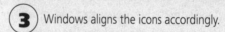

2 To arrange by name, type, size or date, select the **Arrange Icons** command and then select the type of arrangement you want.

Change How Icons Are Displayed

You've probably figured out by now that Windows 95 uses icons to represent everything from hardware components (such as a hard drive or printer) to documents. When you start Windows, you see an icon for each of the tools you can use. Not only can you move and rearrange these icons, but you also can change how Windows 95 displays them.

When you look at the contents of a window, you usually see a large icon with a title below it for each window item. However, you can easily have Windows display the icons in a different way. For example, if the window contains a lot of icons, you may want to display them as small icons so that you can see more of them in the window. If you are looking for an icon by name, you may prefer to see a list. And if you want to see the size, date, or other details of a file in addition to the icon, you can select a detailed view. The following list describes the display options from which you can choose:

- **Large Icons** (default)   In this view, Windows displays the contents of the window using large icons.

- **Small Icons**   In this view, Windows displays the contents of the window as smaller icons. Using smaller icons enables you to see more icons within the window.

- **List**   In this view, Windows displays the contents of the window in a list arranged alphabetically by name.

- **Details**   In this view, you see the name, type, size, and modified date and time for the contents. You may need to scroll the window horizontally or resize the window to see some of the columns.

Begin Guided Tour   Display Different Icon Information

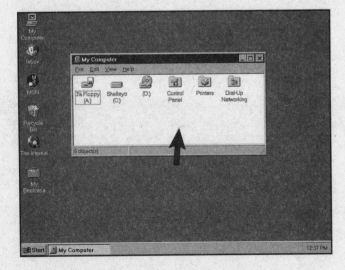

1 Right-click in the window you want to change.

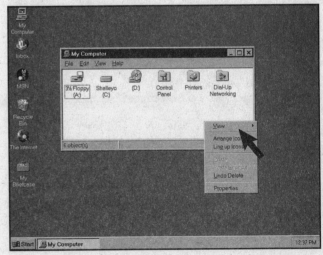

2 In the shortcut menu that appears, select the **View** command.

Begin Guided Tour Display Different Icon Information

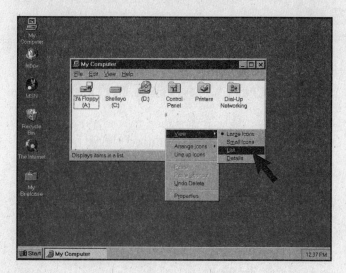
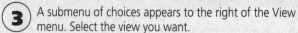

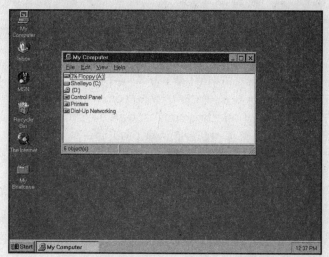

3 A submenu of choices appears to the right of the View menu. Select the view you want.

4 Windows displays the window contents accordingly. In this figure, Windows displays the window's contents in list view.

Windows retains the icon view you select when you exit and restart Windows (until you change to another view).

Select Menu Commands with the Mouse or Keyboard

One task that you will use daily as you work in Windows is selecting menu commands. Luckily, the process of selecting commands is the same in Windows 95 and any Windows program. There are several methods for selecting a command, and you have the option of using the mouse or the keyboard.

Select Commands with the Mouse

By far, the easiest method is to use the mouse. Point to the menu you want to open and click the mouse button. The menu drops down to display a list of commands. To choose a command, point to the command you want and click the mouse button.

You'll find different types of menus in Windows, but they all work the same. From the desktop, you can display the Start menu or a shortcut menu. Within programs, the menus are usually listed along the top of the window in the menu bar.

Depending on the command you select, different things may happen. When you select some commands, they are carried out immediately. When you select a command that is followed by an arrow, another menu (called a submenu) appears. You make a selection from this menu by clicking on the command you want. (To display these sub menus on the Start menu, you don't have to click on the command. You can simply point to the command to display the submenu.) And finally, when you select a command followed by an ellipsis (...), a dialog box appears. (For more information on dealing with dialog boxes, see "Understand Dialog Boxes" on page 28.)

Keyboard Alternatives

Ultimately, Windows is designed for the mouse: you can do almost anything in Windows simply by poking around at menus, icons, and buttons. However, Windows does allow you to use your keyboard, and you may even find it easier and quicker to enter commands with the keyboard than with the mouse. Although the tasks in this book focus mainly on mouse actions, this section shows you how to use keyboard alternatives.

To open a menu, hold down the **Alt** key and press the key that corresponds to the underlined letter in the desired menu name. For example, press **Alt+H** to open the Help menu. Each command on the menu contains an underlined letter (called a selection letter). Press the key that corresponds to that letter to enter the command, or use the down-arrow key to highlight the command and press **Enter**. In addition, the menu lists keyboard shortcuts for selecting some of the commands.

> After you've pressed Alt and activated the menu bar, you can't do anything else until you select a menu, press Alt again or press Esc.

For some commands, you press one key by itself. For example, you might press the **F1** function key to access the Help system. With other commands, you press a keystroke or combination (two or more keys pressed at the same time). For example, if you are told to press **Ctrl+F1**, you hold down the Ctrl key, press the F1 key, and then release both keys. You can use keys and key combinations to open menus, bypass menus, and enter commands directly, as well as to select and run applications.

The only trouble with using the keyboard instead of the mouse is that you have to memorize the key combinations in order to enter the proper command. To help, Windows displays most key combinations on its menus.

The following table summarizes the keyboard options just presented, as well as other keyboard alternatives you might find helpful as you work.

Keyboard Alternatives to Mouse Moves

Press This	To Do This
Esc	Close a menu without making a selection
Alt+F4	Exit an application or quit Windows
Ctrl+Esc	Display the Start menu
F1	Go to Help
Alt+hyphen	Open a group or document window's Control menu
Alt+Tab	Switch among open windows
Tab	Move forward among Help or dialog box items
Shift+Tab	Move backward among Help or dialog box items
Alt+ underlined letter	Select dialog box item with the corresponding underlined letter
Shift+F10	View the shortcut menu for the selected item

Begin Guided Tour   Use the Start Menu

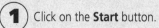

1 Click on the **Start** button.

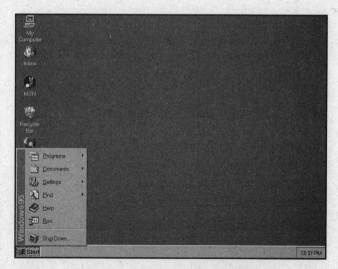

2 The Start menu appears, listing the available options. Click on the command you want. (You also can move the pointer over the command you want to display the next submenu.)

(continues)

Guided Tour   Use the Start Menu   *(continued)*

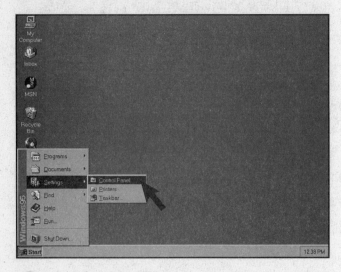

If you have opened a menu and want to close it without selecting a command, press **Esc**.

3 A submenu appears, listing more available choices. Click on the command you want.

Begin Guided Tour   Use Pull-Down Menus

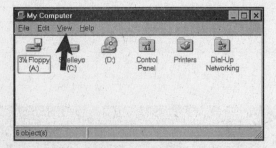

1 Click on the menu name to display the menu.

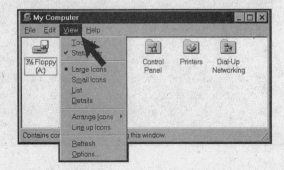

2 The menu opens to display a list of related commands. Click on the command you want.

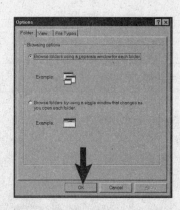

3 If a dialog box appears, make your selections and click the **OK** button.

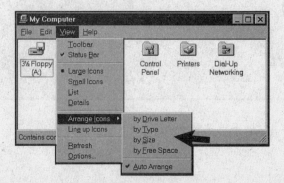

4 If a submenu appears, click on the command you want.

Begin Guided Tour   Use a Shortcut Menu

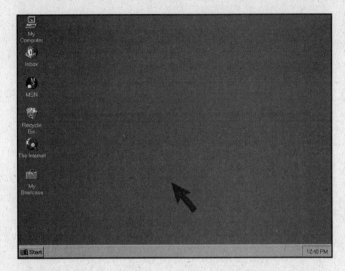

1 Right-click on the item you want to modify. For example, to modify the desktop, right-click on any blank area of the desktop.

2 Windows displays a shortcut menu. Click on the command that you want. If a submenu appears, select the appropriate command from it.

Begin Guided Tour   Select a Command with the Keyboard

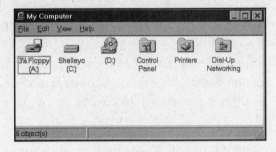

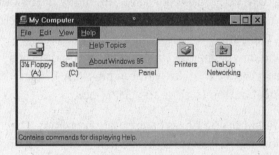

1 To open a menu, press **Alt** plus the menu's selection letter. For example, press **Alt+H** to open the Help menu.

2 Press the selection letter of the command you want, or press the down-arrow key to highlight the command and then press **Enter**.

Understand Dialog Boxes

A dialog box is Windows way of communicating with you. You'll see three types of dialog boxes in Windows 95. The most common type enables Windows to ask you for more information. However, Windows also displays a dialog box when it needs you to confirm an action (such as exiting Windows) or when it needs to give you information (to display disk statistics after you format a disk, for example).

Most Windows dialog boxes ask you for more information. For example, Windows might display a dialog box to ask you which font you want to use, how many copies you want to print, or what type of document you want to create. Like selecting menu commands, working with dialog boxes is the same in Windows 95 and all Windows applications. Once you master the elements of one type of dialog box, you can easily navigate and make choices in any dialog box.

Basically, you make your selections in the dialog box (as described in the following list), and then you click the **OK** button to confirm and carry out the command. If you change your mind or if you display a dialog box by mistake, you can press **Esc** or click the **Cancel** button to close the dialog box.

Different dialog boxes have different options. The following list describes the elements you might find in any given dialog box and explains how to use each one. The Guided Tour shows examples of these dialog box elements.

> **Tab**   Some dialog boxes contain several sets of options, each on a separate "page." To access the other page of options, click on the tab at the top of the dialog box.

> **Text box**   When you are required to type something (such as a file name when saving a file), you use a text box. To enter text in a text box, click in the text box and then type. If the text box already contains an entry, you can drag across it to highlight the entry. Then type the

new entry to replace the existing text or simply press **Delete** to delete it.

List box   A list box contains a number of options from which you can choose. For example, when Windows wants you to select a folder, it displays a list box of folder names. Simply click on the one you want.

Drop-down list box   Sometimes Windows displays only the first item in a list, with an arrow next to it. This type of list box is called a drop-down list box. To display the entire list, click on the down arrow. Then click on the list item you want.

Option buttons   When you can select only one option from among several, you see a set of option buttons. (For example, if you were working on a memo and selected the Print command, you'd need to choose an option button to indicate whether you wanted to print a highlighted selection, a particular page, or the entire memo—but not all three.) To select an option button, click on it. All other option buttons in the set are deselected.

Check boxes   You use check boxes to turn options on or off. With check boxes, you can usually select several options at once (for example, you can make text bold and italic). To activate a check box, click in the box. When a check box is selected (turned on), an X or a check mark appears in the box.

Command buttons   After you make your dialog box selections, you click on a command button to carry out the command. Most dialog boxes include an OK button ("go ahead") and a Cancel button ("I changed my mind"). You also may find other buttons that enable you to make additional choices. For example, if you click an Options button, another dialog box with more options appears.

Begin Guided Tour Select a Tab

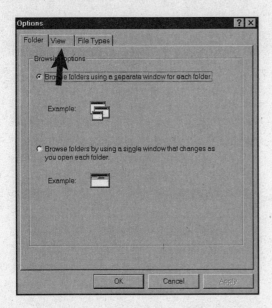

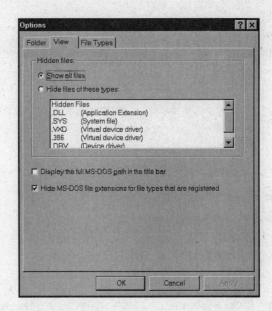

1 When a dialog box includes different sets of options, you see tabs at the top of the dialog box. To select another tab, click on it.

2 Windows displays the selected tab.

Begin Guided Tour Make an Entry in a Text Box

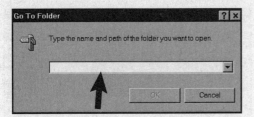

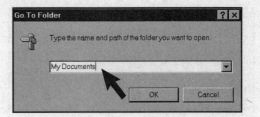

1 Click in the text box.

2 Type the entry you want. For example, to go to a file, type the file name in the text box (as shown here).

Begin Guided Tour Select an Item from a List Box

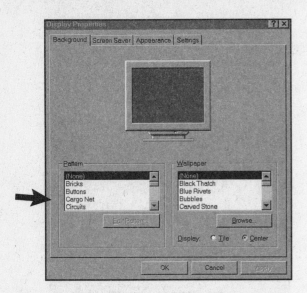

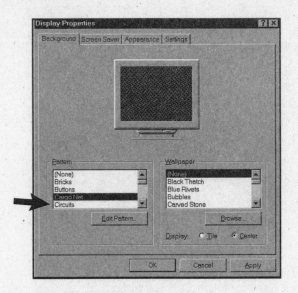

1 To make a selection in a list box, simply click on the item. If the item you want is not visible, use the scroll bar to move through the list, and then click on the item you want.

2 That item appears highlighted.

Begin Guided Tour Select an Item from a Drop-Down List Box

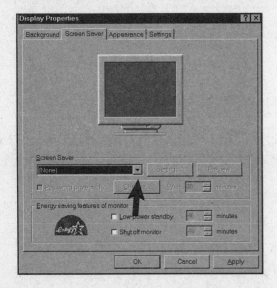

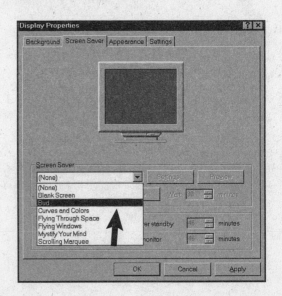

1 To display the items in a drop-down list box, click on the arrow next to the list box.

2 Windows displays a list of choices. Click on the one you want.

Begin Guided Tour Select an Option Button

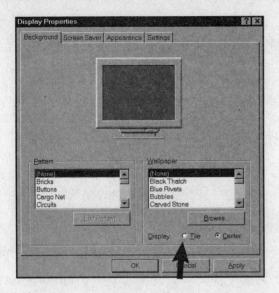

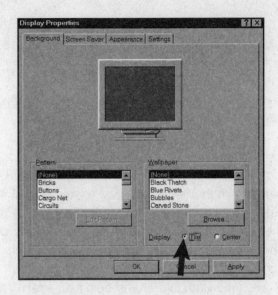

1 To select an option in a group of option buttons, click the button.

2 Windows darkens the selected option button, and deselects whichever button was previously selected.

Begin Guided Tour Select a Check Box

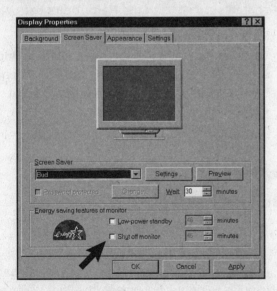

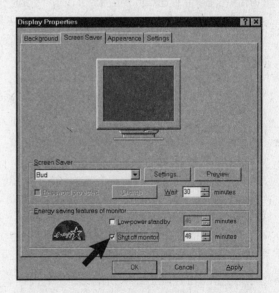

1 When Windows displays a check box, you can choose to turn an option on (a check mark appears) or off (no check mark appears). To change the status of a check box option, click in the check box.

2 Windows displays a check mark in the check box (as shown here) when it is selected.

Get Help

It's practically impossible to remember how to use each and every feature of Windows. When you need a quick reminder of how to do something, instead of looking around for your manual, you can use Windows online Help system.

Think of online Help as a big book with all the information you need about Windows. You can look up information in the Help system just as you would look up information in a book: using the table of contents or the index. You also can search for a particular word or phrase and find related topics in the Help system. Which method works the best? It depends on your goal. The following guidelines should help you make your decision:

- If you are just browsing through the topics and want to learn something about Windows, you may choose to use the Contents tab. The contents page is organized like a book: topics are broken into the categories Introducing Windows, How To, Tips and Tricks, and Trouble-shooting. First you select the general category you want, and then you narrow it down by selecting topics and subtopics until you see the Help information you want.

- If you are looking up a particular feature and don't want to have to figure out how that feature might be categorized, you can use the index. When you use the index, you type the first few letters of the topic, and Windows displays a list of matching topics. You select the topic you want from that list.

- If you can't find help using the contents or index, you can try searching for the word or phrase. When you use this method, Windows displays all topics that include the word or phrase you type. (The first time you use this option, you have to set up the Find feature. A wizard—a series of step-by-step dialog boxes—will lead you through the process of setting up the necessary files to use Find.)

Navigating in Help

In many cases, you will simply display the Help information you want and then close the Help window. In some cases, however, you may want to do more than that. For example, you may want to print the Help topic, or you may be wading through the Help system and find that you need to go back to a previous topic. Or you may want to keep the Help information on-screen so you can review the steps as you work in another program. You can use the buttons in the Help window to do all of these things.

- To print the Help topic, click the **Options** button and select **Print Topic**. To change the font, click the **Options** button, select the **Font** command, and then select **Small**, **Normal**, or **Large**.

- If you want to go back to a previous topic, click the **Back** button. To go back to the table of contents screen, click the **Help Topics** button.

- To keep the Help window on top, click the **Options** button, select the **Keep Help on Top** command, and then select **On Top**. (To change back, follow the same process but select **Not On Top**.)

Getting Help in a Dialog Box

When you select certain commands, Windows displays a dialog box of options. In many cases, the options are self-explanatory. For example, when you tell Windows to print a document, the Print dialog box specifically asks you to select how many copies you want to print. In some cases, however, you may not be sure what a particular option does. The answer, then, is to get help on it. In most dialog boxes, a Help button (a question mark) appears on the right end of the title bar. You can use this button, as explained in the *Guided Tour*, to get help on any dialog box option.

Begin Guided Tour   Use Help Contents

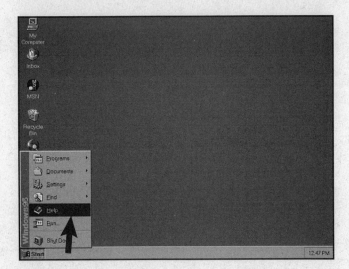

1 Click the **Start** button and select the **Help** command.

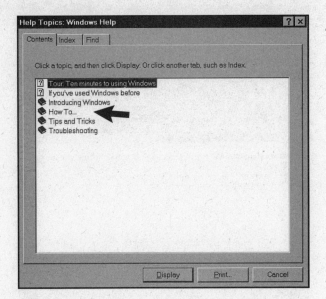

2 The Help Topics dialog box appears, with three tabs of options: Contents, Index, and Find. Windows displays the Contents dialog box, which contains a list of topics, each represented by a book icon. Double-click on **How To** to display subtopics.

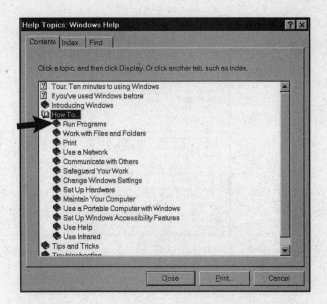

3 Windows displays additional subtopics below How To. Double-click on the **Help** topic for which you want information. For example, double-click on **Run Programs**. (You can use the scroll bar to see any topics that are hidden from view.)

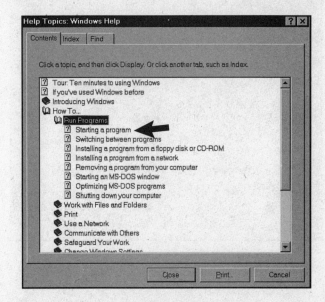

4 Windows displays a question mark icon in front of Help topics. Double-click on the **Help** topic you want. For example, double-click on Starting a program.

(continues)

Guided Tour Use Help Contents *(continued)*

A quicker way to find out about a dialog box option is to right-click on the option. In the shortcut menu that appears, select the What's This? command, and a short description of the item pops-up.

5 A Help window appears, giving detailed information about the selected topic. When you are finished reading the Help information, close the window by clicking the **Close** button.

Begin Guided Tour Use the Help Index

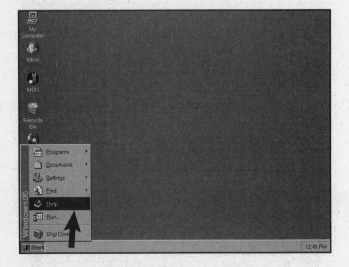

1 Click the **Start** button and select the **Help** command.

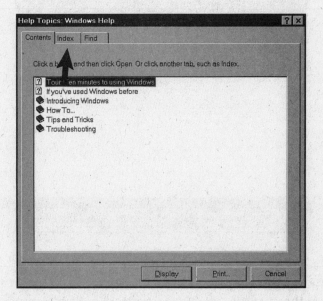

2 In the Help Topics dialog box, click on the **Index** tab.

Guided Tour   Use the Help Index

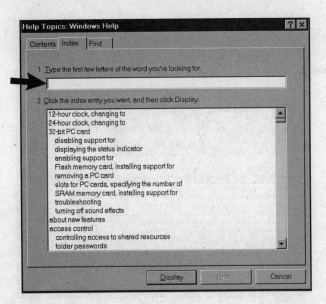

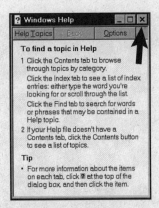

5 Windows displays the Help information for the selected topic. When you finish reading this information, close the window by clicking the **Close** button.

3 The Index tab of the Help Topics dialog box appears. In the text box, type the first few letters of the topic you want help on. For example, to find help on Help, type **help**.

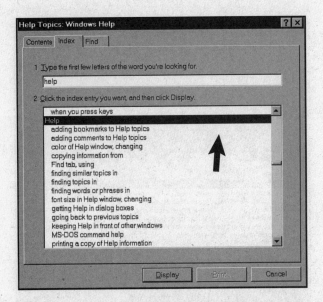

4 Windows displays matching topics in the list box. Double-click on the topic you want. (You also can click once on the topic and then click on the **Display** button.)

Begin Guided Tour   Search for a Help Topic

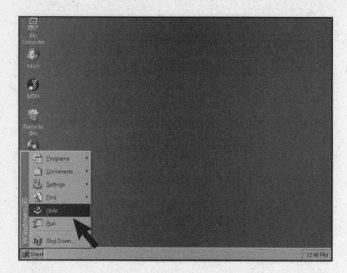

1 Click the **Start** button and select the **Help** command.

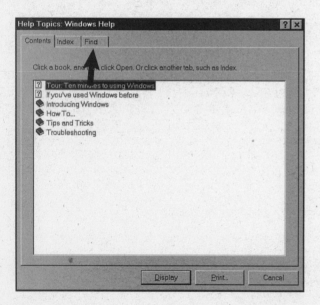

2 In the Help Topics dialog box, click on the **Find** tab. If this is the first time you've used Find, the Find Setup wizard appears. Click on **Next**, then **Finish**. The wizard creates a word list for searching.

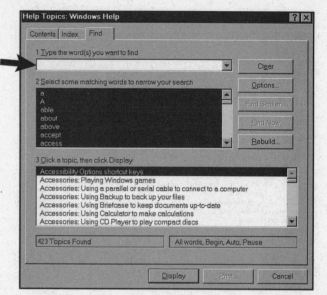

3 The Find tab of the Help Topics dialog box appears. In the first text box, type the word or words that you want to find. For example, type **start**.

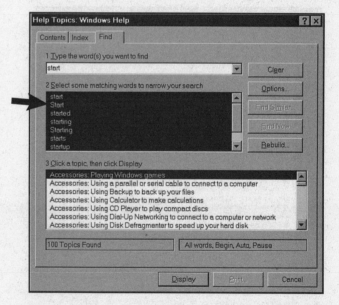

4 Windows displays matching topics in the list box. To narrow the search, click on the matching topic that is closest to what you are looking for. For example, click on **Start**.

Guided Tour   Search for a Help Topic

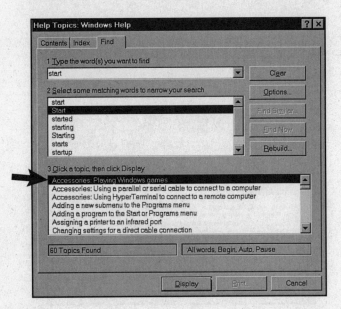

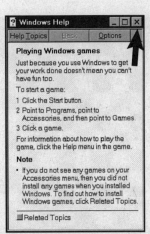

5 Windows displays the topics that contain the word or words you typed. Double-click on the topic you want. For example, double-click on **Accessories: Playing Windows games**. (You also can click once on the topic and then click on the **Display** button.)

6 Windows displays the help information for the selected topic. When you finish reading this information, close the window by clicking the **Close** button.

Begin Guided Tour Get Help in a Dialog Box

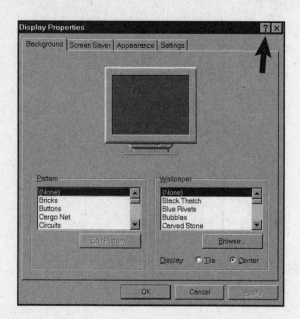

1 If the dialog box contains a question mark button, click on this button.

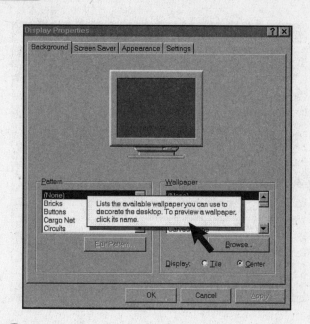

3 A description of the option pops up.

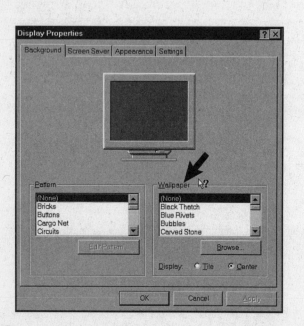

2 The mouse pointer changes to an arrow and a question mark. Click on the option for which you want help.

HOW TO...

Set Up and Run Programs

Even though Windows 95 includes many useful tools, you won't be spending most of your time in Windows. Instead, you will use Windows to start programs, and you will spend most of your time on the computer working in those programs. Windows provides you with tools that make starting and switching among programs easy and convenient. This section covers not only how to start programs, but how to install new programs, customize the Start menu, and more. This section covers the following topics:

What You Will Find in This Section

Use the Start Menu

When you start Windows, you'll see the Start button in the lower-left corner of the window. The Start button, as its name implies, is where you get started in Windows 95. Therefore, you should get familiar with the options on this menu.

When you click the Start button, you see the Start menu, which includes the following items:

 Programs   Use this command to start programs, as described in the *Guided Tour*.

 Documents   Displays the names of the 15 documents you opened most recently. You can open a document and start a program by clicking on the document name. See the task "Start a Program and Open a Document" on page 141.

 Settings   Use this command to change or view Windows settings and options. For example, you can access the Control Panel to change the screen colors. See the section "Use the Control Panel to Customize Windows 95" on page 427.

 Find   This feature is new in Windows 95. Use this command to find a file on your computer using one of several search methods. See "Find a File or Folder" on page 111.

 Help   If you want to get online help, use this command. Help is covered in "Get Help" on page 32.

 Run   To run a program by typing its command, use this command. See the task "Use the Run Command" on page 48.

 Shut Down   Use this command to properly shut down Windows before you turn off the PC. See the task "Start and Exit Windows" on page 7.

The Start menu is a little different from other menus. When a command is followed by an arrow, you don't have to click on it to display the submenu (although you can). You can just point to the arrow with your mouse, and the submenu appears. Sometimes you may have to move through more than one level of submenu to get to the command you want. When that happens, simply move the mouse over the next arrow to display the next submenu until you see the command you want.

Begin Guided Tour   Select Programs and Commands from the Start Menu

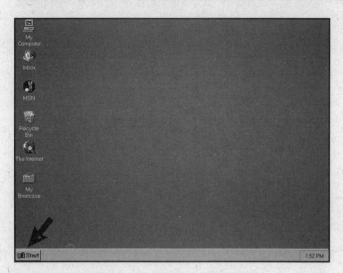

1 Click the **Start** button.

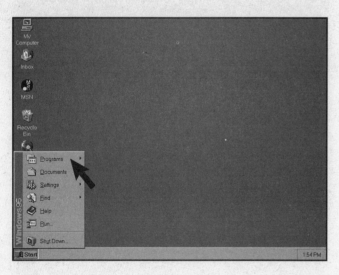

2 When the Start menu appears, move your mouse over the arrow for the command you want.

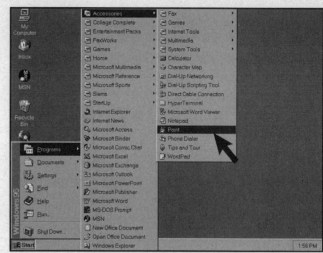

3 If the command contains a submenu, that menu appears. Continue selecting commands until you get the result you want (until a program starts, for example).

Start and Exit a Program

Throughout this section, you'll find a number of ways you can start a program in Windows 95. Because you have a lot of options, you (the user) pick the method that most clearly matches your needs. The most common method for beginning users to start a program is from the Start menu.

To help you keep track of all your programs, Windows 95 organizes the programs into folders. You can think of a folder as a drawer in your desk. You might have one drawer that contains all the tools you need for working with numbers, such as a slide rule, calculator, pencil, and lined accounting paper. Similarly, in Windows 95, you might have a folder that contains your tool for working with numbers: your spreadsheet program.

When you click the Start button and select Programs, you see a submenu listing the folders that contain the programs that are set up on your system. Each of those folders has an arrow to the right of its name. (Below the folders are icons for some of the Windows programs, such as Windows Explorer.) When you select a folder, another submenu appears, displaying the program icons in that folder. For example, if you select Accessories, you see a submenu that lists icons for all of the Windows 95 accessory programs. You can start a program by clicking the program name on the menu.

When you see all the programs in the menu, you may wonder how those programs got there. Programs are added to the Start menu in one of several ways:

- As part of the installation process, Windows automatically sets up some programs and adds them to folders on the Start menu.

- If you installed Windows 95 over Windows 3.1, the program groups and program icons you had set up in Windows 3.1 are carried over to Windows 95. Each program group you had in Windows 3.1 became a folder in Windows 95.

- When you install new programs (as covered in the section "Install a Program" on page 51), the installation program adds a folder and program icons to the Start menu.

- You can customize the Start menu, adding and deleting folders and programs to meet your own needs. You'll learn how to do this in the sections "Add a Folder to the Start Menu" (page 53) and "Add a Program to the Start Menu" (page 55).

> The terms "application" and "program" mean the same thing and are used interchangeably.

Exit a Program

Before you shut down Windows and call it a day, you should save all the documents you are working on (see "Save and Close a Document" on page 130) and close all your applications. If you forget to save a file, most applications remind you when you exit the program.

Most Windows programs provide several methods for exiting the program. The *Guided Tour* shows you how to exit using the File Exit command. In addition, you can double-click on the **Control menu** icon, you can click the **Close** button, or you can press the shortcut key combination **Alt+F4**.

> Try this shortcut. Right-click on the taskbar button for the program you want to close. In the shortcut menu that appears, select **Close**.

Begin Guided Tour   Start a Program

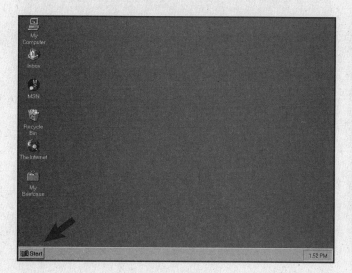

1 Click on the **Start** button.

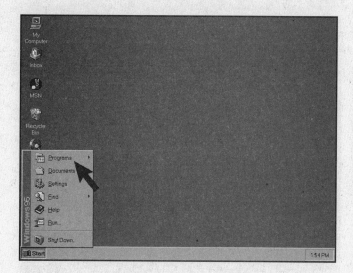

2 The Start menu appears. Select the **Programs** command by moving the mouse pointer over the arrow or click once on the **Program** command.

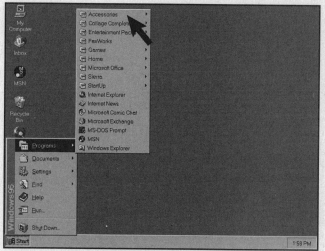

3 The submenu that appears lists the program folders on your system. Point to the program folder that contains the program you want to start. (You may need to move through more than one submenu before you come to the program icon you want.)

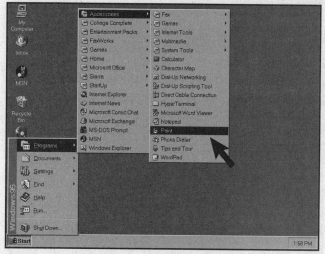

4 When you see the program icon (such as the Paint icon in this figure), click on it to start the program.

(continues)

Guided Tour Start a Program (continued)

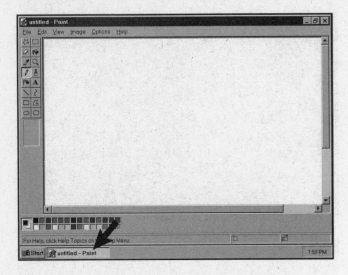

You can quickly start some programs, and start a new document or file, by rightclicking on the desktop. Select **New** from the shortcut menu, then click on the program you want to open from the submenu.

 Windows starts the program and displays a program window. A button for the program appears on the taskbar.

Begin Guided Tour Exit a Program

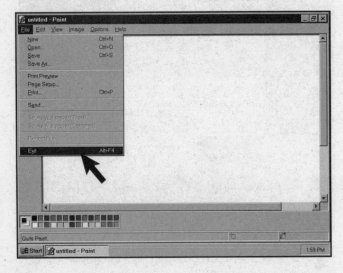

1 After you've saved your document (see "Save and Close a Document" on page 130), open the **File** menu and select the **Exit** command. (If you've forgotten to save, Windows displays a message reminding you to do so.)

2 Windows closes the program.

Start a Program Each Time You Start Windows

Do you use one program all the time—almost every time you use Windows, for example? If so, you can save yourself the time of moving through the Start menu and its submenus to start that program; you can just have Windows start the program each time you start Windows. For example, suppose that 95 percent of the time you spend on the computer, you are using Word for Windows. You could start Windows and then start Word, or you could just have Windows start Word for you.

To start a program automatically, you add it to the StartUp program folder. You can add as many programs as you want (up to the limit of your system's memory). Be selective, though. Don't add every program or you will waste system resources.

The *Guided Tour* shows you how to create a shortcut (a pointer to the original program file) and place it in the Startup folder so Windows will start that program every time you start Windows. When you create a shortcut, the program icon remains in its original location, but you place a duplicate icon in a place that's more convenient so you can start it more quickly. See the section "Add a Shortcut to the Desktop" (page 63) for more information on shortcuts.

> If you don't like the name assigned to the shortcut, you can rename the icon as explained in "Add a Shortcut to the Desktop" (page 63).

To create a shortcut to a program, you have to know a few basic concepts about how Windows treats programs:

- A program is a special type of computer file. Most programs use the extension .EXE, which is short for executable. That means you can start and run a program file.

- Windows 95 stores programs in the folders in which you placed them when you installed the program. To find the program, you have to open that folder. You can open folders and display their contents using either My Computer or Windows Explorer. The section "Manage Folders and Files" on page 67 covers how to navigate through the folders on your system.

- Windows uses different icons to represent different objects. For example, program icons look like a miniature representation of the program, and folder icons look like folders.

- The shortcut is a pointer to the original program file in the original folder. You easily can add or delete these shortcuts without affecting the application.

Remove an Icon from the StartUp Folder

If you change your mind and don't want to start the program each time you start Windows, you simply delete the program icon from the StartUp folder by following these steps:

1. Right-click on the **Start** button and select **Open**.

2. In the Start Menu window, double-click the **Programs** folder. You see the contents of the Programs folder.

3. Double-click the **StartUp** folder. The folder opens, and you should see the program icon.

4. Right-click on the icon and select **Delete**.

5. When you are prompted to confirm the deletion, click the **Yes** button.

Begin Guided Tour Add a Program to the StartUp Folder

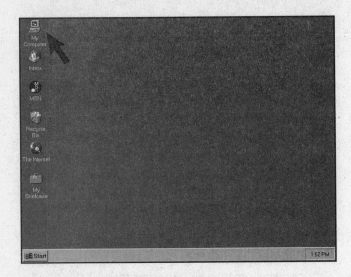

1 Double-click the **My Computer** icon.

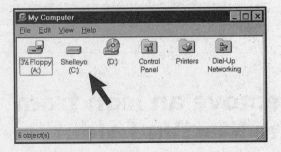

2 The My Computer window shows an icon for each of the disk drives on your computer. Double-click on the drive and then the folder that contains the program icon you want to add to StartUp.

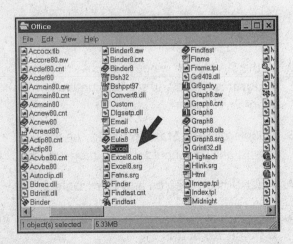

3 When you see the icon for the program you want to start automatically, right-click on it.

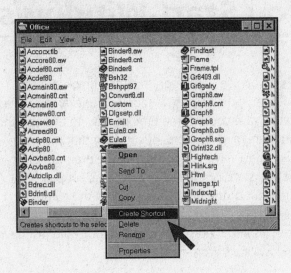

4 In the shortcut menu that appears, select the **Create Shortcut** command.

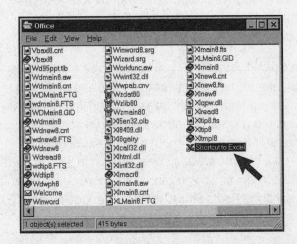

5 Windows displays a shortcut icon in the program window. Now you have to move this icon to the StartUp folder. To do so, right-click on the **Start** button.

For information on navigating in My Computer, see the section "Manage Folders and Files" on page 67.

Guided Tour Add a Program to the StartUp Folder

6 In the shortcut menu that appears, select the **Open** command.

7 Windows displays the Start Menu window, which contains the Programs folder. Double-click the **Programs** folder.

8 A window opens displaying the contents of the Programs folder (which consists of the program icons and folders stored in this folder). Double-click on the **StartUp** folder. Windows displays the StartUp folder window.

9 If necessary, arrange the StartUp folder window and the window that contains the shortcut so you can see both of them. You also can close all of the other windows if you want (see "Open and Close a Window" on page 11). Drag the shortcut icon to the StartUp window.

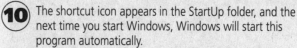

10 The shortcut icon appears in the StartUp folder, and the next time you start Windows, Windows will start this program automatically.

Start a Program Using the Run Command

The easiest way to start a program is from the Start menu. In addition, you can use the Run command to start a program. Although this method is difficult to use because you have to know a lot about the program you want to run, you may want to use it when you are installing a new program or, perhaps, starting a DOS program that you don't use very often.

When you use this command, you have to tell Windows the name of the program file and the path to that file. (A *program file* is a special type of file that is often called an executable file and usually uses the extension. EXE.) A *path* gives the location of the program file on your hard drive or floppy disk and shows exactly how to get to that file. For example, if you want to run Word for Windows (its program file is named Winword) and it is stored in the WINWORD folder, which is in the OFFICE97 folder, which is on the C drive, the path would be:

C:\OFFICE97\WINWORD\WINWORD. EXE

If you don't know the path of a particular file, you can use the Browse button in the Run dialog box to browse through the drives and folders on your system. When you click on Browse, Windows displays the folders and files in the current folder. In the Browse dialog box, use any of the following techniques to find and indicate the correct path:

- To change to another folder, double-click on it. Windows displays the files in that folder.

- To move up a level in the folder structure, click on the **Up One Level** button.

- If you want to change to a different drive, display the **Look in** drop-down list and select the drive you want.

- If you want to change the types of files that are listed, display the **Files of type** drop-down list and select the type of files you want displayed.

- If you want to see detailed information about the folders and files, select the **Details** button. To return to List view, click the **List** button.

Begin Guided Tour   Use the Run Command

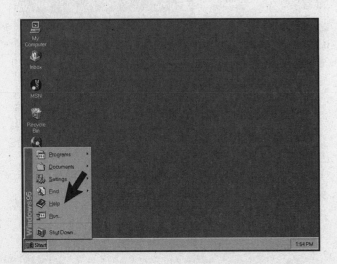

 Click on the **Start** button and select the **Run** command.

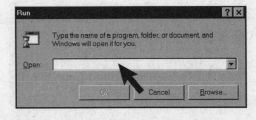

2 The Run dialog box appears. If you know the complete path and file name of the file you want to run, type it in the Open text box. (For example, you might type **C:\OFFICE97\WINWORD\WINWORD.EXE.**)

Begin Guided Tour Use the Run Command

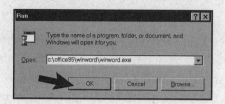

In Windows 3.1, you used the Run command to install a program. In Windows 95, you can use either the Add/Remove Program icon or the Run command to install programs.

3 With the complete path and file name in the Open text box, click on the **OK** button. Windows runs the program.

Begin Guided Tour Use the Browse Dialog Box to Find the Program File

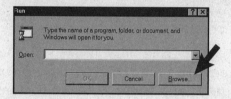

1 If you get to the Run dialog box and you don't know the path, click on the **Browse** button.

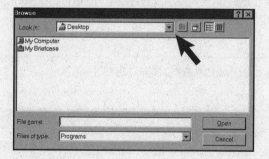

2 In the Browse dialog box, open the **Look in** drop-down list.

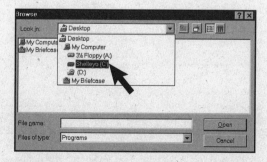

3 Click on the drive you want, and then double-click on the folder(s) until you locate the program file you want.

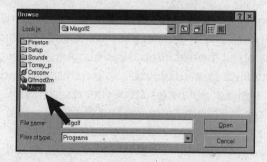

4 When you see the file listed, double-click on it or click once and click the **OK** button.

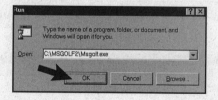

5 Windows returns you to the Run dialog box and inserts the path into the Open text box. Click on the **OK** button. Windows runs the program.

Switch Between Open Applications

If this is your first experience using a computer and Windows, you may be more comfortable using only one program (or application) at a time, or you may not have found a need to use any more than that. However, once you get the hang of using Windows applications and accessories, you'll find yourself wanting to use multiple programs to do more than one thing at a time on your computer. Then you'll realize how useful and convenient it is to have two or more applications open at the same time.

For example, to create a report for your class, church group, or business, you might use WordPad or Word to type up all the text information about the project and then use Excel to provide some worksheets and charts that explain the results of your research. You easily can start both programs and switch between them as needed. (Part 2 gives you ideas for using Windows accessories to create some attractive and useful projects.)

If you used Windows 3.1, you had to remember a key combination to switch between programs. Although you can still use the Alt+Tab key combination to cycle between programs, Windows 95 provides an even easier way to switch to a different application: the taskbar.

> The number of programs you can run at once is determined by the amount of memory your system has.

When you start a program, Windows adds a button for that program to the taskbar. Windows automatically resizes those buttons as you start more programs so that you can always see a button for each program you are currently running. Even at a glance, you can tell which program is active because its taskbar button looks pressed in. To switch to a different program, you simply click on the program's taskbar button.

Begin Guided Tour   Use the Taskbar to Switch Between Applications

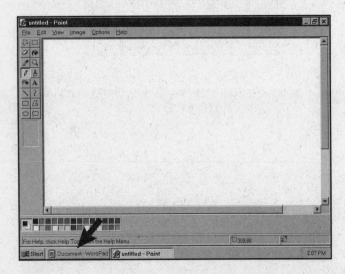

1 With more than one program open, click on the taskbar button for the program to which you want to switch.

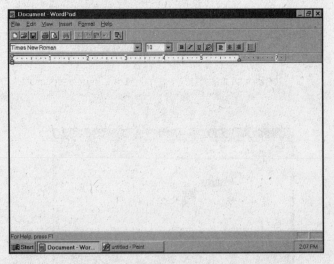

2 Windows displays that program, making it the active program.

Install a Program

When you install Windows 95, it sets up program folders and icons for all the installed programs and accessories that come with Windows 95 (such as WordPad and Paint). In addition, if you install Windows 95 over Windows 3.1, Windows 95 sets up a program folder for each program group and creates a program icon for each one you had in Windows 3.1.

If you had any older DOS programs on your computer when you installed Windows 95, they may not have been picked up during the installation. If they don't appear on the Start menu under Programs, you'll probably have to reinstall them. Whether you need to reinstall one of those programs or install a new program for the first time, eventually you will want to install other programs. When you install a program, a couple of things happen:

- Windows copies the necessary program files to your hard disk.

- Windows adds an icon for that program to the folder you select.

Although the easiest way to install a new program is to use the Add/Remove Programs feature (as described in the *Guided Tour*), you also can use the Run command. To use the Run command, open the **Start** menu and select **Run**. Then type the path and name of the installation program. For example, if you were installing a program named "Install" from drive A, you'd type **A:\INSTALL** in the Run dialog box. Most installation programs are named INSTALL, SETUP, or something similar. Check your program documentation for the specific command to use. See the task "Start a Program Using the Run Command" (page 48) for more help on using this command.

There might come a time when you need to remove old programs that you no longer use to save space on your hard drive. For some programs, Windows also enables you to use the Add/Remove Programs icon to remove a program from your system. To learn how to remove a program in this way, flip to "Remove an Old Program" on page 481.

Begin Guided Tour   Use Add/Remove Program

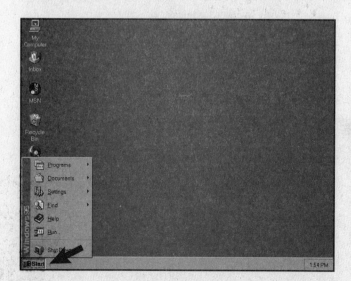

1 Click on the **Start** button to display the Start menu.

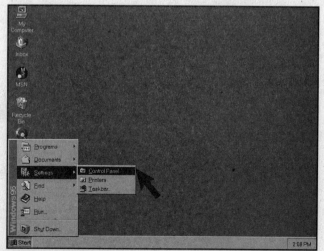

2 Select **Settings** and then select **Control Panel**.

(continues)

Begin Guided Tour Use Add/Remove Program   *(continued)*

3 In the Control Panel window, double-click the **Add/Remove Programs** icon.

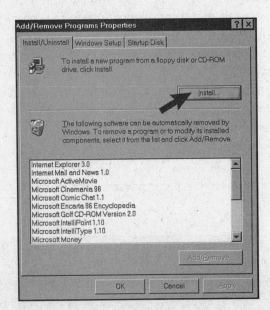

4 The Add/Remove Programs Properties dialog box appears. If necessary, click on the **Install/Uninstall** tab. Then click on the **Install** button.

Note that when you delete a program from the hard drive, without using the Remove Programs feature, the icons that point to the program are not automatically deleted. You must manually delete them, as covered in the task "Remove a Folder or Program from the Start Menu" (page 58).

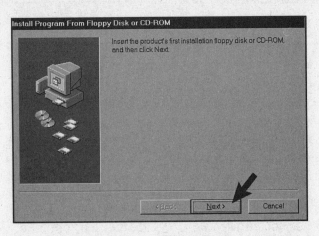

5 You are prompted to insert the floppy disk or CD-ROM that contains the program's setup files. Do so, and then click the **Next** button.

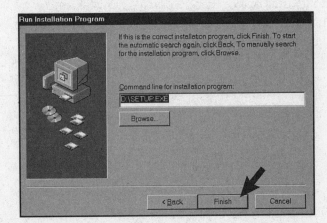

6 Windows searches for the installation program on the drive in which you inserted the disk or CD. When it finds the program, Windows displays the file name for the installation program. Click the **Finish** button, and Windows runs the installation program. Follow the on-screen instructions, which will vary depending on the program you are installing.

If you upgrade from Windows 3.1, it, might help you to think of the folders on the program sub menu as program groups.

Add a Folder to the Start Menu

When you select Programs from the Start menu, you see a list of folders (and program icons) in the Programs menu. When you select one of these folders, you access a submenu. To help you organize your programs in the groups you want, Windows enables you to add new folders to this menu. You can set up as many folders as you want and then add program icons to them to get the programs you want in each folder.

For example, you may want to create one folder that contains all your writing tools (programs you use for writing) and another that contains your financial tools (spreadsheet, check management, and so on.) Another organization technique is to set up folders for each of the programs you have. For example, you may have one folder that contains all the Microsoft Office programs.

When you are setting up folders, keep the following tips in mind:

- You can have multiple program icons for one program. This enables you to start a program from more than one place on the desktop (as described in "Start a Program Each Time You Start Windows" on page 45). For example, if you set up a folder for each person who uses the computer and each person who uses Paint, you can add a Paint program icon to each person's folder for convenience.

- When you create a new folder, it is empty until you add shortcuts to it. You'll learn how to add shortcuts in "Add a Shortcut to the Desktop" on page 63.

- You can nest folders within folders. For example, you could set up a folder for each person who uses the PC, and then set up folders for each person's different tasks. For instance, you might have a folder for Sean that contains folders called Financial, Games, and Work.

- A folder name can contain up to 255 characters, including spaces. However, you can't use any of the following characters:

    \ ? : * , " < > |

Begin Guided Tour Add a Folder

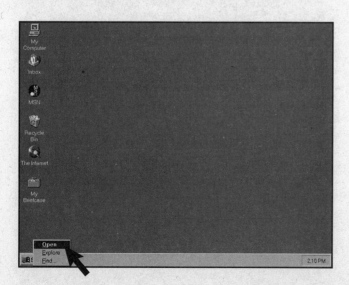

① Right-click on the **Start** button. In the shortcut menu that appears, click on **Open**.

② In the Start Menu window, double-click on the **Programs** icon.

(continues)

Guided Tour   Add a Folder   *(continued)*

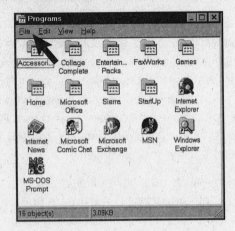

3 The Programs window opens, displaying the folders and icons it contains. If you want to nest the folder you are creating within an existing folder, open that folder by double-clicking on it. Open the **File** menu and select the **New** command.

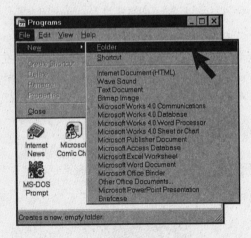

4 From the submenu that appears, select **Folder**.

5 Windows adds a new folder to the Programs folder. Type the name you want to give the new folder (such as Work) and press **Enter**.

6 Windows adds the new folder to the Start menu. (Close all open windows and access the Start menu, and you'll see the new folder in the location you selected.) You now can add other programs to this menu by following the steps in the task "Add a Program."

Add a Program to the Start Menu

If you've ever used someone else's computer, you may find that it is set up much differently from the computer you use. Even if you're using the same type of computer and running the same version of Windows, your systems can be drastically different. How can that be?

Windows enables you to arrange your programs and customize a number of features on the desktop to suit the way you work. Therefore, your neighbor's or your friend's computer may look entirely different than your PC. Basically, to each his or her own.

As I described in the previous task, you can customize the Start menu by adding folders and grouping your programs together to suit your needs. Likewise, you can add a program directly to the Start menu or to a folder within the Start menu. (You also can add a program directly to the desktop, as covered in "Add a Shortcut to the Desktop" on page 63.)

> You can add a program to the Start menu by dragging its icon onto the Start button. The program then appears at the top of the Start menu (not in the Programs menu).

When you add a program to the Start menu or a folder, you are creating a shortcut—a pointer to the original program file. Using shortcuts, you can add a program to more than one folder without ever moving the original file. The *Guided Tour* walks you through adding a program icon (shortcut) to a folder in the Start menu.

Browse Your System

When you add a program, you have to know the program's file name and path. If you know the file name and path, you can type it in the appropriate text box to tell Windows where to find it.

However, if you don't know the path to your program, use the Browse button in the Create Shortcut dialog box to search through the drives and folders on your system and find the program file. When you click the Browse button, Windows displays the folders and files in the current folder. Within the Browse dialog box, you can do the following:

- To change to another folder, double-click on the folder. Windows displays the folders and files within that folder.

- To move up one level in the folder structure, click on the **Up One Level** button.

- If you want to change to a different drive, display the **Look in** drop-down list and select the drive you want.

- If you want to change the types of files that are listed, display the **Files of type** drop-down list and select the type of file you want displayed.

- By default, Windows displays the contents of the folder as a list. If you want to see detailed information about the folders and files, select the **Details** button. To return to list view, click the **List** button.

Create a New Folder

Suppose you're in the middle of adding a new program icon, and you realize that you don't want it in any of your existing folders. You want to create a new folder to put it in, but you don't want to start all over. Don't worry. Windows 95 enables you to create a new folder for the program as you add the program icon. To do so, follow the *Guided Tour* and use the optional step (step 7) to create the new folder.

Begin Guided Tour   Add a Program

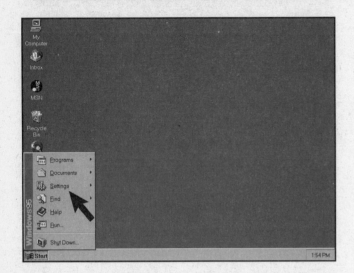

1 Click on the **Start** button to display the Start menu.

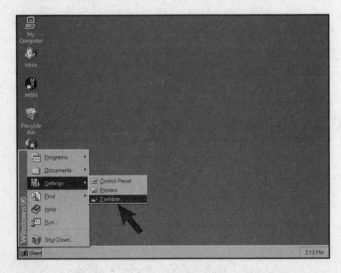

2 Select **Settings** and then **Taskbar**.

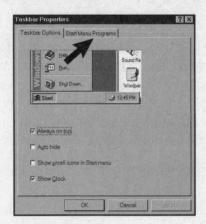

3 In the Taskbar Properties dialog box, click on the **Start Menu Programs** tab.

4 On the Start Menu Programs tab, click the **Add** button.

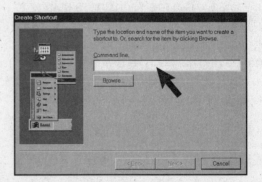

5 The Create Shortcut dialog box appears. In the Command line text box, type the path for the program. If you don't know the path, click the **Browse** button and then locate the program you want to add.

Guided Tour Add a Program

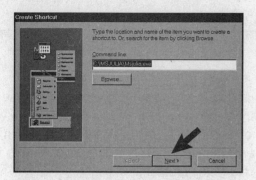

6 With the program name in the Command line text box, click the **Next** button. The Select Program Folder dialog box displays an outline of the folders in your Programs folder.

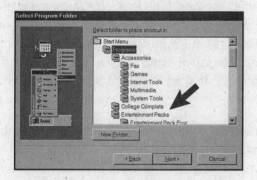

7 (Optional) When you're prompted to select the folder for the program, click the **New Folder** button to create a new folder. Type the name of the new folder and press **Enter**.

8 Click the folder in which you want the program to appear, and then click the **Next** button.

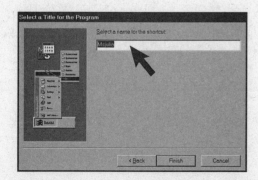

9 You are prompted to type a name for the shortcut. Windows suggests the name of the program file, but you can enter a more descriptive name. Type the name that you want to see on the menu, and then click **Finish**.

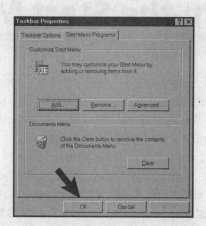

10 Click **OK** to close the Taskbar Properties dialog box.

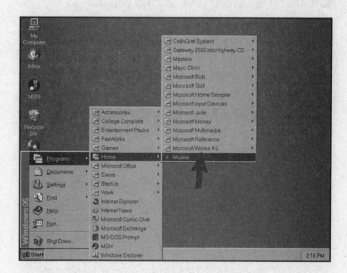

11 To make sure the program is added to the menu, click the **Start** button and select the folder to which you added the program. The program should be listed on the menu.

Remove a Folder or Program from the Start Menu

As you use your computer more and more, your needs may change, and you may find that you no longer like your organization method. Perhaps you originally added all your programs to the Start menu, but you really only use a few of them. Now your Start menu is cluttered with programs you don't need and don't use. Are you stuck with this mess? No. Just as you can add folders or programs to the Start menu, you also can do the reverse: remove folders or programs.

Note that this *Guided Tour* teaches you how to remove the program from your Start menu only—not from your system. Keep in mind that the program icon and the program file are not the same thing. The program file is the set of instructions stored on disk that enables you to run the program. (A program file usually has the extension .EXE and is stored in the folder you selected when you installed the program.) The program icon is a pointer to the program file.

When you delete a folder, you also delete all of its contents. For example, suppose that you have a folder named WORK that contains program icons for Word, Excel, and Power-Point. If you delete this folder, you also delete all the program icons in the folder.

Think of it this way: the program file is something tangible, and the program icon is simply a set of directions to the tangible thing. If you're having a hard time getting it straight, try thinking of them as two presents. If you open a box that contains the program file, you have something to use or play with. If you open a box that contains the program icon, all you have is a piece of paper telling you where to find the box with the program.

When you remove a folder or program icon, you delete the object that points to the program files, but you do not delete the actual program; the program files remain on disk. (This is like throwing away the slip of paper; doing so does not damage the program itself.) You can still run the program (although not using that program icon), and you can re-create the program icon that points to the program file if you want.

In some cases, you may want to get rid of both the program file(s) and the pointer to those files. You can remove the program files using the Add/Remove Programs icon, as covered in the task "Remove an Old Program" on page 481. Or you can use Windows Explorer or My Computer to delete the program files. See the section "Manage Folders and Files" on page 67.

You also can right-click on the program icon or folder icon in the Start Menu window and then click on the **Delete** command to remove a program or folder.

Begin Guided Tour   Remove a Program Icon

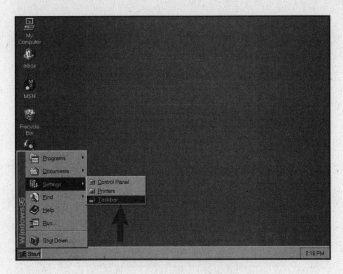

① Click on the **Start** button, select **Settings**, and select **Taskbar**.

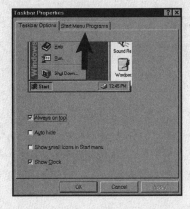

② In the Taskbar Properties dialog box, click on the **Start Menu Programs** tab if necessary.

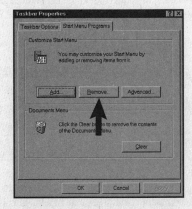

③ On the Start Menu Programs tab, click the **Remove** button.

④ The Remove Shortcuts/Folders dialog box appears. Double-click on the folder that contains the program you want to remove.

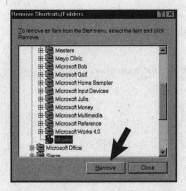

⑤ When you see the program you want to remove, click on it, and then click the Remove button.

⑥ Windows removes the icon. Click the **Close** button and click **OK** to close the dialog boxes.

Begin Guided Tour   Remove a Folder

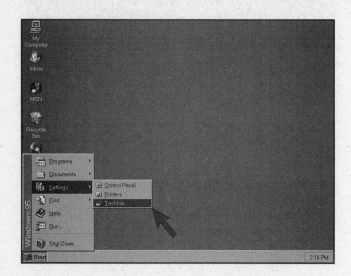

1 Click on the **Start** button, select **Settings**, and select **Taskbar**.

2 In the Taskbar Properties dialog box, click on the **Start Menu Programs** tab if necessary.

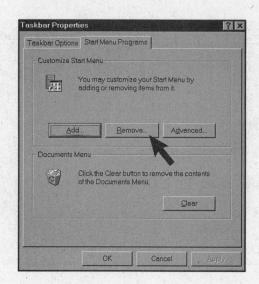

3 On the Start Menu Programs tab, click the **Remove** button.

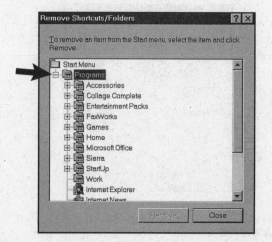

4 The Remove Shortcuts/Folders dialog box appears. To remove a folder, click on it, and then click the **Remove** button.

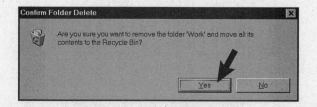

5 You are prompted to confirm that you want to remove the folder and its contents. Click the **Yes** button. Then click the **Close** button and **OK** to close the dialog boxes.

Move a Program to a Different Folder

When you install a program Windows creates a folder for it so you can find it and start it easily. The problem is, sometimes Windows doesn't organize your programs the same way you would. Windows provides yet another way for you to make the Windows desktop more comfortable for your personal working style: it enables you to move your programs and accessories into different folders.

You've learned that the Start menu contains folders and that you can store program icons or other folders within those folders. When you want to do some rearranging, first you need to display the program icon you want to move, and then you need to display the folder where you want to put the icon. To help you visualize this process, think about refiling a piece of paper. You start by opening the folder and taking out the paper you want to move. Then you open the folder where you want to place the item, and you shove it in.

In the Start menu, you don't physically open any folders. Instead, you open on-screen windows. First, you open the folder that contains the program icon (window 1). Then you open the folder where you want to place the program icon (window 2). You can then move the icon from one window to the other.

When you are working with multiple windows, you can arrange them manually by dragging the title bar. Alternatively, you can right-click on a blank area of the taskbar and select a command to have Windows 95 tile or cascade the open windows. See "Move and Arrange Windows" on page 16 for details on moving among windows.

When you move program icons from one folder to another, it does not affect the location of the program files on your hard disk. If you want information on moving a file from one location to another, see "Manage Folders and Files" on page 67.

Begin Guided Tour   Move a Program

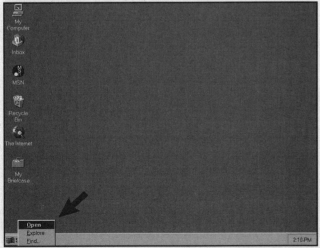

1 Right-click on the **Start** button. In the shortcut menu that appears, select **Open**.

2 In the Start Menu window, double-click on the **Programs** folder.

(continues)

Guided Tour   Move a Program

(continued)

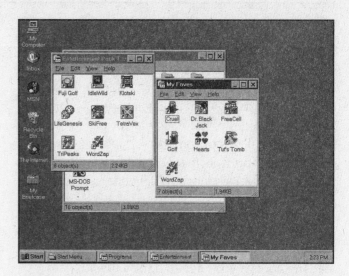

3 The Programs window appears, displaying the contents of the Programs folder. Double-click on the folder that contains the icon you want to move. You may have to open several folders to get to the one that contains the program you want.

5 Rearrange the windows so you can see both the window containing the program icon you want to move and the window containing the folder to which you want to move it. Then drag the icon to the new window.

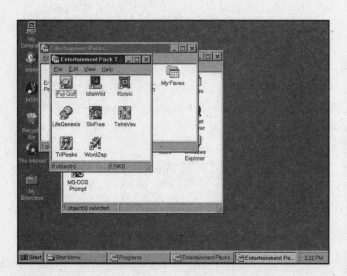

4 In the window that opens, you see the contents of that folder, including the icon you want to move in this example, the program named TriPeaks. Next, double-click on the folder where you want to place the icon (My Faves).

6 Windows moves the icon to the new folder. Click on each window's **Close** button.

7 From now on, when you use the Start menu to start the program, you'll find the icon in this folder.

As a shortcut, you can drag the program icon from its window and place it on top of the other folder icon. (You don't have to open window 2.)

Add a Shortcut to the Desktop

You know how inefficient and harried you become when the top of your desk is cluttered and things are out of place or located in places that are inconvenient. If you think about your desk, you can see that you use a certain organization for the tools and papers you use. Some items you always leave right on top of the desk because you use them constantly. Other items you organize in the desk drawers; smaller or more frequently used items go in the top drawers, and files and items you rarely use go in the bottom drawers.

The same type of organization carries over to your electronic desktop. For example, you can put tools to which you want immediate access right on the desktop. However, you may put other important programs in your StartUp folder so Windows starts them each time you start Windows. And still other programs you may organize into folders on the Start menu.

By default, the desktop includes a few important icons: My Computer, the Recycle Bin, and a few others. You can add other icons to the desktop for programs you use most often so you can have immediate access to them. When you are creating a shortcut, keep these pointers in mind:

- A shortcut is simply a pointer to something else. For example, a shortcut to a program is just a pointer to the program files.

- You can create shortcuts for different types of items. You can create a shortcut to a program (covered here). When you double-click on a program shortcut, Windows starts the program. In addition, you can create shortcuts to folders or documents you use often. See the section

"Manage Folders and Files" on page 67 for help on creating that type of shortcut.

- You can place shortcuts at different levels. You can place a shortcut on the desktop (covered here) or within the Start menu (covered in the task "Add a Program to the Start menu" on page 55).

- You can create a shortcut using either My Computer or Windows Explorer. The *Guided Tour* covers using My Computer; for information on using Windows Explorer see the section "Manage Folders and Files" on page 67.

Note that a shortcut does not change a program, folder, or document's location; it just places an icon on the desktop that enables you to access the file quickly.

Rename a Shortcut Icon

When you create a shortcut, Windows names the icon "Shortcut to *xx*," where *xx* is the original name of the program or document. If you don't like this name, you can use a different name. For example, you may want to use a more descriptive name or a shorter name. Although you can use up to 255 characters (including spaces) to name a shortcut, be frugal with your naming schemes to keep your desktop neat and easy to understand. Make sure your names make sense. A cryptic name can confuse you and waste your time if you have to open a program to see what it is.

Begin Guided Tour   Create a Shortcut

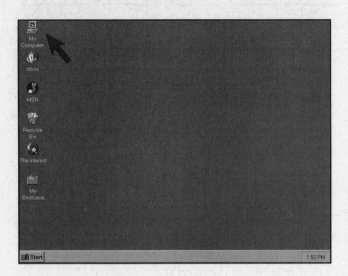

1 Double-click on the **My Computer** icon.

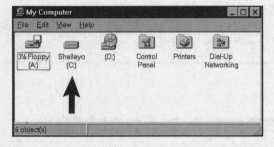

2 The My Computer window displays icons for the contents of your system. Double-click the drive and the folder that contains the icon you want to move to the desktop. You may have to open several folders until you find the program file.

3 When you find the program icon, point to the icon, and press and hold down the right mouse button. Then drag the item to the desktop.

4 Windows adds the shortcut icon to the desktop. You can now double-click on the icon to start the program (program icons), to open the folder (folder icons), or to open the document (document icons).

5 Close all the open windows and move the icon to where you would like it on the desktop.

Begin Guided Tour   Rename a Shortcut Icon

1 Right-click on the icon you want to rename.

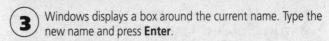

3 Windows displays a box around the current name. Type the new name and press **Enter**.

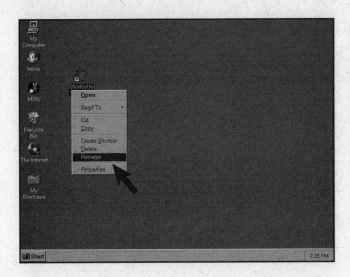

2 In the shortcut menu that appears, select **Rename**.

4 Windows renames the shortcut icon.

Delete a Shortcut from the Desktop

In some cases, you may get over-enthusiastic and put icons for all your programs, most of your folders, and lots of documents right on the desktop. That's the electronic equivalent of having every book, paper, file, and pen you own out on your desk. When this organization gets too cluttered, you need to make changes: You need to delete shortcuts you no longer use.

Keep in mind that when you delete a shortcut from the desktop, you are simply removing the icon from the desktop. You are not deleting the original file or program. At the same time, if you delete the file or program, you must also delete the icon; Windows won't automatically remove the shortcut. See "Install a Program" on page 51 for more on deleting a program.

If you delete a shortcut by accident, you can retrieve it from the Recycle Bin. See "Retrieve Something from the Recycle Bin" on page 118.

Begin Guided Tour   Delete a Shortcut

1 Drag the icon to the Recycle Bin. Or right-click on the icon, select the **Delete** command, and click the **Yes** button.

2 Windows removes the shortcut from the desktop.

HOW TO...
Manage Folders and Files

Look around your office. Do you have filing cabinets filled with important papers? Are they organized into drawers and folders (well, somewhat organized)? This same method of organization applies to the electronic documents you create on a computer. Each document you save—whether it's a report, a chart, or an address list, for example—is stored in a file. Keeping track of those files is part of using any computer.

Windows 95 offers two file management tools: My Computer and Windows Explorer. In many cases, the steps you follow for each are the same or very similar; which method you use is a matter of preference. This section describes how to display, find, organize, and work with the files on your computer using both My Computer and Windows Explorer.

What You Will Find in This Section

Understand Disk Drives, Folders, and Files

Suppose you own your own business and use your computer to keep track of your clients, inventory, and other business details. In your business, you have certain papers that you need to keep track of (invoices, orders, bills, payments received, and so on). Let's say your method of keeping track of these papers is to throw them all in a closet, everything tossed together in one big pile. Can you imagine trying to find a particular piece of paper in that closet? It would be impossible!

To better keep track of your paper documents, you probably use a more organized method, usually some type of filing cabinet with a folder or drawer for each type of paper item you keep (one for invoices, one for orders, and so on). When you need to find something, you simply go to the appropriate folder or drawer and find the one you need. Sound better?

Many new computer users don't realize that the same is true for working with computer files. You should use the same logic and organization to manage your computer folders and files that you use for your paper files.

When you create a document on your computer, the data is stored on your hard disk as a file with a file name. You can think of a file as being like a paper document, and you can think of your hard disk as the filing cabinet in which you store the document. If you have more than one drive, it's like having more than one filing cabinet. All the drives on your system are comparable to a complete set of filing cabinets.

> A *document* is anything you create on your computer: a memo, a letter, a picture, a spreadsheet, or whatever.

Now if you kept all your files together in the same place on the computer, it would be the same as throwing them all in a heap in one closet. Instead, you can divide your hard disk into sections called folders, and then you can organize your files into folders.

> If you're upgrading from Windows 3.1, note that what used to be called a directory is now called a folder.

Folders are an important part of disk organization. The following outline shows a simple folder structure:

```
C:\
    \WORD
    \EXCEL
        BUDGETS
        SALES
```

Using that structure as an example, consider the following statements about folders:

- The structure of folders on a drive is sometimes called the folder tree. You start with one main folder, called the *root*, which is represented by the backslash (\) at the top level.

- All other folders are branches of the root folder.

- You can store folders within a folder. For example, you can have one folder for your Excel worksheet files, and within that folder, you can have folders for each type of worksheet—one for budgets, one for sales, and so on. These folders are sometimes called *subfolders* or *nested folders*.

- The arrangement of folders at different levels is often referred to as the *folder hierarchy*. In this example, you have two top level folders, WORD and EXCEL, and two nested folders within EXCEL.

- The chain of folder names starting at the root and going to a particular folder is called that folder's *path*. For example, the path name to the folder SALES would be C:\EXCEL\SALES. (You separate the divisions of a path with backslashes.)

The Two File Management Tools

To keep track of the drives, folders, and files on your system, you can use either of Windows 95's file management tools: My Computer or Windows Explorer. My Computer provides a graphical view of the drives on your system. (You can think of using My Computer as surveying the various filing cabinets you have.) Most new users will want to use My Computer. To learn how to start and use My Computer, see "View Your Folders and Files with My Computer" on page 71.

The Windows Explorer provides a graphical representation of the entire folder tree (including all drives)

and the contents of the currently selected folder. Users who are upgrading from Windows 3.1 will find that Windows Explorer is very similar to Windows 3.1's File Manager. If you are already comfortable using Windows, you may prefer Windows Explorer. To learn how to start and use Windows Explorer, see "View Your Folders and Files with Windows Explorer" on page 73.

For most tasks, you can use My Computer or Windows Explorer—whichever you prefer. In many cases, the steps are similar if not exactly the same. When the steps are similar and there is no advantage to using either tool, the *Guided Tour* covers both tools. If the method for using one tool is preferred or easier, the *Guided Tour* covers that method.

Understand Icons

To help you distinguish between the types of items on your computer, Windows uses a different icon for each type of item. The following table shows the icons you can expect to see.

Windows 95 Icon Types

Icon	Type	Description
	Drive icon	This type of icon represents a drive. You can display the contents of the drive by double-clicking on the icon.
	Folder icon	This type of icon represents a folder. You can display the contents of the folder by double-clicking on the icon.
	Program icon	This type of icon represents a program. The look of the icon varies from program to program.
	Document icon	This type of icon represents a document. If Windows can identify the program that created the document, it displays a small program icon within the document. If not, it displays a generic document icon.
	Shortcut icon	When you create a shortcut to a program, folder, or file, Windows displays the appropriate icon type with this arrow icon on it to indicate that the item is a shortcut.

Begin Guided Tour View My Computer

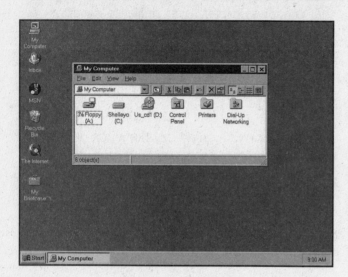

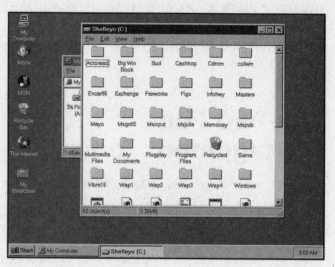

1 My Computer displays an icon for each of the drives on your computer. (Alternatively, you can view the contents of your drives with Windows Explorer.)

2 To keep your files organized, you can create folders. Windows displays an icon that looks like a folder for each folder on your system.

3 Within the folders, you store your files. Windows displays a document icon for each file and (if possible) indicates the type of file with a program icon. (For example, the Word icon indicates that all of these files were created in Word.)

View Your Folders and Files with My Computer

As the previous task explained, Windows provides, you with two tools for viewing and working with the folders and files on your system. One of those tools, My Computer, is essentially designed for the beginning user or for times when you just need to browse through your folders.

The first step in most file management tasks is to find and display the file or folder you want to work with. For example, when you want to create a shortcut to a program (as described in "Add a Shortcut to the Desktop" on page 63), you first have to find the program file. You can use My Computer to look through your drives and folders to find the program file you want. Similarly, you can use My Computer to find a document file (such as a report) that you've created and saved.

> Remember you also can use Windows Explorer to display the contents of your system. See "View Your Folders and Files with Windows Explorer" on page 73.

When you double-click on the My Computer icon, Windows opens a window in which it displays icons that represent the contents of your computer. The drive icons you see indicate the drives you have on your particular system and what they are called

(therefore, your screen may not look quite like the ones in this book). For example, if you have only one hard drive and one floppy drive, Windows displays only two drive icons (C: and A:). In addition to the drive icons, Windows displays icons for the Printers folder and your Control Panel folder. To learn more about printing, flip to "Print Your Documents" (page 157); to learn more about the Control Panel turn to "Use the Control Panel to Customize Windows 95" (page 427). Finally, if you are connected to a network, Windows displays icons for the network drives. See "Use Windows on a Network" (367) for more information.

To display the contents of a drive, double-click on it. A window opens, displaying the folders and programs on that drive. You can continue to open folders by double-clicking on them until you find the file you want. To close all windows in that particular chain of windows, hold down the **Shift** key and click on the **Close** box. Windows closes all the windows in that chain.

You can use My Computer not only to view the contents of your computer, but also to copy files, create shortcuts, create new folders, and so on. The rest of this section describes the tasks you can perform in My Computer and in Windows 95's other file management tool, Windows Explorer.

Begin Guided Tour Use My Computer

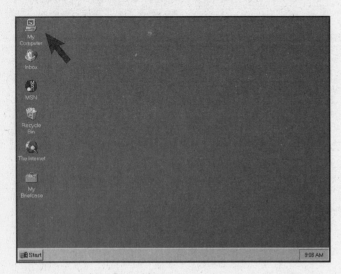

1 Double-click on the **My Computer** icon. The My Computer window opens.

2 Windows displays icons for the drives on your system, the Printers folder, and the Control Panel folder. To open a drive or folder, double-click on its icon.

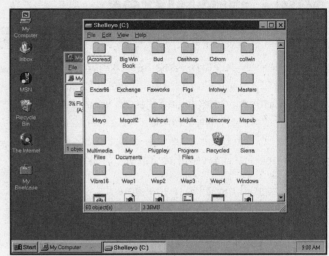

3 Windows opens another window and displays the contents of the drive or folder. Continue opening folders until you find the folder or file you need.

To close all open windows in an application press **Shift** and click on the **Close** button of the active window

View Your Folders and Files with Windows Explorer

The Windows Explorer is one of Windows 95's two file management programs. If you are upgrading from Windows 3.1, you'll find Explorer to be very similar to version 3.1's File Manager. In the Explorer window, Windows displays all the folders on your system as well as the contents of the currently selected folder.

Because Explorer shows all the available drives and folders in one window, some tasks (such as moving a file) are easier to accomplish with Windows Explorer than they are in My Computer. Keep in mind that you can perform most tasks using either My Computer or Windows Explorer; which one you use is basically a matter of preference.

In Windows Explorer, the window is split into two sections. The left side of the window shows all of the drives and folders on your system displayed in a hierarchical structure called a *folder tree*. The right side of the window displays only the contents of the item that's selected in the left side. For example, if you select a folder on the left side, you see the contents of that folder on the right side. The status bar displays the number of objects (files and folders), the amount of disk space that the selected item takes up, and the amount of free disk space on the selected drive.

When you want to look at the contents of a drive or folder, you must select it, by clicking on it once. You can use the following techniques to control what is displayed in the Explorer window:

- Click on the plus sign next to a drive icon to see a list of the folders on that drive. (This is sometimes called expanding the folder tree.)

- Click on the plus sign next to a folder icon to see a list of subfolders within that folder.

- Click the minus sign next to a folder or drive icon to collapse (hide) the folder's or the drive's contents (if you no longer want to view the contents of a particular folder, for example).

- Use the vertical scroll bar to move through the list of drives or folders on the left side to find the one you want. (If your list is expanded and your computer contains a lot of drives and folders, you may not be able to see the entire list.)

- Use the horizontal scroll bar to scroll through the contents list on the right side of the window. (If the selected folder or drive contains many items, you may not be able to see them all on the right side of the window.)

- Select the item at the very top of the folder tree on the left side (it's called the Desktop) to display all the drives on your system (the same contents you see when you open My Computer).

- To quickly go to a particular folder, open the **Tools** menu and select the **Go to** command. In the Go To Folder dialog box, type the path to the folder you want to open and click **OK**.

- When you double-click on a folder in the right side of the window, the folder is opened, and Windows displays its contents on the right side of the window.

You can start Windows Explorer and explore a drive or folder from My Computer. To do so, click on the item you want to explore. Then open the **File** menu and select **Explore**. You also can explore the contents of the Start menu by right-clicking on the **Start** button and selecting **Explore**.

Begin Guided Tour Start Windows Explorer

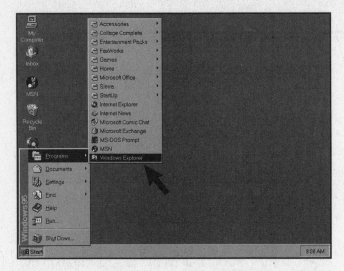

1 Click on the **Start** button to display the Start menu. Select **Programs** and then select **Windows Explorer**.

2 Windows starts Windows Explorer and displays the contents of your computer. Your drives and folders appear in a hierarchical structure on the left side, and the contents of the selected item appear on the right side.

Begin Guided Tour Scroll Through the Drives and Folders

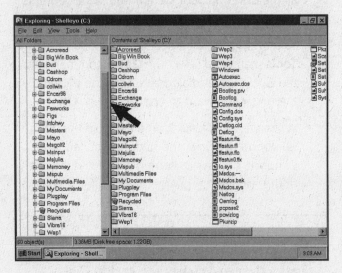

1 To scroll through the folder tree on the left, click the up and down scroll arrows (or drag the scroll box). To scroll through the file list on the right, click on the right and left scroll arrows.

2 When you scroll to the end of the list for the current drive (shown here), you see icons for your other drives.

Begin Guided Tour   Display Additional Folders

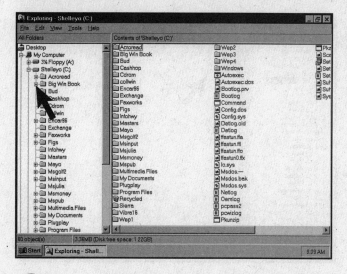

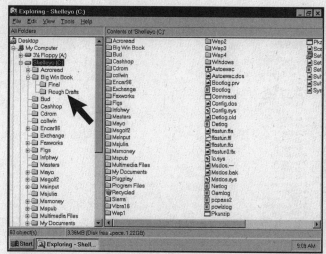

1 Click on the **(+)** next to a folder to display its subfolders.

2 On the left side, Windows displays the subfolders within the selected folder. (Notice that the plus sign changes to a minus sign to indicate that the folder has been expanded.)

Begin Guided Tour   Hide Folders

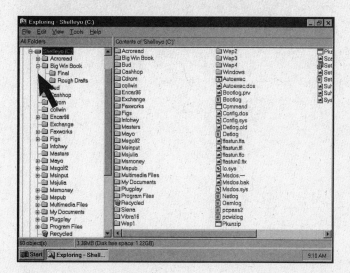

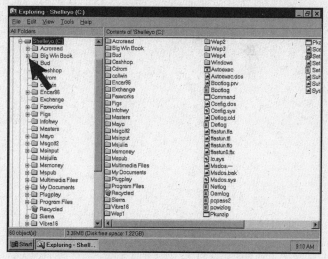

1 Click on the **(–)** next to a folder to hide its subfolders.

2 Windows collapses that "branch" of the folder tree and hides all the folders within that folder.

Begin Guided Tour Select a Drive or Folder

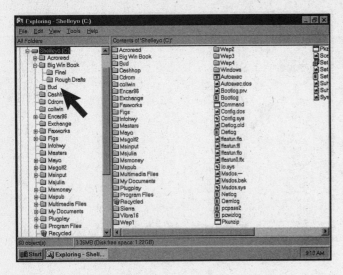

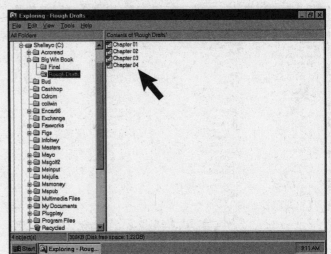

1 To display the contents of another drive or folder on the right side of the window, click on the drive or folder on the left side (or use the arrow keys to highlight it).

2 Windows displays the contents of the newly selected drive or folder.

Change How You View Your Computer's Contents

When you use My Computer or Windows Explorer, you are often looking for a file or group of files. How Windows displays the files often plays a part in how easy it is for you to find the one(s) you want. (For example, a display of the file names might be fine when you're looking for a program file, but you need to see a detailed view that shows the date when you're looking for the newer of two files.) Therefore, Windows enables you to control how files are displayed in the My Computer and Explorer windows.

The View menu in both My Computer and Windows Explorer enables you to control how Windows displays the disks, directories, folders, and files. In addition, the View menu also contains options you can use to select which on-screen tools Windows displays, to select different icon arrangements, and to set options for the types of files Windows displays.

The following guidelines should help you determine which view is best for certain situations:

- If you want to be able to identify the contents by type (according to which program they were created in), you probably want to use icon view.

- If the folder or drive contains a lot of icons, select small icon view so the window can hold more icons.

- If you are looking for a particular file or program by name, try list view.

- Finally, if you want more information (such as the type, file size, and so on) about the contents, use details view.

The View menu also includes commands for arranging the icons and controlling the display of certain on-screen elements. You can choose to have Windows arrange icons by name, size, type, or date. To align the icons in the window, use the Line up Icons command on the View menu. This command is available only in My Computer or when you right-click on the desktop.

By default, Windows displays a status bar that shows the number of items in the window (Windows Explorer and My Computer also display the amount of space available on the current disk). You can turn off the status bar if you want. Likewise, you also can control whether Windows displays a toolbar at the top of the window.

Use the Toolbar

The My Computer and Windows Explorer toolbars contain icons you can use to work with the window's contents. If you choose to display the toolbar, you can use these buttons as a shortcut method of selecting commands. The table on the next page shows the toolbar buttons and describes each one.

Use the Options Command

The View menus in My Computer and Windows Explorer also contain an Options command that gives you access to the Options dialog box. In the Options dialog box, you can change a number of things about the display.

- When you open My Computer and then open a folder, both windows remain open. You can change this so that only the current window remains open. To do so, use the Folder tab in the Options dialog box, as covered in the *Guided Tour*. (This only applies to My Computer–not Windows Explorer.)

- By default, hidden files do not appear in the window. With the options on the View tab, you can change this so that all files are displayed.

- On the View tab, you can choose to display the complete path name in the title bar and to display extensions for files.

- Use the File Types tab to see a list of the registered file types.

Toolbar Buttons

Button	Name	Description
Documents	Folder Drop-down list	Enables you to select another drive or folder.
	Up One Level	Moves you up one level in the folder structure.
	Cut	Cuts a selected file or folder. (See the task on moving files or folders.)
	Copy	Copies selected file(s) or folders. (See the task on copying files or folders.)
	Paste	Pastes a cut or copied file or folder.
	Undo	Undoes the last command.
	Delete	Deletes the selected file(s) or folder(s).
	Properties	Displays or changes file properties. (See "Display and Change File Properties," pg. 108.)
	Large Icons	Changes to large icon view.
	Small Icons	Changes to small icon view.
	List	Switches to list view.
	Details	Switches to details view.

Resize the Columns in Explorer or My Computer

When you use the Details view within My Computer or Explorer, it displays its list of information in four columns. The first column displays the file name, the second column displays the file size, the third column displays the file type, and the last column displays the date and time of the file's creation or most recent modification.

If you work with the Explorer or the My Computer window maximized, the size of these columns is relative; for the most part, each column has enough room to display its data. But if you work with a smaller window, you may need to adjust the width of each column so you can see all the information. In addition, in Explorer, you may want to change the size of the folder list (on the left) to make the files list (on the right) larger.

Begin Do It Yourself Change the Size of the Files List in Explorer

1 Position the mouse pointer on the divider between the folder and files lists. The mouse pointer changes to a two-headed arrow.

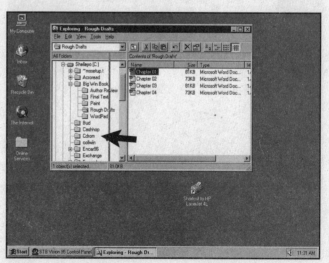

2 Drag the divider to the left to increase the size of the files list, or drag it to the right to decrease the size.

(continues)

Do It Yourself   Change the Size of the Files List in Explorer   (continued)

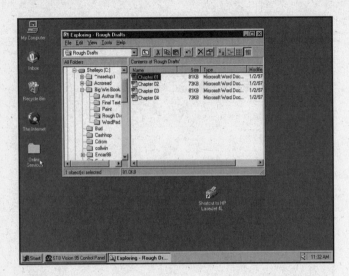

3 Release the mouse button, and the divider is moved to where you indicated.

Begin Do It Yourself   Adjust the Size of the File List Columns in Details View

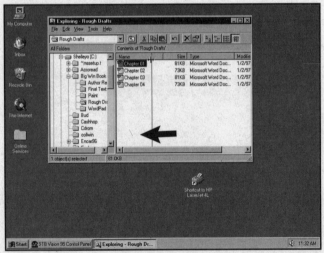

1 In Explorer or My Computer, position the mouse pointer at the right edge of the title area for the column whose size you want to adjust. The mouse pointer changes to a two-headed arrow.

2 Drag the column divider to adjust the size of the column.

Do It Yourself   Adjust the Size of the File List columns in Details View

To adjust the size of a column to fit its contents exactly, simply double-click on the column divider. For example, to make the Name column exactly wide enough for its contents, double-click on the column divider at the right edge of the Name title area.

 3 Release the mouse button, and the column's size is adjusted.

Toolbar Buttons

Button	Name	Description
📁 Rough Drafts ▼	Folder Drop-down list	Enables you to select another drive or folder.
🔼	Up One Level	Moves you up one level in the folder structure.
✂	Cut	Cuts a selected file or folder. (See the task on moving files or folders.)
📋	Copy	Copies selected file(s) or folders. (See the *Guided Tour* on copying files or folders.)
📋	Paste	Pastes a cut or copied file or folder.
↩	Undo	Undoes the last command.
✕	Delete	Deletes the selected file(s) or folder(s).
📄	Properties	Displays or changes file properties. (See "Display and Change File Properties," pg. 108.)

(continues)

Toolbar Buttons   Continued

Button	Name	Description
	Large Icons	Changes to large icon view.
	Small Icons	Changes to small icon view.
	List	Switches to list view.
	Details	Switches to details view.

Begin Guided Tour   Change How the Contents Are Displayed

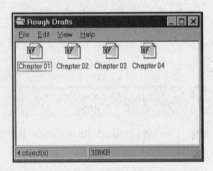

1 Open the window that you want to change.

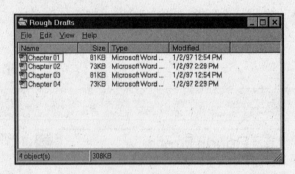

3 Windows displays the contents in the selected view. Here you see the contents in Details view.

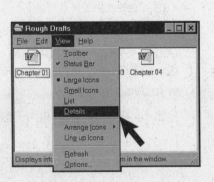

2 Open the **View** menu and select the type of view you want: **Large Icons**, **Small Icons**, **List**, or **Details**.

Begin Guided Tour   Arrange Icons

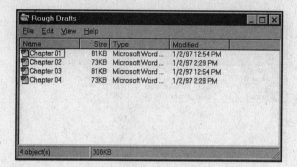

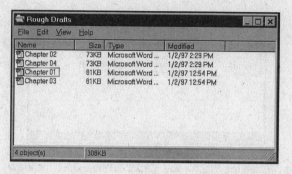

1 Open the window you want to change.

3 Windows arranges the items in the appropriate order. Here the items are arranged by size, from smallest to largest.

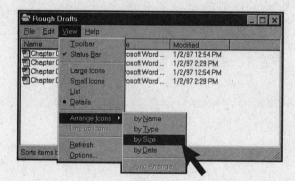

In Details view, you can arrange items by clicking on the column header. For instance, to arrange by date, click on the Date column header.

2 Open the **View** menu and select the **Arrange Icons** command. In the submenu that appears, indicate how you want the items arranged.

Begin Guided Tour   Turn On or Off the Status Bar and Toolbar

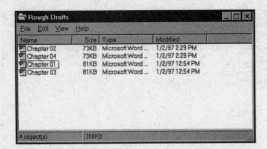

1 Open the window you want to change. Open the **View** menu.

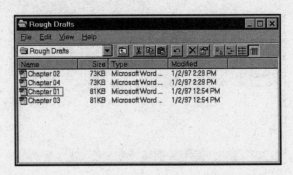

3 Windows makes the changes to the window. Here the status bar is hidden, and the toolbar is displayed.

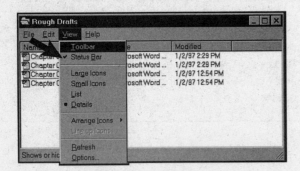

2 If you want to turn on the status bar or the toolbar, select either the **Status Bar** command or the **Toolbar** command so that there is a check mark. If you want to turn off the status bar or toolbar, select the command to remove the check mark.

Begin Guided Tour   Set View Options

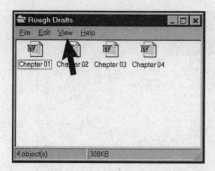

1 Open the window you want to change. Open the **View** menu.

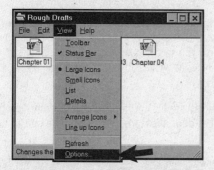

2 Select the **Options** command.

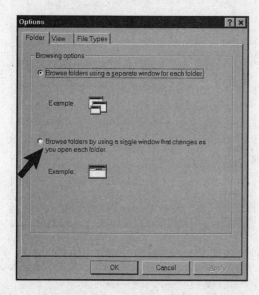

3 The Options dialog box appears. If you are using Explorer, skip to the next step. In My Computer, you see the Folder tab. Indicate whether you want all windows to remain open when you're browsing for files. If you are finished making changes, skip to step 6.

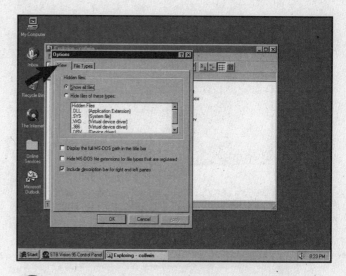

4 To make changes to the view options, select the View tab. On the View tab, indicate whether you want to display all files or hide certain file types. If you want to display the path name in the title bar, hide MS-DOS file extensions that are registered, or include description bar for right and left panes (available for Explorer only), select any of those check boxes.

5 When you are finished making changes, click the **OK** button.

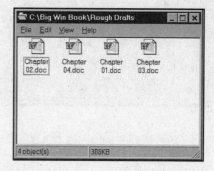

6 Windows makes the changes. Here the path name appears in the title bar, and the file extensions are displayed.

Begin Guided Tour   See a List of Icons

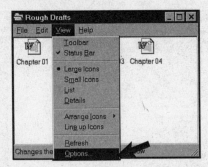

1 Open the My Computer icon or start Windows Explorer. Then open the **View** menu and select the **Options** command.

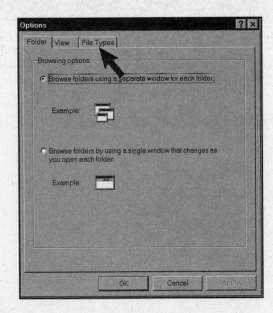

2 In the Options dialog box, select the **File Types** tab.

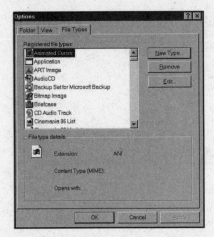

3 Windows displays a list of the registered file types that shows the icon and a short description. In the lower half of the dialog box, you see the extension that's associated with the selected file type, as well as an icon for the program in which it was created.

4 To display the file information about another program, scroll through the icons and click on the one you want.

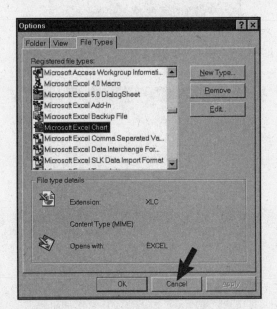

5 Windows displays file information about that icon. When you are finished reviewing this information, close the dialog box by clicking the **Cancel** button.

Create a Folder

You learned earlier in this section that it's a good idea to organize your hard disk so you can keep track of where your files are stored. You also learned that you should organize your computer's contents into folders and subfolders. Now it's time to learn how to create a new folder to meet your needs.

When you first start using your computer, there are already some folders set up on your system. Windows, for example, is stored in its own folder, which contains several subfolders for certain file types. When you install a new program, that program also sets up the folders it needs. In addition to these folders, you can add new folders of your own using My Computer or Windows Explorer; the *Guided Tour* covers both.

You can create a folder anywhere within the structure of your computer. That is, you can create a folder on the desktop, at the top level, or within another folder. The chain of folders that starts at the drive name and goes to your folder is called the path. (For example, if you have a folder named DOCUMENTS in the WINWORD folder on drive C, the path to that folder would be C:\WINWORD\DOCUMENTS.)

Consider the following suggestions when you are creating folders:

- Be sure to use a meaningful file name so that you can easily identify the contents of the folder. When naming folders, you can use up to 255 characters including spaces.

- Before you start creating folders, spend some time thinking of how you want to group your files. You may want to create a folder for each type of document you create, or you may want to organize your folders by project (have one folder for each project or job you are working on).

- It's a good idea to separate your document files from your application files. This makes it easier for you to back up the document files. In addition, if you upgrade your application, you don't have to worry about deleting important document files.

Begin Guided Tour   Create a Folder Using My Computer

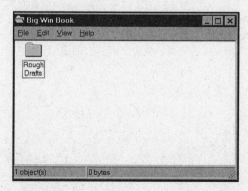

1 In My Computer, open the drive or folder where you want to place the new folder.

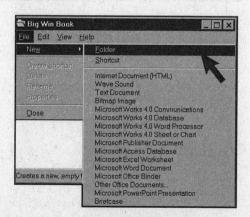

2 Open the **File** menu and select the **New** command. In the submenu that appears, select **Folder**.

(continues)

Guided Tour Create a Folder Using My Computer *(continued)*

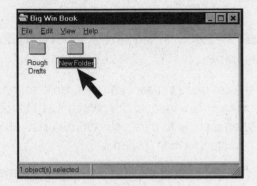

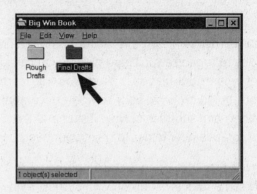

3 Windows adds a new folder (named New Folder) to the window. The name is highlighted so you can type a more descriptive name.

4 Type a name for the new folder and press **Enter**. Windows displays the new folder.

Begin Guided Tour Create a Folder Using Windows Explorer

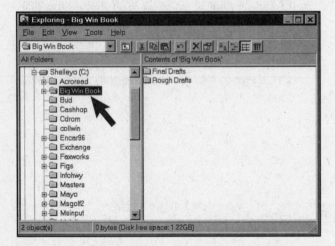

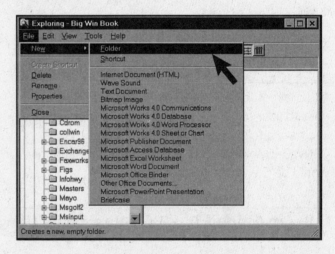

1 Start Windows Explorer and select the drive or folder where you want to place the new folder.

2 Open the **File** menu and select the **New** command. In the submenu that appears, select **Folder**.

Guided Tour Create a Folder Using Windows Explorer

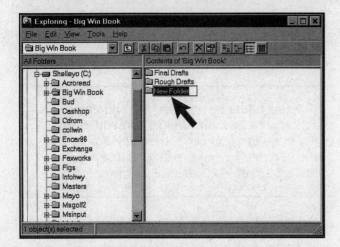
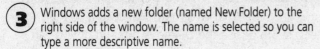

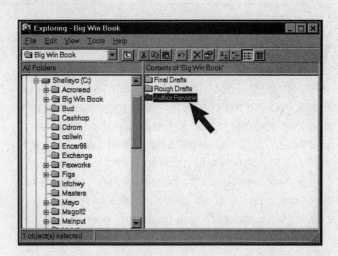

3 Windows adds a new folder (named New Folder) to the right side of the window. The name is selected so you can type a more descriptive name.

4 Type a name for the new folder and press **Enter**. Windows displays the new folder.

Delete a Folder

When you first start using a computer, you will probably think you have more than enough space for all the documents and programs you need. But as you use the computer more and more, you will find that you quickly fill up the available disk space you have. You'll create documents that take up space, and you'll probably add new programs. Eventually, you will have to do a little housekeeping to get rid of files and folders you no longer need or that you created by mistake. Or you might just need to do some reorganizing that results in folders you no longer need. In all these cases, you can delete the folders you no longer need.

When you delete a folder, keep in mind that you are not only deleting the folder, but its contents as well. Therefore, you should always open the folder, look over its contents, and move or copy any files or folders you want to keep to another location before you delete the folder.

> Delete a folder by mistake? Try undoing the action with the **Edit, Undo** command. If that doesn't work, you can retrieve the folder from the Recycle Bin. See the task "Retrieve Something from the Recycle Bin" on page 118.

You can delete a folder from My Computer or Windows Explorer (they work the exact same way), and you can use one of two methods: drag it to the Recycle Bin or use the Delete command. If you can see the Recycle Bin, use that method. If the Recycle Bin isn't visible, use the command method. Both are described in the *Guided Tour*.

Begin Guided Tour   Drag a Folder to the Recycle Bin

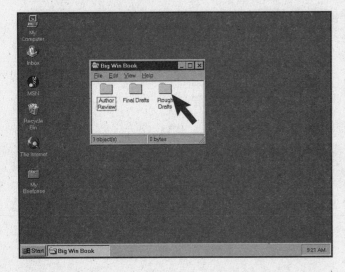

1 Open My Computer or Windows Explorer and display the folder you want to delete. (Be sure that you also can see the Recycle Bin icon.)

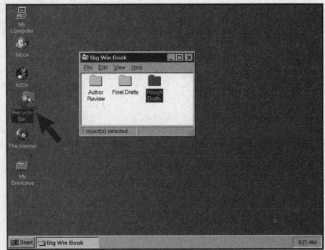

2 Drag the folder to the Recycle Bin. Windows deletes the folder.

Begin Guided Tour   Delete a Folder Using the Delete Command

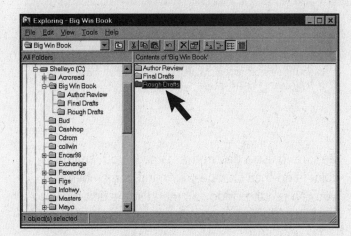

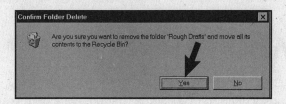

3 A dialog box appears, asking you to confirm the deletion. Click the **Yes** button to delete the folder.

1 Open My Computer or Windows Explorer and display the folder you want to delete.

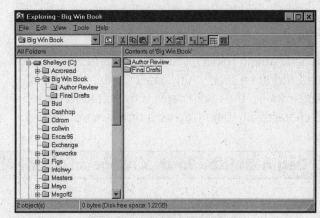

4 Windows deletes the folder.

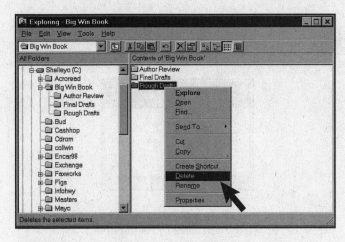

2 Right-click on the folder. In the shortcut menu that appears, select the **Delete** command.

Rename a Folder

When you first start organizing your folders and documents, you may have a good idea of where you want to place each item. But over time, you may need to make some changes. One item you may want to change is the name of a folder. For example, suppose you created a folder for Chapter 2, but then you rearranged your chapters, and Chapter 2 became Chapter 3. No problem. You simply change the folder's name.

When naming folders, you can use up to 255 characters, including spaces. (In some DOS and Windows applications, the folder name is truncated to the old 8-character limitation. When a program truncates a

folder or file name, it adds a tilde ~ to indicate that the name has been shortened.) You cannot use any of the following characters:

\ ? : * " < > |

Be sure to use a descriptive name. If you rename a folder and then change your mind, remember that you can use the Undo command in the Edit menu to undo the change.

You can use My Computer or Windows Explorer to rename a folder. The steps are the same for both and are shown here in the *Guided Tour*.

Begin Guided Tour Change a Folder Name

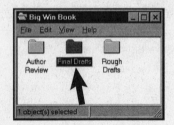

1 In My Computer or Windows Explorer, display the folder you want to rename.

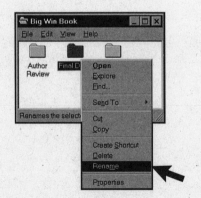

2 Right-click on the folder. In the shortcut menu that appears, select the **Rename** command.

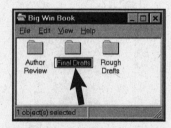

3 The current name is selected so you can type the new name. Type the new name and press **Enter**.

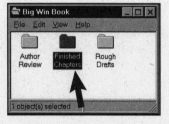

4 Windows renames the folder.

Copy or Move a Folder

After you use your computer for a while, you may find that your original organization plan for folders and files is outdated. Perhaps you started with a structure similar to this, with one main folder for all your work files and a subfolder for each application type.

```
C:\
    WINWORD
    EXCEL
    WORK
        WINWORD DOCS
        EXCEL WORKSHEETS
```

After working with this structure, you've decided that a different organization would work better. You'd rather have the document folders within the program folders like this:

```
C:\
    WINWORD
        WINWORD DOCS
    EXCEL
        EXCEL WORKSHEETS
```

You can create new folders and then move the files accordingly, or you can simply move the folders. As with most file management tasks, you can use My Computer or Windows Explorer to move folders. It is easier to use Windows Explorer, though, because you can see all the folders in one window. Therefore, the *Guided Tour* covers that method only.

You also can use the Cut and Paste commands in the Edit menu to move a folder. To do so, follow these steps:

1. In My Computer or Windows Explorer, select the folder you want to move.

2. Open the **Edit** menu and select the **Cut** command. (If the toolbar is displayed, you can click on the **Cut** button.)

3. Open the folder into which you want to place the cut folder.

4. Open the **Edit** menu and select the **Paste** command.

You also can copy a folder by using Copy instead of Cut. Doing so copies not only the folder, but the folder's contents.

Begin Guided Tour Move a Folder

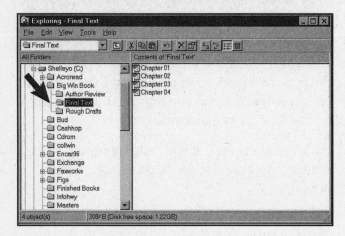

1 In Windows Explorer, select the folder you want to move.

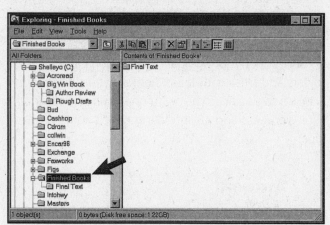

3 Windows moves the folder to its new location. In this figure, the folder that contains the moved folder is expanded so you can see the results.

You can copy a folder by holding down the **Ctrl** key and dragging a copy of the folder to the new location.

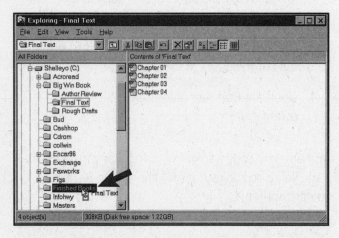

2 On the left side of the window, make sure you can see the folder to which you want to move the folder. Then drag the folder to its new location.

If the tree is too large, you can drag the object past the bottom or top of the pane, and the window will scroll automatically.

Begin Guided Tour   Copy a Folder

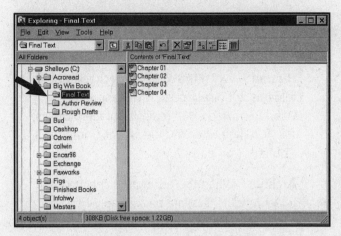

1 In My Computer or Windows Explorer, select the folder you want to copy.

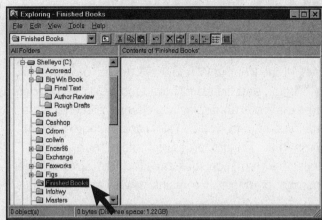

3 Select the drive or folder in which you want to place the copy.

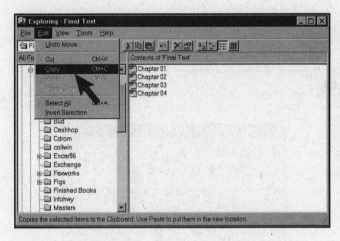

2 Open the **Edit** menu and select the **Copy** command.

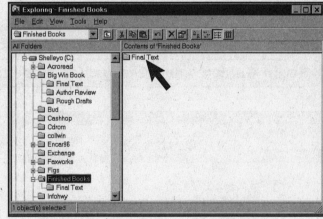

4 Open the **Edit** menu and select the **Paste** command. Windows copies the folder and its contents.

Display and Change Folder Icon Properties

All the icons in Windows 95 (folder, program, disk, and file icons) have features called **properties** that you can display and change. Depending on the type of item, you can view and change different properties. The properties of a folder, for example, include information such as its location, size, and the number of objects it contains, as well as its attributes.

Attributes control which folders appear in a folder's contents list, whether you can delete or change a folder, and whether a folder is backed up (archived). You can set the following attributes for each folder:

Read-Only   When this attribute is checked, the folder cannot be deleted or changed.

Hidden   When this attribute is checked, the folder is not displayed in My Computer or Windows Explorer. To redisplay hidden folders, see "Change How You View Your Computer's Contents" on page 77.

Archive   When this attribute is checked, this folder (and its files) are backed up when you run a backup. (see "Back Up and Restore Files" on page 353.)

You can display and change folder icon properties in My Computer or in Windows Explorer using the steps shown in the *Guided Tour.*

Begin Guided Tour   Change Icon Properties

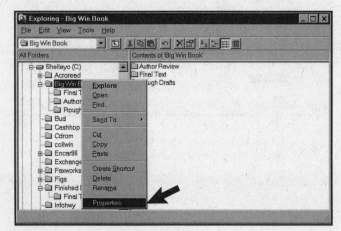

1 Select the folder whose properties you want to view or change. Right-click on the folder and select **Properties** from the shortcut menu that appears.

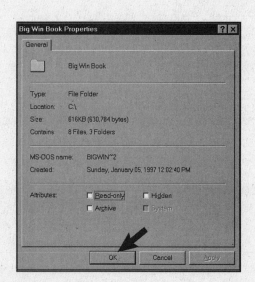

2 The Properities dialog box appears. Review the folder information and make any changes to the attributes. Then click the **OK** button.

Create a Shortcut to a Folder

Suppose you have one important folder that contains the documents you work on most often: you use the computer every day, and you mainly work with the contents of this folder. Although you could go through the process of opening the folder using My Computer or Windows Explorer every day, why waste your time? Instead, you can create shortcuts to save time.

If you use a folder often and want quick access to its contents, you can create a shortcut to the folder. By creating a shortcut, you can put the folder right on the desktop or add it to the Start menu. For example, suppose you are writing a book and keep all the document files together in one folder. If you add the folder's icon to the desktop, you can display the folder's contents simply by double-clicking on the

icon. No more wading through ten or twelve menus and submenus on the Start menu!

> You learned how to create a shortcut on your desktop in "Add a Shortcut to the Desktop" (page 63). The process for creating any type of a shortcut (to a program, a folder, or a file) is the same. This task shows you how to create a shortcut for a folder.

When you create the shortcut, Windows names the icon "Shortcut to *xx*," where *xx* is the folder name. You can use the Rename command to give the icon a more descriptive name. (See "Rename a Folder" on page 92.)

Begin Guided Tour   Create a Shortcut

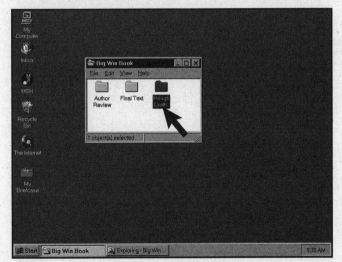

1 In Windows Explorer or My Computer, select the folder for which you want to create a shortcut. Be sure that you can see at least part of the desktop.

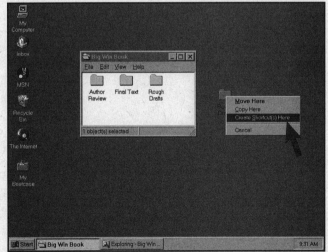

2 With the right mouse button, drag the folder icon from the window to the desktop. You see a shortcut menu. Select **Create Shortcut(s) Here**.

(continues)

Guided Tour Create a Shortcut

(continued)

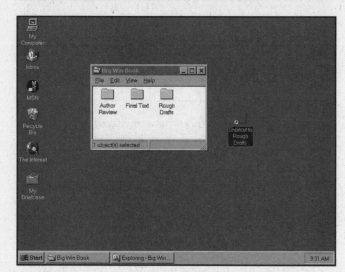

To add the shortcut to the Start menu, drag it to the Start menu.

3 Windows displays the shortcut in its new location (the desktop in this case).

Select Files to Move or Copy

You can also work with the files on your disk. In many cases, you perform an action (such as copying, deleting, or renaming) on a file the same way you do on a folder.

You can select as many files as you want to work with. If you select one file and execute a command, Windows carries out the command on that file only. If you select several files, Windows carries out the command on all the selected files.

When selecting files, you can use the following shortcuts:

- To select a range of files that are next to each other (*contiguous*), click on the first file, press and hold the **Shift** key, and click on the last file. The first and last files and all files in between are selected if you're in list view. If you're in icon view, all files between the two (in a rectangular area) are selected.

- To select a group of files that are not next to each other (*noncontiguous*), click on the first

file, press and hold the **Ctrl** key, and click on each other file you want to select.

- You also can select a group of files by clicking in the upper-left corner of an area and dragging the mouse over all the files in that area. An outline appears and moves with the mouse pointer to indicate the area you're selecting. When you've "captured" all the files you want to select, release the mouse button. All the files are selected.

- To select all files, open the **Edit** menu and choose the **Select All** command, or press **Ctrl+A**.

- To invert the selection (select all unselected files and deselect the selected files), open the **Edit** menu and choose the **Invert Selection** command.

- To deselect a file, click on it again.

Begin Guided Tour   Select Files in My Computer

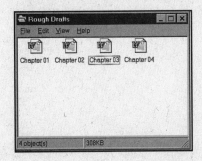

1 Open the window that contains the files you want to select.

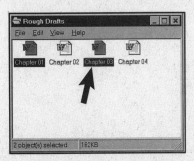

2 Select the file or files you want using the methods described in the text. The document icons appear highlighted.

Begin Guided Tour   Select Files in Windows Explorer

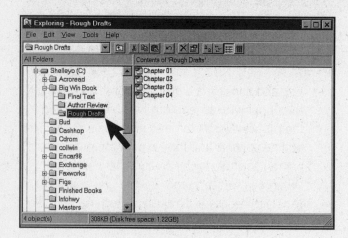

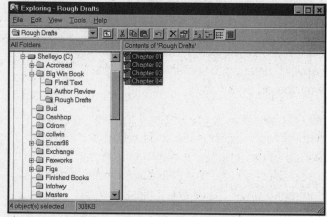

1 Display the file or files you want to select.

2 Select the file or files you want using the methods described in the text. The files appear highlighted.

Move Files

You may want to move files around for any number of reasons: maybe you inadvertently saved a document in the wrong folder, or perhaps your projects have grown so much you need to reorganize your files and put them in different folders. Whatever the reason, you can easily move a file from one folder to another or from one disk to another.

The easiest way to move a file is to drag the file in Windows Explorer (as covered in the *Guided Tour*).

If you move or copy a file to a folder that contains another file with the same name, Windows assumes you want to replace the first file with the one you're moving. Windows displays a dialog box asking you to confirm the replacement. (The date and times the files were last modified are displayed so you can tell which file is more current.)

Begin Guided Tour   Drag Files to Move Them

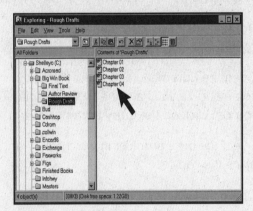

1 In Windows Explorer, display the files you want to move on the right side of the window.

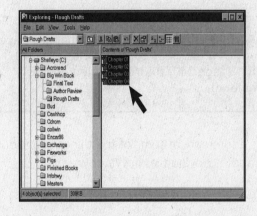

3 Drag the selected file(s) to the folder or drive on the left side of the window.

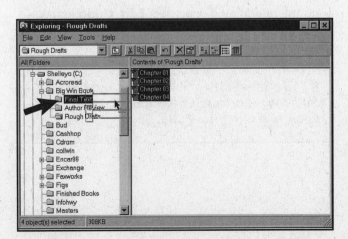

2 On the left side, scroll through the list until you can see the drive or folder to which you want to move the files. Select the file or files you want to move.

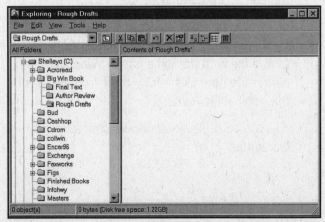

4 Windows moves the selected file(s) to the new drive or folder.

Copy Files

One file management task you will perform often is copying files. You might need to copy a group of files so you have extra copies in case something happens to the originals (for which purpose you also can make a backup as covered in "Maintain Your System" on page 337). Or maybe you need to copy files to a floppy disk so you can take work home from the office. Or perhaps you need to copy files to a floppy disk that you can give to a co-worker (if you need to share documents and you're not on a network). Or maybe you just want to copy a file so you can have two versions, one to keep intact and one to modify.

> You can use the File Save As command to save a copy of a file. See "Save and Close a Document" (page 140) for information on this command.

Here is a summary of some of the things you should know about copying files in Windows.

- You can copy a single file or a group of files.

- You can copy the files to the same drive and folder, to another drive, or to another folder.

- You can create a copy by dragging or by using the Edit, Copy command.

- If you use the Copy command to copy a file to the same folder or to another folder that contains a file with the same name, Windows names the new files "Copy of *xx*," where *xx* is the original file name.

- You can copy files in Windows Explorer or My Computer.

The *Guided Tour* shows you how to copy files by dragging in Windows Explorer because that's the quickest method. It also shows you how to use the Send To command to copy files to a floppy drive (which works the same way in My Computer and Explorer).

Copying with Commands

You can use commands in Explorer or My Computer to copy a file. To do so, follow these steps:

1. Display and then select the file(s) you want to copy.

2. Open the **Edit** menu and select the **Copy** command. (If you have the toolbar displayed, you can click on the **Copy** button instead.)

3. Select the drive or folder in which you want to place the copy.

4. Open the **Edit** menu and select the **Paste** command, or click on the **Paste** button.

If you make a mistake when copying a file, you can undo the operation if you select **Edit, Undo** immediately (or you also can simply delete the copied file).

> If you prefer to use the keyboard, use the following shortcuts: Ctrl+X for Cut, Ctrl+C for Copy, and Ctrl+V for Paste.

Begin Guided Tour   Copy Files by Dragging Them

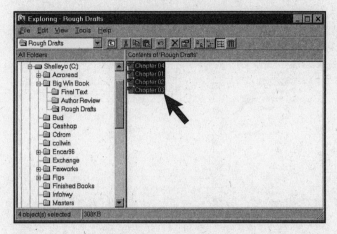

1 In Windows Explorer display the files you want to copy on the right side of the window. Select the files.

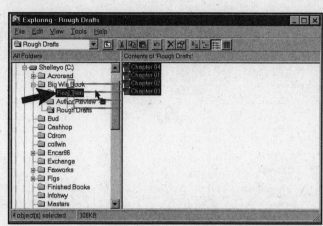

3 Hold down the **Ctrl** key and drag the selected files to the drive or folder where you want to place the copy.

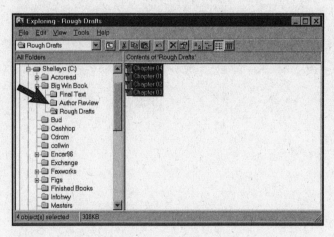

2 On the left side, scroll through the window until you can see the drive or folder in which you want to place the copies.

4 Windows copies the selected files. Click on the folder in which you placed the copies to open it so you can see the results.

If you don't hold down the Ctrl key as you drag, Windows moves the files instead of copying them. Be sure to hold down **Ctrl**.

Begin Guided Tour Copy Files to a Floppy Disk

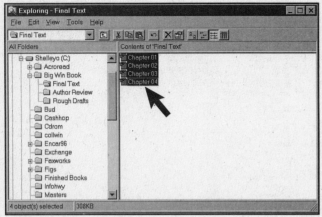

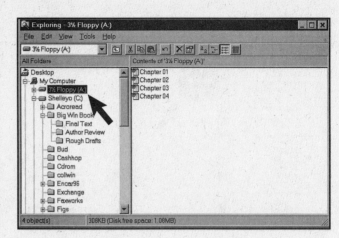

1 In Windows Explorer or My Computer, select the files you want to copy.

4 Windows copies the files. Click on the drive to which you copied the files so you can see the results of the copy.

2 Insert a disk into the drive.

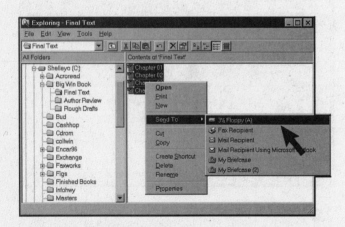

3 Open the **File** menu and select the **Send To** command. In the submenu that appears, select the floppy drive to which you want to copy the files.

Rename Files

When you save a file for the first time, you assign a name to it. Although the name probably seems appropriate at the time, it may not always be. Therefore, Windows enables you to rename files with the Rename command.

Before Windows 95, you had to stick with an eight-character file name and a three-character extension, which was very limiting. Because you ended up with files like CNSDBUDG.XLS, you had to be a pretty good guesser to figure out what some files contained. With Windows 95 you can use as many as 255 characters in a file name, including spaces. This enables you to use much more descriptive

names (such as Consolidated Budget instead of CNSDBUDG). You can use the Rename command to rename older files (those that came from your old DOS or Windows 3.1 files and programs) using more descriptive names.

You also can rename files you have created if you just want to change the name. Perhaps you don't like the name you assigned originally, or perhaps the contents of the file have changed and you want a name that more accurately describes the file.

As with most file management tasks, you can use the same steps in Windows Explorer or My Computer to rename files.

Begin Guided Tour Change the Name of a File

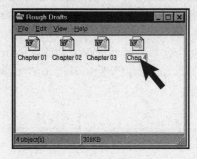

1 In Windows Explorer or My Computer, display the file you want to rename.

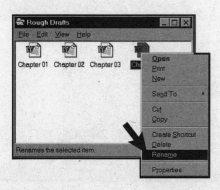

2 Right-click on the file and select **Rename** from the shortcut menu that appears.

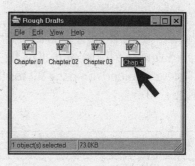

3 Windows highlights the current name and displays a box around it. Type the new name and press **Enter**.

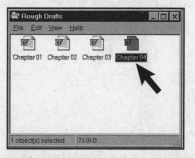

4 Windows renames the file.

Delete Files

The more you use the computer, the more files you have on your hard disk. Although you seem to have plenty of disk space at first, eventually your hard disk becomes cluttered. When that happens, you need to do some housekeeping and get rid of files you no longer need.

You can use My Computer or Windows Explorer to delete any file on your system. Using the Delete command or the Recycle Bin, you can delete a single file or a group of files.

When deleting files, keep the following tips in mind:

- If you think you may need the files again, consider making a backup copy and saving it on a floppy disk. You can then delete the files from your hard disk. If you find later that you need the files though, you still have the copies on the floppy disk.

- If you want to get rid of a whole folder of files, you can delete the folder and all its files at once. See "Delete a Folder" on page 90 for the details.

- If you make a mistake when deleting, try undoing the deletion with the Edit, Undo command. You also can try retrieving the file(s) from the Recycle Bin as described in "Retrieve Something from the Recycle Bin" (page 118).

- When you delete multiple files with a command, you are prompted to confirm the deletion.

- When you delete a program file, Windows displays a dialog box asking you to confirm the deletion. You are reminded that if you delete the program, you can't use it to access the documents created in that program. Be sure to read all prompts carefully, and make sure you know what you are saying OK to.

- When you delete files, be sure not to delete any program files or any files you don't recognize. Applications often have several auxiliary files they use. Although you may think you only need the WINWORD.EXE file, you might actually need many other files in the WINWORD folder. If you don't recognize a file's name, don't delete it!

Begin Guided Tour Delete Files Using a Command

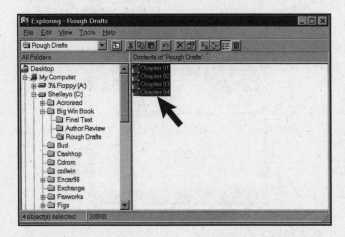

1 In Windows Explorer or My Computer, select the files you want to delete.

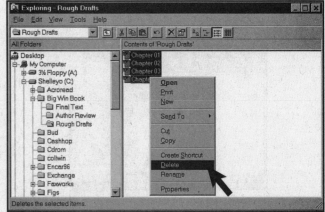

2 Right-click on the files and select the Delete command from the shortcut menu that appears.

Guided Tour Delete Files Using a Command

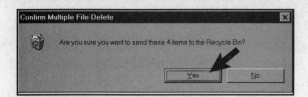

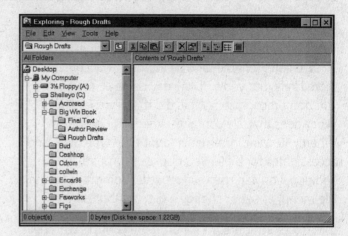

3 You are prompted to confirm the deletion. Click the **Yes** button to delete the files.

4 Windows deletes the file(s).

Begin Guided Tour Delete Files Using the Recycle Bin

1 In Windows Explorer or My Computer, select the files you want to delete.

3 Windows deletes the files.

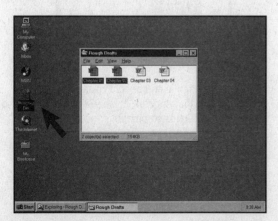

2 Be sure that you can see the Recycle Bin on the desktop. Then drag the selected files to the Recycle Bin.

Display and Change File Properties

As you use the computer more and more and create, rename, and delete files, it becomes more likely that you will one day come across a file you don't recognize. Where did that file come from? What does that file contain? When did I create it? When you want information about the type, size, and access dates for a file, you display its properties. In addition, you can use the Properties command (in the File menu) to set or change a file's attributes.

Like folder attributes, a file attribute controls whether a file can be deleted or changed, whether a file is displayed in file lists, and whether a file is backed up. You can set the following attributes:

Read-Only   When this attribute is checked, the file cannot be deleted or changed.

Hidden   When this attribute is checked, the file is not displayed in My Computer or Windows Explorer. (Using the View tab in the Options dialog box, you can change the view to display

hidden folders; see "Change How You View Your Computer's Contents" on page 77.)

Archive   When this attribute is checked, the file will be backed up when you run a backup. For more information on backing up, see the section "Maintain Your System" on page 337.

Depending on the type of application, you may see additional tabs in the Properties dialog box. For example, for Word for Windows documents, you can save summary information such as keywords or the author's name, and you can display statistics about the file. Therefore, the Properties dialog box has a Summary tab and a Statistics tab. Some utilities also add tabs to all property pages.

You can use the steps in the *Guided Tour* to display and change file properties in My Computer or Windows Explorer.

Begin Guided Tour   Use the File Properties Dialog Box

① In My Computer or Windows Explorer, display the file whose properties you want to view or change.

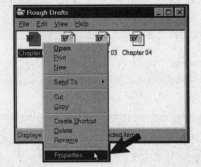

② Right-click on the file and select **Properties** from the shortcut menu that appears, or open the **File** menu and select the **Properties** command.

Guided Tour Use the File Properties Dialog Box

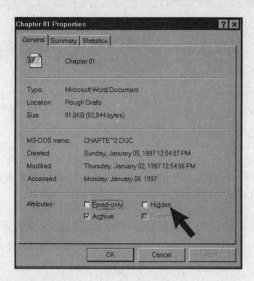

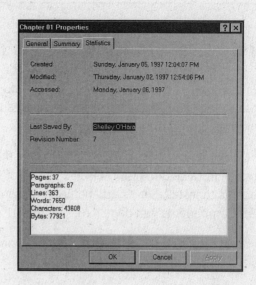

3 The Properties dialog box appears. Click the check box of any attribute you want to change. If the dialog box has other tabs (such as the Summary tab in the Word for Windows Properties dialog box), you can display and change this information as well.

5 Click the **Statistics** tab. This tab displays statistics about the file. Click the **OK** button to close the dialog box.

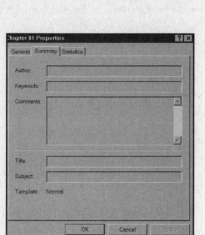

4 If you select the **Summary** tab, you see summary information about the file. If there is no information displayed, the author did not complete the summary box when he or she created the file.

View a File

When you can't remember the contents of a file, you can use Quick View to display the file. Windows can display most types of application files with Quick View. There are some file types, such as sound files, that cannot be displayed.

To use Quick View, you must install this feature. If you did a typical installation, it isn't selected as one of the components to install. See "Add and Remove Windows 95 Components" on page 476.

After you've displayed a quick view of the file, you can do the following things:

- To open the file for editing, click the **Open File for Editing** button, or open the **File** menu and select the **Open for Editing** command.

- To display an overall view, open the **View** menu and select the **Page View** command.

- To scroll through a multipage document, use the scroll arrows or press **Page Down** and **Page Up**.

- To resize and move the Quick View window, use the techniques covered in "Master Windows Basics" (page 3).

You can use the Quick View feature from My Computer or Explorer. The *Guided Tour* shows you how.

Begin Guided Tour Take a Quick View of a File

1 In Windows Explorer or My Computer, select the file you want to view.

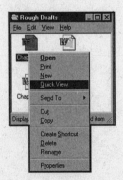

2 Open the **File** menu and select the **Quick View** command.

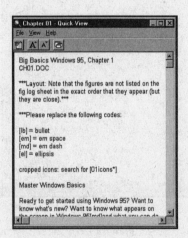

3 Windows displays a window showing the contents of the selected file. If you want to open the file, click the **Open File for Editing** button or open the **File** menu and select **Open File for Editing**.

4 To close the window, click the **Close** button.

Find a File or Folder

Have you ever saved a file and then been unable to find it? You know the file name, and you know the file's somewhere on your hard disk, but where? When you have trouble locating a file, you can use the Find command to tell Windows to search your hard disk for you.

You can use one of three methods to start a search. You can select the **Find** command from the **Start** menu. You can open the **Tools** menu in Windows Explorer, select **Find**, and select **Files or Folders**. Or, you can open **My Computer**, select the drive or folder you want to search, open the **File** menu, and select the **Find** command. Because no one method is preferred over the others, the *Guided Tour* gives an example of each.

With the Find command, you can have Windows search for files or folders, and you may have any or all of the following search options:

- If you know the name or the partial name of the file or folder, you can search using the name.

- If you have some idea of where the file is stored, you can have Windows search in a specific folder. If you don't know the location, you can have Windows search the entire disk.

- If you don't know the name, but you have some idea of the last time you worked on the file, you can search for folders or files modified within a certain time period.

- If you don't know the name or the date last modified, you can use the Advanced feature to search for files that contain a certain word or phrase. You also can use Advanced to search for a particular file type.

You can start the Find command directly from the Start button, from Windows Explorer, from My Computer, and from some applications.

For information on searching for files on the Microsoft Network, see "Use the Microsoft Network and the Internet" on page 312.

When you start the Find process, Windows asks you the name of the file or folder you want to find. By default, Windows doesn't match the case as you type it. For instance, if you enter Chap as the search string, Windows matches Chap, CHAP, and chap. If you want Windows to match the case, in the Find dialog box, open the **Options** menu and select the **Case Sensitive** command.

To search more quickly, you may want to narrow the search to a particular folder or a folder and its subfolders. For example, suppose you have a WINWORD folder that contains several subfolders for the projects you are working on. You know you saved the file in one of the subfolders of WINWORD, but you aren't sure which one. Instead of taking the time to search the entire disk, you can search the WINWORD folder and all its subfolders. To search a particular folder, select it in the **Look in** drop-down list, or click on the **Browse** button and use the Browse dialog box to select the folder(s) you want. Be sure to check the **Include subfolders** check box if you want Windows to check all subfolders in the named folder.

When Windows completes the search, the dialog box expands to display the matches in the lower part. Windows displays the name of the document, the folder in which the document is stored, the size, and type of document. The status bar shows the total number of items found.

In this file list, select the file you want. You can then open the file, delete it, rename it, and so on using the commands on the File menu. You also can open the folder that contains the file.

Use Wild Cards to Search for Files by Name

If you search for a file by name, you can type in all or part of the name, and you can use the wild cards * and ? (which are shortcuts that save some typing). The asterisk wild card, for example, represents any number of characters. So if you enter the search string CH*.DOC, Windows searches for all files that start with CH, have any number of characters after CH, and have the .DOC extension. This search would find CHAP01.DOC, CHAPTER01.DOC, CHILDREN STORY.DOC, and so on. The question mark wild card, on the other hand, represents any one character. For example, the search string CHAP?.DOC would find CHAP1.DOC and CHAPT.DOC, but not CHAP22.DOC.

Search for Files by Date or Contents

Sometimes you may not remember what you named the file, but you remember when you created and saved it (say, within the last week). If you can't remember the name, you can try another search strategy: search by date.

When you search by date, you can search for files modified within a certain date range (for example, all files modified from 7/13/97 to 7/16/97), or you can search for files modified during a certain number of previous month(s) or day(s). If you use the latter, you select the number of days or months (for example, you can search for all files modified in the past four days).

As a backup strategy, you can search for all files modified within the last month. When Windows displays the results of the search, you can easily copy or back up the files in the search results list. This ensures that you get all recently modified files.

Use the Advanced Tab

You can use the Advanced tab of the Find dialog box as a last ditch effort to locate a file. Using the features on this tab, you can search for a particular type of file, you can search for a file by its size (or a size range), or you can search for a file that contains a specified word or phrase. For instance, suppose you know the file you created contains the word "superlative." You can have Windows search for "superlative" and display a list of all files that contain that word.

When you are trying to locate a file by a word or phrase, think of a unique word or phrase to search for. If you search for a common word, the search may take a very long time, and you may have too many matches.

Saving a Search

In some cases, you will search for the same file or group of files more than once. For example, suppose you are writing a book and use the file naming scheme "Chapter x," where x is the chapter number. You often need to find and group all of the chapter files together. In such a case, you can search for the files once and save the search criteria. The next time you want to search for the same group, you won't have to go to the trouble of entering all the search options.

Follow these steps to save a search:

1. Enter the search criteria you want to save.

2. Open the **File** menu and select the **Save Search** command.

When you save the search, Windows places an icon on the desktop. You can double-click this icon to run the search at any time.

Begin Guided Tour   Search for a File by Name

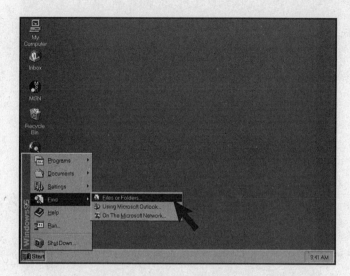

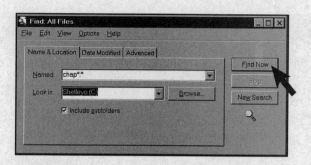

4 When you have entered the name and selected the folder or drive, click the **Find Now** button.

1 Click on the **Start** button, select the **Find** command, and select **Files or Folders.**

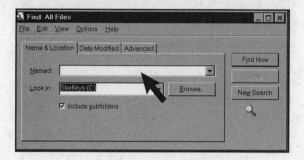

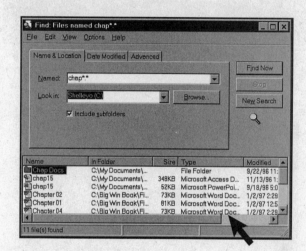

2 In the Find dialog box, click on the **Name & Location** tab if necessary. In the **Named** text box, type a partial or complete name. Remember that you can use wild cards.

5 Windows searches the selected drive(s) and folder(s) and displays the names of any matching files in the lower part of the window. To close the dialog box, click the **Close** button.

If you don't get the search results you want, click the **New Search** button and confirm that you want to start a new search. Try again using a different name or a different search method.

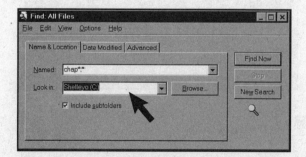

3 With the name completed, click the **Look in** drop-down list and select the drive or folder you want to search. If you want to include subfolders within the selected folder or drive, be sure the **Include subfolders** check box is selected.

Begin Guided Tour   Search for a File by Date

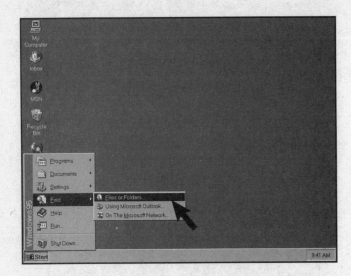

1 Click on the **Start** button, select the **Find** command, and select **Files or Folders**.

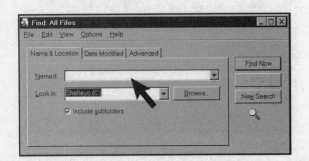

2 In the Find dialog box, click the **Name & Location** tab if necessary. If you want to enter a name or partial name, do so in the **Named** text box; however, you can leave this blank.

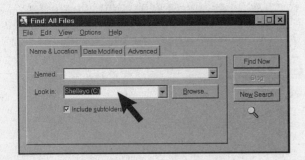

3 Open the **Look in** drop-down list and select the drive or folder you want to search, or click the **Browse** button and use the Browse dialog box. If you want to include subfolders within the selected folder or drive, be sure the **Include subfolders** check box is selected.

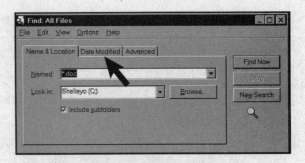

4 After you select the folder or drive, click the **Date Modified** tab.

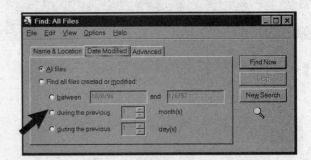

5 To search for files within a certain date range, select this option and enter the start and end dates in the between text boxes. To search for files modified within the past *x* month(s), select this option and enter the number of months. To search for files modified within the past *x* day(s), select this option and enter the number of days.

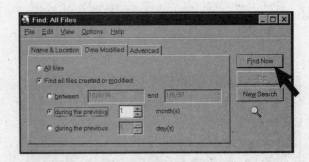

6 When you have completed the date range to search, click the **Find Now** button.

Guided Tour Search for a File by Date

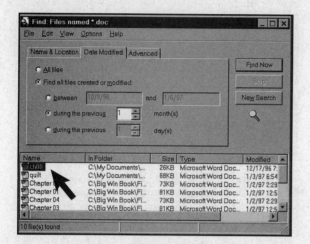

You can combine these search options. For example, you can enter a word or phrase *and* select a date range to limit the search to only files within that date range.

7 Windows searches the selected drive(s) and folder(s) and displays any matching files in the lower part of the window. You can use the commands in the File menu to work with the matching file(s). To close the dialog box, click the **Close** button.

Begin Guided Tour Search for a File with a Certain Word or Phrase

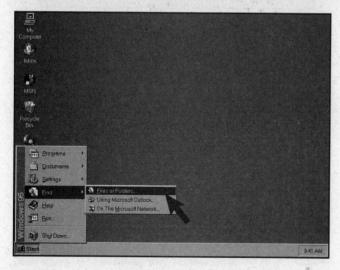

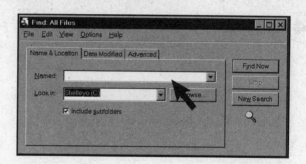

1 Click on the **Start** button, select the **Find** command, and select **Files or Folders**.

2 In the Find dialog box, click the **Name & Location** tab if necessary. If you want to, enter a name or partial name in the Named text box. Select the drive or folder you want to search from the **Look in** drop-down list, or click the **Browse** button and use the **Browse** dialog box. If you want to include subfolders within the selected folder or drive, be sure the **Include subfolders** check box is selected.

(continues)

Guided Tour Search for a File with a Certain Word or Phrase *(continued)*

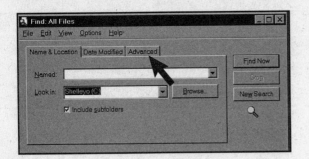

3 After you select the folder or drive, click the **Advanced** tab.

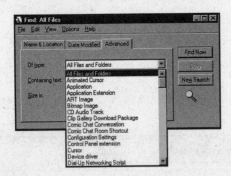

4 If you want to search for a certain type of file, display the **Of type** drop-down list and select the type of file. If this is the only option you want to select, skip to step 7.

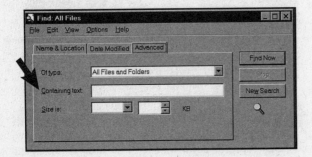

5 If you want to search for a word or phrase, type that word or phrase in the **Containing text** text box. If this is the only option you want to select, skip to step 7.

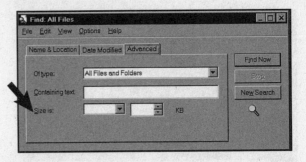

6 If you want to search for a file based on its size, enter the size in the **Size** is text box. You can also use the drop-down list and select at least or at most. Then enter the at least or at most size.

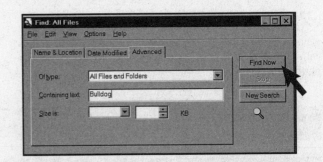

7 When you have completed the search options, click the **Find Now** button.

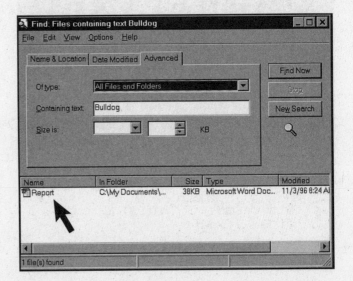

8 Windows searches the selected drive(s) and folder(s). The search may take a while. When Windows finishes the search, it displays the matching files in the lower part of the window. To close the dialog box, click the **Close** button.

Create a Shortcut to a File

Suppose that, as part of your job, you update the same production file or sales report each day or at least a few times a week. Each time you want to use it, you can start the application, display the Open dialog box, change to the drive and folder that contains the file, update the file, and then close it. Or, you can make the file more accessible by adding it to the desktop or the Start menu. For example, you can place a shortcut to this file right on the desktop so that each time you need to update it, you can simply double-click the file icon to start the application and open the document.

Creating a shortcut to a file is similar to creating a shortcut to a program or folder. You start by displaying the file in either My Computer or Windows Explorer. Then you create the shortcut and place it where you want it. You can place the shortcut on the desktop, on the Start menu, or even within another folder. The steps are the same whether you use My Computer or Explorer.

Begin Do It Yourself   Add a Shortcut to the Start Menu or the Desktop

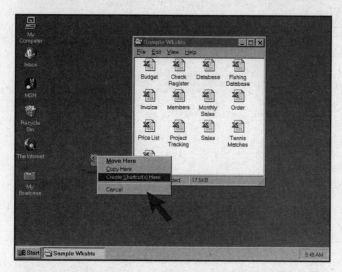

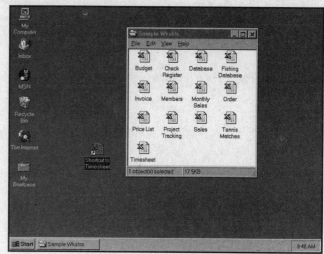

1 In Windows Explorer or My Computer, display the file for which you want to create a shortcut.

2 With the right mouse button, drag the file from the window to the desktop. A shortcut menu appears. Select **Create Shortcut(s) Here**.

3 Windows adds the shortcut to the desktop.

To add the shortcut to the Start menu, drag it to the Start menu.

Retrieve Something from the Recycle Bin

How can you retrieve a deleted file? When you delete something (a file or folder, for instance), the item isn't deleted immediately. Instead, it is placed in the Recycle Bin. So if you change your mind, you can simply open the Recycle Bin and remove the item. (This only works if the Recycle Bin hasn't been emptied since you deleted the file. For information on emptying the Recycle Bin, see "Empty the Recycle Bin" on page 119.)

If you delete something from DOS or from a floppy disk, it is not sent to the Recycle Bin.

When you take something out of the Recycle Bin, you can put the item back in its original location using the Restore command, or you can drag the item to a new folder or drive. If you delete a folder and then restore a file from that folder, Windows re-creates the folder and puts the file back in that folder.

Begin Do It Yourself Retrieve a Deleted File

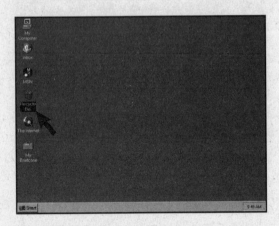

1 Double-click on the **Recycle Bin** icon.

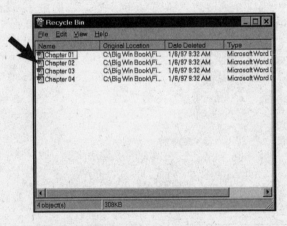

2 Windows displays the contents of the Recycle Bin. Select the file or files you want to restore.

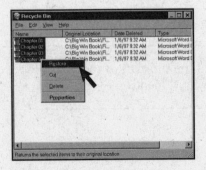

3 Right-click on the selected file(s) and select **Restore** from the shortcut menu, or open the **File** menu and select the **Restore** command.

4 Windows removes the items from the Recycle Bin and puts them back in their original location.

Empty the Recycle Bin

Luckily for you, the Recycle Bin isn't emptied each time you delete something. Instead, you have to call the trash man; that is, you give the command to tell Windows when to empty it. And before you think to yourself that you just won't ever empty the trash so you can always undelete any file that you've deleted, let me warn you that the files in the Recycle Bin still take up space. You aren't recovering disk space when you put files in the Recycle Bin, so you do need to empty it periodically.

Before you empty the Recycle Bin, open it up and take a look through the files and folders to make sure it doesn't contain any files or folders you need. You can't use an Undelete command to undo the deletion after you remove the files from the Recycle Bin. After you are sure you don't need anything, you can safely empty the Recycle Bin.

If you don't like having to empty the trash periodically, you can change the Recycle Bin's properties so that Windows empties the trash automatically. You can set these properties for all drives, or you can set different properties for individual drives, as covered in the *Guided Tour*. For example, on a network drive, you may want Windows to move files to the Recycle Bin for a short period of time. On your own hard drive you may prefer that Windows deletes the files immediately. If you want to set all drives the same, you indicate that on the Properties dialog box's Global tab and set the options once. If you want to set the drives individually, you indicate that on the Properties dialog box's Global tab, select the tab for the specific drive, and set the options as you want them.

Begin Guided Tour   Use the Empty Recycle Bin Command

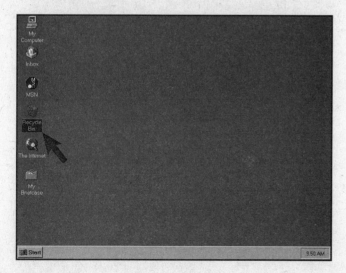

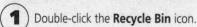

1 Double-click the **Recycle Bin** icon.

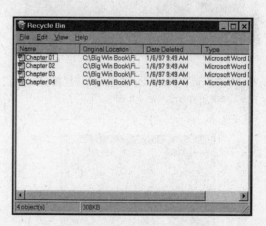

2 Windows displays the contents of the Recycle Bin. (If you see any files or folders that you need, use the Restore command to retrieve them.)

3 Open the **File** menu and select the **Empty Recycle Bin** command.

(continues)

Guided Tour   Use the Empty Recycle Bin Command   *(continued)*

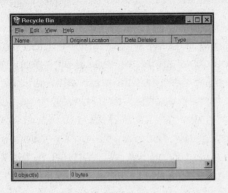

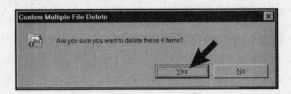

5 Windows empties the Recycle Bin, and all the files are permanently deleted.

4 Windows prompts you to confirm the action. Click the **Yes** button.

Begin Guided Tour   Set Recycle Bin Properties

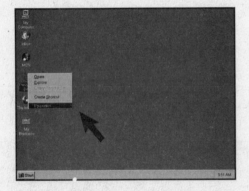

1 Right-click on the **Recycle Bin** and select **Properties** from the shortcut menu that appears.

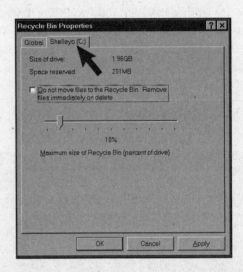

3 If you want to set all drives independently, select each drive tab and indicate whether you want deleted items moved to the Recycle Bin or deleted. Do this for each drive you want to change.

4 When you are finished making changes, click the **OK** button.

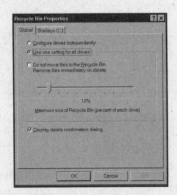

2 Click on the **Global** tab of the Properties dialog box. To configure all the drives the same, click on **Use one setting for all drives**. Indicate whether you want deleted items moved to the Recycle Bin or deleted. Skip to step 4.

Display Disk Properties

Just as you can display detailed information about your folders and files, you can display detailed information about the disks on your system. For example, you can display the disk name (called the label), the amount of disk space used, and the amount of free disk space. This information shows you at a glance how much room you have left, and it can help you decide when you need to do a little housekeeping to free up some space.

Suppose, for example, that you are about to install a new program and you want to see how much space you have on your hard drive. You can access the Properties tab to see how much space is used and how much is free. If you find that you don't have enough disk space, you know you need to delete programs and files you no longer need before you install the new program.

By default, a disk drive's label is the same as its one-letter designation. Your first hard drive is labeled C, and your floppy drive is labeled A. You can assign a different label when you format a drive, or you can use the Properties tab to change the name of a drive to something more descriptive. The name can help you keep track of the contents of the disk.

For example, if you have two hard drives, you can label them so that you can quickly distinguish the C drive from the D drive. If you have a floppy disk that contains your sales reports, you can label the disk SALES so you will quickly know that you have inserted the right disk. In addition, some users like to personalize the PC and assign a unique "pet" name to each drive! When you create a disk name, you can use up to 11 characters.

Another way to personalize your computer is to rename the My Computer icon on your desktop. For example, you may want to use something a little more creative than "My Computer." You may want to assign a more fun name such as "Goody Box."

You can use My Computer or Explorer to display disk properties or rename a disk icon. The steps are the same.

Begin Guided Tour   Display Disk Properties

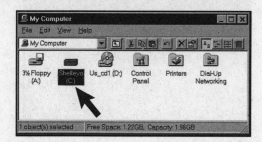

1 In My Computer (shown here) or Explorer, display the drives on your system.

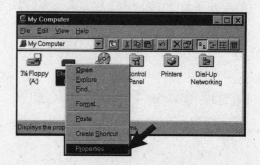

2 Right-click on the drive whose properties you want to check and select **Properties** from the shortcut menu that appears.

(continues)

Guided Tour Display Disk Properties

(continued) .

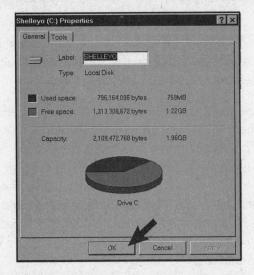

For more information on maintaining your hard disk(s), see "Maintain Your System" on page 337.

3 Click on the **General** tab. Windows displays the label name and the amounts of used and free disk space. Review this information and then click the **OK** button.

Begin Guided Tour Rename a Disk

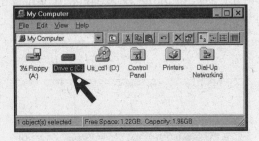

1 In Windows Explorer or My Computer, display the disk you want to rename.

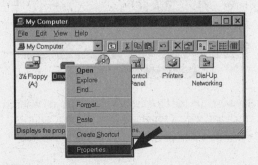

2 Right-click on the disk and select **Properties** from the shortcut menu that appears.

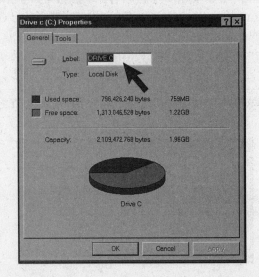

3 The Properties dialog box appears. In the **Label** text box, type the name you want to use, and then click the **Close** button.

Guided Tour   Rename a Disk

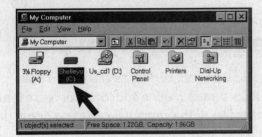

4 Windows renames the disk.

Begin Guided Tour   Rename the My Computer Icon

1 Right-click on the **My Computer** and select **Rename** from the shortcut menu that appears.

2 Windows highlights the name and displays a box around it. Type the new name and press **Enter**.

3 Windows renames the icon.

Format a Disk

Before you can use a disk, you have to format it. Formatting prepares the disk so that you can store files on it. (Think of formatting as being like the process of painting the lines on a parking lot.) Formatting divides the disk up into sectors (parking spaces).

It used to be that when you bought a new computer, you had to format the hard disk yourself. New computers today come with the hard disk already formatted. It is very unlikely that you will ever need to format a hard disk. If you do have to because of disk problems, you should consult a data recovery specialist.

You do have to format floppy disks though. You have to format newly purchased disks (unless you buy them preformatted), and you can format other disks if you want to get rid of all the data on them.

Floppy disks come in two sizes: 3 1/2 and 5 1/4 inch. Most new computers use 3 1/2-inch disks; older computers use 5 1/4-inch disks. You match the disk to the disk drive (that is, if you have a 3 1/2-inch disk drive, you use 3 1/2-inch disks).

Floppy disks also come in two capacities. The *capacity* is a measure of how much information the disk can store. A 5 1/4-inch disk can store 360 kilobytes (abbreviated KB) or 1.2 megabytes (abbreviated MB). A 3 1/2-inch disk can store 720KB or 1.44MB. Just as you must match the disk size with your drive, you must match the capacity with your drive. For example, if you have a 1.44MB drive, you should purchase 1.44MB disks.

> Formatting erases all the information on the disk. You can sometimes retrieve the information with special data recovery software, but don't count on it. Instead, before you format a disk, make sure it doesn't contain data you need.

Create a System Disk

When you start your computer, the system goes through its startup routine and looks for and executes important files. If the computer can't find or run these files, it won't start.

As a safeguard you can make a system disk (a disk that contains all the files necessary for startup) with which you can start the computer if something happens to the files on your hard disk. Think of this system disk as a "spare key" to your computer. When you installed Windows 95, you created a system disk.

As another alternative, you may want to create a system disk if you have a lot of DOS programs (games in particular) that require special memory or configuration commands. You can then start from this disk to run these games.

To make a system disk, follow these steps:

1. Insert a formatted floppy disk into the drive. From Windows Explorer, select the floppy drive containing the disk that will become the system disk.

2. Right-click on the drive and select **Format** from the shortcut menu that appears.

3. The Format dialog box appears. If you need to change the capacity, display the **Capacity** drop-down list and select the capacity.

4. Select the **Copy system files only** check box.

5. If you want to add a label, type a name for the disk in the **Label** text box.

6. Click the **Start** button. Windows copies the system files and displays summary information about the disk.

7. Click the **Close** button.

Begin Guided Tour Search for a File by Name

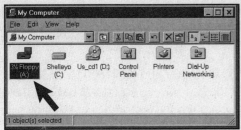

1 In Windows Explorer or My Computer, select the drive you want to format.

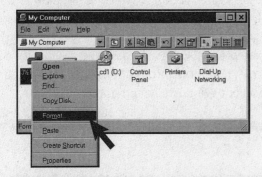

2 Right-click on the drive and select **Format** from the shortcut menu that appears.

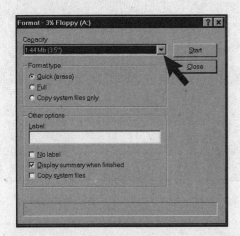

3 The Format dialog box appears. If you need to change the capacity, display the **Capacity** drop-down list and select the capacity. Select the format type: **Quick** or **Full**.

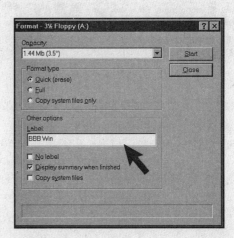

4 After you select the type of format, type a name for the disk in the Label text box. If you don't want a label, select the **No label** option button.

5 Click the **Start** button.

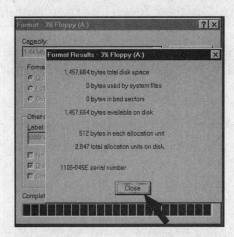

6 Windows formats the disk and displays summary information about the disk. Click the **OK** button.

7 Click the **Close** button.

Start an Application from Windows Explorer or My Computer

Sometimes you will use Windows Explorer or My Computer to find a program you want to start. Perhaps you can't remember where a particular program is stored, or perhaps the program wasn't added to the Start menu when you installed Windows. You can use My Computer or Windows Explorer to find a program, and then you can start the program directly from My Computer or Windows Explorer.

You also can start an application and open a document from My Computer or Windows Explorer. For example, suppose you are looking for a Word document that you can't find. After you find the file using Windows Explorer, you don't have to make a note of where the file is stored, exit Windows Explorer, start the application, and then open the document. Instead, you can start the application and open the document right from Windows Explorer.

How does Windows know which application to open? Usually by the file name extension. Certain file name extensions are associated with particular programs (for example, .DOC files are associated with Word for Windows). For more information on file associations, refer to your Windows documentation.

Begin Guided Tour   Start an Application

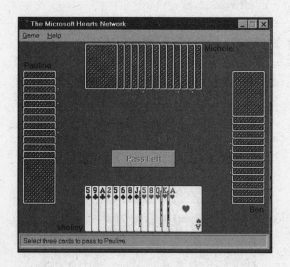

1 In Windows Explorer or My Computer, display the application you want to open.

2 Double-click on the application file.

3 Windows starts the application.

Begin Guided Tour   Start an Application and Open a Document

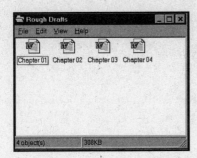

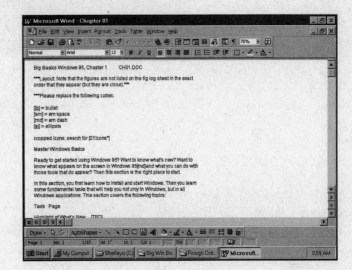

1 In Windows Explorer or My Computer, display the document you want to open.

2 Double-click on the document.

3 Windows starts the program and opens the document.

HOW TO...

Work with Documents

f you ever used a computer when only DOS programs were available, you know how difficult it was to learn and work with multiple programs. Each program had its own set of rules and regulations that you had to follow to perform even a simple task.

One of the benefits that Windows brought to computing was some consistency: Windows applications have to follow certain guidelines. For example, you open a menu the same way in all applications, and most key combinations function the same from application to application (pressing F1 always accesses Help). This means that many skills you learn in one Windows program carry over to other Windows programs.

One concept that is the same in all Windows programs is working with documents: opening, creating, saving, and closing. This section focuses on some of the skills you need to create and work with documents. Specifically, it covers the following topics:

What You Will Find in This Section

Save and Close a Document

If you've used a computer before, you understand the importance of saving. All of your work is stored temporarily in the computer's memory as you create and edit a document. If you don't save and something happens (you lose power or your computer gets hung up), all the information in memory is lost. Therefore, you need to make a permanent copy of the work by saving it to your hard disk. Saving is one of the most important skills you can learn.

When you save a document, you have to tell the program two things: what you want to call the document and where you want to store it. First, you assign a name for the document. Unlike previous versions, in Windows 95, you are not limited to only eight characters for the file name and three characters for the extension. You can enter a file name of as many as 255 characters, including spaces. However, you can't use any of the following characters: \ ? : * , " < > |. Second, you assign a location for the document—that is, you place it in a certain folder on a certain drive.

The Save As Dialog Box

The first time you save a file, you see the Save As dialog box (even if you select the Save command). In this dialog box, you type the file name and select the location for the file. Use the following techniques to select a location:

- Select the drive from the **Save in** drop-down list.

- Double-click on a folder in the list box to see the contents of that folder, and select that folder as the location.

- Click on the **Up One Level** button to move up the folder tree if the folder you want isn't listed.

- Click on the **Details** and **List** buttons to control how the files are listed in the dialog box. In Details view, Windows displays detailed

information (file name, file size, access dates and so on) for all the listed documents. In List view, Windows displays the document names in a list (without icons).

- Create a new folder for the document right in the dialog box, as described later in this task.

After you save the document the first time, you don't have to enter the file name and location each time you save. The program saves the document with the same name and in the same location every time you select save the file.

In some cases, you may not want to save the document with the same name (perhaps you want to use a more descriptive name, or you want to keep the original document intact and make another copy by saving the document with another name). The *Guided Tour* covers how to save a document with another name. Follow the same steps to save the document to another location. For example, if you save a document in the wrong folder, you can save it again in the correct folder and delete the mistake.

> Most programs include shortcuts for accessing the Save command. Look for a Save button on the toolbar or a keyboard shortcut. For example, in both Word and Excel you can click on the Save toolbar button or press Ctrl+S.

Close a Document

When you save a document, the document remains open so you can continue working. If you are finished with the document, you need to close it. You should always close a document when you finish working on it so you don't waste system resources. (To learn more about system resources, turn to "Display System Information" on page 371.

When you close a document, you don't exit the application; you simply remove the document from the screen and from memory. You can then choose to open another document or create a new document.

In most applications, you can close a document by opening the **File** menu and selecting **Close**. You also can close a document by clicking the **Close** (**X**) button in the document window. (Be sure to click in the document window and not the application window.) However, some applications, such as WordPad, don't include a Close command. In such a case, you can close the current document by opening another document, by creating a new document, or by exiting the application.

If you close a document without saving, the program will prompt you to save. If you are just experimenting with a document or if you make changes to a document and don't want to save them, you can abandon the document (close it without saving). To do so,

open the **File** menu and select **Close** command or click the **X** button in the document window. When prompted to save the document, select **No**.

Create a New Folder

In some cases, you may want to put the document you are saving in a new folder. When that happens, instead of going back to the desktop and using My Computer or Windows Explorer to create a new folder, you can create one right from the Save As dialog box. (This feature is new in Windows 95.) To create a new folder, follow these steps:

1. In the Save As dialog box, click on the **Create New Folder** button.

2. Windows adds a new folder with the default name New Folder. Type the name for the folder and press **Enter**.

Begin Guided Tour   Save a Document for the First Time (File Save)

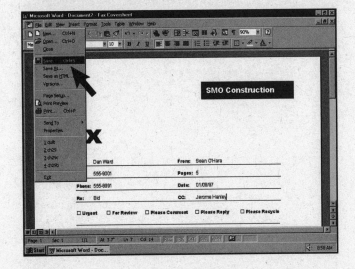

1 Open the **File** menu and select the **Save** command.

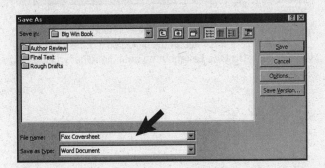

2 You see the Save As dialog box, which will vary somewhat between applications. Type the file name in the **File name** text box. To save the document in the current folder and drive, skip to step 5. To save it to a different drive or folder, continue with steps 3 and 4.

(continues)

Guided Tour　Save a Document for the First Time (File Save)

(continued)

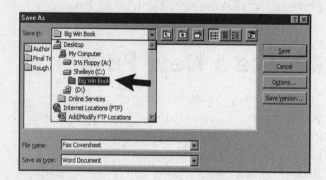

3 To save the document to a different drive, display the **Save in** drop-down list and select the drive you want.

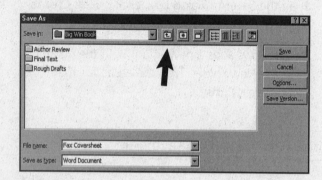

4 To save the document in a different folder, double-click on the folder if it is listed in the dialog box. If the folder isn't listed, click the **Up One Level** button until the folder you want is displayed.

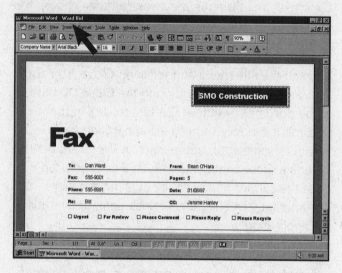

5 When you've selected the location and entered the name, click **Save**.

6 Windows saves the document to the specified folder, and the name of the document appears in the title bar.

To save a document again, open the **File** menu and select the **Save** command. Windows saves the document.

Begin Guided Tour   Save a Document with a Different Name (File Save As)

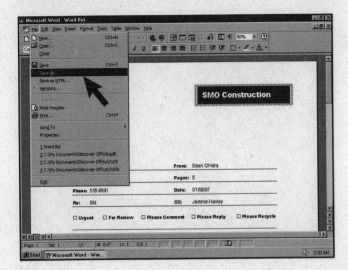

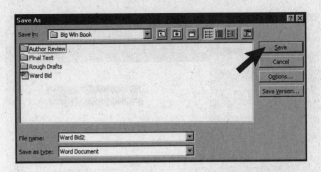

3 When you've selected the location and entered the name, click **Save**.

1 Open the **File** menu and select the **Save As** command.

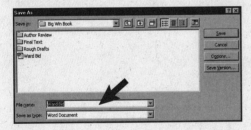

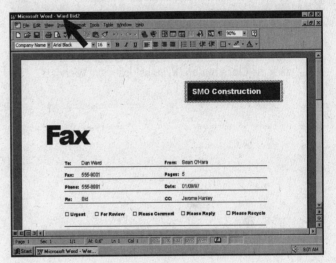

2 You see the Save As dialog box, which varies somewhat between applications. Type the file name in the **File name** text box and select the drive and folder for the document.

4 Windows saves the document, and the new name appears in the title bar.

Begin Guided Tour   Close a Document

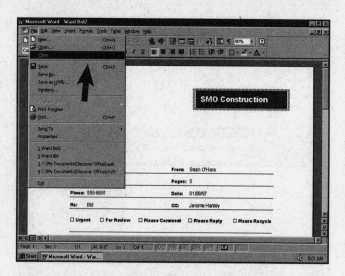

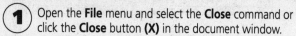

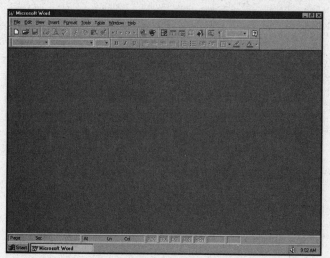

1 Open the **File** menu and select the **Close** command or click the **Close** button **(X)** in the document window.

2 Windows closes the document, but the program remains running. You can open another document or create a new document.

Open a Document

In many cases, you save a document to disk so you can access it later (to edit, reuse, or print it, for example). To use a document again, you need to know how to open an existing document. The Open dialog box (which appears when you select File Open) has standard features that you'll find in most applications. So after you master opening a document in one application, you can figure out the process in any other Windows application.

> Some applications include additional features in the Open and Save As dialog boxes. For example, you may find an Options button for selecting other options for the command. For information on these additional features, use the online help system.

Just as you do when you save a document, you must tell Windows two things when you want to open a document: the document's name and location. When you select the File Open command, the Open dialog box appears, listing all documents in the current folder. If you see the document you want, simply double-click on it. If the document is not listed, you have to change to the drive or folder that contains the document. To do so, use any of the following techniques:

- To display documents on another drive, select the **Look in** drop-down list and select the drive you want. Windows then displays the folders and documents on the selected drive.

- To move up one level in the folder structure, click the **Up One Level** button.

- If you need more information about the document, click the **Details** button. This view

displays not only the file name, but other file information, such as the date the file was modified and the size, that may help you find the file you want.

- If you can't find the document you want, try using the Find command, which is discussed in "Find a File or Folder" on page 111.

- To open a document of another type, display the **Files of type** drop-down list and select the type of document you want to open. The options that appear in this drop-down list will vary depending on the application you are using. For example, in Word, you'll see other types of documents you can import, like other word processing documents.

Work with More Than One Document

Many applications enable you to work with more than one document at a time. For example, you can review the text in one document while you create another document, or you can copy or move information from one document to another. (Copying and moving is covered later in this section.)

To open more than one document, you use the File Open command. Windows opens each document in its own window, and the last document you open becomes the active document. You can switch among documents using the commands on the Window menu (as described in the *Guided Tour*). The number of documents you can have open simultaneously depends on the program you're running and the amount of memory you have.

Begin Guided Tour Open a Document

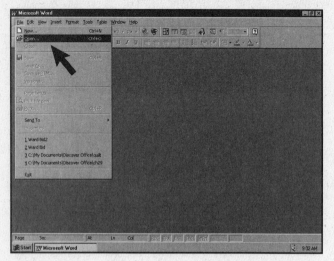

1 Open the **File** menu and select the **Open** command.

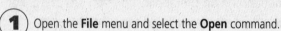
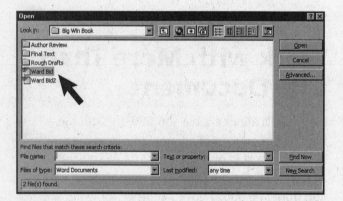

2 The Open dialog box appears, listing the documents in the current folder. If necessary, change to the drive and folder that contains the document you want to open. When you see the document you want to open, double-click on it or click the file and then click the **Open** button.

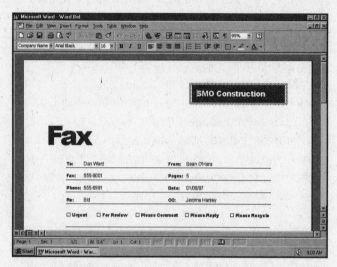

3 The program opens the document in a document window.

Keep in mind that all documents are displayed in a document window within the program window. You can use the window controls to restore, maximize, minimize, resize, and move the windows. Most applications also give you some options for arranging all open documents. For example, you can use the Window Arrange All command in Word to have Word arrange the windows.

Begin Guided Tour   Work with More Than One Document

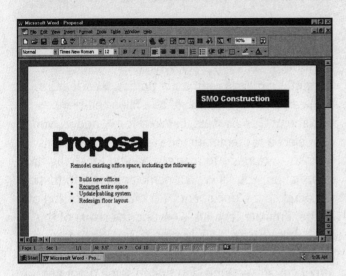

1 Open the **File** menu and select the **Open** command to open the first document you want to work with. The program displays that document on-screen.

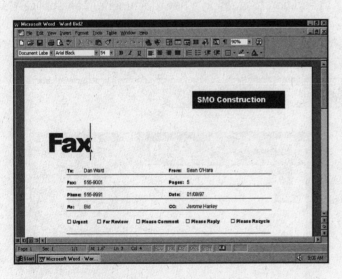

2 Open the **File** menu and select the **Open** command again to open the next document you want to work with. Now the program displays this document on-screen.

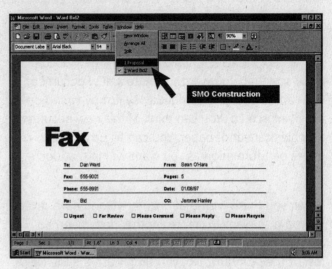

3 To switch to another open document, open the **Window** menu. In the list of currently open documents at the bottom, click on the one you want to make active.

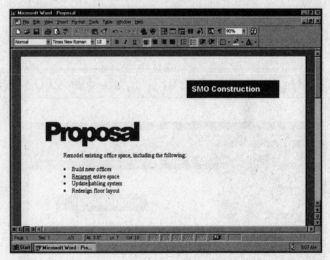

4 The document you selected becomes active.

Create a New Document

When you start almost any application, you see a blank screen, which is really a new document screen. If you want to create a new document, you can begin doing so right away just by typing on the blank screen. You can think of this new document as a blank sheet of paper. You can fill up as many pages of information as you want within that document.

When you finish with that document (and have saved it), you may want to create another document. So how do you get a blank screen again? Do you have to restart the program? No, you simply use the File New command. With this command, you can create a new document at any time.

In some programs, when you select the File New command, a new blank document appears on-screen. In other programs, however, you are prompted to select the style of document you want to create.

Some programs enable you to create a new document based on a template, which may include text, formatting, macros, and other predesigned features (you can think of a template as a fill-in-the-blank document). For example, in Word for Windows, you can select a fax template for a fax cover sheet. This template includes a formatted heading for all the fax information. You fill in your name and fax information to complete the document. A complete discussion of all the template features is beyond the scope of this book, because each application has different templates available. For now, you just need to realize that templates are available and that in some programs you will be prompted to select the template you want to use when you select File New.

In addition to creating a new document in an application, you also can create a new document in a folder or on the desktop, as covered in the *Guided Tour*.

Begin Guided Tour   Create a New Document in the Application

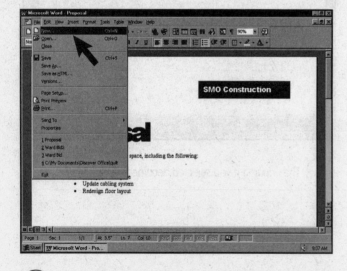

1 From within the open application, open the **File** menu and select the **New** command.

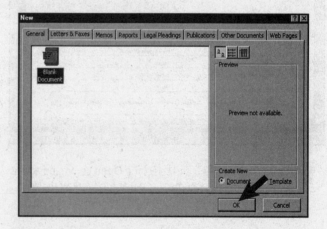

2 If prompted, select the document template or type of document you want to create. Then click **OK**.

Guided Tour   Create a New Document in the Application

A quick way to open a new document is to click the left mouse button on the **New Document** button in the standard tool bar.

3 The new document window appears.

Begin Guided Tour   Create a New Document from a Folder

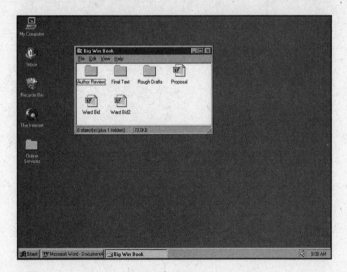

1 From My Computer, open the folder in which you want to create the new document.

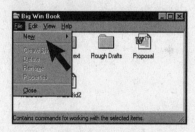

2 Open the **File** menu and select the **New** command.

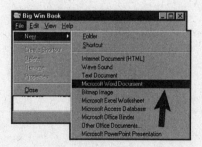

3 You see a submenu of document types. Select the type of document you want to create.

(continues)

Guided Tour   Create a New Document from a Folder

(continued)

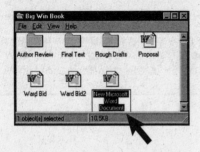 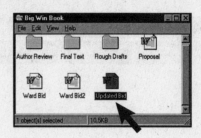

4 Windows creates an icon for the new document and gives it a default name. The default name is selected so you can replace it with a more descriptive name. Type the name you want to assign to the document and press **Enter**.

5 Windows creates the document and displays the document icon. Double-click the document icon to start the program and open the document.

To quickly open a new document, right-click on the desktop. Select **New**, then select the document type you want. For example, you can select **Microsoft Word Document**.

Start a Program and Open a Document

Most of the time when you work in a program, you open and work on a document that you've worked on previously. To make it easy to open recently used documents, Windows provides the Documents command on the Start menu.

When you click on the Documents command, you see a list of the last 15 documents you worked on. When you select one of these documents, Windows starts the program you used to create the document and opens the document. Instead of starting the program and then using the File Open command to find and open the document, you can use this shortcut to get started.

You also can open a document and start a program from My Computer or Windows Explorer. See "Start an Application from Windows Explorer or My Computer" on page126 for information on using these methods.

Begin Guided Tour   Start a Program and Open a Document

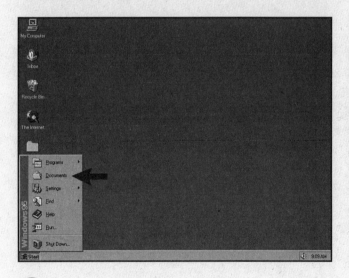

1 Click on the **Start** button and select **Documents**.

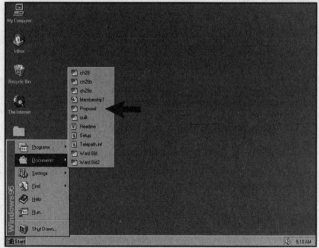

2 Click on the name of the document you want to open.

(continues)

Guided Tour   Start a Program and Open a Document *(continued)*

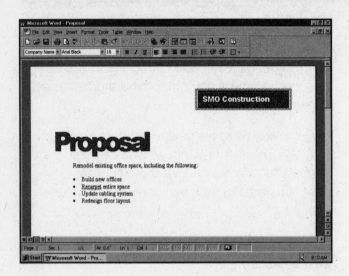

If you want to clear the contents of the Documents menu, you can do so by clicking on the **Start** button, selecting **Settings**, and selecting **Taskbar**. Click on the **Start Menu Programs** tab and click the **Clear** button. Then click on **OK**.

 Windows starts the program and displays that document.

Select, Copy, and Move Text

Copying and moving (cutting) information from one place to another are two of the most common procedures you'll use. Because the Copy and Cut commands work the same in all Windows 95 applications, you can use the same set of steps to move a picture you create in Paint to move a paragraph of text in a Word document. You can move or copy information within a document, from one document to another, and from one application to another. And in all cases, you follow the same basic procedure.

Windows 95 uses the analogy of scissors and paste for moving and copying. When you want to move something, you "cut" it from the original location and then "paste" it in the new location. When you want to copy something, you "copy" it and then "paste" it. To distinguish the difference between moving and copying, remember that when you move an object, it no longer appears in its original location. When you copy an object, it remains in its original location, and a copy is created.

> You can click the left mouse button to select the Cut, Copy, and Paste buttons on the standard tool bar.

When you copy or move information from one place to another in the same document or from one document to another, the information is pasted in the same format. When you copy or move information from one application to another, things can get tricky because the applications may use a different method for storing the data. For example, a spreadsheet document and a word processing document aren't the same type of file. When you copy spreadsheet data to a word processing document, it has to be pasted in a format that the word processing program can understand. How the data is pasted depends on the two applications.

Select Text

The first step in any cut or copy procedure is to select what you want to cut or copy. Text is probably the most common type of item you will cut or copy. To select text, position the mouse pointer at the beginning of the text you want to select, press and hold down the mouse button, and drag across the text. When you reach the end of the text you want to select, release the mouse button, and the text appears highlighted.

In addition, applications often include shortcuts for selecting. For example, you select a picture in Word by clicking once on it, you select a range in Excel by dragging across the cells you want to select, and you select a word in Word by double-clicking on it. How you select items other than text depends on the application. For more information on selecting items, review "Create a Document in WordPad" (page 162) and "Use Paint to Create Pictures and Graphics" (page 197).

When you are copying and pasting, consider these shortcuts and techniques:

- Most programs include toolbar buttons for Cut, Copy, and Paste. You also can use keyboard shortcuts: many applications use Ctrl+X for Cut, Ctrl+C for Copy, and Ctrl+V for Paste.

- The information you cut or copy is placed in a temporary holding area called the Clipboard, and it remains there until you cut or copy something else. This means that you can paste multiple copies by selecting the Paste command again and again.

- You can move or copy the information to another document. To do so, open both documents, cut or copy the data from one document, switch to the other document using the Window menu, and paste the data in the second document. See the task "Open a Document" (page 135) for information on working with more than one document.

- You also can move or copy information from one application to another.

Use the Clipboard Viewer

If you forget or want to check what you have in the Clipboard, you can use the Clipboard Viewer to see what is currently stored there. This mini-application is not installed if you follow the typical installation. You can, however, choose to install this component later. (Installing other Windows components is covered in "Add and Remove Windows 95 Components" on page 476.

When you open the Clipboard Viewer application, you see the contents of the Clipboard. You can use the commands in this mini-application to do the following:

- To save the Clipboard's contents as a file, open the **File** menu and select **Save As**. Type a file name, select a folder, and click on **OK**.

- To delete the contents of the Clipboard, open the **Edit** menu and select the **Delete** command.

- To change how Windows displays the contents, open the **Display** menu and select another display format. The default is Auto; Clipboard Viewer decides and uses the most appropriate format for the contents.

Begin Guided Tour Move Text and Objects

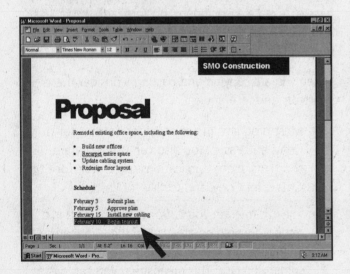

 1 Select the text or object you want to move.

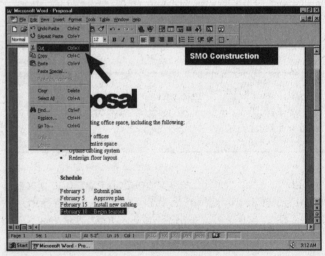

2 Open the **Edit** menu and select the **Cut** command or click on the **Cut** button (the scissors) on the toolbar.

Guided Tour Move Text and Objects

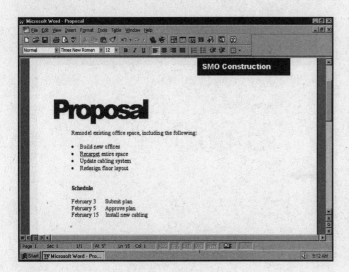

3 The selection is removed from the current location (and placed on the Clipboard Viewer).

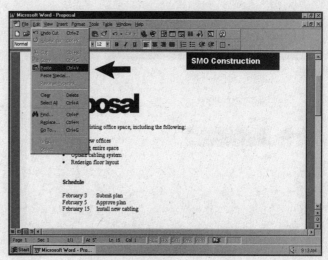

5 Open the **Edit** menu and select the **Paste** command.

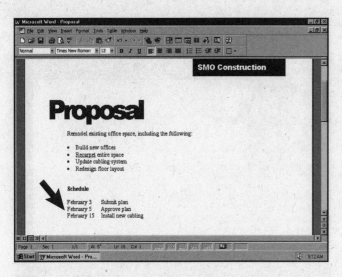

4 Click on the location where you want to place the information. The insertion point appears.

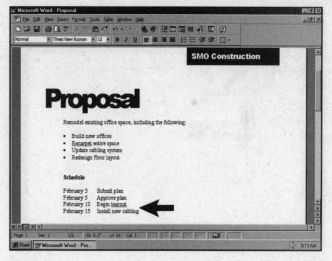

6 The selected information appears in the new location.

Begin Guided Tour   Copy Data

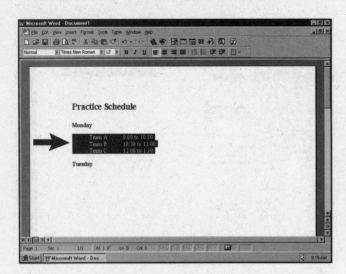

1 Select the text or object you want to copy.

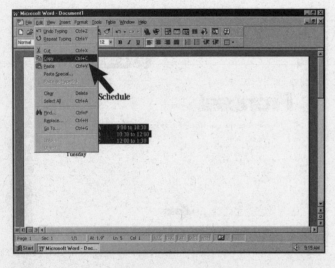

2 Open the **Edit** menu and select the **Copy** command.

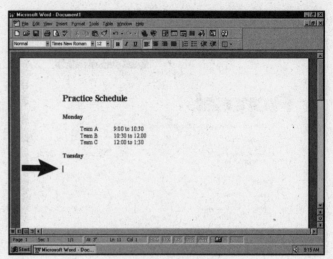

3 The selection is copied to the Clipboard (but also remains at the current location). Click on the location where you want to place the information. The insertion point appears.

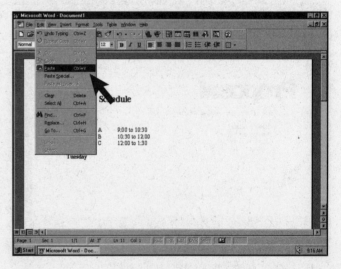

4 Open the **Edit** menu and select the **Paste** command.

Guided Tour Copy Data

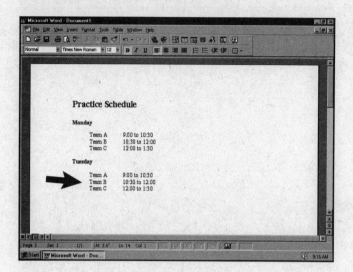

To learn how to cut, copy and paste text or graphics from one application to another, take a look at the projects in "Get It Done with the Accessories," which starts on page 395.

5 The selected information appears in the new location.

Begin Guided Tour Use the Clipboard Viewer

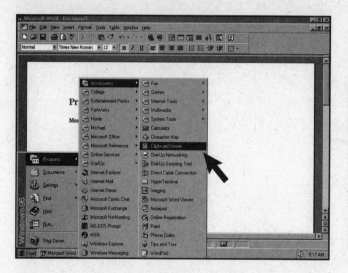

1 Click on the **Start** menu. Then select **Programs**, **Accessories**, and **Clipboard Viewer**.

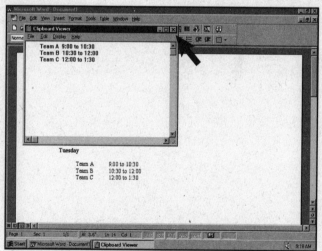

2 Windows displays the contents of the Clipboard—whatever you cut or copied last. To close the Clipboard Viewer, click the **Close** button.

HOW TO...
Print Your Documents

n the pre-Windows computer world, each application you used had to be individually set up to work with the type of printer you had. As a result, printing might have worked well with one application, but not so well with another application.

Windows eliminates all those headaches. With Windows, you set up the printer once, and then all Windows applications can use and communicate with that printer. This section describes some of the Windows features you can take advantage of when you set up and use your printer. Specifically, it covers the following topics:

What You Will Find in This Section

Set Up a New Printer

Windows 95 does its best to take the pain out of installing new hardware. For example, if your printer is hooked up to your system when you install Windows 95, Windows 95 can figure out the type of printer and settings you are using and set up the printer accordingly. You only need to mess with printer settings when you add a new printer or update your printer driver.

Luckily for you, Windows makes the process of installing a new printer easy—with the help of the new Add Printer Wizard. The Add Printer Wizard is a series of dialog boxes that walk you through the specific steps you need to follow to add a printer. You work through the dialog boxes and answer all the questions. To move to the next step in the wizard, click on the **Next** button. If you make a mistake and want to go back to a previous screen, click on the **Back** button. To stop the installation, click on the **Cancel** button.

Before you start this process, make sure you know the following information:

- The name and manufacturer of your new printer. Look for this information on the printer itself or in your printer manual.

- How the printer is connected. A printer is connected to the computer via a cable, and the cable plugs into a port (like a plug-in socket) on the back of the computer. Most computers are connected to a parallel port, called the LPT1 port. Some printers are connected to a serial port (either COM1 or COM2). Check your printer documentation to find out the type of printer connection you must use.

- Printer driver files. Windows sets up a new printer using a printer driver (a file that tells Windows and other programs how to work with your printer). When you purchased your printer, you may have received a disk with printer drivers on it. In addition, Windows 95 comes with some printer drivers on its disks.

> If you have trouble setting up your printer, refer to the printing section in the *Quick Fixes* part of this book.

You also will be prompted to enter a name for the printer. This name will appear in the My Computer window and in all places where this printer is referenced. You can name it anything you want.

Also, you are asked whether you want to use this printer as the default. If you are setting up one printer, you want it to be the default. When you print from an application, that program will use the default printer. If you have more than one printer connected to your PC, you can select the printer you use most often as the default.

Connect the printer to your computer and turn on the printer. Then follow the *Guided Tour* to install the printer so your computer recognizes it and can send documents to it for printing.

> If you're connecting to a network printer, see "Use Files, Programs, and Printers on the Network," page 375.

Begin Guided Tour Use the Add Printer Wizard

(3) Windows starts the Add Printer Wizard and displays the first Add Printer Wizard dialog box. Click on the **Next** button.

(4) If you are hooked up to a network, you are prompted to select a Local Printer or Network Printer. Make your selection and click on Next.

(1) Double-click the **My Computer** icon to display its contents. Then double-click the **Printers** folder.

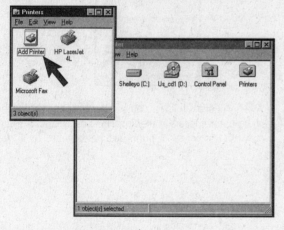

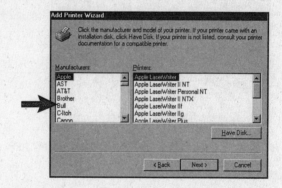

(2) The Printers folder window contains an icon for each printer you have previously set up and an Add Printer icon. Double-click on the Add Printer icon.

(5) To use one of Windows printer drivers, select your printer's manufacturer from the **Manufacturers** list; then select the printer model from the **Printers** list. If you want to use a printer driver on a disk that came with the printer, click on the **Have Disk** button and then select the drive and folder that contains the printer files. Click on the **Next** button.

(continues)

Guided Tour Use the Add Printer Wizard *(continued)*

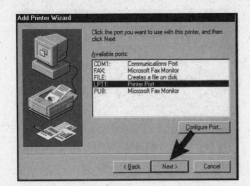

6 You are prompted to select the port to which the printer is attached. Select the port and click on **Next**.

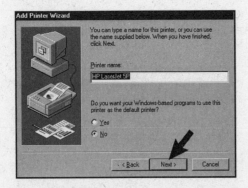

7 Next, enter a name for a printer and indicate whether this printer should be used as the default for all Windows applications. Click on the **Next** button.

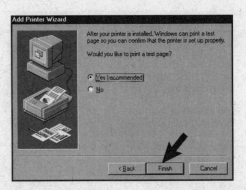

8 When asked whether you want to print a test page, select **Yes**. Then insert the disk with your printer files in the appropriate drive (either a Windows 95 disk or the disk provided with your printer) and click on **Finish**. Windows copies the necessary files to your hard disk.

9 When Windows finishes copying the files, an icon for the new printer appears in the Printers folder window. You can now use this printer to print documents.

Set Printer Options

When you install your printer, Windows automatically sets it up to print according to certain *default* settings. As a result, when you tell a Windows 95 application or accessory to print a document, you will get one copy of the document printed on 8 1/2" x 11" paper with the short side of the page (the 8 1/2" side) at the top. Although Windows 95 tells the printer to use these default settings, you can easily change the print options.

To change such things as the number of copies, the paper size, or the page orientation (which way the page is turned), you need to change the printer settings. Depending on what print jobs you want to affect, you can make these changes in either of two ways:

- To change printer settings for all documents you print in Windows 95, you access the Printer Properties dialog box via My Computer. Any document you print from any application is printed according to these settings.

- To change printer settings for all documents you print in a particular application (such as WordPad or Excel), you open **File** menu and select **Print**, and then click on the **Properties** button. Then any document you print from that application is printed according to the settings you selected in that application (instead of the settings in the Printer Properties dialog box).

The Printer Properties dialog box contains tabs with several types of options you can change. You'll most likely see such tabs as General, Details, Paper, Graphics, Fonts, and Device Options. The following sections describe the most common printer settings you can change, categorized by the tab on which they usually appear. Some printers may provide additional options. If you do not understand what an option is used for, look in the Windows 95 Help system for more information. You also can check out "Printing Problems" (page 537) for some additional help with your printer.

The General options are most useful for users that share a printer (see "Use Files, Programs, and Printers on the Network" on page 375). When you click on the General tab, you can set the following options:

Comment Use this text box to type in any comments about the printer. For example, if you share printers, you may add a comment that describes the printer so others hooked up to it can view the comment.

Separator Page If you select this option, the printer prints a page between documents, which helps you keep track of separate documents on a printer that is shared by several people. You can choose to print a full page with a graphic or simply a page with text by selecting the option you want from the drop-down list. To select the image to use, click on the **Browse** button and then select the file you want.

Print Test Page Use this button to test the printer and print a sample page.

The options on the Details tab are useful when you need to change or update the printer driver, you are having trouble with transmissions, or you need to check the port to which the printer is connected. You can set the following Details options:

Print to the following port Display this drop-down list and select the port to which you want to print. You can use the Add Port and Delete Port buttons to add new ports or delete ports from the list.

Print using the following driver Display this drop-down list and select the printer driver you want to use. To install a new driver, select the **New Driver** button.

Not selected If a printer isn't online, Windows displays an error message. This entry controls how many seconds must pass before Windows displays the message.

Transmission retry If a printer has problems, Windows displays an error message. This entry controls how many seconds Windows waits before reporting the error. (If you are printing a large document, you may want to increase this setting.)

When you change the paper settings on the Paper tab in the Printer Properties dialog box, you change them for every document you print from your computer (so all documents print the same, regardless of which application you're printing from). If you want to set different Paper options (such as changing the paper size) for a document you've created in Word, for example, your best bet is to change those options in the application's Print dialog box so it only affects certain documents.

Whether you're working in the Printer Properties dialog box for all Windows applications or in a particular application's Print dialog box, you can set the following Paper options:

Paper size Select the paper size. Some printers can print on different size papers (for example, legal paper). Select the paper size your printer uses.

Orientation Select portrait or landscape orientation. In portrait orientation, the printer prints down the long side of the page. In landscape orientation, the printer prints across the long side of the page.

Paper source Select the paper tray used for the paper source. Some printers have more than one tray. For example, a printer may have one tray for letterhead and another for blank paper. You can select the tray to use.

Media choice Select the type of print medium. This option is not available on all printers.

Copies Enter the number of copies you want printed.

Layout Select the type of layout you want.

You can use the Graphics tab to control how graphics images print. Keep in mind that the defaults will work fine most of the time, and you won't need to make changes. Also, check the Help system for tips on which settings work best in specific situations. For example, if you display help on dithering, the Help system describes when you might want to select each of the dithering options. These are the options you have on the Graphics tab:

Resolution Display this drop-down list and select the resolution you want to use for printing graphics. The higher the resolution, the better quality the image (and the slower the print job).

Dithering Select how gray shading is handled in graphics. For some printers, there will be halftoning settings instead of dithering.

Intensity Select how dark you want to print the graphics images. Not all printers use this option.

Graphics mode Select Vector for faster printing. If you have problems using Vector, select Raster. Again, not all printers give you this choice.

The Fonts tab enables you to select how TrueType fonts are handled: downloaded (the default) or printed as graphics.

The Device Options tab shows options that are unique to the selected printer. For instance, on my printer, my Device Options include:

Print density Controls how much ink is used.

Print quality Controls the quality for text printing.

Memory tracking The printer has memory that enables it to process the print jobs you send. You can control how the printer handles memory using this option.

Begin Guided Tour   Change Default Printer Options

1 Double-click on the **My Computer** icon and then double-click on **Printers**.

2 The Printers folder window displays an icon for each printer you have set up. Right-click on the printer you want to change and select Properties from the shortcut menu.

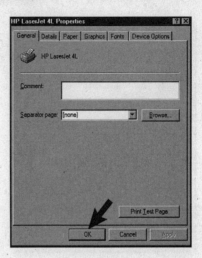

3 The Properties dialog box appears. Click on the **General** tab if it's not displayed and make any necessary changes. (Refer to the list of options on the preceding pages.) Then click the **Details** tab, or click on **OK** if you are finished.

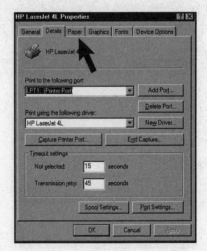

4 Make any necessary changes here. To make changes to the paper used, click the **Paper** tab, or click **OK** if you are finished.

(continues)

Guided Tour Change Default Printer Options

(continued)

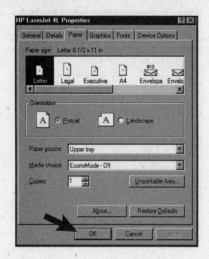

5 In the **Paper** tab, make any changes to paper size, orientation, and so on. If you want to make changes to how graphics print, click on the **Graphics** tab. Or if you are finished making changes, click on the **OK** button.

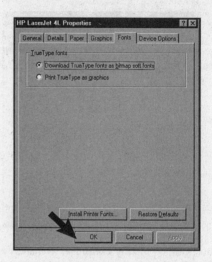

7 In the **Fonts** tab, select to either download TrueType fonts (the default) or print these fonts as graphics. To change other printer options, click on the **Device Options** tab. Or if you are finished making changes, click on the **OK** button.

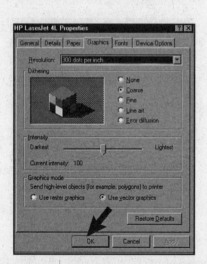

6 In the **Graphics** tab, make any changes to how graphics print. If you want to make changes to how TrueType fonts are handled, click the **Fonts** tab. Or if you are finished making changes, click on the **OK** button.

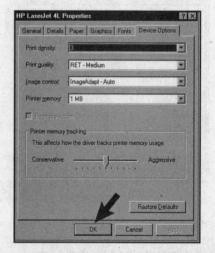

8 Make the changes you want in the **Device Options** tab. When you finish making changes, click on the **OK** button.

Print a Document

The purpose of creating most documents is to share information with others. For example, if you create an annual report for your company, you will most likely print, copy, and distribute the report. You can print a document in two ways: directly from the application you used to create the document, or from My Computer or Windows Explorer.

- To print from an application, use the **Print** command in the **File** menu. In most applications, this opens a Print dialog box, in which you can select such options as the number of copies to print or whether the pages are collated. This dialog box will vary among applications, but it will have similar options. You also can change printer properties from this dialog box.

- To print from My Computer or Windows Explorer, drag the document icon to the printer in your Printers folder, or select the document, open the **File** menu, and select **Print**.

Set Printer Properties

You also can make some selections about how the document prints. In the preceding task, you learned how to make some printer setup changes that affect all print jobs. In many cases, you also will want to make changes to a certain application. For example, you may want to print your Excel reports in landscape. You can select properties for a specific application, as covered in the *Guided Tour*. Refer to the preceding task for explanations of the options that you can change.

Note: You also can change the settings for a particular document. For example, you can select to print a document in landscape orientation. For document-specific changes, use the **Page Setup** command. (Most applications include this command in the File menu.)

Begin Guided Tour   Print from an Application

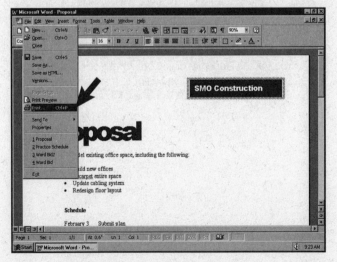

1 In the application, open the document you want to print. Then open the **File** menu and select the **Print** command.

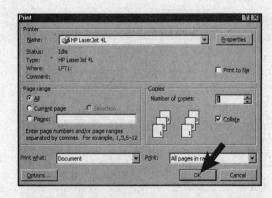

2 The Print dialog box appears (it varies among applications). Click on the **OK** button, and the application sends the document to the printer.

Begin Guided Tour Print from Windows Explorer or My Computer

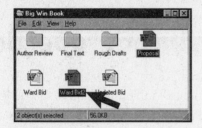

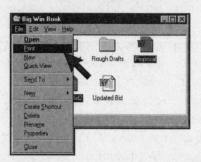

1 Select the file you want to print. If you want to print several files, select all of them.

2 Open the **File** menu and select the **Print** command. Windows opens the application and prints the selected file(s).

Begin Guided Tour Set Printer Properties from an Application

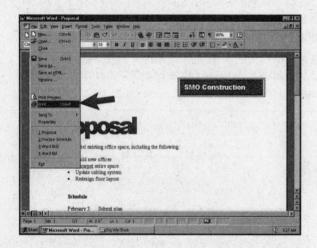

1 Open the **File** menu and select the **Print** command.

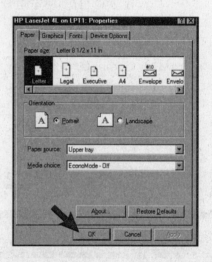

3 You see the Properties dialog box for the selected printer. Select the tab on which you want to make a change, make the change, and then click on the OK button.

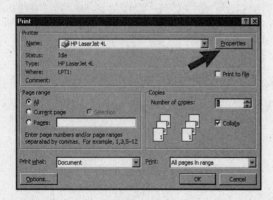

2 You see the Print dialog box. This dialog box varies from application to application but contains similar features. Click on the **Properties** button.

Control Print Jobs

Windows manages the details of each print job you send to the printer so that you can continue working. Because Windows is so efficient at this, you don't have to wait until one document is finished printing to send the next document to the printer. You can send as many documents as you want, and Windows places them in a print queue in the order in which they were received.

The print queue displays the name of the document, its status, its owner, the progress of the print job, and the time the job was started. After you access the print queue, you can pause or cancel all print jobs or any individual job, and you can control the order in which the jobs are printed.

- To pause all print jobs, open the **Printer** menu and select the **Pause Printing** command. To resume printing, open the **Printer** menu and select the **Pause Printing** command again. (This comes in handy when you need to add paper or check the toner cartridge.)

- To cancel all print jobs, open the **Printer** menu and select the **Purge Print Jobs** command.

- To pause a single document, select the document in the print queue, open the **Document** menu, and select the **Pause Printing** command.

- To remove a document from the print queue (cancel the print job), select the document, open the **Document** menu, and select the **Cancel Printing** command.

- To move a document in the print queue, drag it to the new position in the list. (Note that you cannot change the position of the document that is currently printing.)

Begin Guided Tour   Display the Print Queue

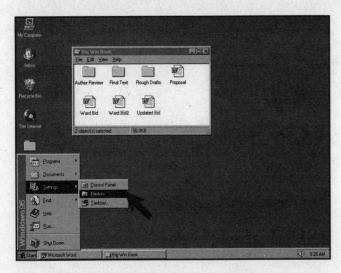

1 To open the Printers folder, click the **Start** button, select **Settings**, and select **Printers**.

2 Right-click on the printer you want to use and select **Open** from the shortcut menu. (Or simply double-click on the printer icon.)

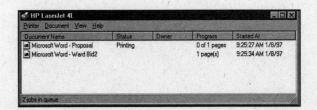

3 Windows displays the print queue, which lists all the current print jobs.

4 Make any changes to the print queue, and then close the window by clicking on the **Close** button.

HOW TO...

Create a Document in WordPad

The most popular type of computer program is a word processing program. Windows 95 comes with a simple word processing program called WordPad that you can use to create simple but professional-looking documents such as letters, memos, and reports.

WordPad includes the most commonly used editing and formatting features. You can add, delete, move, and copy text; you can search for and replace text; and you can make simple formatting changes (which may range from making text bold or italic to changing the margins). If your needs are simple, WordPad may work just fine as your word processing program. (If you need to create more complex documents, you will probably want to purchase a full-featured word processing program, such as Microsoft Word for Windows.)

In this section, you will learn how to perform the following tasks using the WordPad word processor:

What You Will Find in This Section

Get Oriented to WordPad Features

You start WordPad just as you start any other Windows program: click on the **Start** button and select the **Programs** command. Then select the **Accessories** submenu and the **WordPad** program icon.

When you start WordPad, a blank document appears on-screen. Within the blank area of the screen, you see a flashing vertical line, called the *insertion point*. This insertion point indicates where text you type will be inserted.

The WordPad screen includes several standard Windows features: a title bar, a menu bar, and buttons for controlling the size of the window. You can move or resize the window using the skills covered in "Master Windows Basics" (page 3). That section also covers how to select menu commands.

In addition, the window includes two toolbars, a ruler across the top, and a status bar along the bottom. The two toolbars include buttons for commonly used commands and features. The top one contains buttons for opening, closing, printing, and so on; the second toolbar, called the format bar, includes buttons for changing the look of the text. The following table identifies the elements in the toolbars.

WordPad's Toolbar Buttons

Button	Name	Description
Standard Bar		
	New	Creates a new document.
	Open	Opens a previously saved document.
	Save	Saves a document.
	Print	Prints the on-screen document.
	Print Preview	Displays a preview of the on-screen document.
	Find	Searches for text within the document. (See "Find Text" on page 175 and "Replace Text" on page 177.)
	Cut	Cuts or moves text from one location to another. (See "Move and Copy Text" on page 171.)
	Copy	Copies selected text. (See "Move and Copy Text" on page 171 for more information.)
	Paste	Pastes cut or copied text. (See "Move and Copy Text" on page 171.)
	Undo	Reverses the last command.
	Date/Time	Inserts the date and time into your document.

Button	Name	Description
Format Bar		
Times New Roman ▾	Font	Enables you to change the font used for selected text. (See "Change the Look of Text" on page 181.)
10 ▾	Font Size	Enables you to change the font size used for selected text. (See "Change the Look of Text" on page 181.)
B	Bold	Makes selected text bold. (See "Make Text Bold, Italic, or Underline" on page 180.)
I	Italic	Makes selected text italic.
U	Underline	Underlines selected text.
🖉	Color	Enables you to change the color used for selected text. (See "Change the Look of Text" on page 181.)
▤	Align Left	Aligns the paragraph(s) with the left margin. (For more information on alignment changes, see "Align Text" on page 184.)
▤	Center	Centers selected paragraph(s).
▤	Align Right	Aligns selected paragraph(s) with right margin.
☰	Bullets	Adds a bullet to the selected paragraph and indents the paragraph. (See "Indent Text" on page 185.)

Work with WordPad Documents

Part of learning how to use an application is learning how to work with the files. The section "Work with Documents" covers the basics of saving, opening, and closing documents in Windows programs. When you work with WordPad documents in particular, keep the following points in mind:

- Use the **Save** command to save and name a document the first time. To save a document with a different name, use the **Save As** command.

- To open a document that you have saved previously, use the **Open** command. Select the folder that contains the document, then select the document you want.

- When you create a new WordPad document, you can choose one of three document formats: Word 6, rich text (which does not include character formatting), or text (which does not include character formatting).

- You can work with only one document at a time. If you try to open another document or create a new document, WordPad automatically closes the current document.

- WordPad does not include a Close command. When you want to close a document, you must exit the program, open another document, or create a new document.

Begin Guided Tour Start WordPad

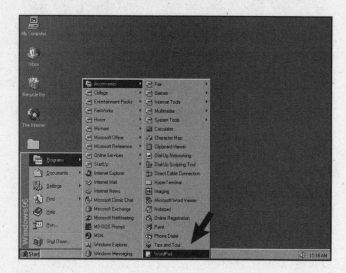

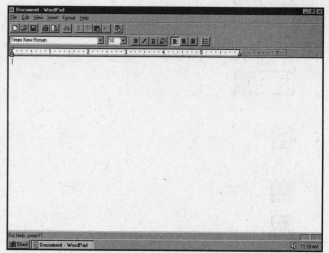

1 To start WordPad, open the **Start** menu, select **Programs**, select **Accessories**, and select **WordPad**.

2 WordPad opens, displaying a new, blank document on-screen with the insertion point at the top. Use the toolbar to access frequently used commands. Use the format bar to make formatting changes to your document. Use the ruler to indent text and set tabs.

Begin Guided Tour Save a WordPad Document

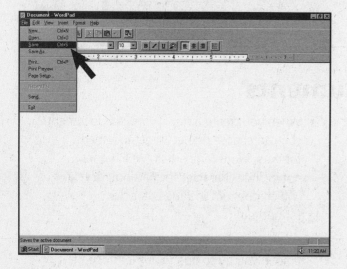

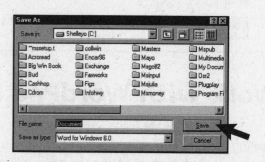

2 The Save As dialog box appears. Type a name and select a folder and then click on the **Save** button.

1 To save a document, open the **File** menu and select **Save**.

Begin Guided Tour   Open a WordPad Document

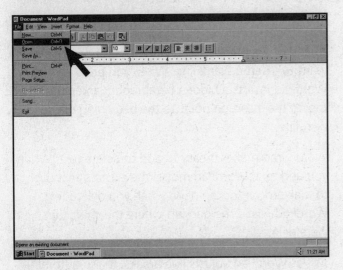

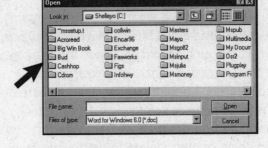

2   In the Open dialog box, double-click on the document you want to open.

1   To open a document you have previously saved, open the **File** menu and select **Open**.

Begin Guided Tour   Create a New WordPad Document

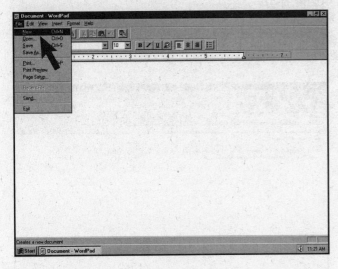

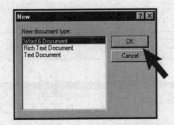

2   Select the type of document you want to create and click on the **OK** button.

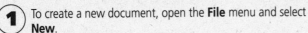

1   To create a new document, open the **File** menu and select **New**.

Type Text

In the simplest terms, a word processing program such as WordPad is just like a typewriter. However, when you type using a word processor, the characters appear on-screen. If you make mistakes, you can easily correct them, because they aren't committed to paper as they are when you type on a typewriter. Press **Backspace** to delete characters to the left of the insertion point, or press **Delete** to delete characters to the right of the insertion point.

Equally convenient is the word processor's word wrap feature. When you type on a typewriter, you have to be careful not to type past the end of the line. When the carriage reaches the end of the line, you must press the return key to go to the next line. With a word processor such as WordPad, you don't have to press a return key (the Enter key on the keyboard) at the end of each line. You just keep typing, and WordPad wraps the words down to the next line

when necessary. You press Enter only when you want to end one paragraph and start another or when you want to insert a blank line. When you press Enter, WordPad inserts a hidden paragraph marker and moves the insertion point to the beginning of the next line.

Word wrap makes it easy to add or delete text. When you add text, WordPad moves the existing text over to make room for the new; when you delete text, WordPad fills in the gap left where the characters were deleted.

Just as WordPad adjusts line breaks, it also automatically inserts page breaks when necessary. When you fill a page, WordPad inserts a break and starts a new page. On-screen, you don't see those page breaks. To do so, preview the document as covered in the task "Preview and Print a WordPad Document" (page 194).

Begin Guided Tour Type Text in WordPad

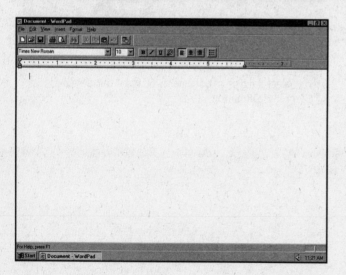

1 Start WordPad. When you start the program, you see a new, blank document on-screen with the insertion point at the top. Just start typing.

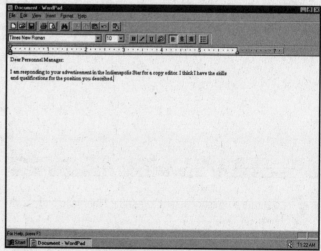

2 As you type, the characters appear on-screen, and the insertion point moves to the right. When the text reaches the margin, WordPad automatically wraps it down to the next line.

Move Around the Document

The insertion point is the vertical flashing line that shows you where new characters you type will appear. When you type a new document, you don't have to worry about placing the insertion point: it moves to the right as you type. However, when you want to change text that's on-screen, you need to place the insertion point in the correct location. For example, when you want to add text, you start by placing the insertion point at the location where you want to add text. You can use the mouse or the keyboard to move the insertion point around in the document.

To use the mouse, click on the location where you want to place the insertion point. The insertion point jumps to that spot. If the location you want isn't displayed in the window, use the scroll bars to scroll

to a different section or page. Click the up and down scroll arrows, or drag the scroll box the relative distance you want to move. Remember that when the page becomes visible, you have to click on it to place the insertion point there.

Sometimes it is faster to move using the keyboard, especially if you are a fast typist and don't like to take your hands away from the keyboard.

If you have not typed anything on-screen (or pressed the spacebar or Enter), you cannot move the insertion point because nothing exists beyond that point. Only after you enter text or spaces on-screen can you move the insertion point. If you try to move and you hear a beep, that's WordPad telling you that you are trying to move past the end of the document.

Begin Guided Tour Navigate a WordPad Document

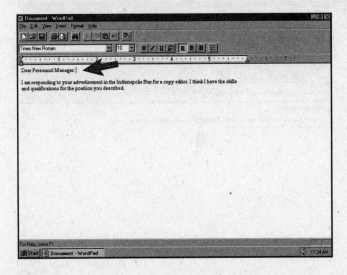

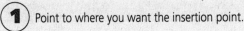

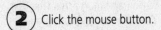

1 Point to where you want the insertion point.

2 Click the mouse button.

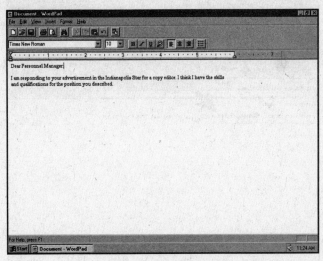

3 WordPad moves the insertion point to the selected location.

Select Text

One of the procedures you will perform over and over again in any word processing program is selecting text. In most formatting tasks and many editing tasks, you start by selecting the text you want to work with. For example, if you want to make the title of your document bold, you start by selecting the title. If you want to delete a paragraph of text, you start by selecting the paragraph.

You can use the mouse or the keyboard to select text. Selecting text with the mouse is similar to dragging a highlighter pen over text on paper. To use the mouse, position the pointer at the beginning of the text you want to select. Then press the left mouse button and drag the pointer in any direction to select the text. As you drag, the text you select appears highlighted.

If you select the wrong text or select text and then decide you want to do something else first, you can deselect it. To do so, click anywhere outside the selected text.

Because selecting text is such a common task, WordPad offers some shortcuts. Use the following selection methods to make the job easier:

- To select a word, double-click within the word.
- To select a line, click once in the selection bar (the thin strip to the left of the text). When the mouse pointer is in the selection bar, it becomes a right-pointing arrow.
- To select a paragraph, triple-click within the paragraph or double-click in the selection bar.
- To select the entire document, open the **Edit** menu and select **Select All**, or press the **Ctrl+A** key combination, or triple-click in the selection bar.

Begin Guided Tour   Learn to Select Text

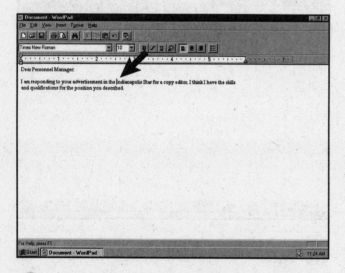

1 Position the mouse pointer at the beginning of the text you want to select.

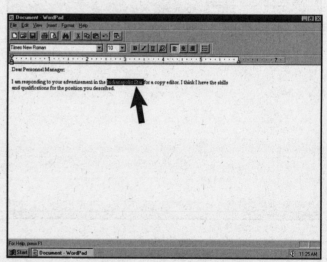

2 Hold down the left mouse button and drag across the text you want to select. As you drag, the text appears highlighted. When all the text you want is highlighted, release the mouse button.

Add and Delete Text

Because the text you type in a word processing program is displayed on-screen (instead of being committed to paper as it is when you type on a typewriter), you can easily add text. For example, suppose you typed a letter and left out the recipient's address. On a typewriter, you'd have to retype the letter. With WordPad, however, you simply move to the place where you want to insert the new text and type it. You can insert as little text or as much text as you want, and WordPad adjusts the existing text to make room for the new text.

Just as easily as you can add text, you also can get rid of text you don't want. (No more Whiteout!) All you have to do is select the text you want to delete, and then press **Delete**. You're rid of it with a simple keystroke. You can delete a single character, a sentence, or a whole section of text.

If you delete text accidentally, you can undo the deletion. To do so, open the **Edit** menu, select **Undo**, or click on the **Undo** button on the toolbar. Note, however, that these methods undo only the most recent action you've taken, so you have to try Undo immediately. (Some programs, like Word, enable you to undo more than just the last action.)

In some cases, you will want to replace existing text with new text. WordPad enables you to do this in two ways. The easiest way is to select the text you want to delete and then start typing the new text. The first character you type deletes the selected text, and your new text is inserted in its place.

The alternative is to turn on Overtype and type over existing characters. This works best when you have an exact match (that is, when you want to type over the same number of characters you want to delete). To use Overtype, press the **Ins** key (sometimes labeled the Insert key) and start typing. WordPad replaces the existing text with the characters you type. When you finish, press **Ins** again to turn off Overtype.

Begin Guided Tour Add Text

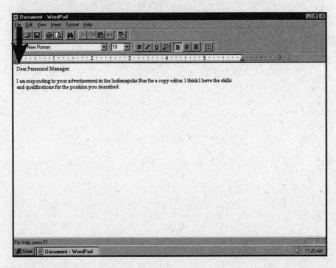

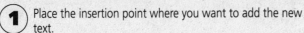

1 Place the insertion point where you want to add the new text.

2 Type the new text.

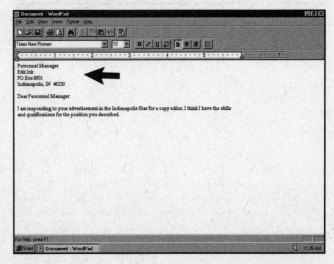

3 WordPad moves the existing text over to make room for the new.

Begin Guided Tour Delete Text

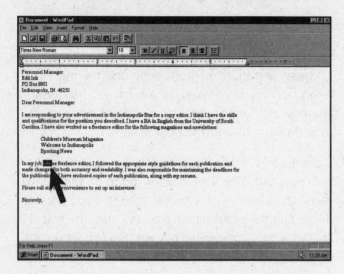

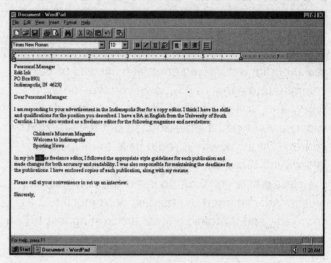

1 Select the text you want to delete. (See "Select Text" on page 168 for details on selecting text.) The text appears highlighted.

2 Press the **Delete** key.

If at any time characters disappear when you start typing, you probably pressed Ins (Insert) by mistake. Press **Ins** again to turn off Overtype.

3 WordPad removes the text, and existing text moves over to fill the gap.

To delete just a few characters, use the Backspace key or the Delete key. Backspace deletes characters to the left of the insertion point; Delete deletes characters to the right. If you have a lot of text, it's faster to select the text and delete it all at once by pressing Delete.

Move and Copy Text

Sometimes you don't know exactly what you want to say when you're composing a document. Therefore, when you review a document after you type it, you often decide that you need to move things around to improve the order of the ideas. Maybe you decide that the closing paragraph would make a better opener, or that the ideas in the body would work better in a different order. You can easily rearrange the text in a WordPad document to put it in the order that makes the most sense. To move text, you use the Cut and Paste commands.

Similarly, you can use the Copy and Paste commands to copy text. Copying comes in handy when you want to repeat the same information—employees' names in a work schedule, for example—more than once in a document. Copying also is a timesaver when you want to use similar text: you can copy the text and then modify the copy.

When you move or copy text, think of scissors and paste. When you move text, you cut it from its

original location using the Cut command, and then you paste it in its new location using the Paste command. When you copy text, you make a copy of it using the Copy command (the original remains intact), and then you paste it in its new location using the Paste command. You can find these commands in the Edit menu, or you can use the buttons in the toolbar.

When you cut or copy text, WordPad places it in a temporary holding place called the Clipboard. The text remains in the Clipboard until it is replaced by something else. (Because the Clipboard is a Windows feature, you can copy text from one application to another. To learn how to copy between applications, see "Select, Copy, and Move Text" on page 143.)

If you open the Edit menu and the Paste command is dim, you haven't cut or copied anything. Select the text first, open the **Edit** menu, then select **Cut** or **Copy**. Move to where you want to place the text, then open **Edit** menu and select **Paste**.

Begin Guided Tour Move Text

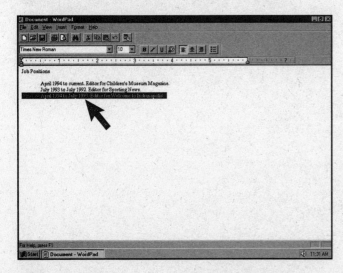

 1 Select the text you want to move. The text appears highlighted.

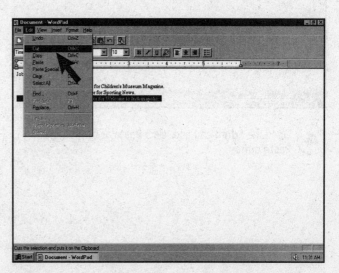

2 Open the **Edit** menu and select **Cut** or click on the **Cut** button.

(continues)

Guided Tour Move Text *(continued)*

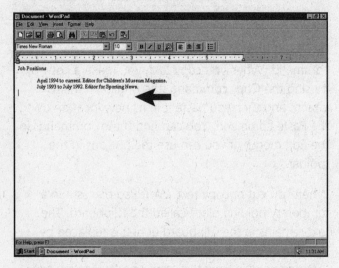

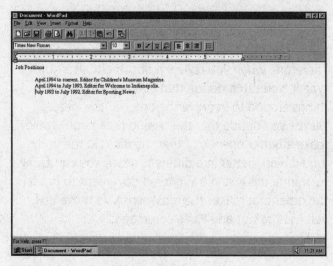

3 WordPad removes the text from the document and places it on the Clipboard. Move the insertion point to where you want to paste the cut text.

5 WordPad pastes the cut text at the new location.

Use these keyboard shortcuts for the Cut, Copy, and Paste commands: after you select text, use **Ctrl+X** for Cut, **Ctrl+C** for Copy, and **Ctrl+V** for Paste.

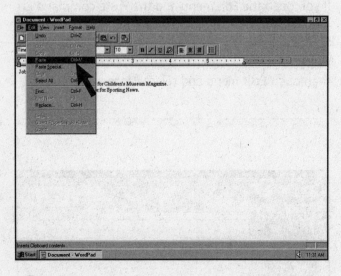

4 Open the **Edit** menu and select **Paste** or click on the **Paste** button.

Begin Guided Tour   Copy Text

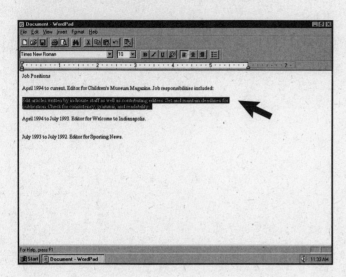

1 Select the text you want to copy. The text appears highlighted.

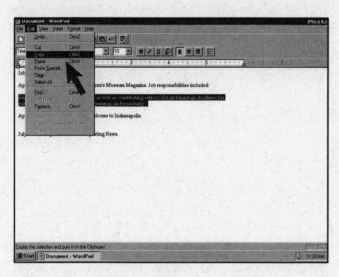

2 Open the **Edit** menu and select **Copy** or click on the **Copy** button.

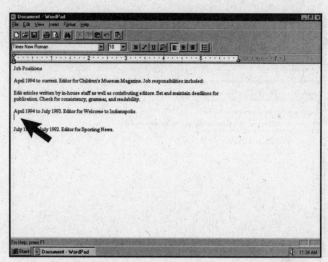

3 WordPad places a copy of the text in the Clipboard. Move the insertion point to where you want to paste the text.

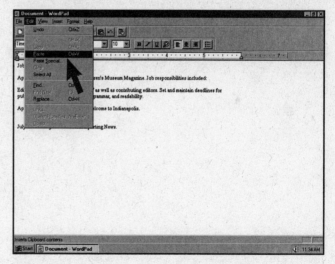

4 Open the **Edit** menu and select **Paste** or click on the **Paste** button.

(continues)

Guided Tour Copy Text *(continued)*

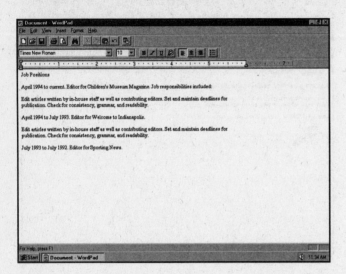

 WordPad pastes the copied text at the new location.

Find Text

In a short document, you easily can scan the text to find a particular word or phrase. In longer documents, though, you may waste a lot of time looking through the text line by line for a particular word. You can use WordPad's Find command to quickly search for a specific word or phrase. This might come in handy, for example, if you needed to look back through a company benefits report for every place where you talked about the 401K plan. You could search for 401K and find all sections that deal with the topic.

When you use the Find command, try to search for a unique word. If you search for a common word, you'll probably have to stop on several occurrences of the word that are not the one you want. For example, suppose you want to find the section of your company benefits report that deals specifically with health benefits. If you search for "benefits," you may have to stop on several sections before you find the one you want. If you search for "health benefits," on the other hand, you have a better chance of moving directly to the section you want.

To fine-tune the search, you also can use the Match whole word only and Match case check boxes. Select the **Match whole word only** check box when you want to stop on whole words. By default, if you type "man," WordPad stops on man, manager, chairman, and any other words that contain man. When you check Match whole word only, WordPad stops only on man. Select the **Match case** check box when you want WordPad to match the word exactly as you type it (for example, if you type "FIG," and want WordPad to stop only on FIG—not fig or Fig).

> If you closed the dialog box, you can repeat the same search. Open the **Edit** menu and select the **Find Next** command, or press **F3**.

When WordPad finishes searching the entire document, it displays a message saying so. If it does not find the specified text, WordPad displays a dialog box. Click on **OK**. Before you try the search again, try changing the search options. Make sure you type the search string correctly.

Begin Guided Tour Use the Find Command

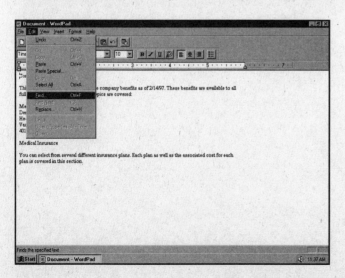

1 Open the **Edit** menu and select the **Find** command.

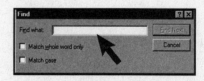

2 The Find dialog box appears. In the **Find what** text box, type the text you want to find. You can type as much or as little text as you want. (If you have searched previously in this document, the last text you searched for may appear in the Find what text box. If so, simply delete the current entry and type the new one.)

Guided Tour Use the Find Command

(continues)

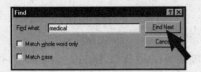

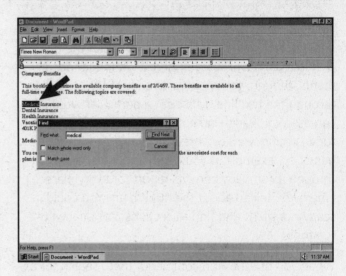

3 When you finish typing the search text, set any options you want to use. (Check the **Match case** check box or the **Match whole word only** check box.)

4 Click on the **Find Next** button to start the search.

Learn how to replace text in the next task "Replace Text," page 177.

5 WordPad searches the document and highlights the first occurrence of the word or phrase. If this is the text you want, click on the **Cancel** button to close the dialog box. If it isn't, click on the **Find Next** button to find the next match.

6 Click on **Find Next** as necessary until you find the match you're looking for.Replace Text

Replace Text

A companion to the Find command is the Replace command. You can use this command to find one word or phrase and replace it with another. For example, suppose you are writing a report and you've cited an author named "Romweber." When you go back to check your sources, you see that the name is actually spelled "Rommweber." You can go through the document line by line and make each change, or you can have WordPad search for the misspelled name and replace it with the correct spelling using the Replace command.

> You can use the keyboard shortcuts Ctrl+F for Find and Ctrl+H for Replace.

When you use the Replace command, WordPad stops on each occurrence individually. At that point, you can choose to replace that occurrence only, skip that occurrence and move to the next one, or replace all occurrences at once. Even though you can replace all occurrences at once, your best bet is to go through and confirm a few of the changes one by one to make sure the process works as you intended because your search string may occur in a form you don't realize. If, for example, you use the Replace command to change the word "plan" to "scheme" throughout a document, and you replace all occurrences without verifying them, you may make some changes you're not counting on. For example, you may end up with the word SCHEMEet instead of PLANet.

If you make a replacement by mistake, you can undo the change. Click on the **Undo** button in the toolbar, or open the **Edit** menu and select the **Undo** command.

Begin Guided Tour   Replace Text

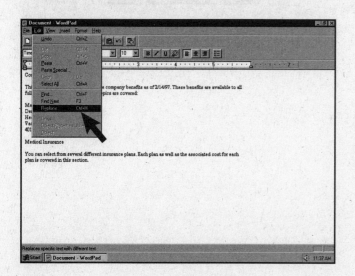

1 Open the **Edit** menu and select **Replace**.

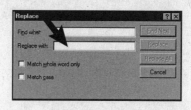

2 The Replace dialog box appears. In the Find what text box, type the text you want to find. (You may have to delete the current entry if one appears; drag across the text and press **Delete**.)

Guided Tour Replace Text

(continued)

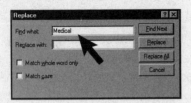

3 When you finish entering the search text, click in the **Replace with** text box and type the text you want to use as the replacement. (If you want to delete the text WordPad finds, leave the Replace with text box blank.)

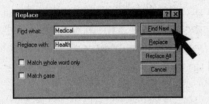

4 With both the find and replacement text filled in, set any replace options. (Check the **Match case** check box or the **Match whole word only** check box.)

5 Click on the **Find Next** button to start the search.

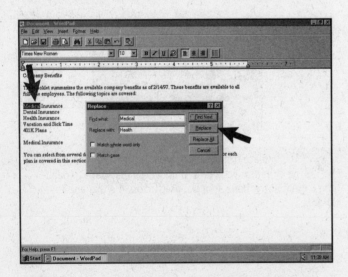

6 WordPad searches the document and highlights the first occurrence of the search text. (The dialog box remains open.) To make the replacement, click on **Replace**. To leave this text as is and move to the next match, click on **Find Next**.

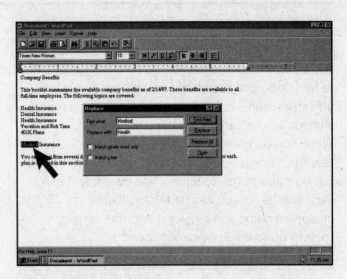

7 WordPad makes the replacement and moves to the next occurrence. Continue the process and click on **Replace** or **Find Next** for each occurrence.

8 (Optional) Click on **Replace All** to make all the replacements at once.

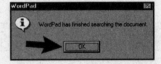

9 When WordPad finishes searching the document, it displays a dialog box. Click on **OK** and then click on the **Close** button to close the dialog box.

Insert the Date and Time

Have you ever sat down to type a letter and then spent five minutes rummaging through your desk for a calendar so you could type the current date? To eliminate this problem, WordPad gives you a shortcut for inserting the date: the Insert Date and Time command. With the Insert Date and Time command, you can choose from several date formats or a combination of date and time formats, and you can even choose whether you want the date spelled out or written in numbers. Not only does this save you from figuring out the exact date, it also saves you from having to type the date.

When you use this command to insert the date and time, it is inserted as ordinary text. That means you can change it or delete just as you would any other text in a WordPad document.

Begin Guided Tour   Insert the Date into a Document

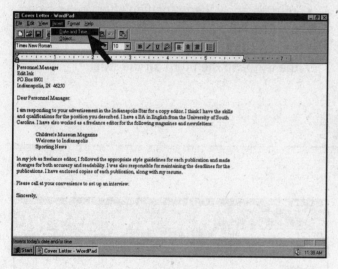

1 Place the insertion point where you want to insert the date. Then open the **Insert** menu and select **Date and Time**. Or click on the **Date/Time** button in the toolbar.

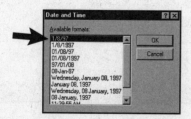

2 In the Date and Time dialog box, select the format you want and click on **OK**.

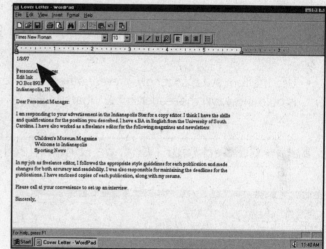

3 WordPad inserts the date in the selected format. (You may have to press **Enter** to separate the date from the existing text, as shown here.)

WordPad uses the date and time from your system clock. If the system's date or time is incorrect, update it using Window's Control Panel. See "Set the Date and Time" on page [15TBD] for details.

Make Text Bold, Italic, or Underline

Many people change the appearance of text to add emphasis. For example, if you want to make the headings in your document stand out, you might make them bold. Or, you might italicize a word or phrase to emphasize your meaning.

The three most common font styles used to emphasize text are bold, italic, and underline. Therefore, WordPad conveniently provides buttons on the format bar for these three styles. You simply select the text you want to change and click on the appropriate button to apply the style you want. To undo a style change, repeat the process.

Before you go crazy making every other word bold or italic, consider these guidelines for making style changes:

- Use the font styles sparingly. If every other word is bold, how will the reader know what's really important? Too much bold makes the document look messy; too much italic is difficult to read.

- You can combine the styles. To make text bold and italic, for example, click on the **Bold** button and then click on the **Italic** button.

- Underlining is the least professional font style. Instead of underlining text, consider italicizing it.

- Some writers tend to use UPPERCASE letters as a way of emphasizing a message. If you use this method, your reader is likely to feel as if you are SCREAMING AT HIM.

- You can apply the formatting after you've typed the text or as you type it. To apply formatting as you type, turn on the style you want to use, type the text, and then turn off the style.

Begin Guided Tour   Change Font Style

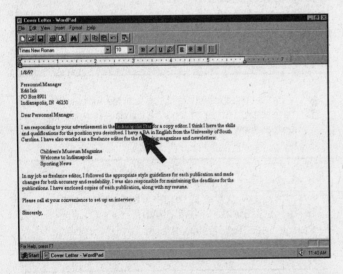

1 Select the text you want to change. Click on the **Bold** button to make text bold. Click on the **Italic** button to make text italic. Click on the **Underline** button to underline text.

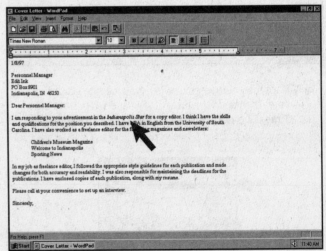

2 WordPad makes the change. Here the text is italic.

Change the Look of Text

The font you use can play an important role in setting the tone of the document. Some fonts are professional looking, some are decorative, and some are just fun. You can choose from a number of available fonts to match the tone you want for your document.

To use a font, the printer has to know how to print that font. All printers have certain built-in fonts that they know how to print. In a font list, you will see a little printer icon next to printer fonts.

If the printer doesn't know how to print a font, it can get that information from the computer in the form of a font file. Before the popularity of Windows and the introduction of TrueType fonts, you would find lots of different font formats and lots of methods for using fonts. Now, however, most fonts are TrueType fonts, fonts that are installed through Windows and stored in files on your hard disk. In a font list, TrueType fonts are marked with TT.

Besides changing the actual font, you can change the font size. For example, you may want to make the headings in your document larger than the body text so the headings stand out. Fonts are measured in points, and there are 72 points in one inch. The larger the point size, the bigger the font.

You can change the color of selected text. Select text and click on the Color button in the format bar. Choose a color from the drop-down list.

The toolbar provides the fastest method for making these types of changes, but you also can make changes in the Font dialog box. Try using the Font dialog box when you want to make several changes at once, when you want to see a preview of the change before you apply it, or when you want access to some other options not available on the toolbar. The *Guided Tour* covers both methods.

Begin Guided Tour Change the Font

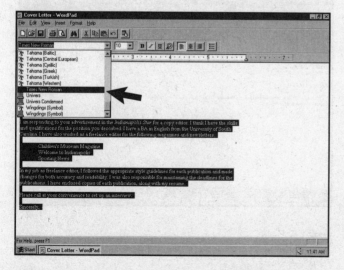

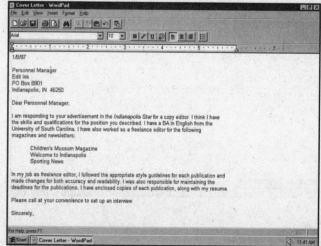

① Select the text you want to change (the entire document in this example). Then click on the **down arrow** next to the format bar's Font list box.

② In the drop-down list, WordPad lists the fonts alphabetically. Click on the font you want.

③ WordPad applies the font and closes the list.

Begin Guided Tour   Change the Font Size

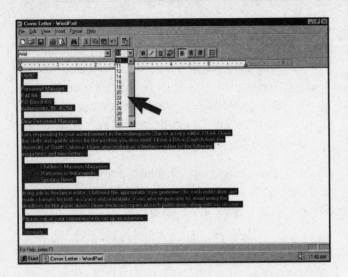

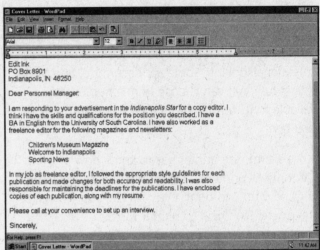

1 Select the text you want to change (the entire document in this example). Then click on the **down arrow** next to the format bar's Font Size list box.

2 In the list of font sizes, click on the size you want.

3 WordPad changes the font size of the selected text and closes the list.

Begin Guided Tour   Use the Font Dialog Box

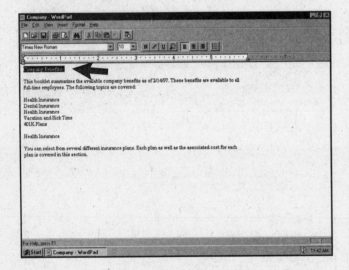

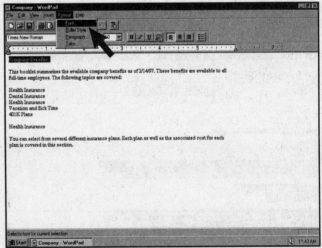

1 Select the text you want to change.

2 Open the **Format** menu and select **Font**.

Guided Tour Use the Font Dialog Box

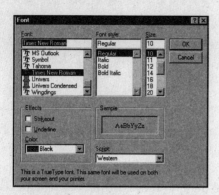

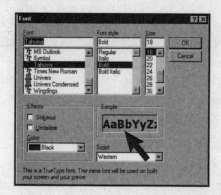

3 The Font dialog box appears. In the Font list, click on the font you want.

4 (Optional) In the Font style list, click on the style you want. In the Size list, click on the font size you want.

5 (Optional) Select the **Strikeout** check box or the **Underline** check box in the Effects area to apply either of those effects.

6 (Optional) If you want to change the color, display the **Color** drop-down list and select a color.

7 As you make changes, WordPad updates the Sample area to show the selected font, style, and size. When you have made all your selections, click on the **OK** button.

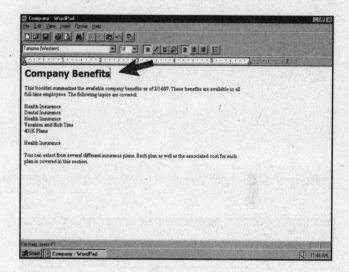

8 WordPad makes the changes.

Align Text

When you start a document in WordPad, all the text is aligned along the left margin. Although this default is fine for most text in a document, you may want to use a different alignment for certain paragraphs.

When you change alignment, that change does not affect just one line of a paragraph; it affects the entire paragraph. (Remember that a paragraph includes the entire section of text down to the hard return.) To change a single paragraph, place the insertion point anywhere in that paragraph. To change several paragraphs at once, select them first.

The fastest way to change alignment is to use the buttons on the format bar: Align Left, Center, and Align Right.

If you change your mind after you make an alignment change, you can undo it with the Undo button, or you can select the paragraph and change the alignment again.

You end one paragraph and create a new one by pressing Enter. When you do press Enter, WordPad inserts a *paragraph marker*, which is very important to formatting. Some formatting features, such as alignment, apply to the entire paragraph. When you make a change to these formatting features (such as tabs, indents, and alignment), the paragraph marker stores that formatting change. This feature can be confusing for two reasons:

- When you format one paragraph and press Enter, all the formatting is carried to the next paragraph.

- When you delete a paragraph marker, the paragraph is combined with the next paragraph and, therefore, takes on the formatting of that paragraph.

Begin Guided Tour Use the Buttons on the Format Bar to Align Text

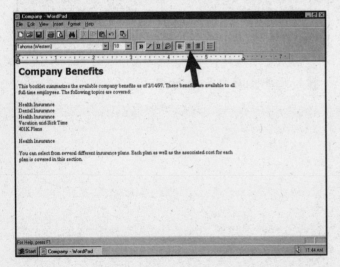

1 To align a single paragraph, place the insertion point anywhere in it. To align multiple paragraphs, select them.

2 Click on the **Align Left** button to left align text. Click on the **Center** button to center text. Click on the **Align Right** button to right align text.

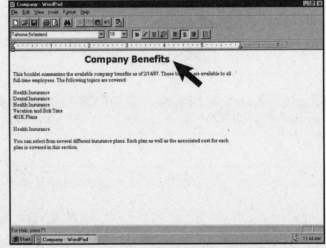

3 WordPad makes the change. Here the text is centered.

...tarted at the left ...ly, it would make ...A reader would ...ght have a hard ...s. As a writer, you ...read by using ...t the first line of ...sily spot where it ...he left and right ...cument.

...**ormat** menu and ...graph dialog box, you ...use the following types of indents:

> **First-line indent** Indents the start of each paragraph

Left indent Sets off text from left margin. Type the amount in inches you want to indent the text in the Left text box.

Right indent Sets off text from right margin. Type the amount in inches you want to indent the text in the Right text box.

You can create a hanging indent. In the Left text box, enter the indent amount for all lines except the first line. Then enter the same amount in the First line text box, but precede it with a minus sign.

Begin Guided Tour   Indent Text

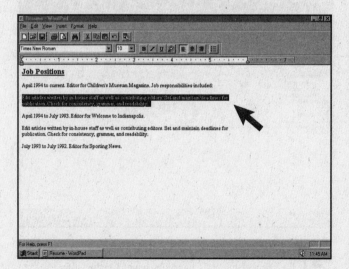

1 Place the insertion point anywhere in the paragraph you want to indent. To indent several paragraphs, select them.

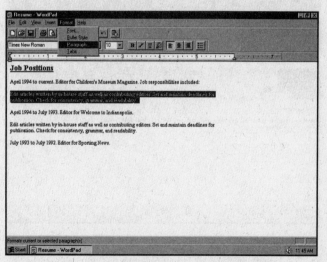

2 Open the **Format** menu and select **Paragraph**.

(continues)

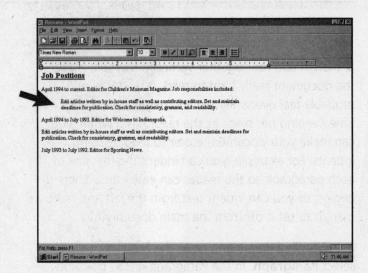

3 Enter the amount in inches for the type of indent you want (see the text discussion for guidance). Click on the **OK** button.

4 WordPad indents the paragraph. This figure shows a 1/2-inch line indent.

Begin Guided Tour Create a Bulleted List

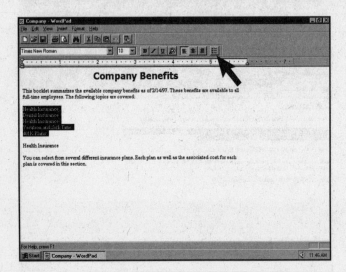

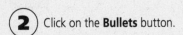

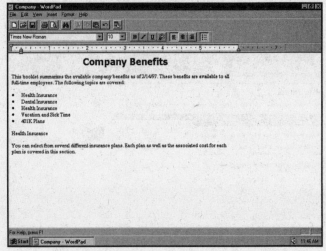

1 To add bullets to existing lines, select the lines first (as shown here). To add a bullet to text you are about to type, place the insertion point where you want to type the new text.

2 Click on the **Bullets** button.

3 WordPad applies the bullet style; it automatically adds bullets and creates a hanging indent for the selected paragraphs.

Set Tabs

To insert a tab in a WordPad document, simply press **Tab**. By default, tabs are set at every one-half inch. If you don't want to mess with setting tabs at different intervals, you can press Tab as many times as you need to line up your text. But it's more efficient to set tabs exactly where you want them. For example, suppose you are setting up a price list or a phone list and don't want to have to press Tab several times to line up the entries. So you set a tab stop at the 2-inch mark (or whatever tab position would work for your document).

Using the Tab dialog box, you can set tabs at any location you want. The Guided Tour shows you how.

Clear a Tab Stop

You also can clear tab stops in the Tab dialog box. To clear a tab stop, follow these steps:

1. Click on it in the Tabs dialog box.
2. Click on the **Clear** button.

You also can click on the **Clear All** button to clear all tab stops that you have set up; this does not, however, clear the default tabs.

Begin Guided Tour   Use the Tabs Dialog Box

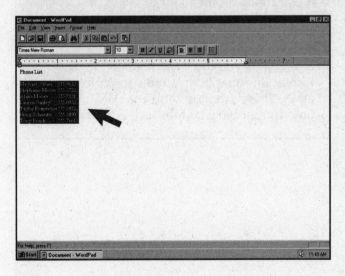

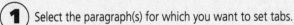

1 Select the paragraph(s) for which you want to set tabs.

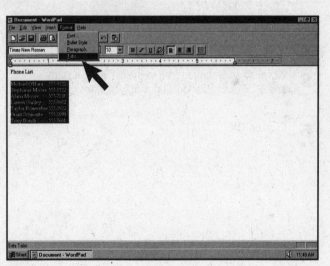

2 Open the **Format** menu and select **Tabs**.

(continues)

Begin Guided Tour Use the Tabs Dialog Box *(continued)*

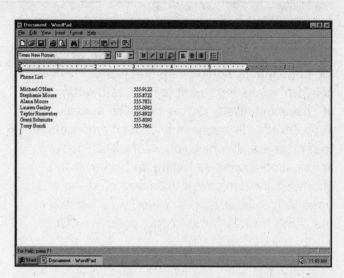

3 The Tabs dialog box appears. In the Tab stop position text box, type the position for the tab (which is measured in inches from the left margin). For example, to set a tab at the 2.5-inch mark, type **2.5**.

4 Click on the **Set** button.

7 WordPad sets up the new tabs. This figure shows a left tab set at the 3-inch mark.

5 WordPad adds the tab stop to the list. Repeat steps 3 and 4 for each additional tab stop you want to create.

6 Click on **OK**.

If you create a tabbed list or a grid of information often, you may want to purchase a more complete word processing program. Most word processing programs have Table features that enable you to set up, manipulate, and format information in a table structure more easily. These programs also enable you to set up different types of tabs such as decimal tabs.

Change Margins and Set Up the Page

Margins are the white area at the top, bottom, left, and right edges of the page. If you don't make any changes, WordPad uses 1-inch top and bottom margins and 1.25-inch left and right margins. However, you can change any or all of these values in the Page Setup dialog box. For example, if you may want to fit more text on a one-page report, you can use smaller margins. On the other hand, you may want a big top margin to make room for a logo.

Most documents generally print on standard size paper (8 1/2 x 11) in standard orientation (portrait). You aren't limited to this paper size and orientation, though. If your printer is capable of printing on legal size paper, for example, you can choose that paper size. Likewise, if you have a document such as a brochure that would look better in landscape orientation, you can change the orientation. Finally, your printer may have more than one bin for your paper

(perhaps the top bin contains plain white paper, and the second bin contains letterhead). You can select the paper source used to print the document.

Change the Measurement Unit

Although WordPad uses inches as the default measurement, you can select a different measurement by following these steps:

1. Open the **View** menu and select **Options**.

2. Click on the **Options** tab.

3. Select the measurement unit you want to use: inches, points, centimeters, or picas.

4. Click on the **OK** button.

Begin Guided Tour   Change Margins

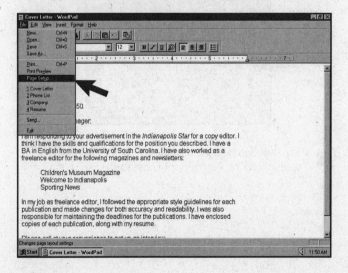

 1 Open the **File** menu and select the **Page Setup** command.

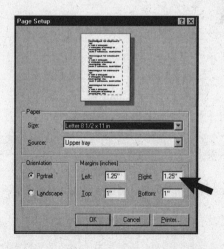

2 The Page Setup dialog box appears. In the Margins section, click in the text box you want to change. Enter the new margin in inches.

Guided Tour Change Margins

(continued)

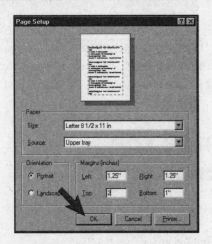

④ When you finish making changes, click on **OK**. WordPad makes the change. (You won't see the effect of margin changes if you're in Normal view; preview the document with File Print Preview to see the change.)

In *portrait orientation*, the printer prints down the long side of the page. In *landscape orientation*, the printer prints across the long side of the page.

③ The example at the top of the dialog box shows the effect of the new margins (here, a 2-inch top margin).

Begin Guided Tour Change the Paper Size, Source, or Orientation

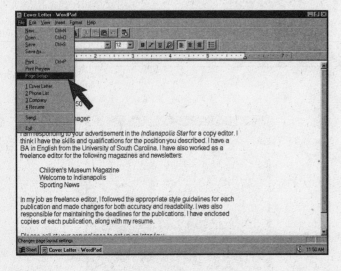
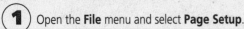

① Open the **File** menu and select **Page Setup**.

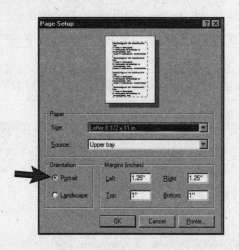

② The Page Setup dialog box appears. In the Orientation section, click on **Portrait** or **Landscape**.

Guided Tour Change the Paper Size, Source, or Orientation

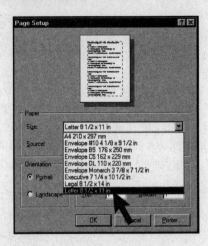

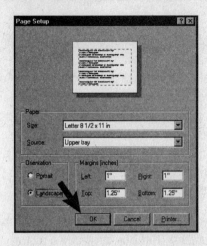

3 To change the paper size, display the **Size** drop-down list. Select the size you want.

4 To change the paper source, display the **Source** drop-down list and select the source.

5 The example at the top of the dialog box gives you a preview of how the document will look using these settings. Here the figure shows a document in landscape orientation. Click on the **OK** button.

To see the effect of margin changes, preview the document, as covered in "Preview and Print a WordPad Document" (page [6TBD]).

Insert an Object

One of the benefits of using Windows and Windows programs is that they enable you to use several types of data in one document. For example, you can create a sales report that includes text, your company logo (a picture), a spreadsheet listing sales information, and a chart. Because you can combine information that you've created in different applications, you can present information to your reader in the most appropriate format.

To combine information in a WordPad document, you insert an *object*. That object can be a picture, a chart, another document, or any element that you created in WordPad or any Windows application. When you select the Insert Object command, you see a list of the types of objects that you can insert. You can choose to create a new object using that type of program, or you can choose to insert an object that you have already created.

After you've inserted the object, you can move it around in the document, change its size, or delete it. To do so, click on the object to select it. WordPad displays black boxes called *selection handles* around the object. Then use any of the following techniques:

- To move an object, position the mouse pointer on a border (but not a selection handle), press and hold down **Alt**, and drag the object to a new position.

- To resize an object, position the mouse pointer on one of the black selection handles and drag.

- To delete an object, press the **Delete** key.

Begin Guided Tour   Create a New Object

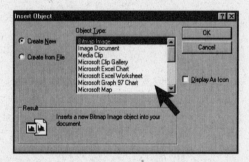

1 The Insert Object dialog box appears. Select the type of object you want to insert. Select **Create New** and click on the **OK** button.

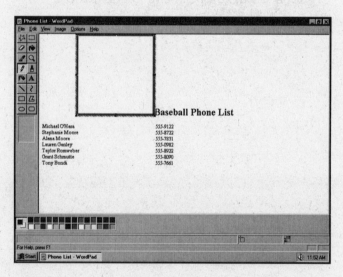

2 The appropriate program starts and displays a blank document (here, a Paint document).

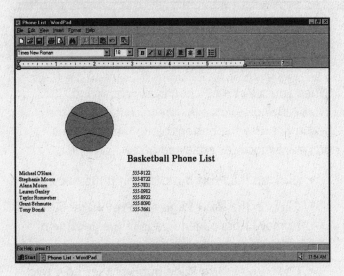

3 Create the object and then click in the document, but outside of the object. The object is added.

Begin Guided Tour   Insert an Object from a File

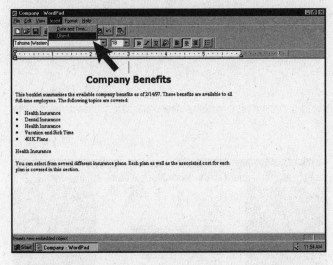

1 Place the insertion point where you want the object. Open the **Insert** menu and select **Object**..

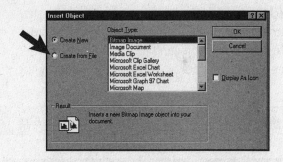

2 The Insert Object dialog box appears. Select the type of object you want to insert. Select **Create from File** and click on the **OK** button.

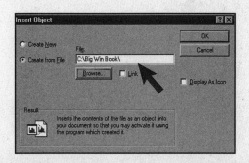

3 Type the file name in the File text box, or click on the **Browse** button and select the file from the Browse dialog box. Click on the **OK** button.

Preview and Print a WordPad Document

You create most documents with the ultimate goal of having your thoughts, ideas, or plans on paper so you can share them with other people. Therefore, you will want to print most of your documents (unless you can gather everyone around your computer screen to read your document). You may print a memo and distribute it to your coworkers, or you may print a letter and then mail it. Whatever the case, when you're ready to print, WordPad enables you to select which printer to use, what to print, and how many copies to print.

> See "Print Your Documents" on page 149 for more detailed information on how to set up your printer and select printer options.

Before you start printing a document, it's a good idea to check its overall appearance and make necessary adjustments. With some formatting elements (margins, for example), you can't just open the document and see how it will look. If you want to see how the entire page will look when it's printed, preview the document.

When you select the Print Preview command, WordPad shows you a mini-representation of the document. Use the buttons along the top of the preview window as explained here.

- Click on the **Print** button to print the document.

- Click on the **Next Page** and **Prev Page** buttons to move from page to page (if the document contains more than one page).

- Click on the **Two Page** button to see how two pages will look side by side.

- Click on the **Zoom In** button to zoom in for a more detailed view of the document. (You can zoom in twice.) Click on the **Zoom Out** button to zoom out.

- Click on the **Close** button to close the preview window when you finish previewing the document.

Begin Guided Tour   Preview a Document

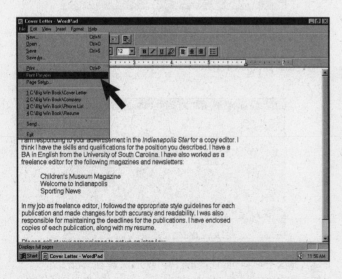

1 Open the **File** menu and select the **Print Preview** command.

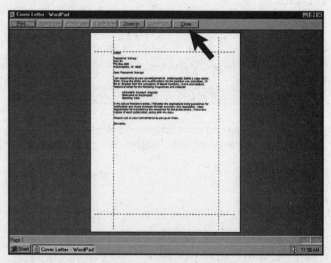

2 WordPad displays a preview of the document. Click on the **Close** button to return to the normal view.

Begin Guided Tour Print a Document

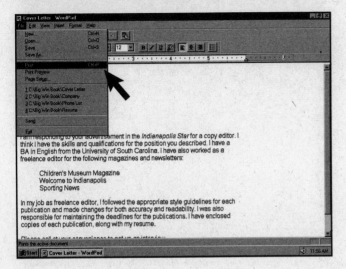

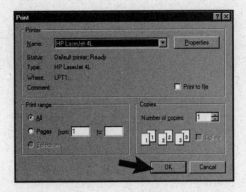

 Open the **File** menu and select the **Print** command.

2 The Print dialog box appears. Make any changes to these options and click on the **OK** button.

Use Paint to Create Pictures and Graphics

Windows 95 includes a paint program called, appropriately enough, Paint. You can use this program to create simple drawings. For example, you could use Paint to create a logo for your company or to create an organizational chart. You can use Paint to create cards, invitations, flyers, and other artistic works. It's fun! In fact, children of all ages enjoy playing with Paint.

The following tasks cover the basics of how to create a drawing using Paint.

What You Will Find in This Section

Understand the Paint Screen

You start Paint just as you start any other Windows program: click on the Start button and select Programs. Then select the Accessories submenu and the Paint icon.

When you start Paint, it displays a blank work area on-screen. You can think of this area as the drawing pad on which you will create your drawing. When you move the mouse pointer within the drawing area, it appears as a pencil. That's because the pencil is the tool selected by default. The following tasks explain how to draw using the other tools.

The Paint screen includes several standard Windows features: a title bar, a menu bar, and buttons for controlling the size of the window. You can move or resize the window using the skills covered in "Master Windows Basics" (page 3). That section also covers how to select menu commands. The screen also includes a status bar, which displays information about the current drawing (such as the size of the shape you are drawing or the location of the pointer).

Along the left side of the window, Paint includes a tool box of drawing tools and a linesize box; along the bottom is a color box. To draw a shape, you select the tool you want from the tool box and then select a foreground and background color from the color box. Depending on the tool you have selected, you can select a line thickness or a shape style, or whether an object is placed on a plain or colored background in the linesize area.

The remaining tasks cover how to draw and format shapes. To become familiar with the various tools before you start drawing, review the following table.

Most of these on-screen elements are helpful to you as you create and format a document. If you find them distracting, however, you can turn them off. See "Change the Display" on page 230 to learn how.

Paint's Drawing Tools

Tool	Name	Use
	Free-Form Select	Use this tool to select a free-form (irregularly shaped) area of the drawing.
	Select	Use this tool to select a rectangular area of the drawing.
	Eraser/Color Eraser	Use this tool to erase part of the drawing or to erase a colored fill from a drawing.
	Fill With Color	Use this to fill a shape with color.
	Pick Color	Use this tool to pick up a color, and then use that color in another part of the drawing.
	Magnifier	Use this to magnify the view of the drawing area.

Tool	Name	Use
	Pencil	Use this to draw freehand (as if you were dragging a pencil across the page).
	Brush	Use this tool to paint an area of the screen. Select the brush shape you want to use.
	Airbrush	Use this tool to create an airbrush effect.
	Text	Use this tool to add text to the drawing. Select the font, size, and style for the text.
	Line	Use this tool to draw a line. Select the thickness or line style for the line.
	Curve	Use this to draw a curved line.
	Rectangle	Use this tool to draw a square or rectangle. You can draw a rectangle with just a border, with a fill and a border, or with just a fill.
	Polygon	Use this tool to draw a polygon (such as a triangle). You can draw an empty, filled, or borderless polygon.
	Ellipse	Use this tool to draw an oval or a circle. You can draw an ellipse that has just a border, has a fill and a border, or has just a fill.
	Rounded Rectangle	Use this tool to draw a rectangle with rounded corners.

Work with Paint Documents

If you've taken the time to create a drawing, you will most likely want to save it so you can use it again or work on it some more later. In addition to saving a drawing after you've finished it, you also should save periodically while you're working. This will keep you from losing all your hard work if your computer loses power. Also, the process of creating a drawing is mostly trial and error, so if you get the drawing in pretty good shape and make a change that looks terrible, you might be stuck with it. Although you can undo most changes, you're better off to save the document before you make a major change. Then, if the change doesn't work, you can revert to the previous version.

The section "Work with Documents" (page 129) covers the basics of saving, opening, and closing documents in Windows applications. When you work with Paint documents in particular, keep the following points in mind:

- You can use the Save command to save and name a document for the first time. By default, Paint documents are saved as bitmap files with the extension .BMP. You can select mono-chrome, 16-color, 256-color, or 24-bit bitmap as the file type. To save a document with a different name, use the Save As command.

- To open a document you have already created and saved, use the Open command. In the Open dialog box, select the folder that contains the document and then open the document you want.

- You can work with only one document at a time. If you choose the command to open another document or create a new document, Paint closes the current document.

- Paint does not include a Close command. To close a document, you must exit the program, open another document, or create a new document.

- You can save part of a Paint document as a separate file. To do so, select the area you want

to save, open the **Edit** menu, and select the **Copy To** command. Then select the folder where you want to place the file and type a name for the file.

- You can import another drawing into the existing drawing. To do so, open the **Edit** menu and select **Paste From** and select the folder and file you want to use.

- As you experiment with Paint, remember that you don't have to save all your work. If you want to start a new drawing but don't want to keep what you're currently working on, open the **File** menu and select **New**. When Paint asks whether you want to save the existing document, click on **No**.

Begin Guided Tour Start Paint

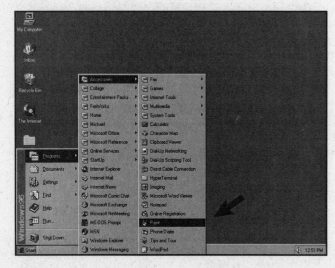

1 To start Paint, open the **Start** menu, select **Programs**, select **Accessories**, and select **Paint**.

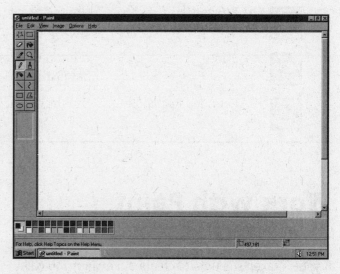

2 Paint opens, displaying a new, blank document on-screen.

Guided Tour Start Paint

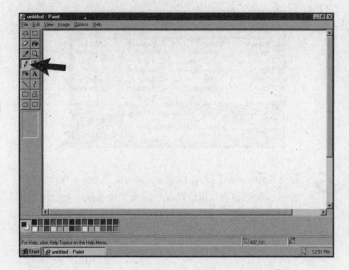

③ Select a drawing tool from the tool box.

⑤ Depending on the tool you select, you can choose different options for drawing the object. For example, when you select the Line tool, you can select the thickness of the line here.

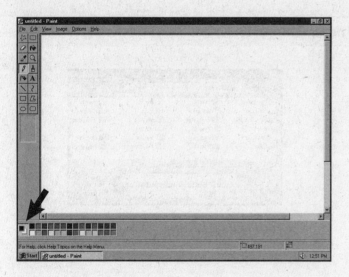

④ Select the colors used for the shape from the color box. The top box displays the selected foreground color; the bottom box displays the selected background color.

Begin Guided Tour   Save a Paint Document

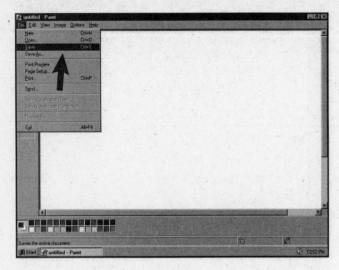

2 The Save As dialog box appears. Type a name and select a folder. Then click the **Save** button.

1 To save a document, open the **File** menu and select **Save**.

Begin Guided Tour   Open a Paint Document

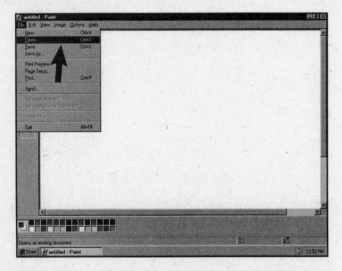

2 In the Open dialog box, double-click on the document you want to open.

1 To open a document you have previously saved, open the **File** menu and select **Open**.

Draw Lines and Shapes

Paint includes a tool box that you can use to create different shapes. These shapes will be the building blocks of your drawing (for example, you can combine a few rectangles and a triangle to create a simple house).

The basic shapes you can draw include:

- Lines
- Curved lines
- Rectangles
- Squares (use the Rectangle tool)
- Polygons
- Ellipses (fancy term for ovals)
- Circles (use the Ellipse tool)
- Rounded Rectangles

To begin drawing a shape, click on the appropriate tool to select it. Depending on the tool, you also might need to select a style for it and a color. For example, if you are drawing a line, you can select a line thickness and a color.

To draw, position the mouse pointer where you want to start drawing, press and hold down the left mouse button, and drag. The techniques for drawing vary from shape to shape. The *Guided Tour* shows you step-by-step how to draw each shape.

Drawing Tips

Depending on the shape you are drawing, different options are available. The following tips will help you make the most of the features Paint has to offer:

- If you make a mistake, open the **Edit** menu and select the **Undo** command (or press **Ctrl+Z**).
- To draw a circle or rectangle, start at the upper-left corner and drag diagonally to the lower-right corner.

- To draw a line that is perfectly straight (horizontal or vertical) or on a 45-degree angle, hold down the **Shift** key as you drag.
- To draw a perfect square, select the **Rectangle** tool and hold down the **Shift** key as you drag.
- To draw a circle, click on the **Ellipse** tool and hold down the **Shift** key as you drag.
- To create a curved line, draw a straight line and then click to place the arcs. A curved line can have one or two arcs. You place and adjust the arc (the curve of the line) when you drag.
- To constrain the angles of a polygon to 45-degrees, hold down the **Shift** key as you drag.
- You can change whether an image is drawn as transparent or opaque. Open the **Options** menu, and check the box next to the option you want.

Work with the Shape

After you've drawn a shape, you have a lot of options for changing its appearance. You can:

Fill the shape with color   You can use a fill to color in the shape, or you can use the Brush and Airbrush tools to add color to the shape.

Move the shape   You can move the shape around within the drawing area as necessary. See "Copy or Move a Shape" on page 222 for more information.

Copy the shape   If you want to use the same shape more than once in a drawing, you can copy it instead of redrawing it. See "Copy or Move a Shape" on page 222 for the details.

Erase the shape   If you make a mistake, you can erase the shape using the Eraser/Color Eraser tool. See "Erase All or Part of a Drawing" on page 217.

Begin Guided Tour   Draw a Line

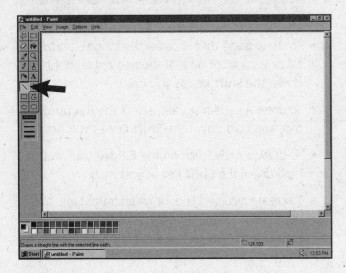

1 Click on the **Line** tool to select it.

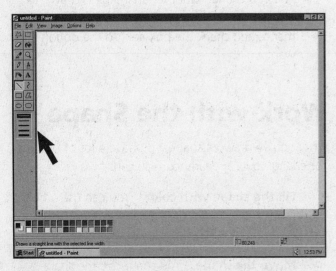

2 The linesize area displays different line thick-nesses. Click on the line size you want to use.

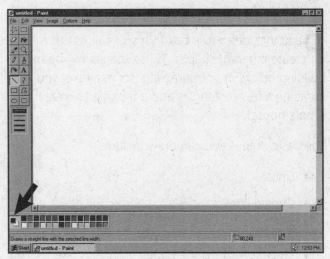

3 In the color box, click on the color you want to use for the line. Then position the mouse pointer in the drawing area where you want to start drawing the line.

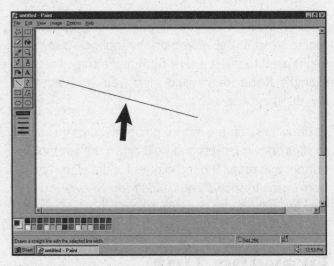

4 Press and hold the left mouse button and drag to draw the line. To draw a straight line, hold down the **Shift** key as you drag. Paint displays your line on-screen.

Begin Guided Tour   Draw a Rectangle or Square

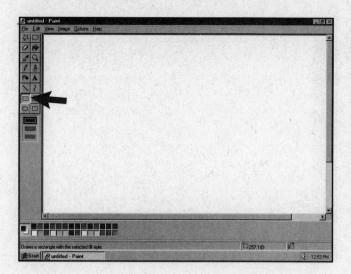

1 Click on the **Rectangle** tool to select it. To draw a rectangle with rounded corners, click on the **Rounded Rectangle** tool.

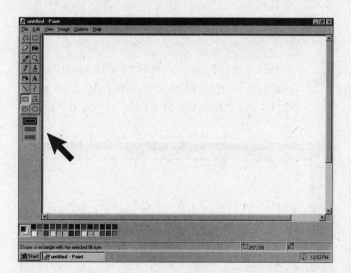

2 The linesize area displays different types of rectangles: one with just a border, one with a fill and a border, and one with just a fill. Click on the style you want to use.

3 In the color box, click on the color you want to use for the border. To select a color for the fill (if you chose to create a filled rectangle), right-click on that color.

4 Paint displays your color selections in the color box. The top color indicates the border color; the bottom color indicates the fill color.

5 Position the mouse pointer in the drawing area. Click and drag to draw the rectangle. To draw a square, hold down the **Shift** key as you drag.

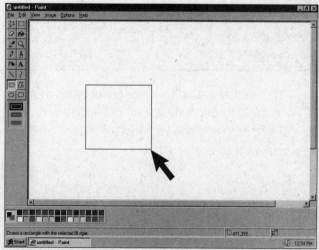

6 Paint displays the shape on-screen (here it's a square).

Begin Guided Tour Draw an Oval or Circle

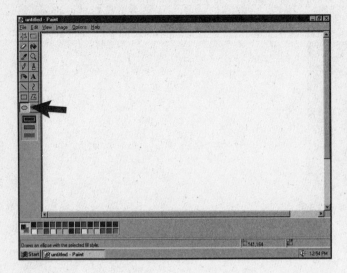

1 Click on the **Ellipse** tool to select it.

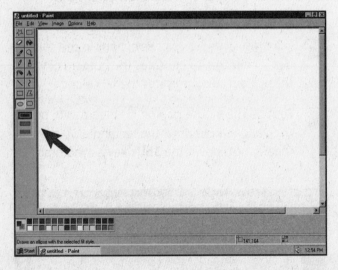

2 The linesize area displays different types of rectangles: one with just a border, one with a fill and a border, and one with just a fill. Click on the style you want to use.

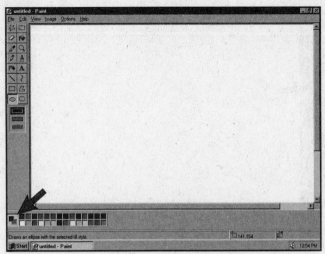

3 In the color box, click on the color you want to use for the border. To select a color for the fill (if you chose to create a filled ellipse), right-click on the color.

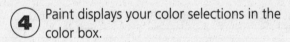

4 Paint displays your color selections in the color box.

5 Position the mouse pointer in the drawing area. Click and drag to draw the ellipse. To draw a circle, hold down the **Shift** key as you drag.

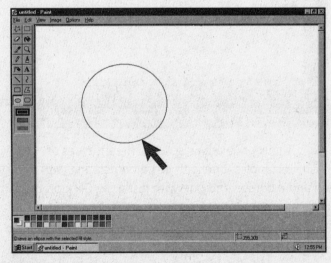

6 Paint displays the shape on-screen.

Begin Guided Tour Draw a Curved Line

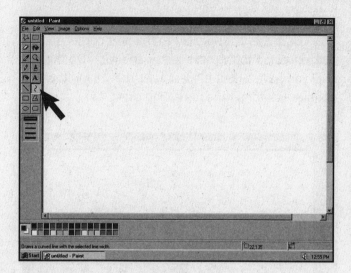

1 Click on the **Curve** tool to select it. Notice the linesize area displays different line thicknesses. Click on the line size you want to use.

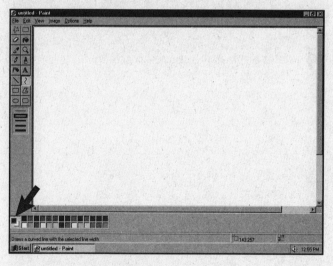

2 In the color box, click on the color you want to use for the line.

3 Position the mouse pointer in the drawing area. Click and drag to draw a line. (To draw a straight line, hold down the **Shift** key as you drag.)

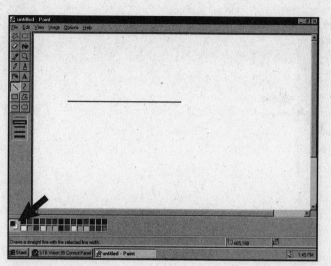

4 Paint displays the line on-screen.

5 Click where you want to place the first arc, and then drag the mouse pointer to adjust the curve. You can place a second arc by clicking at the location where you want the second arc.

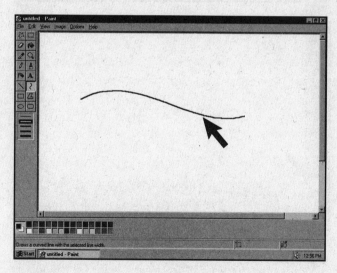

6 Paint displays your line on-screen.

Begin Guided Tour   Draw a Polygon

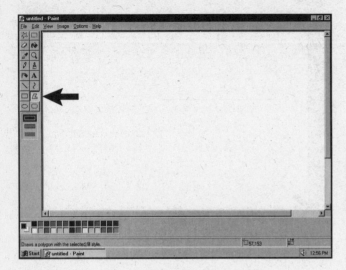

3 Position the mouse pointer in the drawing area. Drag the first side. Go to the next corner and click once. Go to the next corner and click. Do this until you have all but the last sides drawn and then double-click to get the remaining side.

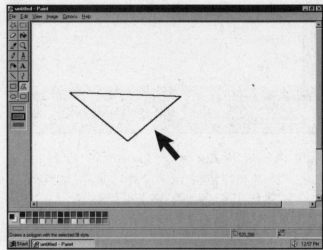

1 Click on the **Polygon** tool to select it. Notice the linesize area displays different types of rectangles: one with just a border, one with a fill and a border, and one with just a fill. Click on the style you want to use.

4 Paint displays the shape on-screen.

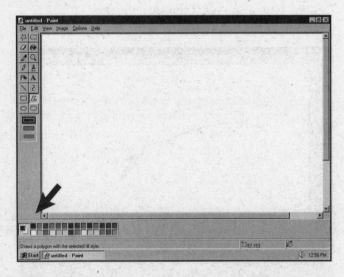

2 In the color box, click on the color you want to use for the border. To select a color for the fill (if you chose to create a filled polygon), right-click on that color.

Add Text

A Paint drawing is not limited to having shapes only; you can also add text to your drawings. For example, you might create a company logo and add your company name, or you might draw rounded rectangles, connect them with lines, and use the Text tool to add names for an organizational chart. You can create birthday cards, invitations, flyers, and other useful projects using the drawing tools and the Text tool.

The first step in adding text to a drawing is to draw the text box (the area that will contain the text). Then you can type the text. When you have drawn the text box and are ready to start typing text, Paint displays the Text toolbar, which contains buttons you can use to format the text. You can choose the formatting before or after you type the text, but you must make your selections before you click in the drawing area again. Use the Text toolbar to format the text in the following ways:

- Select the font used for the text. A *font* is a collection of characters in a certain style. Which fonts you can use depends on your printer and on which fonts you have installed on your system. (For more information on fonts, see "Print Your Documents" on page 149.)

- If you change the font and then add another text box, Paint uses the same font and font size. You can keep these or change to the font and font size you want.

- Make the text bigger or smaller. The size of the text is measured in points (for comparison, there are 72 points in an inch). The larger the number, the bigger the text.

- Make the text bold, italic, or underline.

Begin Guided Tour   Draw the Text Box

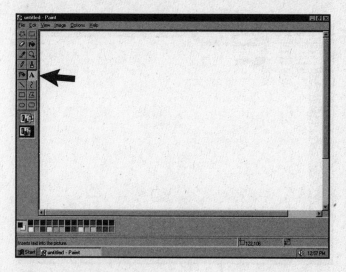

1 Click on the **Text** tool.

2 (Optional) To place the text on a colored background, select the colored background (the bottom option) in the linesize area.

3 To select a color for the text, click on the color you want in the color box. If you selected the option for a colored background, right-click on that color in the color box.

(continues)

Guided Tour Draw the Text Box

(continued)

④ Click and drag in the drawing area to draw the text box.

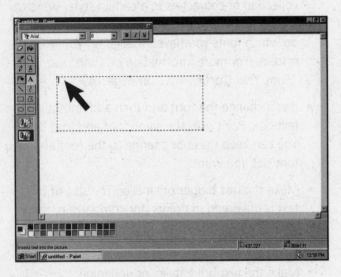

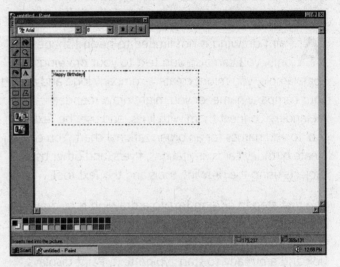

⑤ Paint displays the text box with an insertion point inside, and the Fonts toolbar appears. Type your text.

⑥ Paint displays your text in the text box. If you want to change the look of the text, follow the next set of steps. When you finish typing the text, click in the drawing area.

Begin Guided Tour Format Text

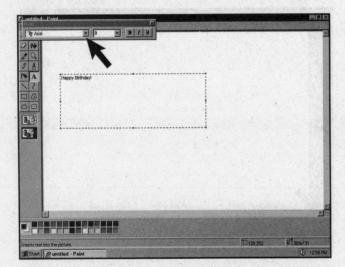

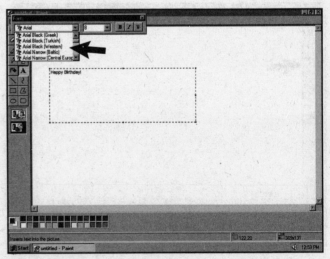

① You can format text before or after you type it (but you have to do it before you click in the drawing area). Here the text is already typed so you can see the results of the formatting changes. Notice the Fonts toolbar is now displayed. To change the font that is used, display the **Font** drop-down list.

② In the drop-down list, click on the font you want to use.

Guided Tour   Format Text

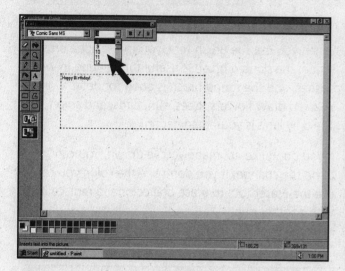

3 Paint displays the text in the selected font. To change the size, display the Size drop-down list and select the size you want. (Remember, the larger the number, the bigger the text.)

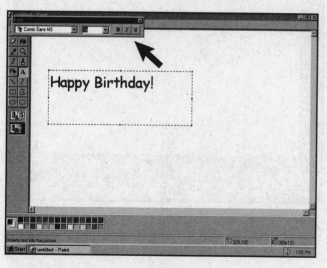

4 Paint formats the text with the size you selected. To make the text bold, italic, or underline, click on the appropriate button.

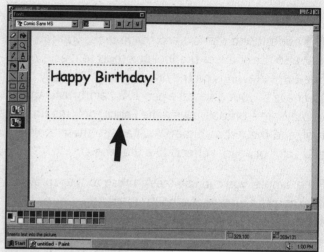

5 When you finish making changes, click in the drawing area.

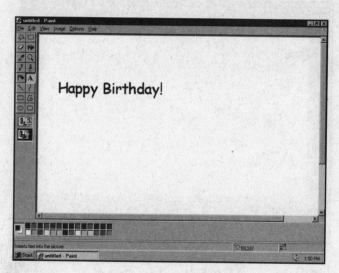

6 Paint adds the text to the drawing.

Create Free-Form Drawings

Besides using the text and shape tools, you can also use some of the tool box tools to create free-form drawings on the drawing area. Basically, you have at your disposal a pencil, a paintbrush, and a spray can—officially called the Pencil tool, the Brush tool, and the Airbrush tool. You can use these tools to add color or special effects to a drawing.

For example, you can use the Airbrush tool to spray blue across a picture of a house to add the sky, or to spray a green color on some bushes in the yard.

When you use the Brush tool, you can select a brush shape: the slanted brush is useful for painting in wide slashes, and the round brush is good for detail work. You can draw flowers, trees, sun, birds, and so on. The only limit is your imagination!

If you don't like an image you've drawn, you can undo the change. If you don't like the color, you can use the Eraser tool to erase one color and replace it with another one.

Begin Guided Tour Draw a Free-Form Shape

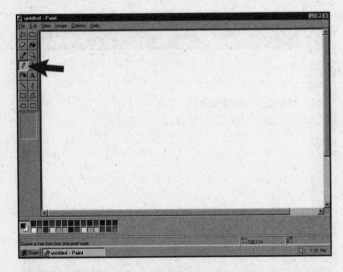

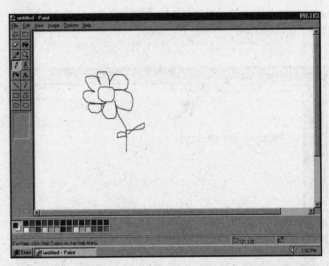

1 Click on the **Pencil** tool to select it.

2 In the color box, click on the color you want to use for the drawing. Paint displays your color selections in the color box.

3 Position the mouse pointer in the drawing area. Drag the pencil across the drawing area just as you would move a real pencil across paper.

4 Paint displays the shape on-screen.

A drawing is composed of little squares called pixels. You can edit the drawing pixel by pixel by magnifying the view and using the Pencil or Brush tools for detailed work. For more on using the Magnify tool, see "Change the Display" on page 230.

Begin Guided Tour   Use the Brush Tool

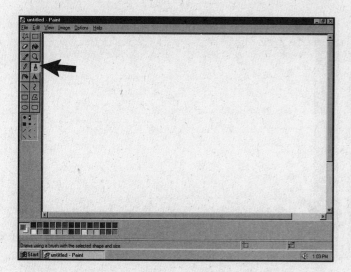

1 Click on the **Brush** tool to select it.

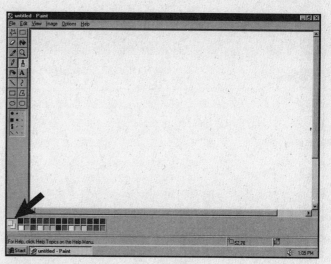

3 In the color box, click on the color you want to use.

4 Position the mouse pointer in the drawing area. Click and drag the brush across the drawing area, using the same motion you would with a paintbrush.

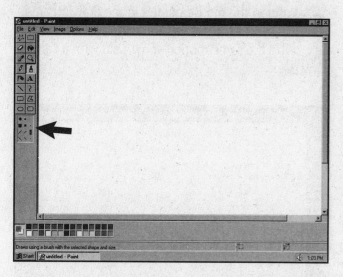

2 In the linesize area, click on the style and size of brush you want to use. For example, you can select a small round brush or a big slanted brush.

5 Paint paints the area.

Begin Guided Tour Spray Paint On-Screen

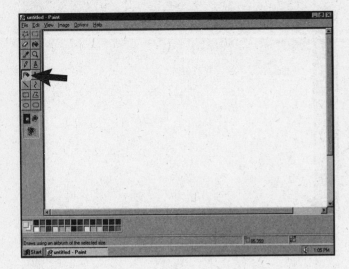

1 Click on the **Airbrush** tool to select it.

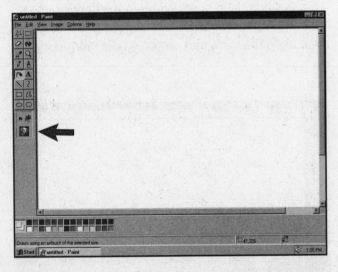

2 In the linesize area, click on the size of the spray area (how much you want the paint to splatter).

3 In the color box, click on the color you want to use.

4 Position the mouse pointer in the drawing area, click and drag the airbrush across the drawing area, using the same motion you would with a can of spray paint.

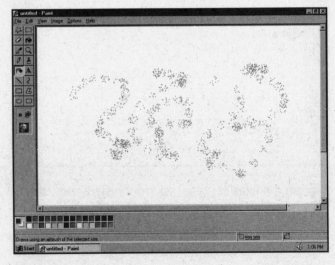

5 Paint displays the results of the airbrush tool.

To spray paint using the background color, use the right mouse button to drag the spray can across the screen.

Fill a Shape with Color

When you draw a shape, you can indicate that you want to fill it with color by selecting the appropriate shape style in the linesize area. However, you can add color to a shape even if you don't select a filled shape initially. You can easily fill a shape with any color you want later, and you can change the color of filled shapes or the color of lines. The *Guided Tour* shows you how to perform each of these actions.

When you are filling shapes, keep the following points in mind:

- You can only fill a closed shape. If you try to fill a shape that isn't closed, the color spills out of the hole and runs all over the drawing area. (If this happens, undo the change and then close up the hole.)

- You can add spot color to an object using the Pencil, Brush, or Airbrush tools. See "Create Free-Form Drawings" on page 212 for more information.

- If you have trouble selecting a line to change the line color or finding and closing a hole in a shape you want to fill, magnify the view.

- You can fill a shape with the background color by clicking the right mouse button instead of the left.

Begin Guided Tour   Fill a Shape

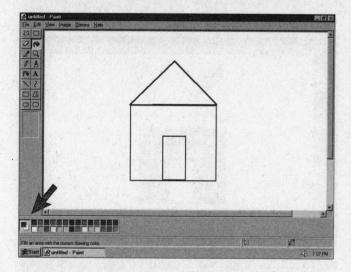

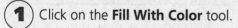

1 Click on the **Fill With Color** tool.

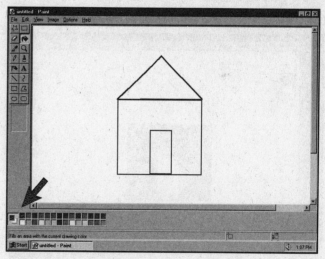

2 In the color box, select the color you want to use for the fill.

(continues)

Guided Tour   Fill a Shape   *(continued)*

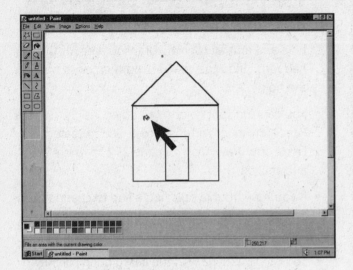

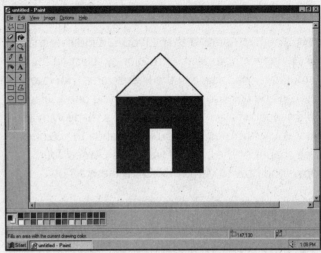

3   Click on the shape you want to fill.

4   Paint fills the shape with color.

Begin Guided Tour   Change the Line Color

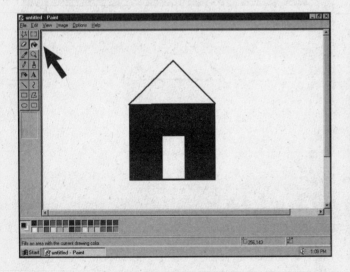

1   Click on the **Fill With Color** tool.

2   In the color box, select the color you want to use for the line.

3   Position the tip of the paint can right on the line. You may want to magnify the view so you can make sure you get the pointer in the right spot. Click the mouse button.

4   Paint changes the color of the line.

Erase All or Part of a Drawing

There are many ways to undo a change you've made to the drawing. If you make a change and immediately decide you don't like it, use the Undo command. You can undo up to the last three changes this way. To reverse the Undo action, open the **Edit** menu and select the **Repeat** command.

If Undo isn't available, you can use the Eraser/Color Eraser tool in the tool box. For example, if you added a shape that isn't quite right, or you want to redo part of a drawing, you can erase a small part of the document, a large part, the entire working area, or just a certain color using the steps in the *Guided Tour*.

One caution to keep in mind is that when you erase, Paint colors over the area with the current background color. So if you want to go back to white, make sure white is selected as the background color (right click on it).

Erase Color

Besides erasing an object, you can replace one color with another. This concept can be confusing because the color change doesn't happen automatically when you select the object to change. You have to drag across the area with the Eraser to change the color.

Here's how the Eraser works. You select the color you want to replace as the foreground color. Then you select the color you want to use for the replacement as the background color. Finally, you select the Eraser tool and right-click and drag across the area you want to change. Paint replaces anything in the foreground color with the new background color.

Suppose you have several red shapes on-screen and want to change them to blue. To make the change, select red as the foreground color and blue as the background color, and then right-click and drag across the shapes you want to change. If you drag across a red item, Paint changes the color. If you drag across a black item the color remains unchanged.

Begin Guided Tour   Erase a Small Part of the Drawing Area

1 Click on the **Eraser/Color Eraser** tool.

2 The linesize area displays several sizes of erasers. The larger the eraser, the wider the path it erases when you use it. Select the size you want.

(continues)

Begin Guided Tour   Erase a Small Part of the Drawing Area   *(continued)*

3 Move the pointer into the drawing area and drag across the area you want to erase.

> If your drawing is really detailed and you want to erase a fine line, magnify the drawing area so you can see an enlarged view. You can do detail work more easily in this view. See "Change the Display" on 230.

4 Paint erases the selected area.

Begin Guided Tour   Erase a Big Part of the Drawing Area

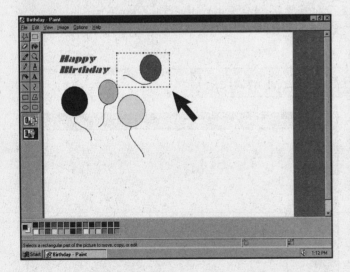

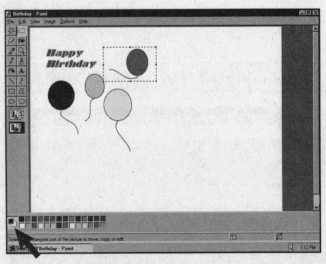

1 Use either of the Select tools to select the area you want to erase. See "Select a Shape" on page [7TBD] for more information on selecting shapes.

2 Check the background color. Paint will fill the entire selected area with this color. You can select a different background color by right-clicking on the color you want to use.

Guided Tour   Erase a Big Part of the Drawing Area

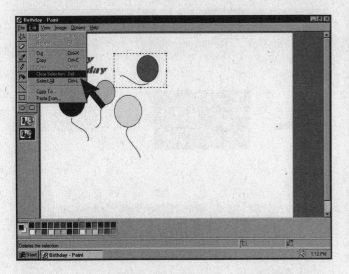

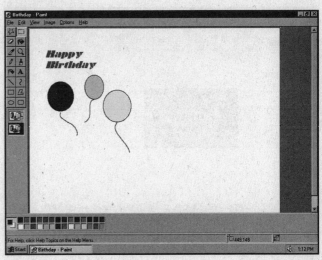

3 Open the **Edit** menu and select the **Clear Selection** command, or press the **Delete** key.

4 Paint clears the selected area.

Begin Guided Tour   Erase Only a Color

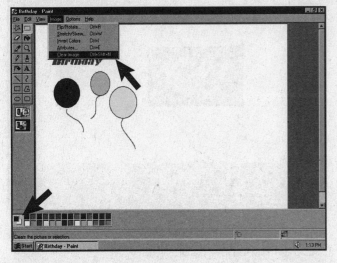

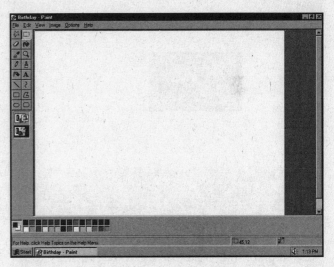

1 Check the background color. Paint will fill the entire drawing area with this color.

2 Open the **Image** menu and select the **Clear Image** command.

3 Paint fills the entire drawing area with the selected background color.

You can press **Ctrl+Shift+N** to select the Clear Image command.

Begin Guided Tour   Erase Only a Color

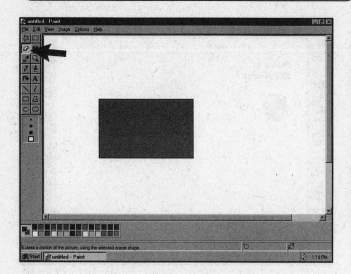

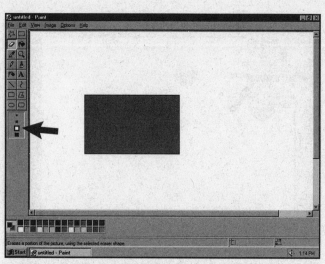

① Click on the **Eraser/Color Eraser** tool.

② The linesize area displays several eraser sizes. The larger the eraser, the wider the path it will erase when you use it. Select the size you want.

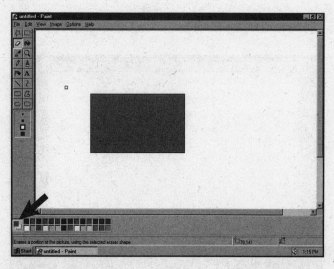

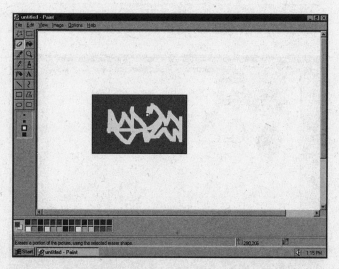

③ In the color box, click on the color you want to replace. Right-click on the color you want to use as the replacement.

④ Position the pointer in the drawing area. Right-click and drag across the area you want to erase.

⑤ Paint erases the selected color and replaces it with the new color.

Select a Shape

After you've created a shape, you have to select it so Paint knows which shape or area you want to work with.

To select the shape or area you want to work with, use either the Free-Form Select or the Select tool. The Free-Form Select tool works like a lasso: you draw a circle around the shape or area you want. This tool works best for objects that are irregularly shaped or are close to other objects. The Select tool draws a rectangle around the selected area and is more suited to regularly shaped objects.

When you select an area with either tool, Paint draws a selection box around the area. You can remove the selection box by clicking outside of it.

After you select the shape, you can do any of the following:

- Copy or move the shape
- Delete the shape
- Change the appearance of the shape—for example, rotate it.

> To select an entire drawing, open the **Edit** menu and select **Select All** (or press **Ctrl+L**).

Begin Guided Tour   Select an Area of Your Drawing

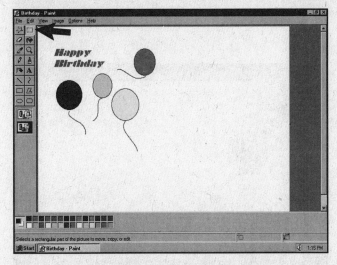

1 Click on the **Free-Form Select** tool or the **Select** tool.

2 In the drawing area, select the area you want to work with. To select an area with the Select tool, drag diagonally downward to draw a box around it. To select an area with the Free-Form Select tool, drag around the area (like a lasso).

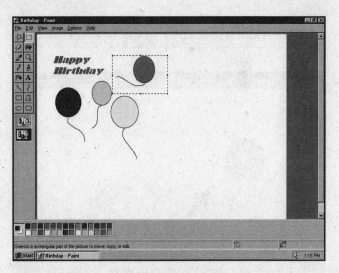

3 Paint displays a selection box around the area.

> If you select the wrong area, click on the screen anywhere and then try again.

Copy or Move a Shape

Suppose you spend a lot of time getting a shape to be just the way you want it: the colors are great, the size is just right, the image is perfect. In fact, this shape looks so good you want to use it again in the same document. Do you have to go through each of the steps to re-create your perfect image? No, you can copy it. For example, if you draw a house, you can create one window and then copy that shape to add all the other windows.

Copying a shape is similar to copying text or any other object in a Windows program. You select what you want to copy, and then select the **Edit Copy** command. To paste the shape, you use the **Edit Paste** command. When you paste the shape, Paint places it in the upper-left corner of the selected document, then you can move the shape to the location you want. You can paste multiple copies by

holding down the **Ctrl** key as you drag the pasted object to its new location.

You can move other shapes, too (not just shapes that you have copied). Part of getting a drawing right is getting each item in the right spot. So if you draw a bicycle and decide after you finish that the front tire needs to be higher to make it even with the back tire, you just select the front tire shape and move it.

You can cut or copy a shape to another application by switching to that application and selecting the **Edit Paste** command.

Use the following keyboard shortcuts when copying and moving shapes: **Ctrl+C** for Copy, **Ctrl+X** for Cut, and **Ctrl+V** for Paste.

Begin Guided Tour   Copy a Shape

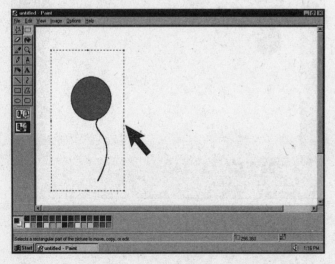

1 With the Free-Form Select tool or the Select tool, select the shape or area you want to copy.

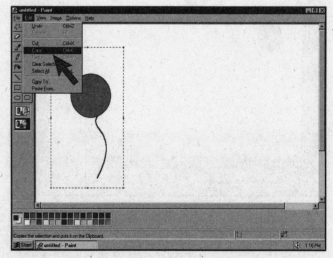

2 Open the **Edit** menu and select **Copy**.

Guided Tour Copy a Shape

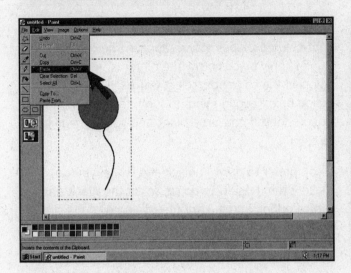

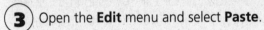

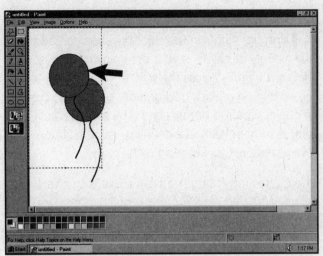

3 Open the **Edit** menu and select **Paste**.

4 Paint places the copy in the upper-left corner. You can move the copy to the location you want.

Begin Guided Tour Move a Shape

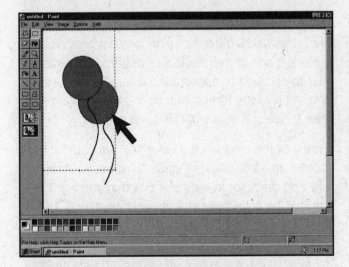

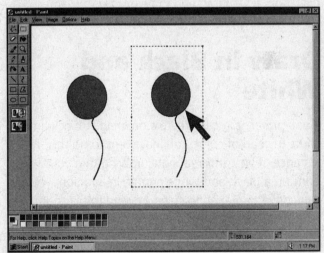

1 With the Free-Form Select tool or the Select tool, select the shape or area you want to move. This figure shows selected the shape that was copied in the preceding *Guided Tour*.

2 Position the pointer anywhere inside the selection box. The pointer changes to a four-headed arrow.

3 Drag the area to the location you want.

4 Paint moves the selected shape to its new location.

Work with Colors

Using the colors in the color box, you can add a variety of colors in your drawing. You can spray paint red writing across the screen; you can create yellow text on a black background; or you can create an object with red borders and a blue fill. Because color is so important in a drawing, Paint includes several features for working with colors.

One interesting change you can make is to invert colors. When you invert colors, you change a color to its complement. Black turns to white, yellow becomes blue, red becomes green. Experiment with the inversions to see what the complementary colors are.

You can create custom colors (as covered later in this section), and you can pick up a color used in a drawing and use that color in another part of the drawing. Being able to pick up a color and reuse it comes in very handy when you've created a custom color and don't want to have to re-create it. If you pick it up, it's guaranteed to be exactly the same.

Draw in Black and White

If you prefer, you can create a drawing in black and white instead of color. You may want to do this, for instance, if you are creating a drawing that you will print on a black-and-white printer. In addition, you can convert an existing color drawing to black and white. If you select this option, however, keep in mind that you cannot undo the change. For example, you can't convert a drawing to black and white just to see what it looks like and then return it to the color version.

When you select the Black and white option from the Attributes dialog box, Paint changes the drawing so that all the colors in the drawing appear as some combination of black and white. Be aware that some

light-colored shapes may disappear. The color box displays only black-and-white patterns. To redisplay colors in the color box, select **Colors** in the Attributes dialog box. Keep in mind, though, that selecting this option doesn't convert a black-and-white image back to color.

If you prefer to draw in black and white, you can make it the default. To do so, select the **Black and white** option in the Attributes dialog box and click the **Default** button.

You also can use the Attributes dialog box to select the dimensions for a picture. In the dialog box, select the measurement you want to use. (Pels, the default, means pixels.) Then enter the dimensions and click the **OK** button.

Create Custom Colors

In the color box at the bottom of the Paint screen, Paint displays 28 different colors and patterns. You can select any of these colors or patterns to use as your foreground or background color. Click on a color to select it as the foreground color; right-click on a color to select it as the background color.

If none of the colors in the color box suit your fancy, you can create a different color. To do so, you start by selecting the color in the color box that you want to replace (the color box can hold only 28 colors). Then you select the **Edit Colors** command from the **Options** menu. After you've displayed and expanded the Edit Colors dialog box (as covered in the *Guided Tour*), you can define the color you want in one of three ways:

- You can click on the color you want in the color matrix and drag the selection arrow around until you get just the color you want. (This is the easiest method.)

- You can type the values for hue, saturation, and luminance to define the color. (This may be difficult unless you are a color expert.)

- You can type the values for green, blue, and red to define the color.

If you spend a lot of time modifying the colors, you may want to save them so they are available again for later drawings. To save a custom color scheme, follow these steps:

1. Open the **Options** menu and select **Save Colors**.

2. In the Save Colors dialog box, change to the folder where you want to save the new color box, type a file name, and click the **Save** button.

To use this same color scheme in another drawing, open the **Options** menu and select the **Get Colors** command. Select the folder where you stored the color file, select the file, and click the **Open** button. The custom colors you saved are now available in the color box.

Begin Guided Tour   Invert the Colors in a Drawing

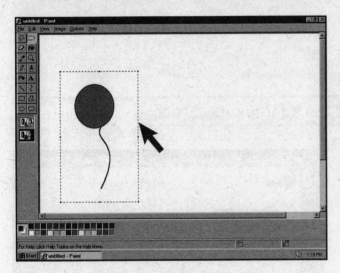 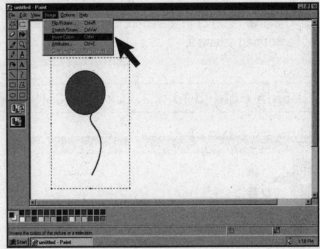

① If you want to invert color in only part of a drawing, select that part using either of the selection tools. To invert colors in the entire document, you don't need to select anything.

② Open the **Image** menu and select **Invert Colors**.

(continues)

Guided Tour   Invert the Colors in a Drawing   *(continued)*

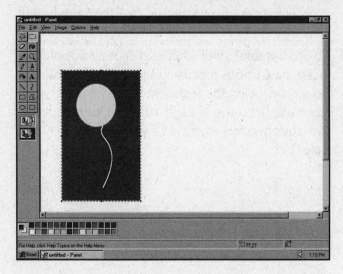

If you want to keep a color version and a black-and-white version, use the **Save As** command to save a copy of the color version. Then you can convert the copy to black and white, but leave the original drawing in color.

3 Paint inverts the colors in the selected area (as shown here) or in the entire drawing if you had nothing selected.

Begin Guided Tour   Pick Up a Color and Use It for Another Shape

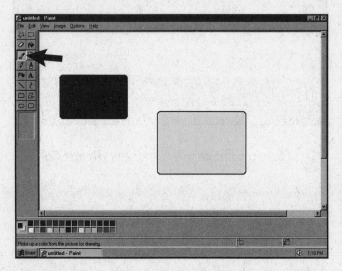

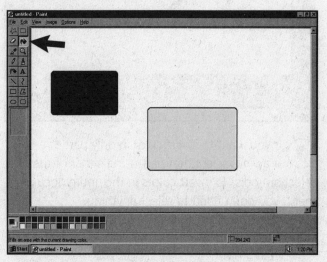

1 Click on the **Pick Color** tool. Then, in your drawing, click on the color you want to pick up and use.

2 Select the tool you want to use with the new color. For example, if you want to use this color as a fill, click on the **Fill with Color** tool.

Guided Tour   Pick Up a Color and Use It for Another Shape

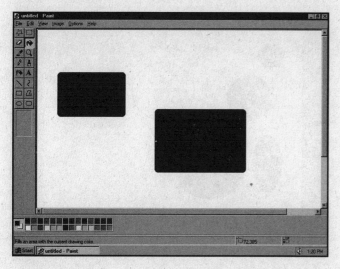

3 Use the tool as you normally would. Here you see the results of filling an object with a picked-up color.

Begin Guided Tour   Convert a Drawing to Black and White

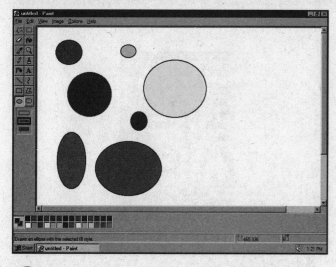

1 Display the drawing you want to convert.

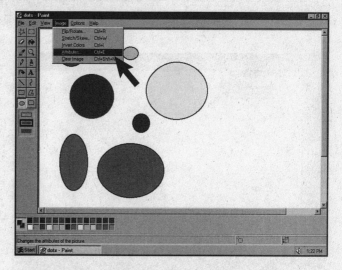

2 Open the **Image** menu and select the **Attributes** command.

(continues)

Guided Tour   Convert a Drawing to Black and White   *(continued)*

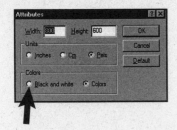

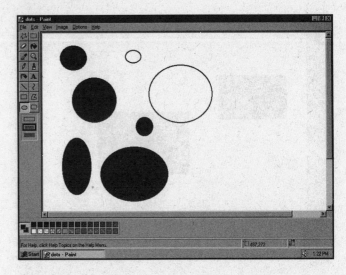

3 In the Attributes dialog box, select **Black and white** and then click **OK**.

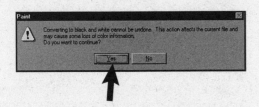

4 Paint displays a dialog box reminding you that this change cannot be undone. To proceed, click the **Yes** button.

5 Paint converts the colors in the drawing to variations of black and white. Notice that the colors in the color box are replaced with black-and-white patterns.

Begin Guided Tour   Customize Color

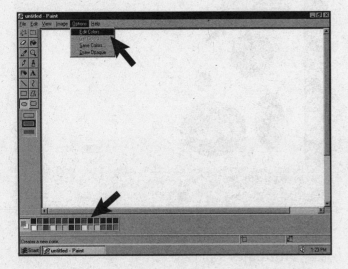

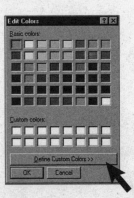

3 In the Edit Colors dialog box, click the **Define Custom Colors** button.

1 In the color box, click on the color you want to replace.

2 Open the **Options** menu and select **Edit Colors**.

Guided Tour   Customize Color

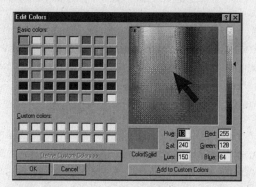

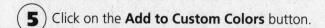

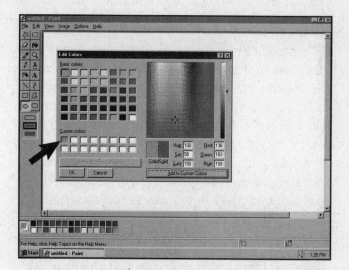

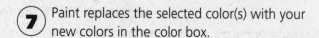

4 The dialog box expands to display the color matrix for selecting a custom color. In the color matrix click on the color you want to use, or enter the values you want in the Hue, Sat, and Lum boxes or in the Red, Green, and Blue boxes.

5 Click on the **Add to Custom Colors** button.

6 Paint adds the new color to the Custom colors list. (Optional) To replace another color, select it in the Basic colors area and repeat steps 4 and 5. Do this for each color you want to change. When you finish making changes, click the **OK** button.

7 Paint replaces the selected color(s) with your new colors in the color box.

Change the Display

To make it easier for you to create and change your drawings, Paint provides multiple ways to view the drawing. For example, you can hide the on-screen tools to see more of a working area; you can zoom in (blow up one area of the drawing) to work on its finer details; and you can zoom out to get an overall view of the drawing. Zooming in on the drawing is great for detailed work; you can edit the drawing pixel by pixel (dot by dot). Paint provides several zoom levels that enable you to see as much or as little detail as you need.

When you choose a zoomed view, you also have two other view options available: Show Grid and Show Thumbnail. You can select Show Grid to have Paint display gridlines that make it easier for you to align objects in the drawing. The Show Thumbnail command tells Paint to display a thumbnail view of the selected area. You can then watch the thumbnail view to see how the changes you make in the zoomed area will affect the overall selected area.

When you zoom the picture, you may see nothing but white and think that the picture has disappeared. Remember, though, that in a zoomed view, less of the drawing fits in the window. You may just be looking at a blank area of the drawing. Use the scroll bars to scroll to the area you want to view or change.

If you prefer to use the keyboard, you can use the following keyboard shortcuts to change the view without opening the View menu:

Keyboard Shortcuts for Changing the View

To Do This...	Press...
Change to normal size (zoom out)	Ctrl+PgUp
Change to large size (zoom in)	Ctrl+PgDn
Hide or display the tool box	Ctrl+T
Hide or display the color box	Ctrl+A
Display gridlines	Ctrl+G

You can drag the tools from one side of the screen to the other. To do so, put the pointer on a gray area of the tool box (not on a tool). Then drag the tool box to the location you want.

Begin Guided Tour   Hide or Display On-Screen Tools

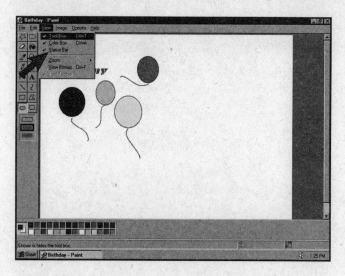

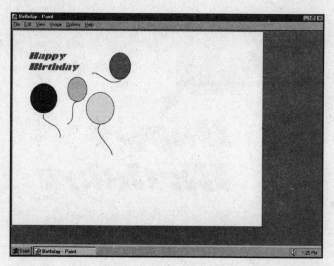

1 Open the **View** menu and select the item (Tool Box, Color Box, Status Bar) you want to hide or display. When an item is displayed, a check mark appears next to its name. Select the item (and remove the check mark) to turn off the display.

2 Paint makes the change. Here you see the Paint screen with the tool box, status bar, and color box turned off.

Begin Guided Tour   Zoom the View

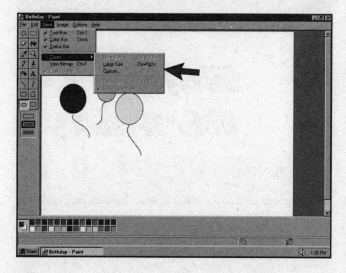

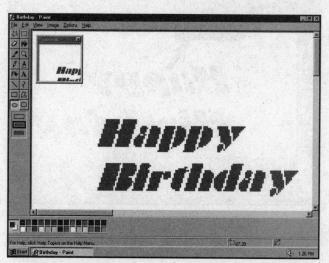

1 Open the **View** menu and select **Zoom**.

2 In the submenu that appears, select a zoom size (normal, large, or custom). If you select custom, select a magnification size (100, 200, 400, 600, or 800%) from the submenu that appears. Then click **OK**.

3 Paint zooms the view. In this figure, the view has been zoomed 400%.

Begin Guided Tour   Display Gridlines

1 In a magnified view, open the **View** menu, select **Zoom**, and select **Show Grid**.

2 Paint displays gridlines. You can use these lines to align shapes in your drawing.

Begin Guided Tour   Display a Thumbnail

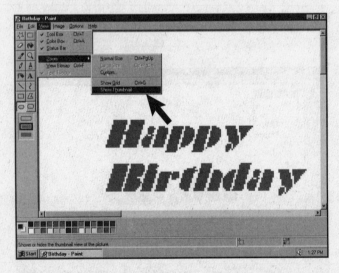

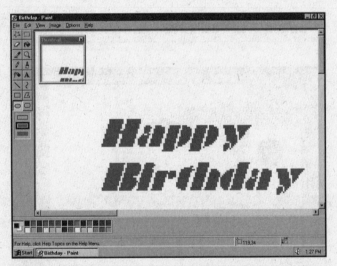

1 In a magnified view, open the **View** menu, select **Zoom**, and select **Show Thumbnail**.

2 Paint displays a thumbnail of the selected area. You can see how the changes in the zoomed area affect the overall area.

Begin Guided Tour   Use the Magnify Tool

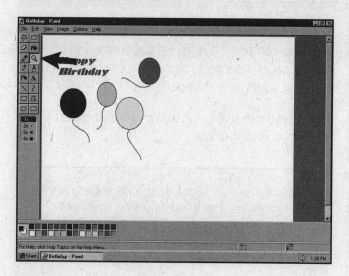

1 Click on the **Magnify** tool.

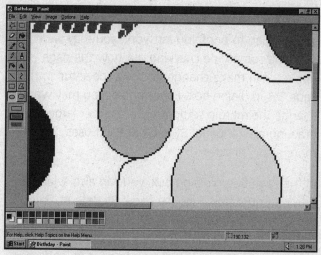

3 Paint magnifies the selected area.

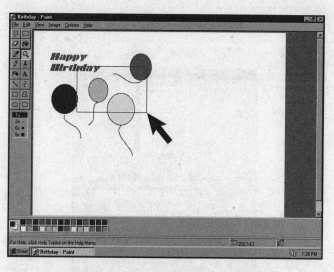

2 Move the pointer into the drawing area and select the area you want to magnify. Then click the mouse button.

The Show Grid and Show Thumbnail commands are not available if you are not in a zoomed-in view. To use these features, you must have zoomed in (magnified) the view.

Set Up the Page

If you plan to print your artwork, you may want to spend some time checking out how the page is set up. You can make changes to the page setup in the Page Setup dialog box. For example, you may want to change the margin settings to fit a rather large drawing on the page. By default, Paint uses .75" margins on all sides.

In the Page Setup dialog box, you can also select a different orientation for the page. By default, Paint prints in *portrait orientation*, or 8 1/2" x 11", where the long edges of the paper are the right and left sides. However, you can choose to print in landscape orientation, or 11" x 8 1/2", where the long edges of the paper are the top and bottom sides.

You also can select a different paper size and source. Which paper sizes and sources you can use depend on what your printer supports.

Finally, you can use the **Printer** button to select the printer you want to use.

To get an overall sense of the page before you print, preview the drawing using the Print Preview command. See "Preview and Print the Picture" on page 236 for information on this command.

Begin Guided Tour   Set Up the Page

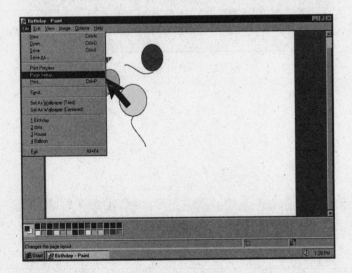

(1) Open the **File** menu and select **Page Setup**.

(2) The Page Setup dialog box appears. To change the margins, click in the Margins area text box for the margin you want to change. Then enter the new setting in inches. (You can delete or edit the current entry.)

(3) In the Orientation area, click on **Portrait** or **Landscape**.

Guided Tour   Set Up the Page

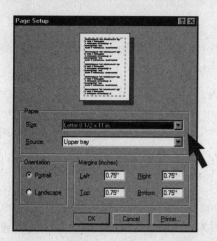

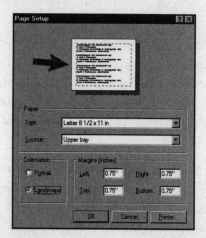

(4) To change the paper size, display the **Size** drop-down list and select the size you want.

(5) To change the paper source, display the **Source** drop-down list and select the source.

(6) The example at the top of the dialog box changes to show you how the document will look using these settings. Here the figure shows a document in landscape orientation with a .75" margin on all sides.

(7) Click the **OK** button. Paint uses the new setup.

Preview and Print the Picture

You'll most likely create some artwork that you will want to print and share with others. For example, you may use Paint to design a birthday card or invitation. Or if your children use the program to create artwork, you can print the drawing and hang it on the refrigerator.

Before you print a document, it's a good idea to check its overall appearance and make any necessary adjustments. With some formatting elements (orientation, for example), you can't tell just by looking at the document in normal view how it will look when printed.

Select the Print Preview command to see a preview of the drawing. Use the buttons along the top of the preview window as explained here.

- Click the **Print** button to print the document.

- Click on the **Next Page** and **Prev Page** buttons to move from page to page (if the document contains more than one page).

- Click on the **Two Page** button to see how two pages will look side by side.

- Click the **Zoom In** button to zoom in for more detail of the document. (You can zoom in twice.) Click the **Zoom Out** button to zoom out.

- Click the **Close** button when you finish previewing the document.

When you have previewed the document and are sure you like how it looks, you're ready to print. Select the **Print** command, and then select the printer to use, the number of copies to print, and other print options.

You might want to use your finished drawings as wallpaper for your desktop. When you select to tile the wallpaper, the entire desktop is covered. When you select to center the wallpaper, just a small patch appears in the center of the screen. For more information on wallpaper, see "Customize Windows 95" on page 429.

Begin Guided Tour Preview a Document

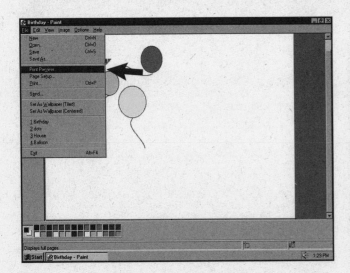

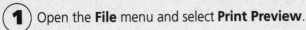

1 Open the **File** menu and select **Print Preview**.

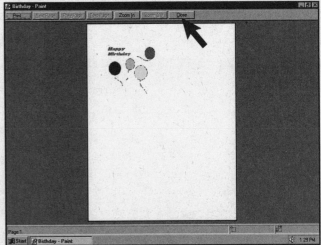

2 Paint displays a preview of the document. Click the **Close** button to return to the normal view.

Begin Guided Tour Print a Document

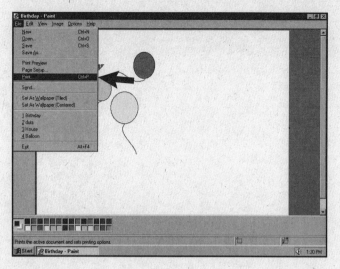

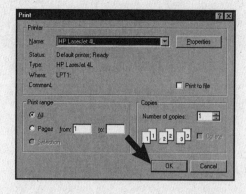

2 In the Print dialog box, make any necessary changes. Then click the **OK** button.

1 Open the **File** menu and select **Print**.

Begin Guided Tour Use a Drawing as Your Desktop Background

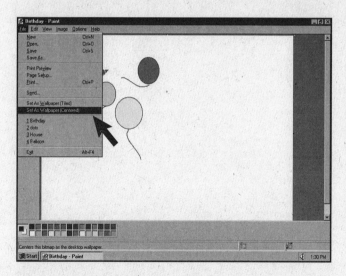

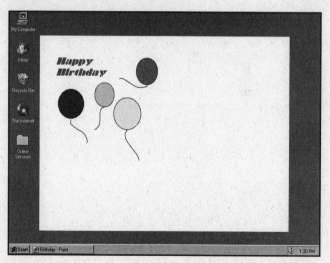

1 Create or open the drawing you want to use. Then open the **File** menu and select **Set As Wallpaper** (**Centered**). Select the (Tiled) command if you want the selected image tiled across the desktop.

2 Windows centers the selected image as the wallpaper. You may have to close or minimize open windows to see the effect of the change.

Use Multimedia Programs

One of the greatest things to hit computing in the last few years is multimedia. *Multimedia* is the combination of multiple communication media. For example, a multimedia presentation may include text, graphics, video, animation, and sound. All of these media combined create a richer, more powerful presentation than the text presentations of yesteryear (which were often dry and hard to sit through).

Windows 95 includes some multimedia applications that you can use if you have the appropriate equipment. Basically, you need a sound card and a CD-ROM drive. Most new computers come with these components already installed; you can add them to your system if necessary.

If you have a multimedia PC, you may want to review this section to find out about Windows 95's multimedia programs. If you don't have the equipment, you may want to review this section to see what is possible. This section includes the following tasks:

What You Will Find in This Section

Play a CD

Does music boost your creativity? Do you think better with some soft music playing in the background? Or do you just want to have fun and blast out some rock and roll? If you have a CD-ROM drive and a sound card installed on your computer, you can use CD Player (included with Windows 95) to play your audio CDs. Yes, you can jam with Patti Rothberg or Hootie and the Blowfish, or you can play some Mozart to soothe your nerves as you work.

Keep in mind that the sound quality isn't going to be as great as if you were playing the CDs on your CD player. Even though most sound cards come with speakers that are adequate for playing sounds, don't expect excellent quality. If you really want stereo-quality music, you can invest in some better speakers for your computer. Speakers range in price from $25 to several hundred dollars.

With CD Player, you can play the tracks on the CD in order or you can change to the track you want. You can even create your own personal play list. Here are some of the options you have when playing a CD with CD Player:

- You can select the track to play using the Track drop-down list or the buttons in the CD Player.

- When you play a CD, you see generic names like Artist and Track 1 in the CD Player window. When that's all that's displayed, it's difficult to select the track you want. You can enter the artist, CD name, and track names so that you can easily switch to the song you want. When you do, CD Player remembers these titles the next time you play the CD.

- If you play the CD without any changes, CD Player plays the tracks in order. However, you can choose to play the songs in random order, or if you are really particular, you can create a play list as covered in the *Guided Tour*.

- The newest computer compact disc drives can handle multiple discs (as can most audio CD players). If you have one of these multidisc CD

drives, you can select not only the track to play, but the artist and the tracks from several CDs. You also can create a play list that combines tracks from several CDs. The number of CDs you can play depends on the number your CD drive can handle.

Play the CD

When you start the CD Player, Windows opens the CD Player window. The CD Player gives you a lot of information about what is playing currently, the current track number, and how much time has passed. At the bottom of the window, the CD Player displays the total play time and the time the current track has played.

> You can minimize the CD Player window, and the CD will continue to play.

In addition, the CD Player includes buttons that enable you to start a song over, switch to a different song, stop a song, and so on. The following table identifies the buttons in the CD Player window.

Besides these buttons, you can use menu commands to select what is played and how the CD is played.

As I mentioned, CD Player plays the tracks in the order they appear on the CD. If you prefer to be surprised, select **Random Order** from the **Options** menu, and CD Player plays the tracks in a random order. Also by default, when CD Player gets to the end of the tracks, it stops. If you want it to continue playing, open the **Options** menu and select **Continuous Play**.

Suppose you want to hear just a little bit of a particular CD to see if you like the music or to find a particular song. If you select **Intro Play** from the **Options** menu, CD Player plays the beginning of each track only. You can set the amount of time you want it to play in the Preferences dialog box.

If you play your CD a lot, you can create a shortcut to the CD Player. The *Guided Tour* covers this procedure.

Setting View and Other Preferences

When you play a CD, you see information about the current track and play time in the CD Player window. If you don't want that much information or if you want more information, you can change the view preferences in the View menu. Remember that when a view command is checked on the menu, it is turned on. You can remove the check and turn off the display by clicking on the command. You can select the following options from the View menu:

- **Toolbar** Tells Windows to display a toolbar with buttons for common commands (such as editing the play list).

- **Disc/Track Info** Controls the display of the name of the artist, title, and track (all shown by default) in the CD Player window.

- **Status Bar** Controls the display of the status bar at the bottom of the CD Player window. The status bar is on by default and displays the total play time and track play time.

- **Track Time Elapsed** Toggles between whether or not CD Player tracks the amount of time that has elapsed since you started playing the CD. This is turned on by default.

- **Track Time Remaining** Enables you to see how much time is remaining for a particular track.

- **Disc Time Remaining** Enables you to see how much time is remaining on the disc.

You also can set the following options via the Options Preferences command.

CD Player Buttons

Button	Name	Description
	Play	Starts playing the CD.
	Pause	Pauses the CD. To resume play, click on the Play button again.
	Stop	Stops the CD.
	Previous Track	Plays the previous track.
	Next Track	Plays the next track.
	Skip Forward	Moves forward within the current track.
	Skip Backward	Moves backward within the current track.
	Eject	Ejects the CD.

Create a Play List

For the most possible control over how a CD is played, you can create a play list. This feature is easy to use if you enter the names of the CD, artist, and tracks as described in the *Guided Tour*. Then you can select the tracks and play them in the order you want.

When creating the play list, keep the following tips in mind:

- If your CD drive can hold more than one CD, you can choose tracks from different CDs to play in the play list.

- All the songs on a CD are included in the default play list. You create your new play list by removing the ones you don't want. To do so, click on the track you want to remove and then click on the **Remove** button. Or, if you prefer, you can clear all the tracks and then add the ones you want as covered in the *Guided Tour*.

- If you want to go back to the original play list (all the tracks in the order they appear on the CD), click on the **Reset** button.

Option	Description
Stop CD	If you want CD Player to stop playing the CD when you exit CD Player, keep this check box checked.
Save settings	To save any changes you make on exit keep this check box checked.
Show tool tips	If you use the toolbar, you can put the mouse pointer on the button edge to see the tool's name. To turn off this feature, uncheck this check box.
Intro play	If you choose to play just an intro of the tracks on the CD, enter the time (in seconds) you want it to play.
Display font	Select the size of the font (Small font or Large font) used for time tracking information.

Begin Guided Tour Play a CD

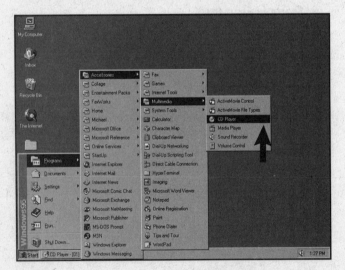

1 Click on the **Start** button, select **Programs**, select **Accessories**, select **Multimedia**, and (finally) select **CD Player**.

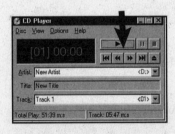

2 Windows starts the CD Player program. Insert a disc into your CD drive and click on the **Play** button.

You also can insert the CD into the drive, and it will automatically start CD Player and play the CD. If CD Player is running, the CD won't auto-play. Also, you can hold down the Shift key to prevent auto-play.

Guided Tour Play a CD

You can change the volume using the Volume Control command in the View menu. See "Set the Volume" on page 248 for more details.

3 CD Player plays the first track on the CD. You can see the current track number and amount of time the CD has been playing in the CD Player window.

Begin Guided Tour Set Play Options

When you enter the names for the artist, title, and tracks, CD Player remembers them the next time you play the CD. You won't have to reenter the names.

1 Open the **Options** menu and select the play option you want to turn on or off. Remember that when an option is on, there's a check mark next to the command. Select the command again to turn if off.

2 CD Player makes the changes.

Begin Guided Tour Play a Different Track

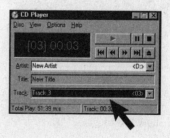

1 In the CD Player window, display the Track drop-down list to see a list of the available tracks.

2 CD Player moves to and plays the selected track (track 3 in this case).

Begin Guided Tour Change the View Options

1 Open the **View** menu. Select the play option you want to turn on or off. Remember that when an option is on, there's a check mark next to the command. Select the command again to turn it off.

2 CD Player makes the changes. Here you see the window with the toolbar displayed and the status bar turned off.

To find out what a toolbar button does, place the mouse pointer on the button. The tool name pops up.

Begin Guided Tour Set Play Preferences

1 Open the **Options** menu and select **Preferences**.

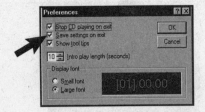

2 The Preferences dialog box appears. Check or uncheck any of these options: Stop CD playing on exit, Save settings on exit, and Show tool tips.

3 If you chose to play the intro, enter the time to play in seconds in the Intro play length spin box (or click the up and down arrows to adjust the number that's there).

4 To change the font used in the CD Player window, select **Large font** in the Display font area. When you finish making changes, click on the **OK** button.

Begin Guided Tour Enter the CD Name and Track Names

1 Insert the CD into the drive. Then open the **Disc** menu and select the **Edit Play List** command.

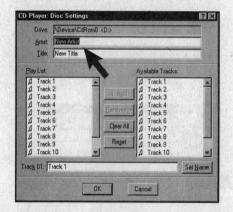

2 The Disc Settings dialog box appears. Start by typing the artist or band's name in the Artist text box. Click in the Title text box and type the CD title. (You can highlight the generic title and then start typing to replace the old title with the new one.)

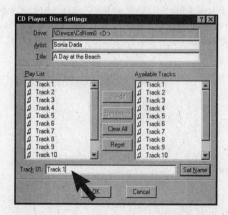

3 Select a track name in the **Available Tracks** list. Then in the **Track** text box, select the current name and replace it by typing the actual track name.

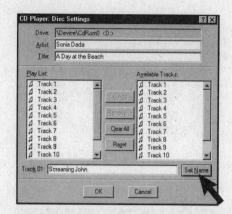

4 After you type the name, click on the **Set Name** button.

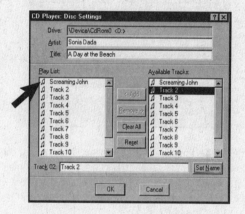

5 CD Player updates the name of the selected track in the Play List and Available Tracks list.

6 Repeat steps 3 through 5. Do this for each track. When you finish naming the tracks, click on the **OK** button.

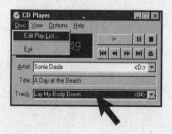

7 When you play the CD, CD Player displays the name of the current track in the Track list.

Begin Guided Tour   Create a Play List

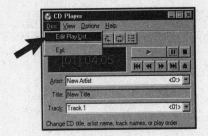

1 Open the **Disc** menu and select **Edit Play List**.

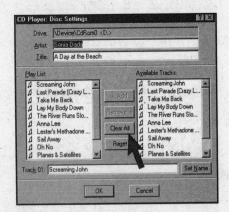

2 The Disc Settings dialog box appears. The Play List displays the tracks in order, and all tracks are selected for play. The Available Tracks list contains all the tracks on the CD. (Here the track names have been entered.) Start by clearing the current Play List: click on the **Clear All** button.

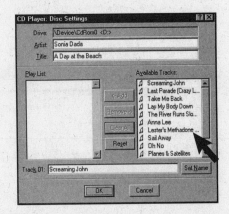

3 CD Player clears the Play List. In the Available Tracks list, click on the track you want to play first.

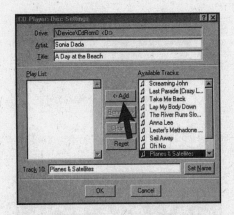

4 Click on the **Add** button.

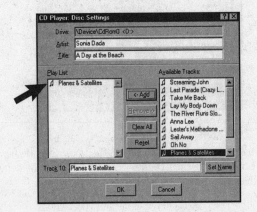

5 CD Player adds the track to the Play List. Repeat steps 3 and 4 for each track you want to include in the Play List. When you finish making changes, click on the **OK** button.

6 When you play the CD, CD Player plays the songs in the order you selected.

Begin Guided Tour Create a Shortcut to the CD player

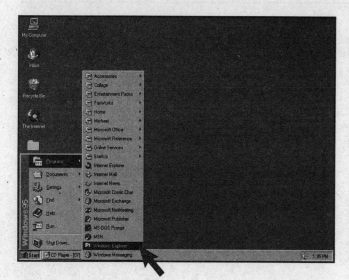

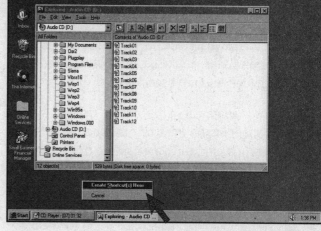

1 Click on the **Start** button, select **Programs**, and select **Windows Explorer**.

3 When you release the mouse button, you see a shortcut menu. Select **Create Shortcut(s) Here**.

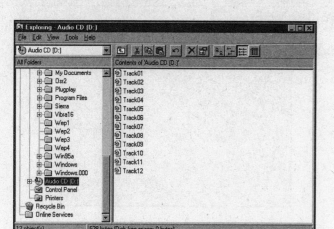

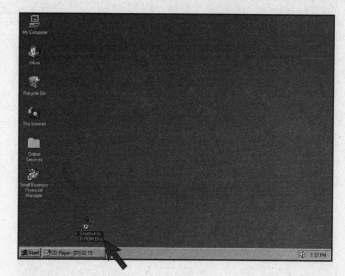

2 With the right mouse button, drag the icon representing your CD-ROM drive onto the desktop.

4 The shortcut is added to the desktop. You can double-click on the CD's shortcut icon. If you have a regular CD-ROM disc in the drive, Windows 95 displays the contents of its directory. If you have an audio CD in the drive, Windows starts CD Player, and it plays the CD.

Set the Volume

Music too loud? Music too soft? Music just right? With the Volume Control program, you can adjust the playback volume for your CDs and other system sounds. You also can adjust the balance between the left and right speakers.

The options that appear in the Volume Control dialog box vary depending on the type of sound card you have. Different sound cards are capable of playing different types of sounds. For example, some are capable of playing synthesized sound, in which case, you also can adjust the volume of the synthesizer. You can adjust the volume of audio CDs using the Audio CD volume control. Also, you can adjust the volume of sound files (WAV files) by setting the Wave option.

> To mute all sounds, check the **Mute all** check box.

Although your Volume Control dialog box may have different options from those described here, you make a change in the same way: drag the control bar up to increase the volume or drag the control bar down to decrease the volume. Drag the balance control left or right to adjust the balance between the left and right speakers.

Begin Guided Tour Use the Volume Control Program

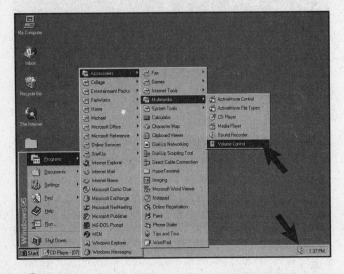

1 Double-click on the tiny speaker icon in the right corner of the taskbar. Or, if you prefer, click on the **Start** button, then select **Programs**, **Accessories**, and **Multimedia**, **Volume Control**.

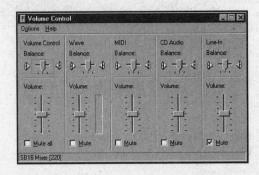

2 The Volume Control dialog box appears. To increase the volume, drag the Volume Control bar up. You can also drag the Volume Control Balance bar right or left to adjust the volume between the two speakers.

3 Depending on your sound card, you may be able to adjust other settings. For example, you can adjust the wave balance, synthesizer balance, MIDI balance, Line-In Balance, and CD Audio balance by dragging the appropriate controls.

4 When you finish making changes, click on the **Close (X)** box.

Play Sounds and Record Your Voice

Not only can you play audio CDs on your computer, you also can play other sounds, called WAV files, and record your own sounds with the Sound Recorder. You can use this program for something useful (such as attaching a sound message to a file for a coworker) or something fun (such as recording silly sounds like your dog barking).

You can assign a sound to a Windows event so that when that event occurs (when an alert dialog box appears, for example), you hear a sound and see the alert message. You can change the sound, and you can assign sounds to other system events.

You can play back most sounds without a sound card; Sound Recorder can use the computer's speaker. The sound will play better, though, if you have a sound card. Sounds, like all information on a computer, are stored in files. Most sound files use the extension

WAV and are also called wave files. You can play back sounds that you have recorded, or sounds provided with some other application. For example, Windows comes with some sample sounds (found in the WINDOWS\MEDIA folder). You also can download sounds from bulletin board systems or purchase sound files.

To record sounds, you need a sound card and a microphone, and the microphone must be plugged into your sound card. Most sound cards come with a microphone, but it may not have been connected. Check your sound card manual for help on where to plug in the microphone.

Play the Sound

After you start the Sound Recorder and open a sound to play, you can use the buttons in the Sound Recorder window to play, rewind, or fast forward the sound. The following table identifes the buttons for playing and recording sounds.

Sound Recorder Buttons

Button	Name	Description
◀◀	Seek To Start	"Rewinds" the sound (goes back to the beginning).
▶▶	Seek To End	"Fast forward" the sound (goes to the end).
▶	Play	Plays the sound.
■	Stop	Stops playing the sound.
●	Record	Records a new sound.

Besides playing the sound, you can change certain qualities of it. You can make the following changes by selecting the appropriate command from the Effects menu:

- To make the sound louder, select the **Increase Volume (by 25%)** command.

- To make the sound softer, select the **Decrease Volume** command.

- To play the sound more quickly, choose the **Increase Speed (by 100%)** command.

- To play the sound more slowly, choose the **Decrease Speed** command.

- To add an echo effect, select the **Add Echo** command.

- To play the sound back in reverse order (end to start), select the **Reverse** command.

To adjust the playback volume, use the **Audio Properties** command as covered in the *Guided Tour*.

Record Your Voice

Sometimes it's easier to explain something than to write a note. Therefore, you might use Sound Recorder to record a message for your coworker that explains what she needs to do with a file, to record a message for your husband reminding him to update the checkbook register, or to have fun recording silly sounds.

When you record a sound, keep the following points in mind:

- You need a microphone to record a sound.

- If you want to use the sound again, you must save the sound (as covered in the *Guided Tour*). Because sound files can be really huge, you should try to keep your message short and concise. Also, be sure to delete any recorded messages you don't need. No reason to hog valuable disk space with worthless files.

- For complete information on opening and saving files, see "Work with Documents" on page 129.

- To adjust the recording volume, use the **Audio Properties** command.

Begin Guided Tour   Play a Sound

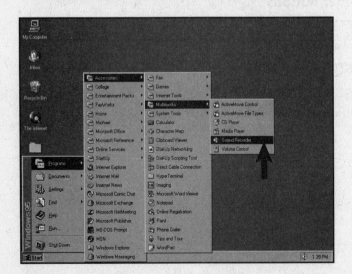

1 Click on the **Start** button, select **Programs**, select **Accessories**, select **Multimedia**, and select **Sound Recorder**.

2 Windows displays the Sound Recorder window.

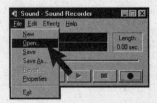

3 To play a sound, open the **File** menu and select **Open**.

Guided Tour Play a Sound

4 The Open dialog box appears. Change to the drive you want in the Look in drop-down list. Then select the appropriate folder from the list.

> Windows includes some sample sound files in the WINDOWS\MEDIA folder.

5 When you change to the folder that contains the files, you see the available sound (WAV) files. Click on the file you want, and then click on the **Open** button.

6 In the Sound Recorder window, the name of the sound now appears in the title bar. To play the sound, click on the **Play** button.

7 Sound Recorder plays the sound. As it plays, you see the sound wave in the Sound Recorder window.

Begin Guided Tour Change the Sound Effects

1 In the Sound Recorder window, open the **Effects** menu and select the option you want.

2 Click on the **Play** button to play the sound.

Begin Guided Tour Record a Voice Message

1 In the Sound Recorder window, open the **File** menu and select **New**.

2 Click on the **Record** button to start recording.

3 Speak into the microphone to record your sound. You see a visual representation of the sound wave as you make your recording.

4 When you finish recording, click on the **Stop** button. You can play back the sound by clicking the **Play** button.

5 To save the sound, open the **File** menu and select **Save**.

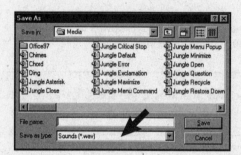

6 In the Save As dialog box, change to the drive and folder where you want to store the file. Then type a file name in the File name text box and click on the **Save** button.

7 Sound Recorder saves the sound and displays its name in the title bar.

Play Media Clips and Movies

Multimedia is the combination of different types of communication media (sound, print, video, and so on). A good example of multimedia is a multimedia encyclopedia. When you look up an entry for Beethoven, you can read a text account of his life and accomplishments, and also play a sample of one of his symphonies. The entry might also include a picture of the famous composer. Similarly, in an encyclopedia entry on spacecraft, you may be able to view a video clip of the launching of a mission or hear the recorded countdown from the control center.

Multimedia presentations are becoming more and more prevalent. These types of presentations are being used not only in encyclopedias and other reference tools, but for selling a product or teaching a new concept. For example, the Windows 95 tour includes some animated features that show you how to perform such tasks as drag-and-drop.

If you have multimedia presentations, you can use the Windows 95 Media Player to play them back. (Windows includes some sample files in the WINDOWS\MEDIA folder.) You can play back the following types of files:

- Video for Windows (AVI files)
- Sound (WAV files)
- MIDI music files (MID and RMI)

Many Internet sites also include movies that you can playback if you have the appropriate program. Internet Explorer 3.01 has an add-on called ActiveMovie Control. You can use it to playback MPEG and other movies files.

Use Media Player

The buttons in the Media Player window enable you to play, rewind, and stop the playback. The following table identifies each button.

Media Player Buttons

Button	Name	Description
▶	Play	Plays the file.
❚❚	Pause	Pauses the file. This button is available when a file is being played.
■	Stop	Stops playing the file.
⏏	Eject	Ejects a disc (if you are playing a disc).
◀◀	Previous Mark	Moves to the previous mark (if you have marked a selection of the file to play using the Start and End Selection buttons).

Button	Name	Description
◀◀	Rewind	Rewinds the file.
▶▶	Fast Forward	Fast forward through the file.
▶▶|	Next Mark	Moves to the next marked section (if you have marked a selection or portion of the file to play).
⊻	Start Selection	Specifies the starting point (so you can play part of a file).
⊼	End Selection	Tells Media Player where to end a selection (when you play part of a file).

To set the volume for multimedia files with sound, use the Volume Control command in the Device menu. For more information on adjusting the sound, see "Set the Volume" on page 235.

Media Player includes many other features for working with media files. You can copy a media file to a document, or you can control how the media file is played back, for example. Here are some of the features you may want to experiment with:

- If you want to place a media file in the document, open the media file. Then open the **Edit** menu and select the **Copy Object** command. Move to the document where you want to place the object. Then select the **Edit Paste** command. You can play the media file in the document by double-clicking on it.

- You can select to rewind or repeat the playback of the media file automatically. To do so, open the **Edit** menu and select the **Options** command. Check the **Auto Rewind** and/or **Auto Repeat** check boxes.

- To change the scale of the playback, open the **Edit** menu and select the **Scale** command. Select the scale you want. For sound files, you can select a range in seconds. For video or animation files, you can select a range in frames.

Begin Guided Tour Use the Media Player Program

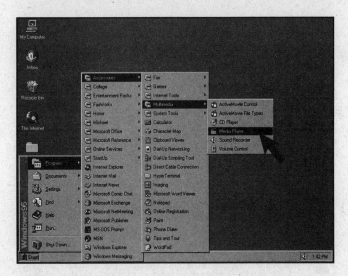

1 Click on the **Start** button, select **Programs**, select **Accessories**, select **Multimedia**, and select **Media Player**.

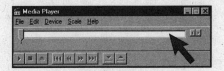

2 Windows displays the Media Player program. From this application, you can play back media clips.

3 Open the **File** menu and select **Open** (as shown here), or open the **Device** menu and select the type of file you want to play (MIDI sequences, Video for Windows, or sound).

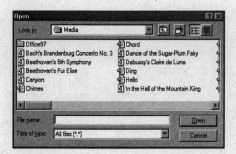

4 The Open dialog box appears with the Media folder selected. You can open files in this folder. Or if necessary, change to the appropriate drive in the **Look in** drop-down list. Then select the appropriate folder from the list.

5 After you change to the folder that contains the multimedia file you want, click on the file and then click on the **Open** button.

6 When you return to the Media Player window, the name of the file appears in the title bar. To play the clip, click on the **Play** button.

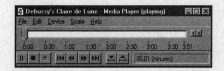

7 Media Player plays back the media clip.

Begin Guided Tour Play a Movie with ActiveMovie Control

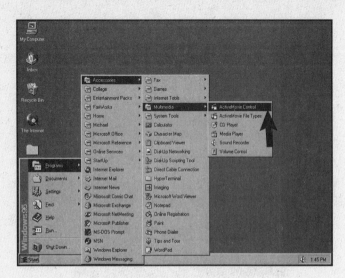

1 Click on the **Start** button, select **Programs**, select **Accessories**, select **Multimedia**, and select **ActiveMovie Control**.

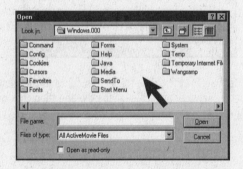

2 The Open dialog box opens automatically. Change to the appropriate drive in the Look in drop-down list. Then select the appropriate folder from the list.

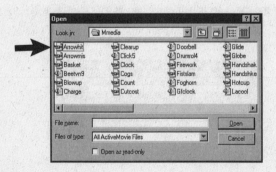

3 After you change to the folder that contains the movie you want, click on the file and then click on the **Open** button.

4 You see the ActiveMovie window with the selected starting image. The name of the file appears in the title bar. To play the clip, click on the **Play** button.

5 ActiveMovie plays the movie.

HOW TO...

Get Your DOS Programs to Run

A DOS program is one that was written specifically for MS-DOS, an operating system in which the user types commands at an on-screen prompt. DOS programs are designed to run one at a time. For example, when you finish using your word processor, you have to exit to the DOS prompt before you can start another program (such as a spreadsheet program).

The problem with running a DOS program in a multitasking environment such as Windows 95 is that the DOS program thinks that it's running by itself with all of the computer's resources at its disposal. (Multitasking means that more than one program can run at once, and you can switch between them.) This can cause problems in Windows 95, where you can run many programs at once, including several DOS programs if you want. As a result, some DOS programs may not run at all or they may run rather slowly. However, this is mostly true of older DOS programs and some DOS games.

If you encounter a problem, or if you simply want to run your DOS programs more efficiently, the tasks in this section will help you.

What You Will Find in This Section

Run a DOS Program

The very first edition of Windows was designed with the intent of running multiple DOS programs at the same time, in their own windows. At first, there were only two applications designed specifically for Windows: PageMaker and Excel. By the time Windows 3.1 came out in 1992, however, many Windows programs were available. Yet, many people still use DOS programs, so the capability of Windows 95 to run DOS programs is still an important feature.

What is unusual is how Windows 95 handles DOS programs. Unlike any previous version (not counting Windows NT), Windows 95 creates a new "simulated computer" of sorts each time it runs a DOS application or a new DOS session. (Windows 3.1, in comparison, created an area in which the DOS program ran, but it didn't copy device drivers and other programs in memory into that area, which limited how well it could run the DOS program.) A DOS program run under Windows 95 doesn't have to run in a limited environment. It can have all the memory and internal device drivers it needs to run, without Windows intruding in its private space. (I'll show you how to manage each DOS program's private environment in "Optimize How a DOS Program Runs" on page 264.)

For quicker access to a DOS program, you can add it to the Start menu, or you can create a shortcut and open it right from the desktop. See "Add a Program to the Start Menu" (page 55) and "Add a Shortcut to the Desktop" (page 63) to learn how.

For now, let's start with how to bring your old DOS world into Windows 95. When you start a DOS program (as explained in the *Guided Tour*), the program starts in a window, which makes it easy to switch between that program and other programs as needed. Alternatively, you can start a DOS program in a full window if you want to so that the DOS program occupies the entire screen. You also can switch a DOS

program from windowed mode to full-screen mode while it's running. Or, if you prefer, you can go to the DOS prompt to enter commands and run programs. And for those stubborn DOS programs (such as some games) that just don't run well under Windows, you can restart your computer and run them from DOS. The *Guided Tour* also shows you how to run your DOS program in each of these ways.

More on Running Stubborn Programs

If you try to start a DOS program and it just doesn't work, then you can restart your computer with just DOS and try to run it again. Microsoft calls this procedure "running in MS-DOS mode," and it creates as close to an old DOS environment as possible, What kind of programs might these be? Well, you might have trouble running some games and computer-aided design (CAD) programs, among others.

In any case, you can restart in MS-DOS mode by selecting the appropriate **Shut Down** command from within Windows 95, or you can start fresh in MS-DOS mode at the time you boot your computer. (You'll learn in the *Guided Tour* the steps to restart in MS-DOS mode from within Windows 95.) To start your computer in MS-DOS mode, simply turn it on and when you hear the first beep, press **F8**. If you select **Command prompt only** from the list, then Windows 95 starts with DOS and processes the commands in your CONFIG.SYS and AUTOEXEC.BAT. This provides the same environment that you'll get if you follow the steps in the *Guided Tour*.

If you select **Safe mode command prompt only** instead, then Windows 95 loads only the minimum drivers, such as your mouse and monitor drivers. This gives your DOS program more memory to use, but it will prevent you from using your CD-ROM, and sound card.

If you set up your computer for dual boot mode (by installing Windows 95 in a separate folder from your previous version of Windows), you have another way to restart your computer with your old operating system. Restart the PC, wait for the beep, and then press **F4**. Windows 95 immediately restores your old AUTOEXEC.BAT and CONFIG.SYS files and starts your old DOS.

What You Should Know Before You Run a DOS Program in a Window

You can minimize and maximize a DOS program window as you would any other Windows window. Note, however, that a DOS program running in a window may only fill a portion of the screen (depending on the video resolution of the program) when you click on the Maximize button.

If you run your DOS program in a window, you can resize it as you would any other by simply dragging one of its sides. However, you won't be able to make the window larger than its normal Maximized size.

In addition, you can resize a DOS window by changing its font size. To do that, simply select a new font size from the Font size list box located on the window's toolbar. If you select **Auto**, then the font size is automatically adjusted when you resize the window. You also can change the font style, as you'll learn in the *Guided Tour*.

This table shows you the toolbar buttons available in a DOS window, and gives a description of what they're used for.

Toolbar Button	What It Does
	Marks text to copy to another document
	Copies selected text
	Pastes text into the document
	Switches to a full-screen session
	Displays the window's properties dialog box
	When this option is ON, the program will not be allowed to do anything when the window is not active. If you turn this option off, the program is run in the background, which means that it can use system resources even while the window itself is not active.
	Changes the font style of text

Begin Guided Tour Run a DOS Program in a Window

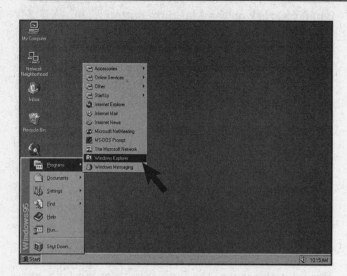

1 Click on the **Start** button, select **Programs**, and then select **Windows Explorer**.

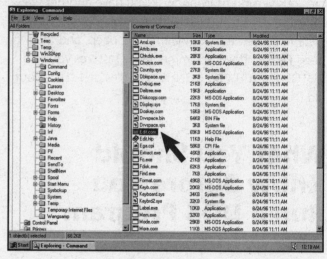

3 To start the DOS program, double-click on the icon next to the program's executable file.

2 On the left side of the Explorer window, change to the folder that contains the program you want to run.

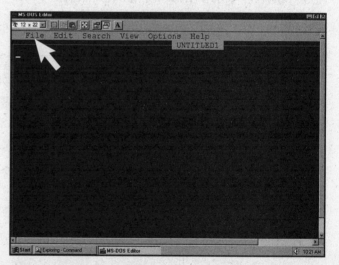

4 The DOS application starts. When you're through, exit the program by opening its **File** menu and selecting **Exit**. The window closes.

Every DOS-based program has different commands. If your program does not have a File menu or an Exit command, you will have to read the program's documentation to find out how to exit.

If you bought a new computer with Windows 95 preinstalled on it, you'll find the traditional DOS utility programs in the WINDOWS\COMMAND folder rather than in \DOS.

Begin Guided Tour   Run a Program at the DOS Prompt

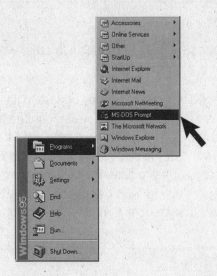

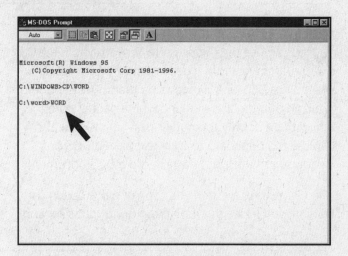

1 Click on the **Start** button, select **Programs**, and then select **MS-DOS Prompt**.

3 Type the name of the program and press **Enter**. (Don't type the .EXE.) For example, type **WORD** and press **Enter**.

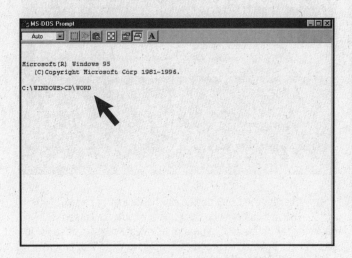

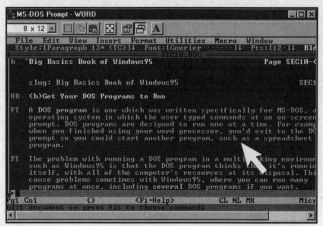

2 Change to the folder where the DOS program is located by typing **CD**, followed by the name of the folder in which the program is located (as in **CD\WORD**). Press **Enter**.

4 The program opens. The title bar tells you which program you're in and that you opened it via the MS-DOS prompt. To exit the file, open its **File** menu and select **Exit**.

Copy and Paste Text into a DOS Window

You can use the Clipboard to copy text from a DOS program to another document whether that document is in a DOS or a Windows program. The Clipboard is a kind of data "waystation" where data is stored while it's on its way to another destination. You also can use the Clipboard to copy text from a DOS or Windows program and paste it into a DOS document.

Keep in mind that when you copy or move text in this fashion, you'll lose the formatting (font, font size, and

attributes such as bold or italic). In other words, all you get is the text.

The process by which you copy or paste data into a DOS document is different from the standard method you learned in the section "Select, Copy, and Move Text" (page 143). But the steps are fairly easy. Note that, for you to copy or paste data, the DOS program must be running in a window. So be sure to press **Alt+Enter** if necessary to place it in a window before you start.

Begin Guided Tour Copy Text from a DOS Program

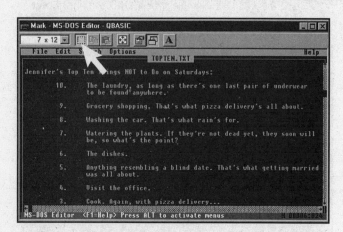

1 If necessary, place your DOS program in a window by pressing **Alt+Enter**. Click on the **Mark** button.

3 Click on the **Copy** button on the toolbar or press Ctrl+C. The text can now be pasted into another document. To paste the text into a DOS program, follow the next set of steps. To paste it into a Windows program, simply switch to that program and click on the **Paste** button.

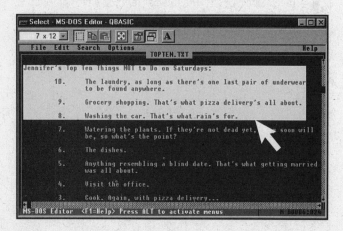

2 Click and drag the pointer over the text to be copied.

Begin Guided Tour   Paste Text to a DOS Program

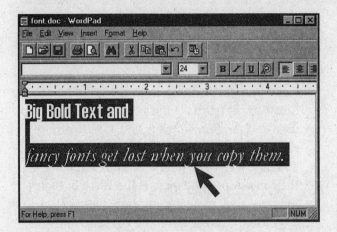

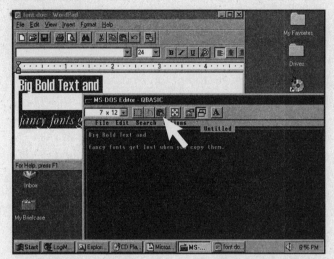

1 Make sure that you've selected and copied the text from your document to the Clipboard. In our example, I've copied text from WordPad to the Clipboard.

2 Switch to your DOS program (which is running in a window) and click in the document where you want to paste the text and click on the **Paste** button. The text appears. Notice that none of the formatting from the WordPad document was carried over to the DOS document.

Optimize How a DOS Program Runs

Most DOS programs run under Windows 95 without your having to do a thing. Some programs, however, do not run smoothly (if at all). In that case, you're stuck with the problem of "optimizing" them (customizing them) so that they will run. The process of optimizing a DOS program involves making the right selections in a series of tabbed sections within the Properties dialog box. This is not easy, and it's not fun. So get someone more experienced to help you if you can.

Let me say this again: If your DOS program is currently working, leave it alone; your attempts to "optimize it" may very well result in it no longer working.

With that warning out of the way, let me begin by explaining some of the things you'll need to know to make the right choices in all those tabbed sections. First of all, you need to know what kind of memory requirements your DOS program has. Check the program's manual; it will usually tell you exactly what you need to know. To understand what the manual is telling you, however, you need to know that there are different kinds of memory:

- *Conventional memory* is memory up to the first 640KB (kilobytes). This is the area in which your program runs, so if it gets crowded with too many other things such as device drivers (for example, the mouse driver) and memory-resident programs (for example, an antivirus program), then you won't have enough conventional memory left.

- *Upper memory* is the area above 640KB and below 1MB; normally this is reserved for DOS to use. To clear device drivers and TSRs (memory-resident programs) out of conventional memory, you can have them load themselves up here. At the top of upper memory is the HMA or high memory area, in which you can place part of DOS itself, to clear out more conventional memory.

- *Extended memory* is any memory above the 1MB mark.

- *Expanded memory* (which most programs don't use anymore) is memory that is accessed through a gateway in upper memory (the area of memory between 640KB and 1MB). Usually, you convert some of the extended memory into expanded memory through the EMM386 command in your CONFIG.SYS.

More About Each Properties Tab

As you go through the steps in the *Guided Tour*, you may encounter some options for which you want a more detailed explanation. Come back to this section for more help.

The Font Tab

Option	What It Does
Available types	Determines the type of fonts available. Use TrueType unless you encounter a problem (such as speed degradation); then use a bitmap font.
Font size	Sets the size of the text in the DOS window.

The Program Tab

Option	What It Does
Cmd line	Shows the path to the program. You can add switches such as /S to control how the program starts if you need to. See your program's manual for a list of the switches it supports.
Working	Shows the name of the folder in which you want to save the files you create with this program.
Batch file	If you type the name of a batch file here, Windows will run the commands in the batch file before it starts the DOS program. For example, you might run a batch file to load an interpreter for your database program. (An interpreter translates the database instructions into something that your PC can understand.)
Shortcut key	You can start your DOS program by pressing a combination of keys. For example, if you assign the combination Ctrl+Shift+E to a program, that program will start when you press these three keys at the same time.
Run	Controls the type of window (such as maximized) in which the DOS program starts. A normal window usually fills about three-quarters of the screen.
Close on exit	Windows automatically closes the program on exit (instead of sitting dormant in a window marked "Finished").

The Memory Tab

Option	What It Does
Conventional memory total	Determines the total amount of conventional memory in which the program needs to run. Leave this set to Auto unless the program manual specifies an exact amount.
Initial environment	This setting controls the size of the environment, a kind of scratch-pad area that DOS uses to keep track of things such as the DOS search path and what type of prompt you're using. The environment also is used by programs to keep track of their own stuff; for example, Windows uses it to track where it should place temporary files. Increasing this setting decreases the amount of conventional memory in which the DOS program can run. If you choose Auto, this is set to the amount specified in the SHELL= line of the CONFIG.SYS.
Protected	Keeps the DOS program from making changes to the way in which Windows has set up memory, which might in turn prevent a poorly written program from corrupting your data. This does cause the program to run a bit slower, however.
Expanded (EMS) memory	Consult the program's manual to see if it needs this type of memory. Your system may not be configured for Expanded memory because most programs do not use it. The amount you specify here reduces the amount of extended memory available.

(continues)

The Memory Tab   Continued

Option	What It Does
Extended (XMS) memory	Extended memory is the amount above the first 1MB. A DOS program must be specifically designed to use this memory, so check your program's manual.
Uses HMA	Allows the program to use the high memory area. Normally, DOS itself is loaded here to give a program more room in conventional memory, so selecting this box usually has no effect.
MS-DOS protected mode	Change this setting if your program requires memory to be set up under the DPMI standard. You might need to do this for point-of-sale software or to run a UNIX-X type program in a DOS window. Basically, leave this set to Auto unless you know for sure that your program needs DPMI memory. Then, set it to the amount it needs.

The Screen Tab

Option	What It Does
Usage	Starts your DOS program in a window or in a full-screen session.
Initial size	If your DOS program needs to start in a specific size window because it does not support a variable number of lines, you may set a specific number in the Initial size list. If you choose Default, Windows opens the program in a standard size window. If the program is designed to reset the screen size on its own, it may override this setting automatically.
Display toolbar	Displays the DOS window toolbar, which provides easy access to the Properties dialog box, fonts, and the Mark, Copy, and Paste commands.
Restore settings on Start up	Windows opens the DOS window in the startup exact location it occupied the last time you used it. Also, the window is set to its former size.
Fast ROM emulation	This option tells Windows to handle the screen display, which is faster than allowing the DOS program to go through the PC's internal ROM to do it. If you're having problems with the way in which your program appears, you may want to deselect this option.
Dynamic memory allocation	If you check this box, Windows will take memory away from your DOS program when it is displaying only text, and it will provide that extra memory to other programs you're currently running. If you run into problems as you switch from displaying just text to displaying text and graphics in your DOS program, then deselect this option.

The Misc Tab

Option	What It Does
Allow screen saver	Allows Windows to continue to run its screen saver at the appropriate time, even when the DOS program is running full-screen.
QuickEdit	Allows you to select text with the mouse without first clicking on the Mark button (for purposes of copying that text to another program). But, if your DOS program is a word processor and you want to be able to select text to copy or move within the program, do not select this option.
Exclusive mode	If you select this option, you will lose the use of the mouse beyond the boundaries of the DOS window. In addition, you won't be able to use the mouse with the DOS toolbar. You can, however, switch to Windows by pressing Ctrl+Esc, and you'll get your Windows mouse back. Only select this option if you're having problems with using a mouse within the program and that's more important to you than using the mouse generally.
Always suspend	Select this option to prevent your DOS game from "playing on without you" when you're in another window. Otherwise, not checking this option allows the program to continue working even while you're working on something else.
Warn if still active	To allow you to exit the DOS program immediately by clicking on its Windows close box, uncheck this option. Warnings that might normally appear (such as the warning that some work is unsaved) will not appear if this option is checked.
Idle sensitivity	If a DOS program remains untouched (idle) for very long, Windows devotes less system time to running the program. To increase the amount of idle time before Windows starts reducing the program's resources, slide the Idle sensitivity knob toward Low.
Fast pasting	Lets Windows try a faster and less system costly method of pasting text from the Windows Clipboard into your DOS program. (Not all DOS programs work well with this setting checked, but you can try it if you want.)
Windows shortcut keys	Prevents the selected shortcut keys from activating their standard Windows functions. This allows these same shortcuts to be used by your DOS program instead.

Begin Guided Tour   Use the Properties Dialog Box to Optimize Programs

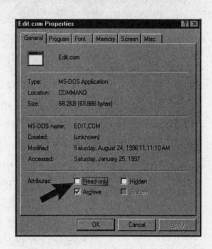

1 Start Explorer and change to the folder in which the program resides.

2 Select the program file.

4 Click on the **General** tab and you can change the attributes of the program's file by clicking on the appropriate check boxes. Because these attributes have little effect on whether your DOS program will run or not, you can skip them.

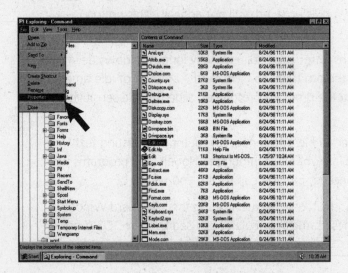

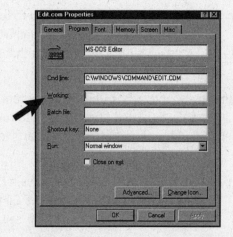

3 Open the **File** menu and select **Properties**.

5 Click on the **Program** tab and you can change information that Windows uses to communicate with DOS and start the program.

6 To have Windows run a DOS batch file before it runs this program, type the path and name of this file in the Batch file text box.

If you're currently running the DOS program you want to change, just click on the **Properties** button instead of following steps 1 through 3.

Guided Tour   Use the Properties Dialog Box to Optimize Programs

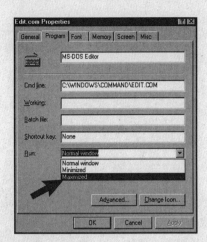

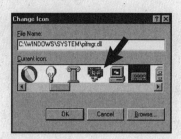

11 Select an icon from the Current icon list and click on **OK**.

7 To assign a shortcut key that you can use to automatically start this program, click in the **Shortcut key** text box and press the keys you want to use. (You must press them all at the same time.)

8 In the **Run** drop-down list, select the type of window you want to start this program with.

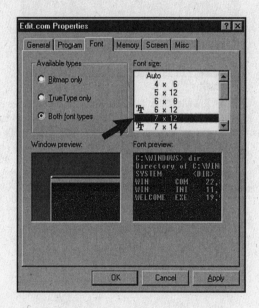

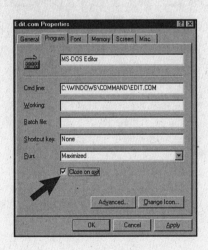

12 Click on the **Font** tab to change the size of the text.

(continues)

9 If you want, check the **Close on exit** box.

10 To change the icon for the DOS program, click on the **Change Icon** button.

Guided Tour Use the Properties Dialog Box to Optimize Programs

(continued)

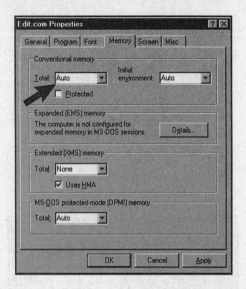

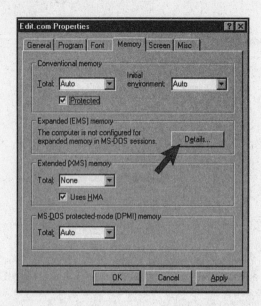

13 Click on the **Memory** tab to select the precise types and amounts of system memory you want Windows 95 to allocate to the DOS program.

14 Check your program's manual for its exact requirement for conventional memory, or select **Auto**, and the program tells Windows 95 what it needs at start-up.

17 If your program requires expanded (EMS) memory, select the amount it needs.

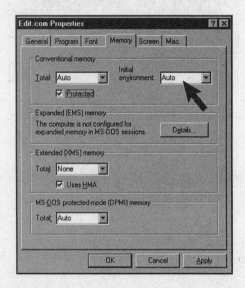

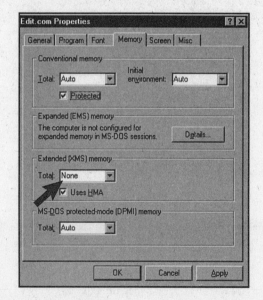

15 Adjust the **Initial environment** setting if necessary.

16 If needed, check the **Protected** box.

18 Increase or decrease the amount of extended (XMS) memory as necessary.

19 Check the **Uses HMA** box, if needed.

Guided Tour   Use the Properties Dialog Box to Optimize Programs

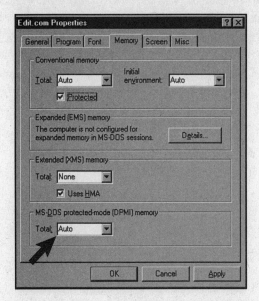

20 Change the setting under **MS-DOS protected-mode (DPMI) memory** *only* if your program specifically needs it.

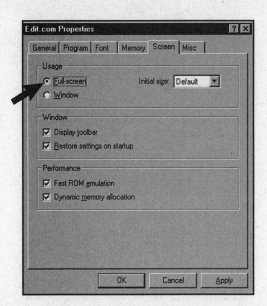

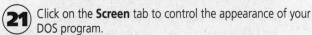

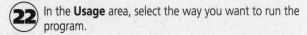

21 Click on the **Screen** tab to control the appearance of your DOS program.

22 In the **Usage** area, select the way you want to run the program.

23 Change the **Initial size** setting only if your program must start with a specific size window. (A drawing program might require this.)

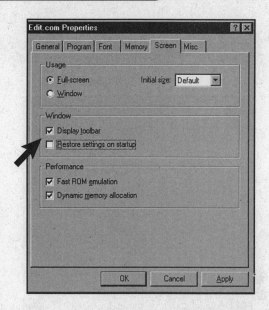

24 If you want your DOS window to display the Standard toolbar, check **Display toolbar**. To learn what each of the toolbar's buttons does, see the section, "What You Should Know Before You Run a DOS Program in a Window," page 259.

25 To have Windows remember where the DOS program window was located on-screen when you last exited it and have it reappear there next time, check **Restore settings on startup**.

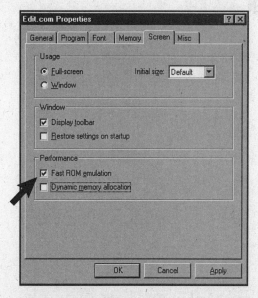

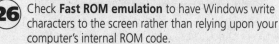

26 Check **Fast ROM emulation** to have Windows write characters to the screen rather than relying upon your computer's internal ROM code.

(continues)

Guided Tour Use the Properties Dialog Box to Optimize Programs

(continued)

 Check **Dynamic memory allocation** if you want Windows to reclaim graphics memory for itself whenever it switches the DOS program back to character mode.

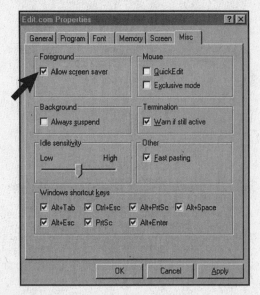

 Click the **Misc** tab to access some additional options.

Check **Allow screen saver** to allow the Windows screen saver to work with this program.

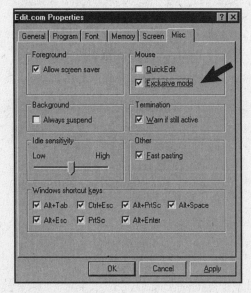

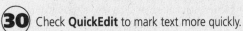

 Check **QuickEdit** to mark text more quickly.

To have the mouse pointer function exclusively as the DOS pointer while the pointer is over that program's window, check **Exclusive mode**.

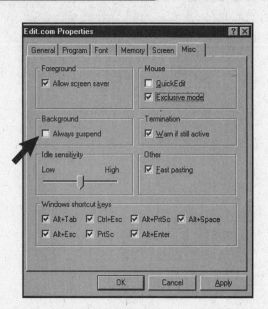

Check **Always suspend** to suspend all program activity when the window is not active.

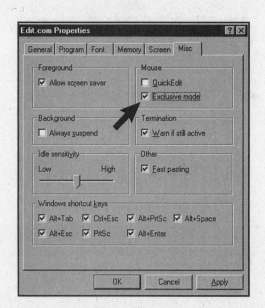

Deselecting the **Warn if still active** box will allow you to quickly exit your program even if files are still open and unsaved.

Guided Tour Use the Properties Dialog Box to Optimize Programs

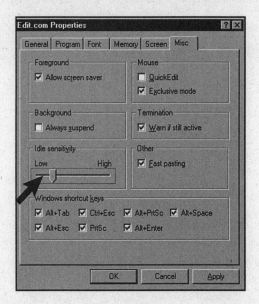

 34 To adjust the amount of time your program can remain idle and yet still command attention from Windows, adjust the **Idle sensitivity**.

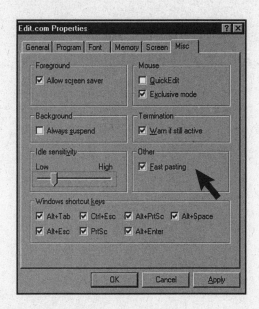

 35 Select the **Fast pasting** option if you want to increase the speed of the Paste function.

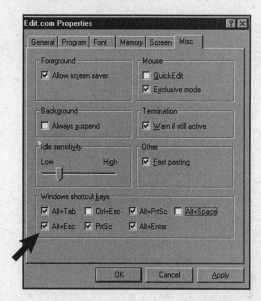

 36 If your DOS program utilizes any of the normal Windows shortcut keys for its own purposes, deselect them from this list.

37 When you've changed the DOS program settings to meet your needs, click on **OK**.

After you set the properties for a DOS program for the first time, Windows creates a shortcut icon to the program. If there is more than one way in which you can use this DOS program, create a different shortcut in Explorer and then customize its properties. Double-click on whichever shortcut icon fits the way in which you want to start the program at that time.

HOW TO...

Communicate with Other Computers

An electronic message, through a fax or via a direct connection to a service such as CompuServe, is just one example of how you might use your computer to communicate. You also might connect, while you're away on a business trip, from a laptop computer to access your files. In this section, you'll learn how to perform all these tasks and more.

You communicate with your computer through a device called a modem. A *modem* translates computer information into sounds that are transmitted through an ordinary telephone line to another modem, which converts the sounds back into computer information. In this section, you'll learn how to set up your modem to work with Windows 95.

The following tasks will get you up and running with your modem and Windows 95's various communications programs:

What You Will Find in This Section

Set Up a Modem

If your PC had a modem when you installed Windows 95, your modem is already set up. However, if you've added or changed your modem since installing Windows 95, you need to perform some simple steps for it to work properly.

If you've never tried to install and configure a modem before, don't panic! With Windows 95's new Plug and Play technology, getting a modem (or any other new piece of hardware) to work correctly couldn't be easier. The concept of Plug and Play is that Windows 95 issues a signal to your new hardware (in this case, the modem), and the modem signals back, identifying itself. This information helps Windows 95 know how to correctly send data to the particular brand of modem you're using.

You might have an external modem, which is located outside the computer and is connected to the computer by a cable. Because it is a separate device, you must turn on an external modem before you attempt to use it. If you don't have an external modem, you're using an internal modem, which is hidden inside the computer itself (it's actually a card sitting in one of the computer slots). You won't need to turn on an internal modem; it is "powered up" when you turn on the computer.

To physically connect your modem to the outside world, follow these steps:

1. Plug a phone line into the phone jack located at the back of the modem. If the modem is internal, you'll find this jack on the back of the computer. Plug the phone line into the jack marked "To Line" or "To Wall."

2. Connect the other end of the phone line to a phone jack in the wall.

3. If you only have one phone jack in your office, run a second phone line from the modem's "To Phone" connector to the phone itself. You'll end up with a line running from the wall to the modem, and another running from the modem to the phone. You won't be able to use both devices at the same time, but you'll be able to easily use one or the other without having to reconnect the phone lines first.

> If you are using one phone line for both your modem and your telephone and you have call waiting, you should disable call waiting when you use your modem. If you don't, and an outside call comes in while you're using your modem, the call waiting signal interrupts the modem and causes it to disconnect. For most systems, you need to have the modem dial *70 before you make your connection. In the Dialing Properties dialog box, you can set your modem to disable call waiting.

Although Plug and Play makes it easy to install your modem under Windows 95, you may run into a problem if you're using more than one serial device. A *serial device* communicates by sending one bit at a time. Each serial device is connected to a particular communications port (COM port) at the back of the PC. Common serial devices include your modem, an old-style serial printer, a serial mouse, or an alternative access device. If you assign two serial devices to the same COM port, you'll run into problems when you install your modem. Luckily, Windows 95 includes a diagnostic program that helps you in this case. It will appear automatically if there's a conflict and step you through the resolution.

After you configure your modem, you need to set up your dialing preferences. These establish your area code and whether you need to dial an access number to get an outside line. You also can enter calling card information to charge long distance connections.

Begin Guided Tour   Configure Your Modem

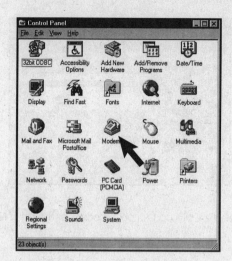

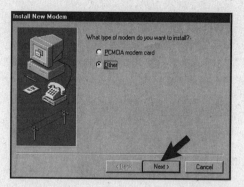

(3) If you happen to have a laptop computer with a built-in modem, you may see this screen. Click on **PCMCIA modem card** (If not, then click on **Other**). Click on **Next**.

(1) Click on the **Start** button, select **Settings**, and select **Control Panel**. Then double-click on the **Modems** icon.

If you're installing a new modem and you have an old modem you don't plan to use anymore, access the Modems Properties dialog box, select the modem from the list, and click on **Remove**.

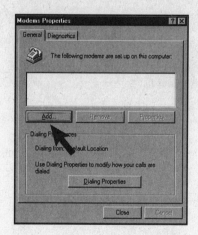

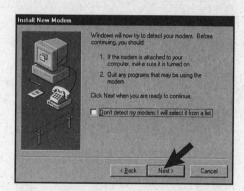

(2) In the Modems Properties dialog box, click on **Add**.

(4) It's recommended that you let Windows 95 try to identify your modem. To do so, continue to step 5. If you prefer to select your modem from a list, select the **Don't detect my modem** option.

(5) Make sure that your modem is turned on. Click on **Next**.

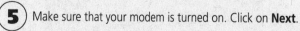

(continues)

Guided Tour Configure Your Modem

(continued)

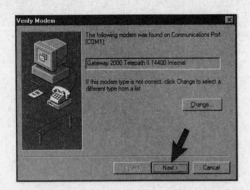

6 Windows 95 displays the name of the modem it detected, as well as the COM port to which it's connected. (If the modem that's listed is incorrect, click on **Change** and select the correct modem from a list.) Click on **Next** and skip to step 11.

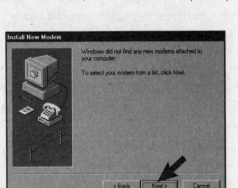

7 If Windows 95 can't determine what kind of modem you're using, you'll see this message instead. Click on **Next**.

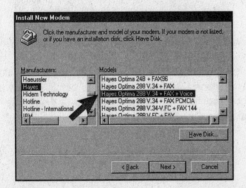

8 Select your modem from those listed. (Or, if you have an installation disk, click on **Have Disk**.) Click on **Next**.

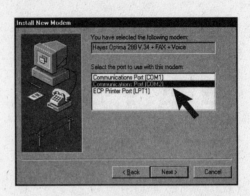

9 Select a COM port for your modem, and click on **Next**.

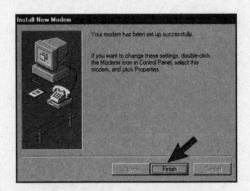

10 Your modem has been installed. Click on **Finish**.

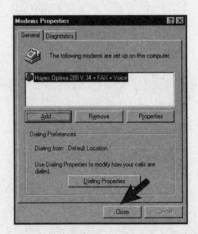

11 Click on **Close** to close the Modems Properties dialog box. You can access this dialog box at any time if you need to change your modem's configuration for some reason.

Begin Guided Tour Set Up Your Dialing Preferences

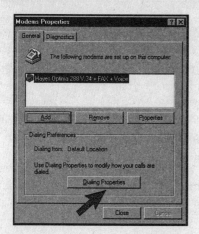

(1) From the Modems Properties dialog box, click on **Dialing Properties**.

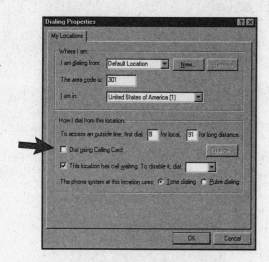

(2) Enter your area code, country, and outside access codes (if necessary). If you want to use a calling card, select the **Dial using Calling Card** option.

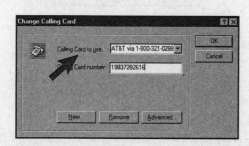

(3) In the Change Calling Card dialog box, enter the calling card information. Click on **OK**.

(4) Disable call waiting if necessary. In most systems, you dial *70; however, you should check with your local phone service.

(5) If you use a pulse (rotary) dialing system, select **Pulse dialing**. Click on **OK**.

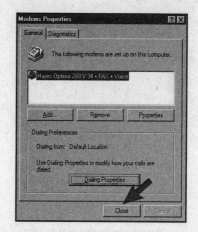

(6) Click on **Close** to close the Modems Properties dialog box.

Get Windows 95 to Dial Your Phone

Phone Dialer is a Windows accessory program that dials your phone for you. Why would you bother to use your computer to dial the telephone? Well, before you make a call, you probably have to drop what you're doing, page through the phone book, find the number, and then dial the phone. Phone Dialer automates the process: you store the numbers you call frequently in Phone Dialer, and then let the program dial the phone for you. Once it dials the number, you just pick up your phone and talk as usual.

Before you can use Phone Dialer, you need to connect your modem to your telephone. To do so, follow these steps:

1. Connect a phone line from the wall jack to the Wall or Line connector in the back of the modem.

2. Run another phone line from the modem's Phone jack to the telephone.

Begin Guided Tour Use Phone Dialer to Make Your Calls

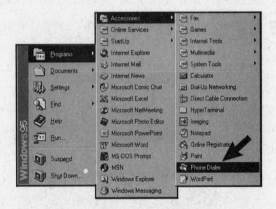

1 Make sure your modem is turned on. Click on the **Start** button, select **Programs**, select **Accessories**, and select **Phone Dialer**.

2 The Phone Dialer window appears. Type the number to dial in the Number to dial text box and click on **Dial**.

3 When you hear the modem connect and the Call Status dialog box appears, pick up the receiver and click on **Talk**. If you get a busy signal, click on **Hang Up**.

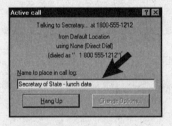

4 When you finish the call, type a description in the text box labeled **Name** to place in call log. Hang up the receiver and click on **Hang Up**.

Use HyperTerminal

HyperTerminal is a general purpose communications program that enables you to connect to any other modem, BBS, or online service. Your modem converts computer data into tones (beeps) that can be sent over a phone line, and the modem at the other end converts those tones back into computer information.

Modems transmit data at various speeds called *baud rates* or (to be more accurate) *bps* (bits per second). Just a few years ago the best modem speed was 9600 or 14,400 bps, but modems sold today can transmit 28,800 bps or faster. When a modem sends data over a phone line, it uses a *protocol*, a set of rules by which data is sent and verified. When both modems send data at the same speed and use the same protocol, data can be sent back and forth safely without error.

With HyperTerminal and your modem, you can connect to a *bulletin board service (BBS)*. A BBS is like an electronic version of your bulletin board at work. After you connect to a BBS, you can post messages, ask questions, and even send a file for someone else to pick up, and other users of the BBS can leave messages and files for you. Sending a file is called *uploading* and receiving a file is called *downloading*. A BBS is usually inexpensive because it's run on a small scale using a single computer and several modems. A particular BBS is usually geared toward one interest, such as sailing, dog breeding, or computer games. Some BBSs are set up for general computing; these are good sources for advice that you can use when you run into a problem. To find out about a good BBS, ask at your local computer store.

Online services such as CompuServe, PRODIGY, Delphi, America Online and the Microsoft Network are like BBSs but are much bigger. An *online service* offers more information, caters to more interests, and provides more help and advice. (As a result, you'll pay more to use an online service than to use a BBS.) One nice feature of both BBSs and online services is their file service, which enables you to locate and download (receive) updated files for your programs and equipment. You also can send and receive e-mail through an online service. In addition, most online services provide access to the Internet—something a BBS can't afford to do. Because most online services provide the software you need to access them, you probably won't use HyperTerminal to connect with one.

HyperTerminal contains a toolbar you can use to connect to a BBS, an online service, and so on. The table on the next page shows you each of the buttons and explains its purpose.

Special Note About Uploading and Downloading Files

Before you send a file, you should *compress* it. A compression program translates the file into a "shorthand" form that takes less time to transmit. The faster a file is transmitted, the smaller the chance is that an error will occur. When someone receives the compressed file, she decompresses it to return it to its original state so she can use it.

Most files are compressed with a utility called PKZIP, which is a shareware program. You can download this utility from almost any BBS or online service. Once it's installed, you need to pay a minimal fee to use it (shareware is not freeware). With PKZIP, you can compress your files before you send (upload) them, and you can decompress the files you receive (download) from an online service or BBS.

There are other compression utilities, such as LHARC and QZIP, but they are not as widely used. If you plan to use PKZIP, look for another shareware utility called WinZip, which makes it easy to use PKZIP within Windows. It's well worth the additional small fee.

HyperTerminal's Toolbar Buttons

Button	Function
	Creates a new connection
	Opens an existing connection
	Connects to current connection
	Disconnects from current connection
	Sends (uploads) a file
	Receives (downloads) a file
	Changes the properties of the current connection

Also, be sure to check whatever you download for viruses. A *virus* is a program that hides itself inside another file. When you use the file, the virus becomes active (although some viruses wait until a particular date or time to activate). The virus can then cause damage to your PC by wiping out files or making them unusable. Some viruses don't do any real damage; but quite a few do, so you should protect yourself by using an antivirus program to check new files for viruses before you use them. Even if you get a file from a reputable source, it's not guaranteed to be virus free.

You can purchase virus checking programs from your local computer store (lots of different types are available), or even search the Web for companies and download a trial version to see if it has the features you prefer.

Begin Guided Tour   Use HyperTerminal the First Time

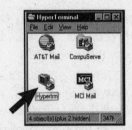

1 Click on the **Start** button, select **Programs**, select **Accessories**, and select **HyperTerminal**.

2 Double-click on the **Hypertrm** icon.

3 In the **Name** text box, enter any description for your connection. For example, to dial into the Small Business Administration online service, you type **Small Business Administration** (or SBA, or another description). Select the icon you want Windows to use for this connection and click on **OK**.

Guided Tour   Use HyperTerminal the First Time

④ In the Phone Number dialog box, enter a phone number for the connection and click on **OK**.

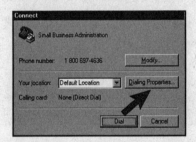

⑤ The Connect dialog box appears. Click on **Dialing Properties**.

⑥ Change settings as needed. Then click on **OK**.

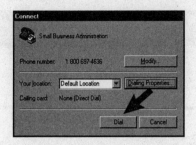

⑦ If you have an external modem, make sure it's turned on now (internal modems are always ready to go) and click on **Dial**. Perform any tasks you want following the steps provided by your BBS or online service. (To upload or download files, see the following subtasks in this *Guided Tour*.)

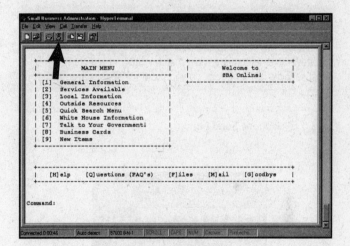

⑧ When you finish using HyperTerminal, click on the **Disconnect** button. To dial another new connection without exiting HyperTerminal, click on the **New** icon and repeat these steps. To dial an existing connection, click on the **Open** icon and select the connection from the list.

⑨ When you exit HyperTerminal, it asks you if you want to save your new connection. Click on **Yes**, and Windows adds an icon in the HyperTerminal folder. You can double-click that icon at any time to redial the connection.

Begin Guided Tour Upload Files

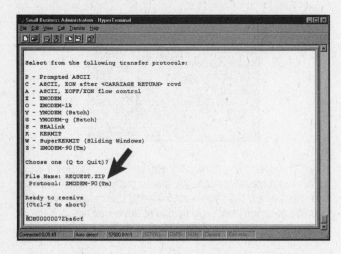

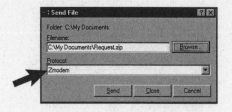

⑤ (Optional) If necessary, change the Protocol.

⑥ Click on **Send**. HyperTerminal uploads the file.

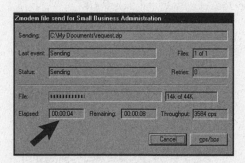

① After you connect, issue the necessary command to indicate you want to upload a file. (This varies from service to service.) You will probably be asked to select a protocol. Whatever you select here must match what you select in step 5. Most services use Zmodem, so you should probably choose that if given a choice.

② Click on the **Send** button.

⑦ HyperTerminal displays a dialog box showing the file's progress. When HyperTerminal finishes uploading the file, you're automatically returned to the terminal window.

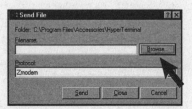

③ In the Send File dialog box, click on **Browse**.

The protocol you choose here must match the one that the BBS, online service, or other modem is using. (You probably selected a protocol in step 1. Make sure that what you choose in step 5 matches that.) Most services use Zmodem, which is the default, so you probably won't need to do anything in step 5.

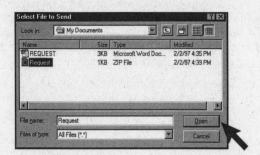

④ Select the folder that contains the file you want to send, and then select that file from the list. Click on **Open**.

Begin Guided Tour　Download Files

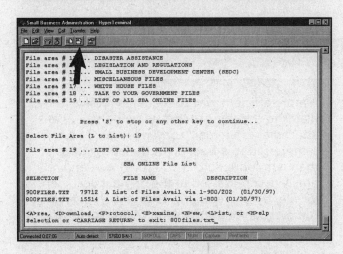

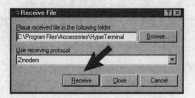

5 Click on **Receive**.

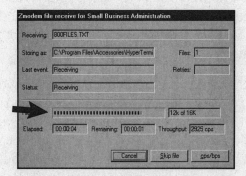

1 After you connect, issue the necessary command to indicate you want to download a file. (This varies from service to service.) If you're downloading from a service, you will probably be asked to select the protocol you want to use from a list. Whatever you select here must match what you select in step 4. Most services use Zmodem, so you should probably choose that if given a choice.

2 Click on the **Receive** button.

6 HyperTerminal displays a dialog box showing the file's progress. When HyperTerminal finishes downloading the file, you automatically return to the terminal window.

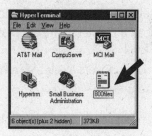

3 If you want to save the file in a different folder, enter the folder's path in the text box labeled **Place received file in the following folder**. (If necessary, click on Browse and select the folder's path from the resulting dialog box.)

7 Your file appears in the folder you indicated in step 3.

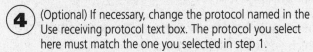
4 (Optional) If necessary, change the protocol named in the Use receiving protocol text box. The protocol you select here must match the one you selected in step 1.

Use Microsoft Exchange to Send and Receive E-Mail

Microsoft Exchange is like the "Grand Central Station" for all electronic mail and faxes on your computer. You can use Microsoft Exchange to receive e-mail or to send it to such places as your company's network, an online service (such as Microsoft Network), and even the Internet. In addition, you can use Microsoft Exchange to send and receive faxes (facsimiles) through your modem or a fax printer.

The Exchange serves as a single central area in which you can organize all of your incoming and outgoing mail. Prior to the Exchange, e-mail and faxes were generally stored in the folder of the program you used to send or receive them. For example, maybe you used to keep your faxes in the WinFax Pro folder and your e-mail in several folders: cc:Mail, WinCim (for CompuServe), and Iquest (your local Internet provider). Now you can organize them all in one place.

When you install Windows 95, the Exchange automatically provides a connection to Microsoft Network and Microsoft Mail. You can set up connections to other services using drivers available from the programs' manufacturers.

You can send an e-mail message through any of the services you choose to use, and you can attach a file as part of the message. Each message you create is placed in the Outbox until you connect to the service you want to use. At that time, your messages are sent. In addition, any e-mail addressed to you is automatically received. You can set up most services to automatically send and receive mail at a specific time, or you can initiate the process manually, as you'll learn in the *Guided Tour*.

A more efficient way to send and receive large files is to compress them and send them as an attachment to e-mail. Large files can be safely compressed to a fraction of their original size, then sent more quickly over the Internet, and finally decompressed to the original document (or file) by the recipient. To do this you need a compression/decompression utility like WinZip or PKZIP, as mentioned in the previous section.

When you log onto a service to receive mail, you receive all your mail. If you want to view your messages before downloading them, you need to use the Remote Mail service explained later in this section. Remote Mail enables you to connect to a service and download the headers for the mail you've received. A header tells you who sent the message and gives a short description. This information is usually enough for you to decide whether a particular message is worth the time it would take to receive it right now, or whether you can wait until a better time. It takes only a few moments to receive headers, while it could take much longer to receive a message (particularly if it contains a file).

The Exchange contains a toolbar from which you can select several common commands. The following table shows those buttons.

The Remote Mail feature also contains a toolbar from which you can select commands.

Exchange Toolbar Buttons

Button	Description
	Moves one level up the folder list
	Displays (or hides) the folder list
	Creates a new e-mail message
	Prints the selected messages
	Moves the selected item to another folder
	Deletes the selected items
	Creates a reply to the sender of the selected message
	Creates a reply to everyone who received the selected message
	Forwards the selected message to someone else
	Accesses your address books so you can make changes
	Enables you to view the items you've received
	Displays a description of what an item does (click on this button and then click on the item in question)
	Moves the selected item to your Favorites folder

Remote Mail Toolbar Buttons

Button	Description
	Connects to the service
	Disconnects from the service
	Marks message for retrieval
	Marks message to receive a copy (this enables you to retrieve the message again at a later time)
	Marks message for deletion (the message will not be retrieved)

(continues)

Remote Mail Toolbar Buttons   Continued

Button	Description
	Unmark all messages
	Displays a description of a particular item (click on this button and then click on the item)

In addition, the New Message window contains a toolbar. Use this table to determine what each button does.

Create Message Toolbar Buttons

Button	Description
Send	Sends message
Save	Saves message in Inbox to send later
Print	Prints message
Cut	Moves selected text to Clipboard
Copy	Copies selected text to Clipboard
Paste	Pastes text from Clipboard
Address Book	Accesses the address books so you can add, change, or delete entries
Check Names	Checks names you've typed to make sure they're valid
Insert File	Attaches a file to e-mail message
Properties	Requests a receipt, changes the priority, and sets other properties of the message
Read Receipt	Indicates you want to receive notification when the recipient reads your message
Importance: High	Lets the recipient know that your message is important
Importance: Low	Lets the recipient know that your message is low priority
Help	Displays a description of a particular item (click on this button and then click on the item)

Microsoft Exchange provides a Microsoft Network address book that you can use to look up addresses on the Microsoft Network. In addition, the Exchange provides a Personal address book in which you can store frequently used e-mail and Internet addresses, plus additional information such as a client's address, phone numbers, company, department, title, and assistant's name. You can even dial a phone number in the Personal address book with the Phone Dialer. For help using the various address books, see "Maintain Your Address Book" on page 472.

Begin Guided Tour   Send E-Mail

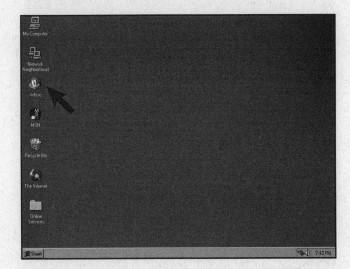

1 Turn your modem on, and double-click on the **Inbox** icon.

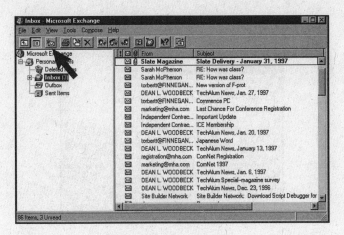

2 Click on the **New Message** button.

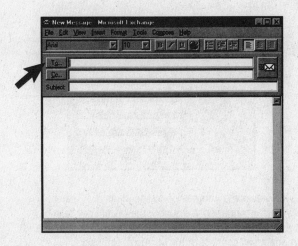

3 Click on the **To** button.

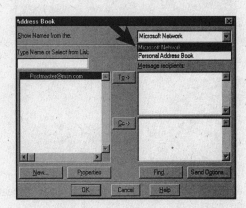

4 Select the address book you want to use. If you choose the Microsoft Network, you will be asked for additional information before going online to the address book. If you choose Personal Address Book, skip to step 7.

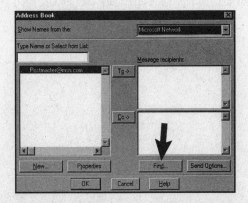

5 Click the **Find** button.

(continues)

Guided Tour   Send E-Mail   *(continued)*

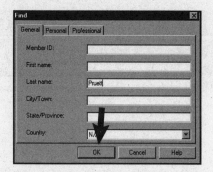

6 Provide some information to speed up your search. The more information you supply, the faster your search through the Microsoft Network Address book. Click on **OK** and your modem will connect to the Microsoft Network.

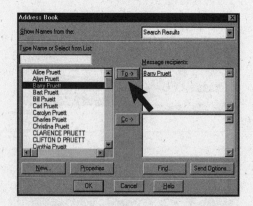

7 Select a name from the list and click on **To ->**. Repeat to add more names.

8 If you want to forward a copy of your message to someone, select a name from the list and click on **Cc ->**. Repeat to add more names.

9 When you finish adding names, click on **OK**.

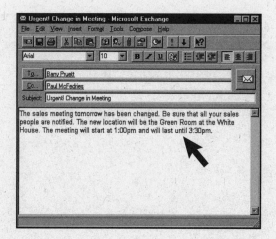

10 Type a **Subject** for your message, and then type your message.

11 If you want to attach a file to send with your message, click on the **Insert File** button.

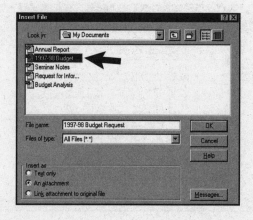

12 The Insert File dialog box appears. Change to the folder that contains the file you want to attach. Select the file from the list and click on **OK**.

Guided Tour   Send E-Mail

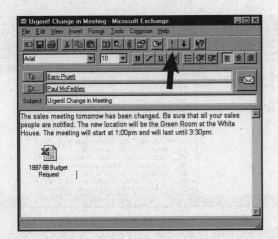
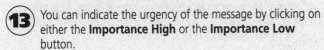
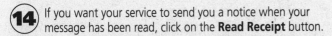

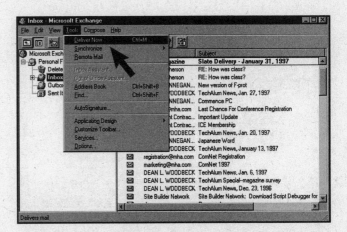

13 You can indicate the urgency of the message by clicking on either the **Importance High** or the **Importance Low** button.

14 If you want your service to send you a notice when your message has been read, click on the **Read Receipt** button.

15 To check the spelling of your message before you send it, press **F7**.

17 If you've set up this service for automatic sending and receiving of e-mail as explained earlier, you don't need to do anything. Your message will be sent at the desired time. Or, if you connect to the service to receive e-mail, your message will be sent then. However, if you prefer to initiate the Send sequence now, select the message, open the **Tools** menu, select **Deliver Now**, and then select the service you want to use. The message is sent immediately.

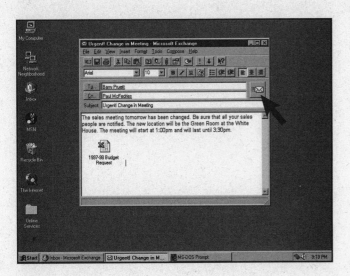

16 Click on the **Send** icon. The message is placed in the Outbox.

Begin Guided Tour   Receive E-Mail

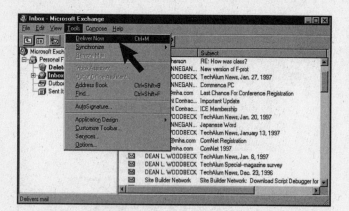

1 Open the **Tools** menu and select **Deliver Now** or **Deliver Now Using**.

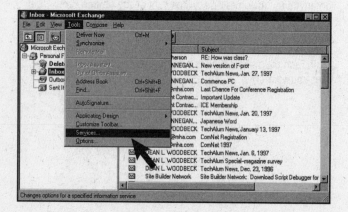

2 If necessary, select the service from which you want to receive e-mail or select **All Services**.

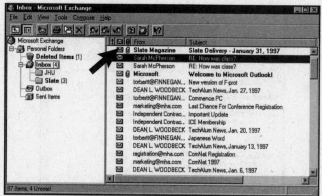

3 If you have unsent mail, your messages are automatically sent at this time. In addition, you receive any new mail, which is placed in the Inbox. Unread messages appear in bold type. To read a message, double-click on it.

Begin Guided Tour Reply to a Message

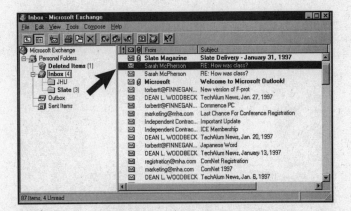

1 Click on the message to which you want to reply.

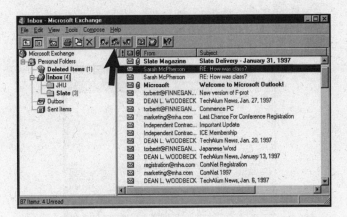

2 Click on the **Reply to Sender** button, the **Reply to All** button (to reply to the sender and all of the original recipients), or the **Forward** button.

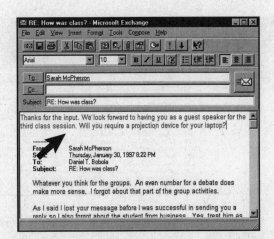

3 Type your reply above the text of the original message. (If you prefer, you can delete the original message.)

If you don't want to include the original messages with your replies, open the **Tools** menu and select **Options**. Click on the **Read** tab and deselect the **Include the original text when replying** option.

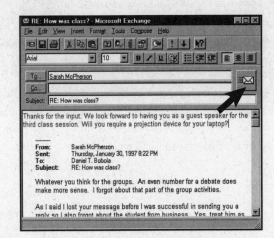

4 To check the spelling of your reply, press **F7**.

5 Click on **Send**. The reply is placed in the Outbox to await outgoing delivery.

Begin Guided Tour Save an Attachment

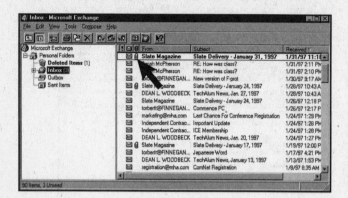

1 Messages that contain an attachment (an attached file) are marked with a paper-clip icon. Select a message that contains an attachment you want to save to your hard disk, and double-click on it.

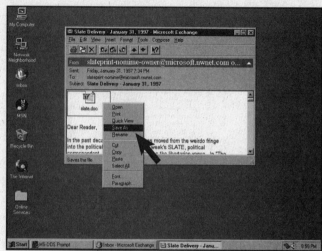

3 Right-click on the icon, and and select **Save In** on the shortcut menu that appears.

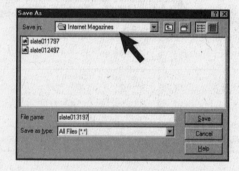

4 In the Save As dialog box, select the folder in which you want to save the attached file and click on **Save**.

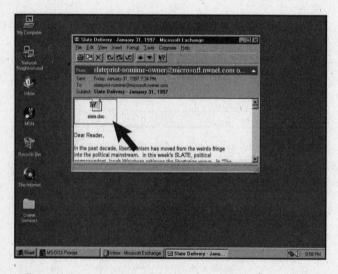

2 Click on the attached file's icon to select it.

Guided Tour Save an Attachment

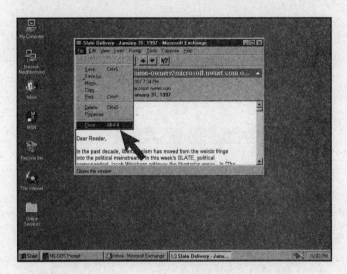

5 Open the **File** menu and select **Close** to close the
message.

Begin Guided Tour Receive E-Mail from a Remote Location

1 Open the **Tools** menu and select **Remote Mail**. If you
have more than one service, select the one you want to
use from the list that appears.

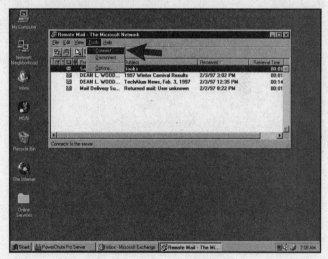

2 Open the **Tools** menu and select **Connect**.

(continues)

Guided Tour Receive E-Mail from a Remote Location *(continued)*

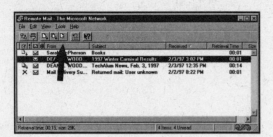

3 Select a message and mark it by clicking on one of these buttons: **Mark to Retrieve** (to receive the message now), **Mark to Retrieve a Copy** (to receive a copy of the message; this enables you to receive the original later, such as after you return to your office PC), or **Mark to Delete** (which deletes the message without retrieving it). Any unmarked messages are left alone.

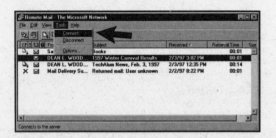

4 When you finish marking messages, open the **Tools** menu and select **Connect.**

5 Microsoft Exchange displays its progress as it transfers your mail. Click on **Cancel** to interrupt the process if you need to.

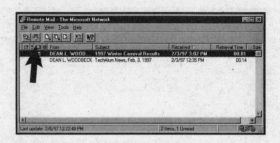

6 Click on the **Disconnect** button.

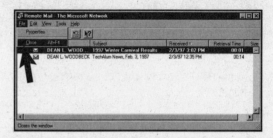

7 Open the **File** menu and select **Close** to return to the main Exchange window. Messages you've received appear in the Inbox.

Send or Receive a Fax

If you have a fax modem, you can send and receive faxes using Windows 95. Windows 95 includes its own fax program called Microsoft Fax. To receive a fax, you start up Microsoft Exchange, which in turn places Microsoft Fax in waiting mode for the incoming fax.

Windows 95 provides several methods for sending faxes, all of which involve starting the Fax Wizard. A *wizard* is a series of dialog boxes that walks you step-by-step through the process of completing a particular task. The Fax Wizard walks you through the process of creating your fax and sending it. Your options for sending a fax include the following:

- **Compose New Fax command** This command is located on the Programs Accessories Fax menu, and it enables you to quickly send a fax.

- **Microsoft Exchange** You can both send and receive faxes through the Exchange.

- **Explorer** You can send a file to your fax program through Explorer, and the file makes up the body of the fax.

- **An Application** You also can fax a document from within most applications, as you'll see in the *Guided Tour*.

> If you prefer your own fax program, such as WinFax Pro, you can use it instead of Microsoft Fax.

All of these options are fine for sending a fax. They all work much the same way, as you'll see when you go through the *Guided Tour*. Use whichever option seems the most convenient for you. However, keep in mind that when you want to receive a fax, you have only one option: the Exchange.

If you choose to use Microsoft Fax instead of another fax program, you can create a customized cover page with your company's logo (see "Create a Custom Fax Cover Page" on page 396).

To send a fax, you can use any of the options listed earlier. To receive a fax, you must start Microsoft Exchange (it can be minimized). Starting the Exchange starts Microsoft Fax and places its icon on the taskbar. Whether Microsoft Fax answers the incoming call immediately depends on how you set it up. For example, if you use the same phone line for your phone and your modem, you may want to set up Microsoft Fax so it doesn't answer each phone call automatically. After you've received a fax, you can view and print it with the Fax Viewer or with Microsoft Exchange.

Windows 95 includes everything you need to send and receive faxes. You can even dial up a remote service to request a fax. For example, the IRS has a service from which you can request a copy of a specific filing form, along with the corresponding instructions. With the Request a Fax option, you'll be able to dial up the service and request the form you want. The service then calls you back, and you receive the fax automatically.

You can send a one-time fax to any location, or you can save your favorite fax numbers in the Address Book so they are easier to reuse. See "Maintain Your Address Book" on page 472 for more information on using the Address Book.

Begin Guided Tour Send a Fax with the Fax Wizard

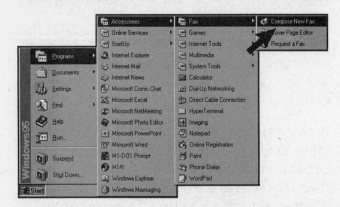

1 Click on the **Start** button, select **Programs**, select **Accessories**, select **Fax**, and select **Compose New Fax**.

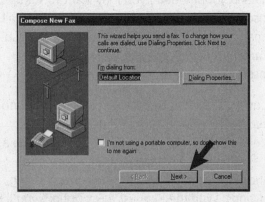

2 The first Fax Wizard dialog box appears. Click on **Next**.

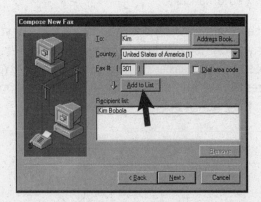

3 Type the name of the person to whom you want to send the fax, and enter his or her fax number. If you want to send to more than one person, click the **Add To List** button after each entry. Click on **Next** to continue.

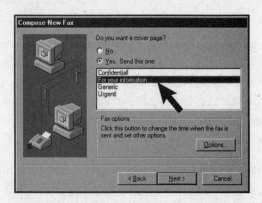

4 Select a cover letter for your fax and click on **Next**.

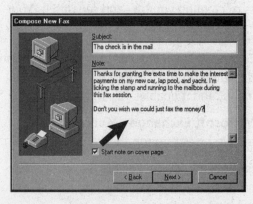

5 Add a description under Subject, and add a note if you want. Click on **Next**.

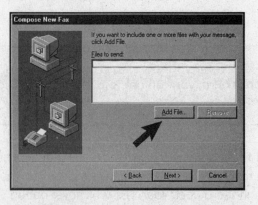

6 If you want to send the contents of a file with your fax, click on **Add File**.

Guided Tour   Send a Fax with the Fax Wizard

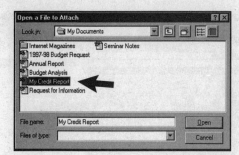

7 In the dialog box that appears, change to the folder that contains the file you want to send, select the file, and click on **Open**.

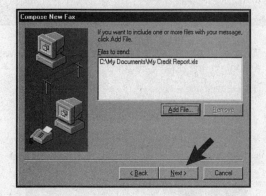

8 The name of the file you selected appears in the Files to send box. Click on **Next**.

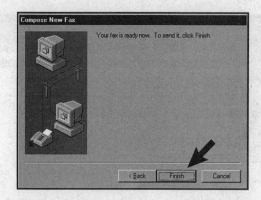

9 Turn on your modem and click on **Finish**.

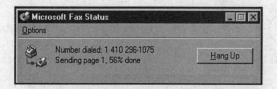

10 Microsoft Fax prepares your fax and displays its progress. If you need to cancel the fax for any reason, click on **Hang Up**. A copy of your fax is placed in Microsoft Exchange's Sent Items folder.

Begin Guided Tour   Send a Fax with Microsoft Exchange

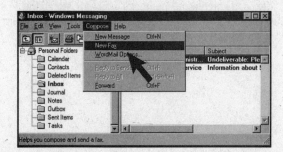

1 From within Microsoft Exchange, open the **Compose** menu and select **New Fax**.

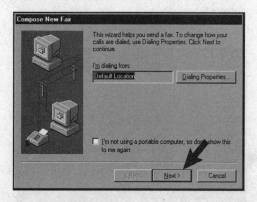

2 The Fax Wizard dialog box appears. Follow steps 2 through 11 of the previous *Guided Tour* "Send a Fax with the Fax Wizard."

Begin Guided Tour Send a Fax from Within a Program

1 Within the program, open the **File** menu and select **Print**.

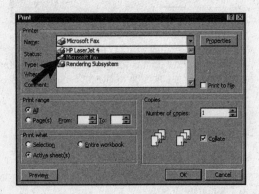

2 In the Print dialog box, select **Microsoft Fax** from the printer list.

3 Now select what you want to fax (using the **Print Range** and **Print What** area) and click on **OK**.

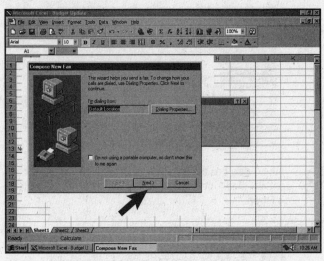

4 When you "print" to the Microsoft Fax printer from within a program, the Fax Wizard starts. Click on **Next**.

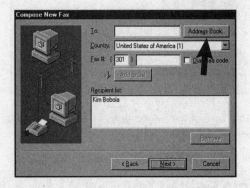

5 Type the name of the person to whom you want to send a fax, and enter his fax number. If you have stored the number, click on **Address Book**; select the number from the list and click on **Next**.

Guided Tour Send a Fax from Within a Program

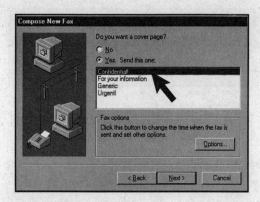

6 Select a cover letter for your fax and click on **Next**.

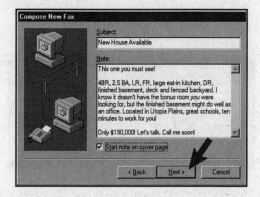

7 Add a description under Subject, add a note, and click on **Next**. Turn on your modem and click on **Finish**.

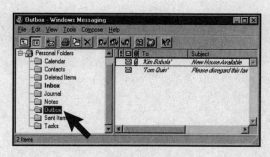

8 If you need to cancel the fax during transmission, click on **Hang Up**. A copy of your fax is placed in Microsoft Exchange's Sent Items folder. If the fax transmission was interrupted, a copy of your fax will remain in your Outbox folder to try again later (or you can delete it).

Begin Guided Tour　Receive a Fax

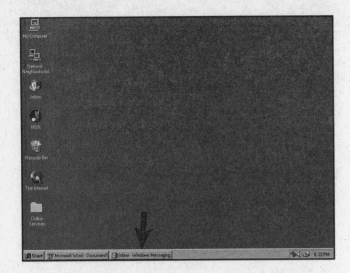

1 Make sure Microsoft Exchange is running (even if it's minimized).

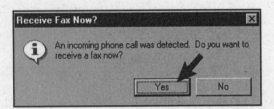

2 When a call comes in, if you've set the modem to answer automatically, it answers the fax. If you've set the fax up for manual answering, this dialog box appears. Click on **Yes** and skip to step 5.

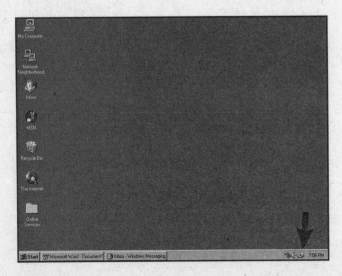

3 If you've set the modem so that it doesn't answer automatically, double-click on the **Fax** icon on the taskbar.

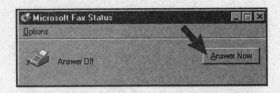

4 The Fax Status dialog box appears. Click on **Answer Now**.

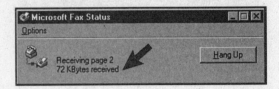

5 Microsoft Fax displays the status of the incoming fax.

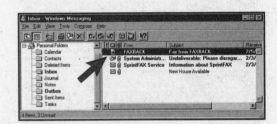

6 The incoming fax is placed in Microsoft Exchange's Inbox. Double-click on it to view its contents.

Begin Guided Tour Receive a Fax from an Automatic Service

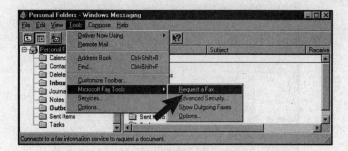

1 From within Microsoft Exchange, open the **Tools** menu, select **Microsoft Fax Tools**, and select **Request a Fax**.

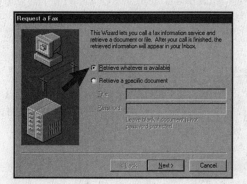

2 Select what you want to retrieve. If you don't know the name of the document you are requesting, select **Retrieve whatever is available**. If you have the name of a specific document, enter it under **Title**. If it's password-protected, enter the password and click on **Next**.

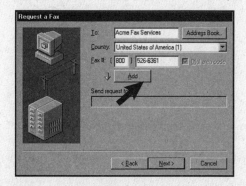

3 Enter the name and phone number of the service from which you want to receive a fax, and click on **Add**. If you've stored the number, click on **Address Book** and select the number from a list.

4 Click on **Next**.
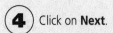

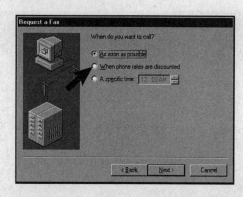

5 Select an option button to indicate when you want to call. Click on **Next**.

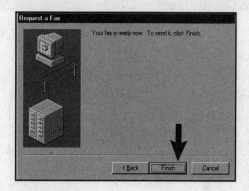

6 Turn on your modem and click on **Finish**. The request is sent at the time you indicated. The service then calls you back and sends the fax.

Begin Guided Tour   View and Print a Fax

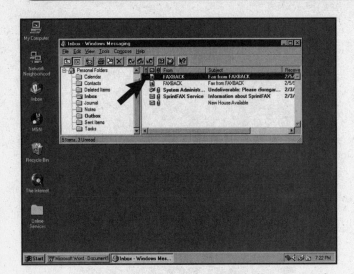

1 In the Microsoft Exchange Inbox, double-click on the fax you want to view.

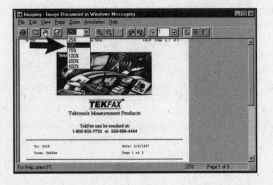

2 To change the zoom, select a different zoom level from the list in the toolbar.

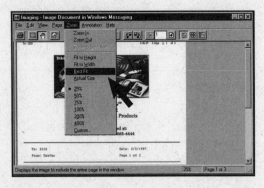

3 You can zoom to fit as much of the page on the screen as you can by opening the **Zoom** menu and selecting **Fit to Width**, **Fit to Height**, or **Best Fit**.

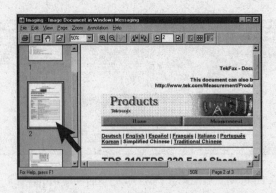

4 If your fax is several pages, open the **View** menu and select **Thumbnails**. You can then jump from page to page by clicking on the appropriate thumbnail. (Alternatively, you can open the **Page** menu and select the page you want to jump to.)

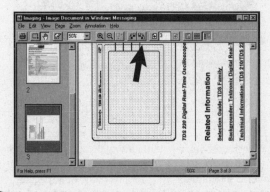

5 Sometimes you'll receive several pages that are not facing the correct direction. Rotate a fax page to the left or right by clicking on either the **Rotate Left** button or the **Rotate Right** button.

Guided Tour　View and Print a Fax

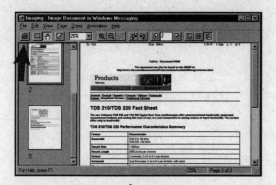

6 To print the fax, click on the **Print** button.

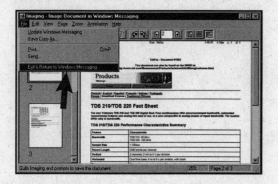

7 When you finish viewing the fax, open the **File** menu and select **Exit & Return to Microsoft Exchange**.

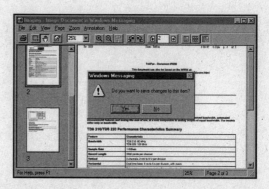

8 If you've made any changes to the fax, Microsoft Fax displays this dialog box. Click on **Yes** to save your changes.

HOW TO...
Use the Microsoft Network and the Internet

Microsoft Network (MSN for short) is an online service (similar to CompuServe, PRODIGY, and America Online) run by Microsoft Corporation. You connect to MSN through your modem. Like most online services, Microsoft Network enables you to send and receive e-mail, "chat" with other members (by typing what you want to say), download and upload files, and get information on a variety of topics, such as current news, sports, and entertainment information. You also can use services such as travel and shopping.

MSN also provides you a quick way to get connected to the Internet. You also can get connected to the Internet using other commercial services such as America Online or through an independent service provider. After you are connected to the Internet, you can browse its many sources.

This section gives you a quick idea of some of the things you can do with MSN and with the Internet:

What You Will Find in This Section

Sign Up for an Online Provider

Windows 95 provides several options for getting connected to different online providers. For example, you can use the MSN icon to sign up for Microsoft's online service. You also can try any of the other online commercial companies. You'll find sign up icons in the Online folder on your desktop. For instance, you can use the America Online icon in this folder to sign up for this service.

Most services offer similar features:

- News areas where you can read up on current events, sports, entertainment, history, health, and many other topics. You can find online magazines as well as newsletters and other sources of current information.

- Service areas which enable you to plan a trip, check the weather, shop, research purchasing a car, and so on.

- Forums where you can find information relating to a particular topic. For instance, you can find software forums where you can post and review messages from other users, download or upload files, review product information, and more.

- Chat areas where you can discuss various topics of interest with other members. You also can participate in special symposiums with important guests.

- Access to the Internet.

What you'll find specifically for each service varies, as do the fees for using that service. You can get detailed information about each service during the sign up process.

> The best fee arrangement is one where you get unlimited access for a set monthly amount. Be sure to shop around and check out the various options before you pick an Internet provider.

To sign up for a service, double-click the sign-up icon and then follow the on-screen instructions. You are prompted to enter your name, billing address, user name (the name you pick will identify you when you sign on and are using the service), a billing plan, and a payment method. For payment method, you use a credit card number and your account will be billed monthly. Some ISPs may also bill customers or bill you through your phone company.

After you sign up the first time, you won't need to enter this information again. Instead, you enter the particular sign-on information for your service. The *Guided Tour* covers how to sign on and exit MSN.

Begin Guided Tour Sign onto the Microsoft Network

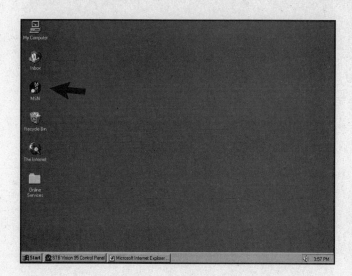

1 Double-click on **The Microsoft Network (MSN)** icon.

3 You are connected to MSN and see MSN On Stage (MSN's home page).

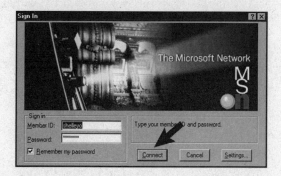

2 In the Sign In window, enter your member ID and password (if necessary) and click on **Connect**.

To have MSN remember your password, check the Remember my password check box. Then you won't have to type it each time you sign on.

Begin Guided Tour　Sign Off the Microsoft Network

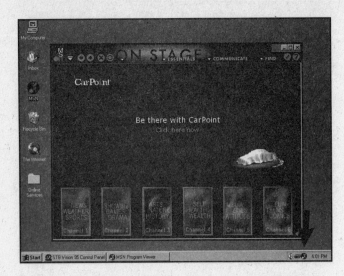

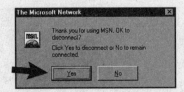

3 MSN prompts you to confirm the disconnect command. Click on **Yes**.

1 Right-click on the **MSN** icon that appears next to the clock on the taskbar.

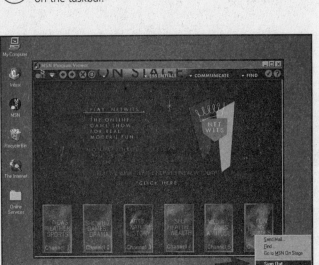

2 In the shortcut menu that appears, select **Sign Out**.

Explore Microsoft Network

When you connect to MSN, you see On Stage, MSN's home page. This area contains several "channels" which you can select. The channels appear along the bottom of this screen and include such topics as news, sports, and weather.

Along the top of the screen you see the other MSN areas. The Microsoft Network gives you direct access to the following areas:

- **On Stage**   Provides several channels of information where you can find "programs" for topics like News, Weather, and Sports; Showbiz, Games, and Drama; Arts, Nature, and History; Self, Health, and Wealth; Media, Zines, and Attitude; and Fun, Teens, and Comics.

- **Essentials**   The majority of MSN's services are available here. You can get local information; find features relating to personal finance, travel, shopping, and computers; look up information in the reference section, and more.

- **Communicate**   To participate in chats, send e-mail, get information from member services, visit forums, go to this area. MSN's electronic mail can be handled through Microsoft Exchange, which was covered in "Communicate with Other Computers" on page 275.

- **Find**   Use this area to find information on MSN.

You can quickly go to any of these areas by clicking the appropriate topic at the top of the MSN window. You can go to a particular site or service within an area by clicking on the down arrow next to the name and then selecting the site you want. You also can use the MSN toolbar to navigate back and forth among the pages you have viewed.

MSN is organized like the Internet. You can go to other sites or services by clicking on the appropriate link. Links appear underlined or in a different color.

MSN Navigation Bar Buttons

Button	Name	Description
▼	Reveal the Internet Toolbar	Display a toolbar for going to Internet addresses. When toolbar is displayed, click this arrow to hide the toolbar.
◄	Back	Go back to the previously viewed page or area.
►	Forward	Go forward (after going back) to the last viewed page.
✖	Stop	Stop the display of the page. Use this button if the display is taking too long.
↻	Refresh	Redisplay the page.
✓	Favorites	Add this site to your list of favorites.
?	Member Services & Support	Takes you to the Member Services & Support page where you can get information about using MSN and about your account.

Begin Guided Tour Tour MSN

1 On Stage is the MSN home page. You see this page each time you sign on to MSN. Here you can find programs relating to weather, sports, entertainment, and more.

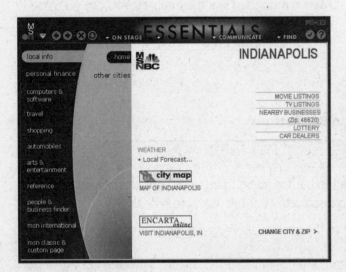

2 To go to Essentials, click on **Essentials**. You see the different categories from which you can select along the left edge of the window: travel, shopping, arts & entertainment, and so on.

3 To go to the Communicate area, click on **Communicate**. You see the features for using MSN to communicate: Chat World, E-mail, Member services, Forums, Internet Community, and Customize This Page.

4 To go to the Find area, click on **Find**. You see the features you can use to find information including looking up something by subject, by calendar, or by word.

The screens and available services in MSN change frequently, so your windows may look slightly different than those in the *Guided Tour*.

View an On Stage Program

MSN's home page is On Stage. The top part of this page displays previews—advertisements and links to services and sites on MSN. If you see something of interest, you can click that page to go to that site.

Along the bottom of the screen are different channels. You can click the channels to view various "programs." Here are the available channels:

- **Channel 1**   Provides links to MSNBC Front Page (a joint effort by MSN and NBC to provide the latest news), Personal Page, Weather, World, Commerce, Sports, SciTech, Life, and Opinion.

- **Channel 2**   Includes Entertainment programs such as the Star Trek: Continuum; Entertainment Tonight; 475 Madison Avenue, described as "an interactive online comedy/drama; How Long?, (914), another online comedy/drama; and NetWits, a game show.

- **Channel 3**   Programs on this channel devoted to Arts, Nature, and History include Retrospect 360, Riff, Mungo Park, and Slate.

- **Channel 4**   Produces programs relating to Self, Health, and Wealth. You can "watch" V-Style, UnderWire, Vinsight, AMC Presents, or MotorSite.

- **Channel 5**   Includes MINT, 15 Seconds of Fame, One Click Away, and Second City News, programs relating to Media, Zines, and Attitude.

- **Channel 6**   Has programs relating to teens, fun, and comics. Visit Spike's World or get a horoscope from Mr. Zodiac at this channel.

When you select a channel, you see the available programs. To view the page for that program, click it. Keep in mind that MSN is continually changing, so the programs that are available may change.

> You can go directly to a program by clicking the down arrow next to On Stage. From the drop-down menu that appears, click the channel you want, then click the program you want.

Begin Guided Tour   View On Stage Productions

1 Each time you start MSN, you see On Stage and the Preview channel. To select another channel, click on the channel you want at the bottom of the screen.

2 You see the programs for that channel. Click on the program you want to view.

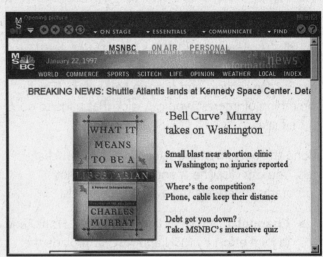

3 You see the page for that particular program.

Begin Guided Tour Go Directly to a Program

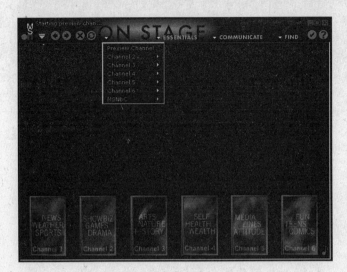

1 Click on the down arrow next to On Stage.

3 You see the programs for that channel. Click on the program you want.

2 You see a list of the available channels. Click on the channel you want.

Use MSN Services (Essentials)

To try out the services and reference information links on MSN, use the Essentials page. You can get to this page by clicking **Essentials** at the top of the MSN Program Viewer window.

Here's a brief run-down of each of the available links on this page. Keep in mind that MSN is updated a lot, so these links as well as the contents of these links may change.

- **Local Info**   You can customize the news you receive using this page. To set up this page, select the metropolitan area, enter your ZIP code, and click the button to set the city. After that, this page will display movie listings, TV listings, nearby businesses, local stock information, weather forecast, and current headlines for your city.

- **Personal Finance**   Select this link to use Microsoft Investor, an investment tool that includes a portfolio manager, quote lookup, market summary, and more.

- **Computers & Software**   This link takes you to Computing on MSN where you can read a daily magazine, check out computer forums, and review a guide to Microsoft.

- **Travel**   Select this link to plan a trip with Microsoft Expedia.

- **Shopping**   Visit the Plaza on MSN and purchase items from such online companies as Tower Records, Avon, American Greetings, and more.

- **Automobiles**   Use Microsoft Carpoint to get information about car models. You can read expert opinions, learn dealer costs, and more, using this service.

- **Arts & Entertainment**   Try Music Central for up-to-date music information or Cinemania for all you need to know about the movies (reviews, biographies, articles, and so on).

- **Reference**   This service includes Microsoft Encarta (an encyclopedia), a parent handbook, and a wine guide.

- **People & Business Finder**   Includes services for finding people, e-mail addresses, businesses, or company web sites.

- **MSN International**   Select links to Australia, Canada, France, Germany, Japan, UK & Ireland, or the United States from this site.

- **MSN Classic & Custom Page**   If you are upgrading from the previous version of MSN, you can view the classic categories of MSN from this site.

Each service provides unique features. For example, if you are using Microsoft Cinemania, you can read current feature articles, check out the release dates of videos, look up movie information, and more. Simply click on the feature you want and then follow any other links or on-screen instructions.

Begin Guided Tour   Use MSN Services

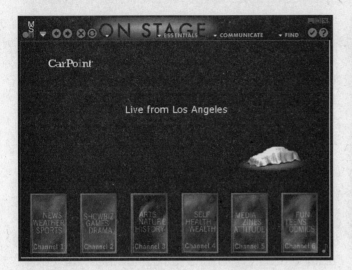

1 From the MSN home page, click on **Essentials**.

3 You see the available services. Use the links to select what you want to do.

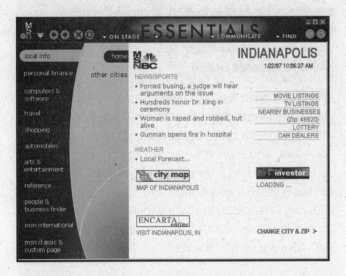

2 You see the Essentials page with links to different categories along the left edge of the screen. The default local information is page is displayed. Click the category or service you want to investigate. If there's more than one, click the category and then select the service you want.

Use MSN to Communicate

Besides giving you access to information, MSN provides you with access to people. You can communicate with other MSN users in three ways: by electronic mail (e-mail), through online chat, or via messages posted to a forum. All of these are available from the Communicate page.

E-mail messages are private correspondences between you and selected recipients; only the recipients whom you designate actually see the messages you send to them. Electronic mail is covered in more detail in "Communicate with Other Computers" on page 275.

The second way to communicate with another member is by direct conferencing, also known as online chat. To chat, several users are linked together directly in real-time, and each user in the connection sees what the others are typing.

In formal chat sessions, an MSN system operator plays the role of moderator. Like in a seminar, the moderator gives a guest the "podium," and that guest speaks (types) for a short time. The moderator then poses questions from the session spectators. In these sessions, you can take part in discussions with leaders from such fields as computing, science, or politics—all while dressed in your pajamas. These moderated sessions are held in areas called auditoriums or *pavilions*.

Informal chat sessions can take place anytime or anywhere, as long as two or more people are online and have at least one common interest. You "listen" to a conversation by reading it; MSN displays the text of the conversation as it happens. When you comment, the text you type appears in a small box in the bottom of the window. When you press Enter, that text appears in the upper window, and everyone else in the conversation sees it.

The third way in which online users communicate is through publicly posted messages on a forum. When you post a message to a forum, even if you direct it to someone specific, its headline is visible to everyone, and anyone can view the message. So when you have a problem with Windows or you want to engage in a political debate, everyone can get involved. You post a question or comment on the forum, and anyone who reads it can reply directly to you. Both the original message and the response are visible to everyone else who visits that forum. MSN has a number of forums ranging in topics from the Ale & Lager Beer Brewing forum to Generation X to Women Online to Science Fiction.

When you open a forum, MSN displays the headings for the messages that have been left there. You can browse through these headings, comment on those you want, and even leave a message on a new subject by posting a message of your own. Responses to that message, and responses to the responses, show up later beneath that headline. The result is a thread that links all the messages that pertain to a particular subject, in the order of their creation.

You also can get information about MSN or change MSN options using the Member Services link.

Begin Guided Tour   View Communication Features

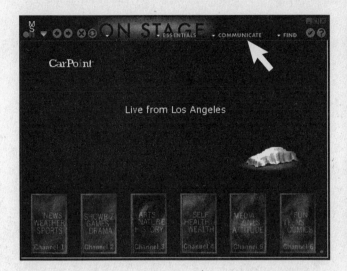

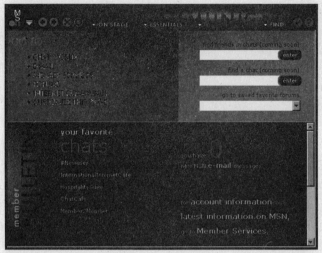

1 From the MSN On Stage page, click on **Communicate**.

2 You see the available communication features. MSN also checks for any e-mail messages and displays a reminder of the number of new e-mail messages waiting. To check your e-mail, click on **E-Mail**. See "Communicate with Other Computers" on page 275 for more information on e-mail.

Begin Guided Tour   Visit a Chat Room

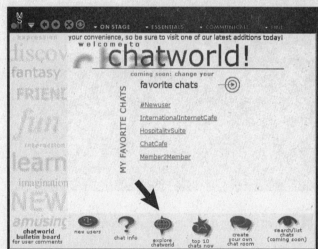

1 From the Communicate page, click **Chat World**.

2 Initially, you see a list of favorite chats. (Some default rooms are selected if this is your first visit and you have not customized.) Chat areas are marked by a "cartoon bubble." To enter one of these areas, double-click on its icon.

(continues)

Guided Tour Visit a Chat Room *(continued)*

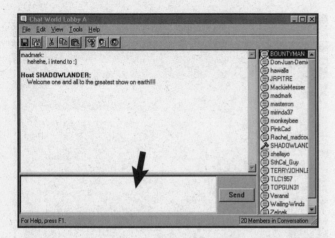

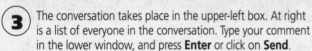

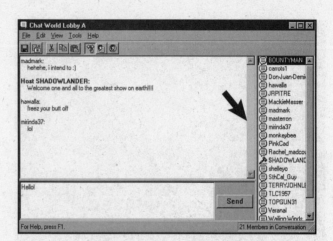

3 The conversation takes place in the upper-left box. At right is a list of everyone in the conversation. Type your comment in the lower window, and press **Enter** or click on **Send**.

4 Use the scroll bars to move through the conversation to view earlier comments.

Begin Guided Tour View a List of Forums

1 From the Communicate page, click **Forums**.

2 Initially, you see a list of favorite forums. To view all forums, click **View all forums**.

Guided Tour View a List of Forums

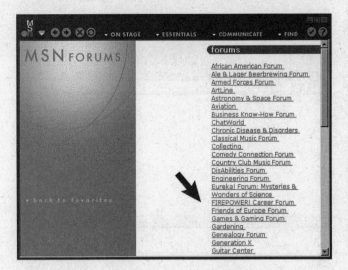

3 You see a complete listing. To select a forum, click on it.

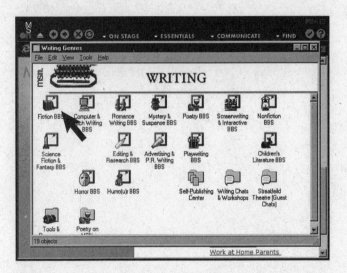

4 You see folders for the different forums within this category. If you see a folder named BBS with a stick-pin, it is a bulletin board to which you can post and review messages. Double-click the specific forum you want to view.

Keep in mind that the content of MSN is always being updated. What you see may vary, especially as this new version is introduced and tweaked.

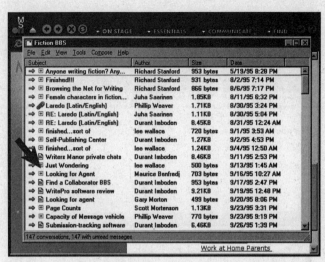

5 You see a list of messages. To read a message, double-click on the message title. MSN displays a message's responses below the message headline. Double-click on the message or response you want to read.

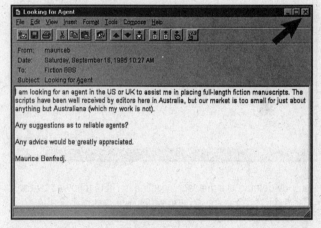

6 MSN displays the message or response in its own window. When you finish reading the message, double-click on its **Close** button.

Begin Guided Tour   Post a Reply to a BBS Message

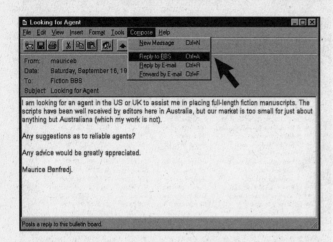

1 Open the message to which you want to reply. Then open the **Compose** menu and select **Reply to BBS**.

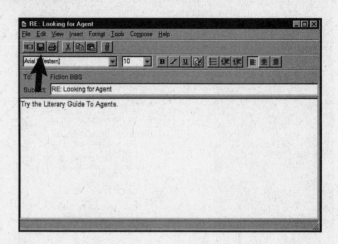

3 When you've completed your message, click on the **Post** button.

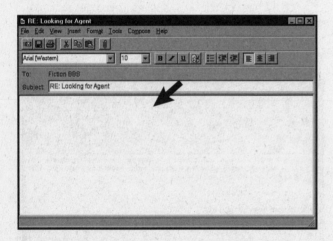

2 By default, the message headline is "RE:" followed by the subject of the message to which it responds. Type the message in the message area.

Find the Information You Need on MSN

MSN includes a lot of features. Using this service to do something useful first means finding what you want. If you are looking for something in particular, you may want to skip browsing from page to page and try looking for it directly. If so, click **Find**. This page includes three tabs for each of the three methods you can use to search.

You can use the Subject tab to browse through categories and subtopics until you find the available links. Select the category you want to investigate: arts & entertainment, computers, Microsoft products, lifestyles, personal finance, education, reference, sports & leisure, health & medicine, or travel. Select

the category and you see topics with the category. Continue clicking until you see the links available for that topic.

Use the Word tab to search for a word or phrase. You can use this feature to search not only MSN, but also the Internet using search tools like Alta Vista, Excite, and Infoseek.

Use the Calendar tab to display special events, new features, system events, contests, activities, and scheduled chats.

The *Guided Tour* covers each of these search methods.

Begin Guided Tour   Find a Topic by Browsing Subjects

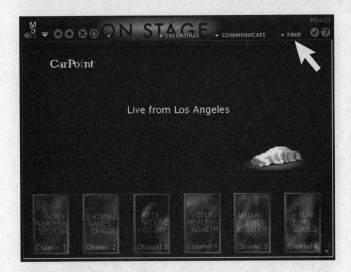

1 From the On Stage page, click on **Find**.

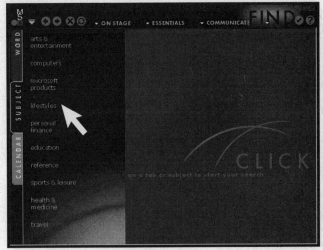

2 You see the Subject tab. Click on the subject in which you are interested.

(continues)

Guided Tour Find a Topic by Browsing Subjects

(continued)

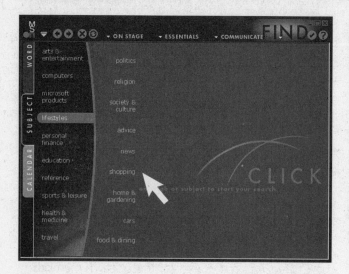

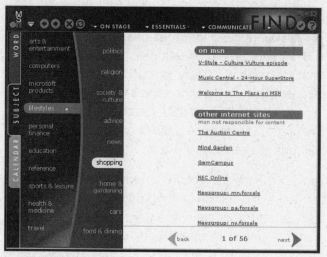

3 You see subtopics relating to the category. Click on the subtopic you want.

4 MSN displays the available links related to this topic. Click on the one you want.

Begin Guided Tour Look Up Something on the Calendar

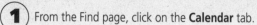

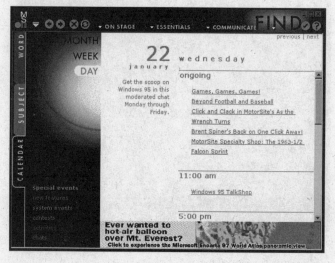

1 From the Find page, click on the **Calendar** tab.

2 MSN displays the current day's events. To see other events, use the links in the lower-left corner.

Begin Guided Tour Find a Topic by Searching for a Word or Phrase

1 From the Find page, click on the **Word** tab.

3 You see a list of matching links. To go to any of these pages, click on the link you want.

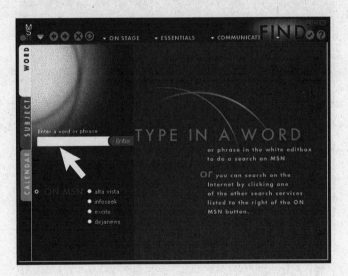

2 MSN displays the directions for searching. Type the word or phrase you want to find and then click on the **Enter** button.

Connect to the Internet

If you have MSN, you can use it to connect to the Internet. CompuServe and America Online also offer access to the Internet, or you can use an independent service provider (ISP) through which you can gain access to the Internet.

The difference between providers is what you pay (although most are fairly competitively priced) and what services are provided. For example, some ISPs offer help on setting up Web pages and more.

To get connected, you need an account and you need to follow the instructions for installing the software. This *Guided Tour* assumes you are using MSN, but if you are not, follow the sign-on instructions for your provider.

You also need a browser—a program you can use to view the information on the World Wide Web (part of the Internet). The new version of MSN installs Internet Explorer for you. This section uses Internet Explorer 3.01 as the browser.

Begin Guided Tour Start Internet Explorer

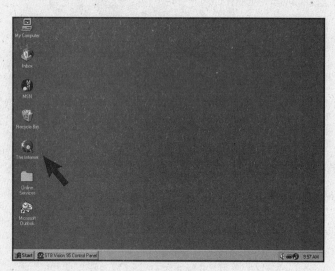

1 Double-click on the **Internet** icon.

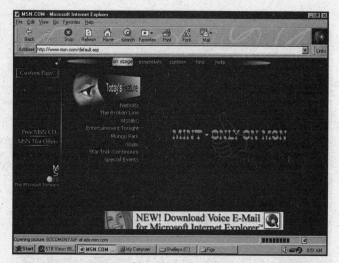

3 When you connect, you see your home page. This figure shows the MSN home page, similar to what you see if you are using MSN. Your home page may vary.

2 If prompted, sign on to your Internet provider (for instance, MSN).

Navigate the World Wide Web

Two of the most popular types of information available via the Internet include the World Wide Web and Usenet (covered later in this section). The Web makes it easy to locate information on the Internet. Everything on the Web is displayed as a document page, and a Web page can contain text, graphics, sounds, movies, and links to other Web pages. These links are what make it possible to browse the Web. When you click on a link, you're taken to another page on the Web, which contains information as well as other links.

To navigate around the Web you can click on the links until you find the page you want. Links usually appear underlined. Images also may be links to other sites. You can tell when your pointer is over a link because the pointer changes to a hand with a pointing finger.

To keep track of where you've been, you can use the Internet Explorer toolbar to move among pages:

Internet Explorer Toolbar

Button	Name	Description
Back	Back	Go back to the previously viewed page.
Forward	Forward	Go forward (after going back) to the last viewed page.
Stop	Stop	Stop the display of the page. Use this button if the display is taking too long.
Refresh	Refresh	Redisplay the page.
Home	Home	Return to your home page.
Search	Search	Search the Web for a topic (see page 329)
Favorites	Favorites	Display a list of your favorite sites.
Print	Print	Print the current page.
Font	Font	Increase or decrease the font size of the text on the current page.
Mail	Mail and News	Use the Mail and News features. See page 331 for more information on browsing newsgroups.

If you don't like browsing, you also can go directly to a site. Each Web page has a unique address called a URL or uniform resource locator. For example, here's the address for the National Basketball Association (NBA): **http://www.nba.com.** You can type this address to go directly to the page.

Begin Guided Tour Go to a Link

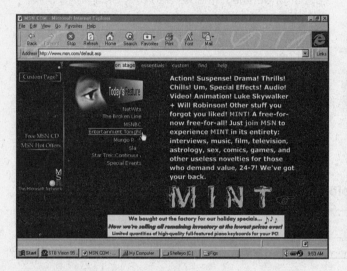

1 From any Web page, click on the link. Links are usually underlined and/or may appear in a different color. Icons and other graphic images may also be links or hot spots.

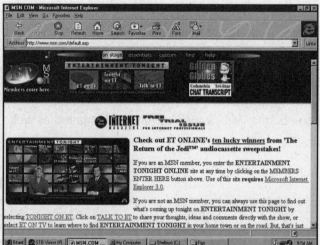

2 That page is displayed. Continue clicking on links until you find the information you want.

Begin Guided Tour Go Directly to an Address

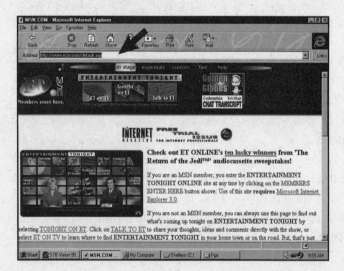

1 Click in the Address text box. The entire address should be highlighted. Type the address you want to go to and press **Enter**.

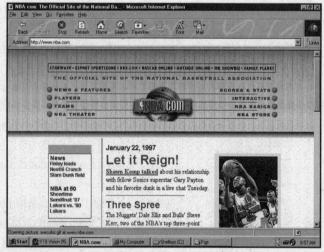

2 Internet Explorer displays that page.

Search for a Topic on the Web

Browsing around is time-consuming (but fun). You never know where you'll end up. You might start out researching a legitimate project and end up checking out pictures of bulldogs on the bulldog page. When you have an idea of what you want to find and want to see what's available, you can search the Web.

> You can also visit Symantec's Internet Fast Find, which contains Web Find. Web Find uses all eight of the most popular search engines at once, discards links, and formats the list sorted by site. The address for this site is http:www.symantec.com/iff/.

To search the Web, you use a search engine, and there are many different search engines available. They all work basically the same: you type the word or phrase you want to find and click the search button. The search engine then displays matches. (You also can fine-tune the search using different search options.)

The search tools differ in how they search—where they look for matches for your words. That means the results will vary. Also, how the results are displayed varies. Some display a short description. Some include some indication of how well the listed site matches the criteria you entered. Some may provide reviews of sites.

The MSN home page provides links to some popular search engines, including Yahoo, Magellan, InfoSeek, Alta Vista, Lycos, and Excite. In your exploration of the Web, you also may find other search engines. (To use a different search engine, just go to that page.) You can experiment to see which one you like best. You may simply prefer the results of one over another. Also, if you search for a topic with one and don't get the results you like, try another one.

> If you have trouble searching—you can't find a match or find too many—try narrowing the search. Look for a button or link that provides an explanation of the different search options you can set.

When you perform a search, you see a list of possible matches, and each one of these are links to that particular page. To go to that page, click the link.

Begin Guided Tour Search the Web

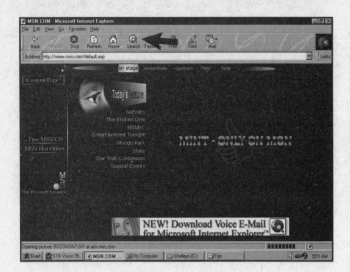

1 Click on the **Search** button in the Internet Explorer toolbar.

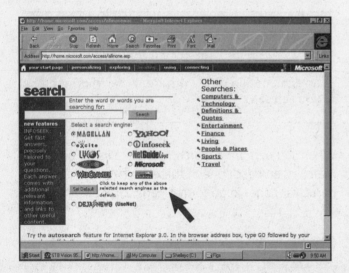

2 You see a list of the different search engines from which you can select. Select the search engine you want to use.

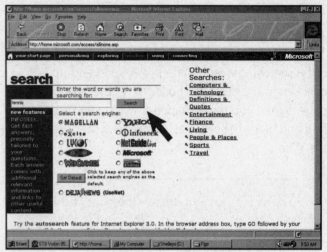

3 In the text box, type the word or phrase you want to find and then click on the **Search** button.

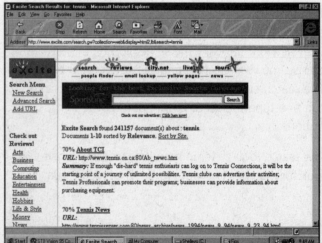

4 You see the results of the search. Here you see the results of a search using Excite. To go to any of the found sites, click on the link to that site. If additional sites were found, you can also display the next set of sites. Look for a link at the end of the list to display the next set of matches.

Participate in Newsgroups

One other popular form of Internet information comes from Usenet, a quarter-century-old system for transmitting text messages about various topics. The Usenet system employs private file servers to maintain messages pertaining to a set of topics. These servers make messages available to any computer that uses Internet protocol. So what you get when you connect all these Usenet servers to the Internet is something like what you get when you subscribe to several specialty magazines for cooking, computer gaming, hunting, and so on.

There are literally tens of thousands of Usenet topics, with cryptic (though telling) names such as **rec.games. pinball**, **israel.russian-jews**, **comp.os.ms-windows. apps**, and **alt.fan.mst3k**. Each part of the name tells you a bit about the information you'll find there. Here's a list of common abbreviations:

alt	Alternative ideas. Typically you find the wildest ideas here. You also run into a lot of pornography and other strange things in the alt sections, so be careful.
rec	Recreational topic, such as boating, hunting, fishing, photography, reading, or films.
comp	Computer-related topics, such as computer games, multimedia, or hardware.
news	Usenet-related topics.
sci	Science and technology topics.
soc	Social issues such as sex, religion, and politics.
misc	Miscellaneous topics that don't fit anywhere else.

While some groups support messages written by the finest scientific minds currently alive, others are of the kind you've probably heard about on the news (in other words, they're not really *news* and some are not exactly in the best taste). Keep in mind that the messages in these newsgroups are not screened for objectionable content.

Internet News gives you access to these Usenet newsgroups. To read the messages and participate in the newsgroup, you subscribe to the groups you want. The first time you use Internet News, you are prompted to select the groups to which you want to subscribe.

> If you are using a local ISP or anything other than MSN, you need to configure Internet news to access your ISP's news server. Otherwise, you will only see the MSN newsgroups. Check with your provider for specific information.

When subscribing, you can do any of the following:

- To select which News server to use, click the one you want in the News servers list. The list of groups is downloaded to your PC; this may take a while.

- You may just see a select list of newsgroups. (Keep in mind that there are thousands and thousands of groups.) To see a list of All newsgroups, click the **All** button. To see a list of just new ones (recently added newsgroups), click the **New** button.

- To display newsgroups with a particular theme or content, type the topic in the Display newsgroups which contain text box.

- To select a newsgroup, click on it. To select multiple groups, click the first one, hold down the **Shift** key, and click the last one. All the newsgroups in between are selected. You also can hold down the **Ctrl** key and click each newsgroup you want to select.

- To subscribe to the selected newsgroups, click the **Subscribe** button. To unsubscribe, click the **Unsubscribe** button.

Begin Guided Tour Subscribe to a Newsgroup

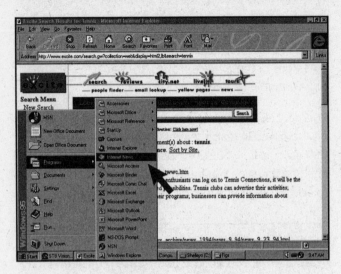

1 Click on **Start**, **Programs**, and **Internet News**. If you have not subscribed to any newsgroups, you see a message telling you so. Click the **Yes** button.

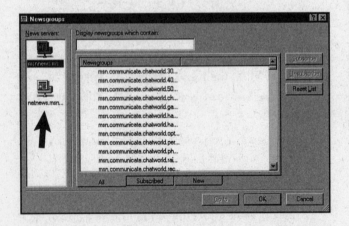

2 You see the Newsgroups dialog box, where you can select the newsgroups to which you want to subscribe. Select the News server you want to select from.

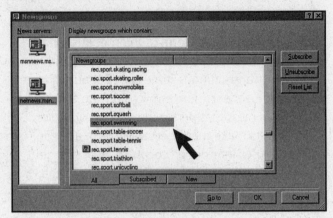

3 Select the groups you want to subscribe to.

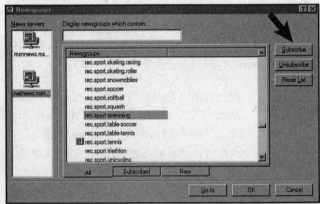

4 Click the **Subscribe** button and then click the **OK** button.

Begin Guided Tour Read a Usenet Newsgroup

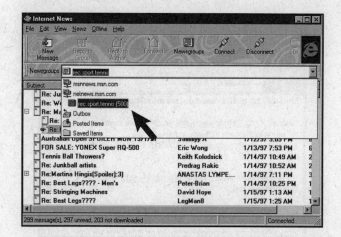

1 From the Internet News window, click on the **down arrow** next to Newsgroups and select the newsgroup you want to review.

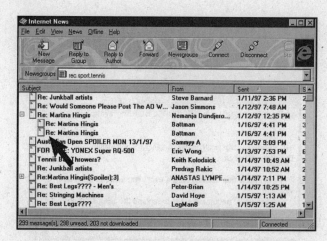

3 To read a message, double-click on its name in the list.

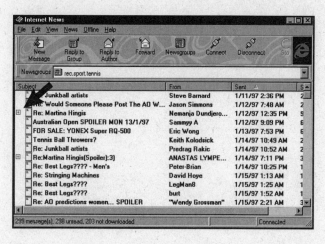

2 Internet News retrieves the messages. Messages that have replies posted to them are marked with a plus sign. To see the list of replies for a message, click on the **plus** sign.

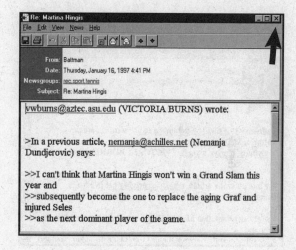

4 You see the message. When you finish with the message, close the window by clicking on its **Close** button.

Begin Guided Tour Post a Usenet Message Reply

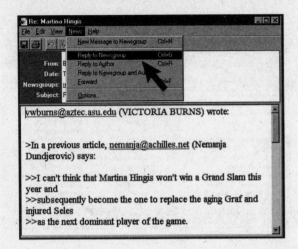

1 From the window of the message to which you're replying, open the **News** menu and select **Reply to Newsgroup**.

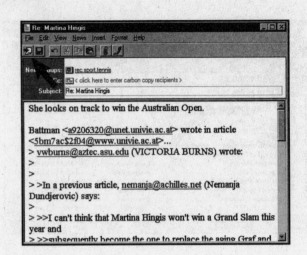

3 When you finish entering your message, click on the **Post Message** button.

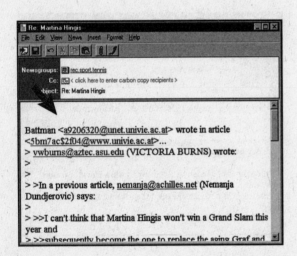

2 Click in the message area, and type your reply.

Begin Guided Tour Post a New Usenet Message

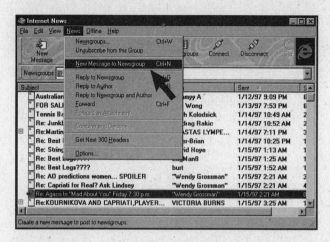

1 From the newsgroup's message headline list, open the **News** menu and select **New Message to Newsgroup**.

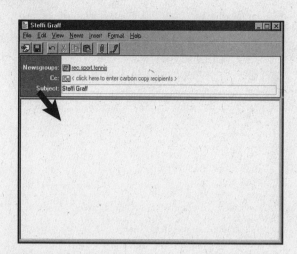

3 Click in the message area and type your message.

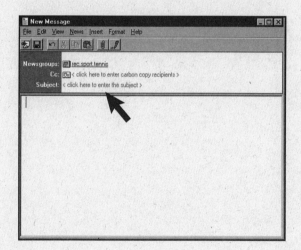

2 Type a subject in the Subject line.

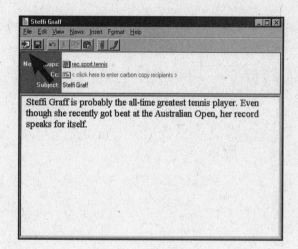

4 Click on the **Post Message** button to post the message.

HOW TO...

Maintain Your System

One of the most important aspects of using a PC is taking care of it—and that doesn't mean just dusting it off every now and then. Maintenance involves keeping your hard disk in optimum working condition, checking for errors, and backing up important files. Maintenance tasks also include adding new hardware to your system and updating the files that control your hardware (called drivers). In this section you find out how to complete all these tasks and more. Specifically, you'll learn how to perform the following tasks:

What You Will Find in This Section

Add New Hardware

The more you use your PC, the more you may find to do with it. You can add features by adding new software, by adding Windows 95 components, or by adding new hardware. In this *Guided Tour,* you'll learn how to add new hardware.

Suppose, for example, your PC doesn't have a modem. You want to get one so you can take advantage of some of Windows 95's communication features: to connect to Microsoft Network or use Microsoft Exchange to send e-mail and send and receive faxes. You can easily purchase a fax/modem and install it. As another example, suppose you want to add a CD-ROM drive so you can take advantage of the multimedia features. Or maybe you already have a modem and a CD-ROM drive, but you are running out of disk space. You may decide to add a second hard drive.

To learn how to add new software, see "Set Up and Run Programs" on page 39. To learn how to add Windows 95 components, see "Add and Remove Windows 95 Components" on page 476.

Basically, adding a new hardware component to your computer is a two-step process:

1. Install or connect the component to the PC.

2. Tell Windows about your new component.

Some hardware items, such as a printer, are separate units and are connected to the PC via a cable that you plug into the appropriate port on the back of the PC. Some hardware items, such as an internal modem, are actually electronic boards that are housed inside the system unit (the boxlike part of the computer). These boards (which are also called controllers, adapters, or cards) plug into empty slots inside the

PC. Other hardware components are actually two parts; for example, some disk drives include the actual drive in its drive bay (an empty shelf in the PC) and a card that fits into a slot. To connect any of these components, follow the instructions in the hardware manual.

So that Windows knows about your new hardware equipment, you have to install it through Windows. Windows receives instructions on how the hardware works and what features the hardware includes from a *driver* and uses the driver file to set up the component. With Windows 95's new Plug and Play technology, you hardly have to worry about the driver. Basically, Plug and Play enables Windows 95 to automatically detect and install many different kinds of hardware drivers. You sit back and let Windows do the work.

If Windows can't detect and set up your hardware component, you can do it manually. Both methods are covered in the *Guided Tour.*

Types of Hardware

The following list outlines the most common hardware items you might need to install:

- **CD-ROM controllers** You can add a CD-ROM drive to your PC so that you can take advantage of the multimedia features. For example, with a CD-ROM drive, you can purchase and use an encyclopedia on a CD. The controller is an electronic card that plugs into one of the slots inside the PC.

- **Display adapters** A monitor is actually two parts: the adapter or card inside the PC and the TV-like component. The inside part—the adapter—is the most important part of the combination because it controls the quality and features of the monitor.

- **Floppy disk controllers** You might add another floppy drive to your system or, if you have an older system, you might need to replace a floppy drive that doesn't work anymore.

- **Hard disk controllers** If you need more disk space, you can add a second hard disk to your PC. The controller is a card that connects to the expansion slot. Newer drives have the controller built into the drive so you simply connect the hard disk to the motherboard with the controller cable.

- **Keyboard** Don't like your current keyboard? Want to opt for one of the newer keyboards that help prevent repetitive stress injuries? You can easily add a new keyboard.

- **Memory Technology drivers** Use these types of drivers to optimize the memory on your PC.

- **Modem** Short for MOdulator-DEModulator, this is a hardware component you must have to use your PC for communication. The modem enables you to connect to other PCs via the phone lines. To install a modem see "Set Up a Modem" on page 276.

- **Mouse** If your mouse quits working or if you want a different one, you can purchase a new mouse.

- **Multifunction adapters** Some cards have more than one function. For example, a sound card may function as a sound card and as a telephone answering machine.

- **Network adapters** If you want to be connected to a network (a group of other computers), you need a network adapter. See "Use Files, Programs, and Printers on the Network" on page 375 for information on using Windows on a network.

Begin Guided Tour Use the Add New Hardware Wizard

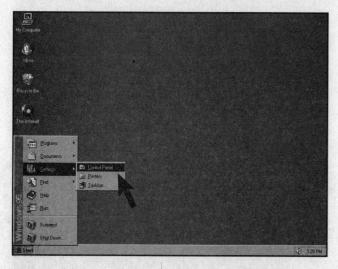

1 Connect your hardware component according to the manual's instructions. Then click on the **Start** menu, select **Settings**, and select **Control Panel**.

2 In the Control Panel window, double-click on the **Add New Hardware** icon.

(continues)

Guided Tour Use the Add New Hardware Wizard *(continued)*

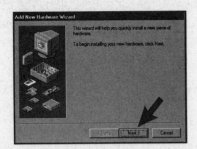

3 The first dialog box of the Add New Hardware Wizard appears. Click the **Next** button.

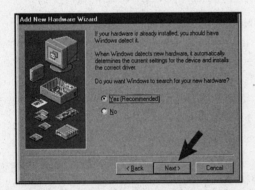

4 Select the **Yes (Recommended)** option to have Windows automatically search your system and detect any new components. Click the **Next** button.

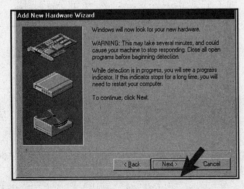

5 Windows displays a reminder that the detection may take a while. Click the **Next** button.

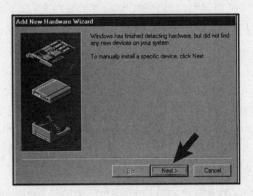

6 If Windows detected your hardware, it is set up automatically. You may be prompted to insert the disk that contains the software for the component. If so, follow the on-screen instructions and skip the remaining steps. If it didn't detect the new hardware, a message tells you to manually install the component (shown here). Click the **Next** button.

7 A list of the types of hardware components you can install are displayed. Select the type you want and click the **Next** button.

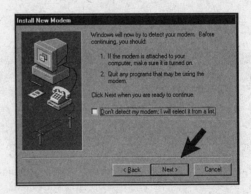

8 If you see a screen like the one above, click the **Next** button to have Windows try to detect this type of component. If not, skip to step 10.

Guided Tour Use the Add New Hardware Wizard

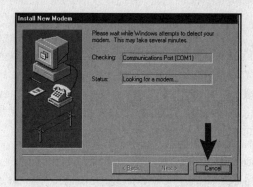

9 Windows checks your system and displays a status message. If Windows finds your component, it sets up the new hardware piece. You may be prompted to insert any necessary set up disks to install software for the hardware. Follow the on-screen instructions. If the component is not found, continue with the remaining steps.

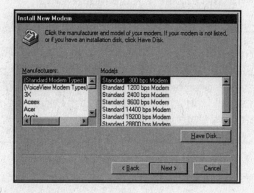

10 If Windows cannot detect your component, you can select it from the list that appears. This figure shows a list of modems; depending on the type of component you are installing, your list of options may be different. Select the manufacturer and model.

If the manufacturer isn't listed and you have a disk that came with the hardware component, click the **Have Disk** button. Then enter the drive and folder that contains the hardware files and click the **OK** button. (Check the instructions that came with the disk for precise instructions on installing the driver.)

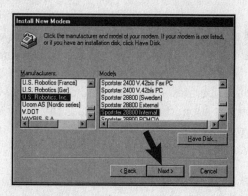

11 Click the **Next** button.

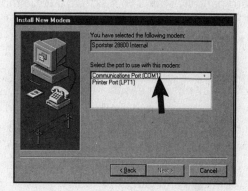

12 You may be prompted to enter other information about the component. For example, for a modem, you select the communication port to which the modem is attached (shown here). Make your selections and then click the **Next** button.

13 When the setup is complete, Windows displays a message to that effect. Click the **Finish** button.

Change a Mouse or Video Driver

Most hardware components rely on a software file, called a *driver*, to set up the hardware. The driver, for example, tells Windows how the hardware operates and what features the hardware component supports. Windows reads the driver each time you start Windows so that you can use your hardware component effortlessly.

One of the most touted features of Windows 95 is Plug and Play technology. This technology enables Windows 95 to detect most hardware devices. Windows 95 comes with more than 100 drivers and can automatically search your system and, in most cases, match the component you're installing with the correct driver.

If you purchase a little-known hardware component, Windows may not come with a driver for it. However, the hardware component should come with a disk that includes the necessary files. You can install the component using this disk. (See "Add New Hardware" on page [12TBD] for information on setting up new hardware.)

After you get the hardware set up, you may need to make some adjustments. For example, when hardware manufacturers improve their products (optimizing the hardware and adding new features), they include new drivers with the hardware. Therefore, you may need to update your driver.

Suppose the company that makes your monitor comes out with a new driver optimized to work with Windows 95. They distribute this driver via the online communication services. Then, to have the most recent driver, you need to install it through Windows. If, on the other hand, your current driver just doesn't work correctly, you need to try another driver. The *Guided Tour* covers how to install a display driver (used with the monitor) and a mouse driver.

> Microsoft introduced a new mouse called the IntelliMouse. This mouse includes features that software programs can use. For example, you can scroll using the mouse (not the scroll bars in the program window).

Begin Guided Tour   Change Display Drivers

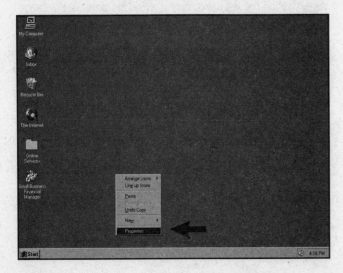

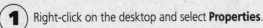

1 Right-click on the desktop and select **Properties**.

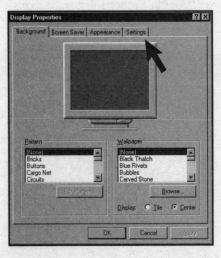

2 The Display Properties dialog box appears. Click on the **Settings** tab.

Guided Tour Change Display Drivers

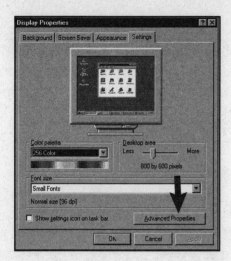

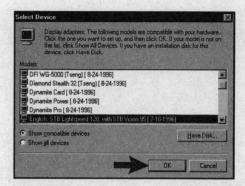

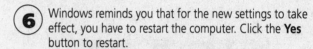

5 The Select Device dialog box appears. In this dialog box, Windows lists all compatible video drivers. If the driver you want is listed, select it and click the **OK** button. If you are installing a driver from a disk, click the **Have Disk** button, insert the disk, enter the drive and/or folder that contains the driver file, and then click **OK**.

3 On the Settings tab, click on the **Advanced Properties** button.

6 Windows reminds you that for the new settings to take effect, you have to restart the computer. Click the **Yes** button to restart.

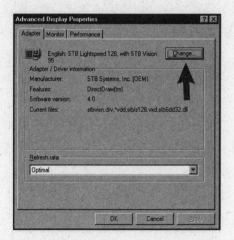

4 Windows displays the Advanced Properties dialog box with the Adapter tab selected. Click on the **Change** button.

Begin Guided Tour   Set Other Monitor Options

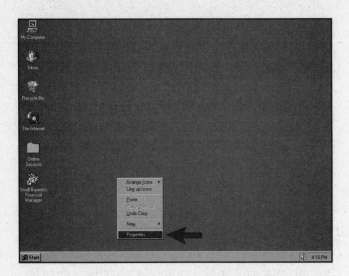

1 Right-click on the desktop and select **Properties**.

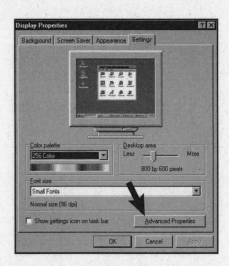

3 On the Settings tab, click on the **Advanced Properties** button.

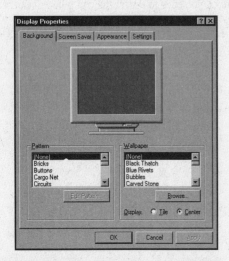

2 The Display Properties dialog box appears. Click on the **Settings** tab.

4 Windows displays the Advanced Properties dialog box with the Adapter tab selected. Click on the **Monitor** tab.

Guided Tour Set Other Monitor Options

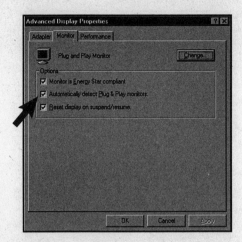

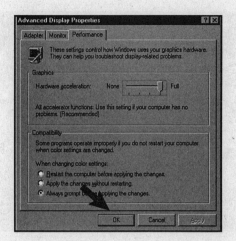

5 Check or uncheck any of the available monitor options. (The one you have available will vary depending on the type of monitor you have.)

6 To check or change performance options, click the **Performance** tab.

7 You see the Performance tab options. Make any changes. For instance, you can control whether the computer is restarted when you make color changes. Then click on the **OK** button.

Begin Guided Tour Install a New Mouse

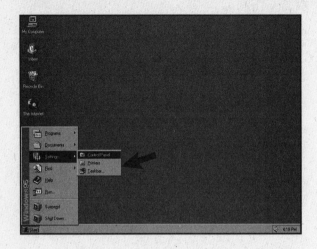

1 Click on the Start button, select **Settings**, and select **Control Panel**.

2 In the Control Panel group, double-click on the **Mouse** icon.

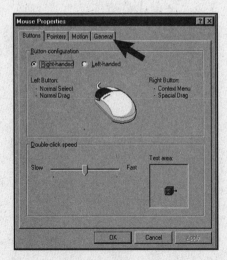

3 The Mouse Properties dialog box appears. Click on the **General** tab.

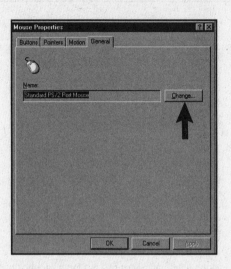

4 On the General tab, click on the **Change** button.

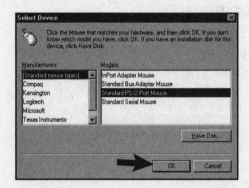

5 In the Select Device dialog box, Windows lists all compatible mouse drivers. If the driver you want is listed, select it and click **OK**. If you are installing a driver from a disk, click the **Have Disk** button, insert the disk, enter the drive and/or folder that contains the driver file, and then click **OK**.

6 Windows reminds you that for the new settings to take effect, you have to restart the computer. Click the **Yes** button to restart.

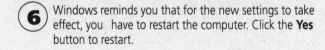

Display Disk Information

After you use your PC for a while, you'll see how you can quickly fill up the hard disk with files. If you're wondering how much space you had to start with or how much space is left, you can use the Properties dialog box to display a pie chart showing the total disk space and space used. This information can help you determine when you need to do some disk housekeeping (such as getting rid of old files, using a disk compression program, or defragmenting your disk).

Disk space is measured in bytes. One byte is equal to about one typed character. One thousand bytes equal a kilobyte, which is abbreviated K or KB; one million bytes equal a megabyte, abbreviated M or MB; and one billion bytes equal a gigabyte (G or GB).

Windows 95 now uses FAT 32 for handling hard drives. FAT 32 uses a different cluster numbering for data storage which allows the operating system to address a partition greater than 2GB (the old limit), and increases storage efficiency by reducing the minimum cluster size.

For information about changing the disk label, see "Format a Disk" on page 124.

Begin Guided Tour Display Available Disk Space

1 Double-click the **My Computer** icon to display the contents of your computer.

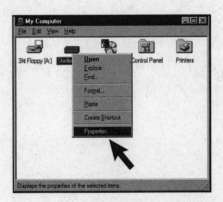

2 Right-click on the disk for which you want to display information. Select **Properties** from the shortcut menu that appears.

(continues)

Guided Tour   Display Available Disk Space   *(continued)*

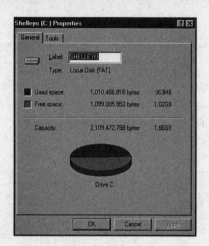

As a general rule of thumb, when the amount of disk space available is 20 percent or less, you should attempt to start freeing up hard drive space by backing up old programs and files and then deleting them from your hard drive.

3 The drive Properties dialog box appears. The General tab displays the name of the disk, the type of disk, and information about how much space is used and how much is available. When you finish reviewing the information, click **OK**.

Check a Drive for Errors

If you think of your drive as a filing cabinet, you can imagine how that filing cabinet can get out of order at times. For example, you may find a document loose in the cabinet and not know which folder it belongs in, you may find part of a document and not be able to find the rest of it, or you may find a folder labeled BUDGETS that contains newsletters. These are all signs that you need to spend some time getting the cabinet back in ship-shape order.

The same is true of your hard drive. Sometimes parts of a file get lost and are left floating around on the disk, and sometimes file names don't match up with the folders in which they're stored.

Use ScanDisk to Straighten Out Your Hard Disk

You don't need to know too much about how ScanDisk works because the program flags and fixes the errors automatically. If you are curious about disk errors, however, you need to know a little bit about how files are stored on a hard disk. Your hard disk is divided into little cubbyholes, called *clusters*. Clusters are further divided into *sectors*. All the clusters on one hard drive are the same size, but the size of clusters may vary from one hard drive to another.

When you save a file, Windows puts as much of the file as possible in the first cluster it finds. If the file won't fit into one cluster, Windows moves to the next available cluster and puts more of the file in it. This continues until Windows finds room for all the pieces of the file. The file allocation table, or FAT, keeps track of where the files are stored. When you open a file, Windows can go to the first cluster and get that part of the file, go to the second cluster and get that part of the file, and so on until it reads the entire file.

FAT32 allows the drive to have a larger File Allocation Table; therefore, the operating system can address a larger hard drive.

Select Scan Options

You can select the type of test you want to perform, a standard test or a thorough test. When you select a thorough test, you can control how ScanDisk operates by setting Scan and Advanced options. You can do the following:

- You can control what ScanDisk checks: the system and data areas, the system area only, or the data area only. The system area contains key information about your system and doesn't take a lot of room. The data area is the rest of the hard disk space and contains your data files. If you want to check your system area for errors, you would want to scan this area.

- You can choose whether ScanDisk checks the disk for read errors only or for read and write errors. When you save a file, the information is written to disk. When you open a file, that information is read from the disk. You can check for both types of errors (reading data or writing data).

- You can control whether bad sectors in hidden and system files are repaired. (You shouldn't be concerned if your hard disk has some bad sectors; that's common. But if you notice a pattern of increasing numbers of bad sectors, consider replacing the drive.)

- For advanced options, you can select whether ScanDisk displays summary information always, never, or only if errors found.

- ScanDisk keeps a log of the disk errors. Using the advanced options, you can control how the log file is handled: Replace log, Append to log, or No log.

- You can control what ScanDisk does (Delete, make copies, or Ignore) to fix a cross-linked file.

- For lost file fragments, you can have ScanDisk delete the files or convert the fragment to files.

- You can have ScanDisk check files for invalid file names and invalid dates and times.

Begin Guided Tour   Check the Drive

1 Double-click the **My Computer** icon to display the contents of your computer.

2 Right-click on the disk you want to check. Then select **Properties** from the shortcut menu that appears.

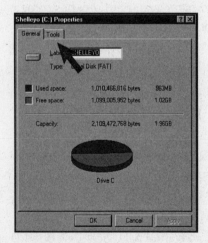

3 In the drive Properties dialog box, click the **Tools** tab.

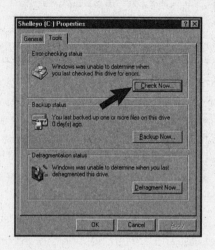

4 The Tools tab contains programs you can use to manage and optimize your disk drives. Click on the **Check Now** button.

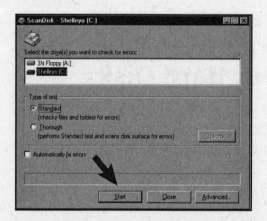

5 Windows displays the ScanDisk dialog box. The drive you selected in step 1 is selected here. (If you want to check another drive, select it from this list.) Click the **Start** button to start checking the drive.

Guided Tour Check the Drive

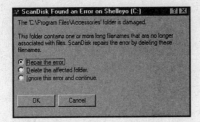

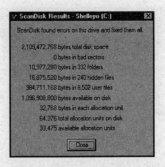

6 Windows checks your drive. If it finds any errors, it displays a dialog box that explains the error and gives you options for repairing the error, deleting the file, or ignoring the error. Select a correction method for each problem, and then click **OK**.

7 When ScanDisk is complete, you see a summary of its findings. Review this information and then click the **Close** button.

After you've corrected the errors on your drive, you can then use the Defrag program to improve its performance. See "Improve the Performance of Your Hard Drive," page 369.

Begin Guided Tour Select Checking Options

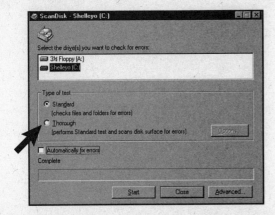

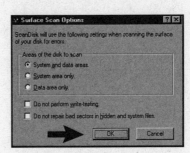

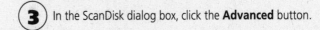

1 In the ScanDisk dialog box, select **Thorough** as the type of test. Then click the **Options** button.

2 The Surface Scan Options dialog box appears. Make your selections and click **OK**.

3 In the ScanDisk dialog box, click the **Advanced** button.

(continues)

Guided Tour   Select Checking Options   *(continued)*

4 Choose a correction method for each type of error, and then click **OK**. The ScanDisk dialog box reappears. Click the **Start** button to check the drive using these settings.

Back Up and Restore Files

The data on your computer is valuable. You may use your PC as your business center and store information about clients, orders, inventory, and so on. Your PC, then, is really the backbone of your business; without the information it contains, you would be lost.

As insurance, then, you should back up the data on your PC on a regular basis. Then if something goes wrong, you can use the backup files to restore your data. What can go wrong? Well, on a rare occasion, a hard drive does fail, and then the user can't access the information it contains. In addition, mistakes happen. If your spouse accidentally deletes your entire customer database and you don't have a backup, you are in real trouble. If you do have a backup, you simply restore the customer database files.

Backing up essentially copies all the files on your system in a compressed format to another drive. You can back up to floppy disks, to another hard drive, or to a special tape backup drive. Backups, especially complete backups, can take up a lot of space. If you must do a lot of backups, consider getting a tape backup unit. (Actually, when you run Backup for the first time, it attempts to detect and set up a tape drive. If you don't have one, select another drive to use as the backup.)

> If you get a tape backup drive later, you can have Backup detect it by opening the **Tools** menu and selecting the **Redetect Tape Drive** command. The **Add New Hardware** command does not work for tape drives.

Set Up a Backup Plan

When you do a backup, you can select which files (called the *backup set*) you want to back up. Which files you back up and when you back up are your

decisions. There are entire books devoted to helping you determine the best method for backing up your PC. Basically, you should set up a systematic backup plan and then follow it. The routine you should follow depends on your particular situation. Regardless, keep these tips in mind:

- So that you have a complete copy of all the programs and files on your PC, you should do a complete system backup. When you start the Backup program, this is the type of backup that is recommended.

- You don't have to do a complete backup each time you back up. You may want to do a complete backup once or twice a year or before you make any drastic changes to your system.

- After you make a complete backup, you may want to back up only key files at certain intervals (for example, at the end of the day, end of the week, or end of the month). How often you should back up depends on how critical the data is to you and your business. If you get daily orders, you may want to back up daily. If you use your PC a few times a week to create documents, you may want to back up once a week or once a month.

- As I mentioned, you can select which files to include in the backup set. Backup gives you several options for selecting files for backup: you can select files in certain folders, you can select files based on whether they have been modified, or you can select files by type.

- When you back up only the key files, consider rotating two sets in case something goes wrong during the backup. If you reuse the original backup set of disks and something goes wrong, you've destroyed your only backup copy. Instead, create one backup set and then use another set of disks or tape for the next backup. When you back up for the third time, reuse the first set, and the second set becomes the extra copy. Make sure you carefully label each backup set so you know its contents and the date of the backup.

- Be sure to put your backup copies in a safe place away from your computer. In case of some types of catastrophe (fire or theft, for example), you will want your backup copies in a secure location.

Select Which Files to Back Up

When you create a backup set, you can select which files are included. One way to do that is to select the individual files and folders you want in the Select files to back up list.

Initially, this list displays only the names of the drives on your PC. You can expand this list to display the folders by clicking the plus (+) sign next to the drive. When you click on +, Backup expands the view to show the folders. Any folder that contains another folder has a plus sign next to its name. You can continue to expand the list until you see the folder you want.

To select a folder, check the check box next to its name. When you do, Windows displays (on the right side of the window) a list of all the folders and files in the selected folder. By default, all the folders and files in that folder are selected. You can select or deselect individual folders or files by clicking in the check boxes next to their names. If all the folders and files within a folder are selected, a check mark appears next to the folder's name. If only some of the folders and files are selected, a check mark on a gray background appears next to the folder's name.

Creating a backup set by selecting folders works well when you keep all your files in one folder and want to make a quick backup. For example, if you were a writer and kept all your chapters in one folder, you could simply back up that folder. If your files are scattered around on the disk, however, you may need to use a different method.

You can use the Backup options to select a differential backup. With this type of backup, all files that have changed since the last full backup are automatically included in the backup set. As an alternative, you can select to back up only certain types of files. For example, if you were a financial planner and created mostly worksheets, you could choose to back up only that type of file and exclude the files you don't want to back up. The *Guided Tour* covers how to back up certain file types only.

Besides selecting files, you also can set options that control how the backup is made, as shown in the *Guided Tour*. You can choose from the following options:

Verify backup by automatically comparing files after backup is finished   If you want to be sure that the backup was done correctly, you can turn on this option. When you verify the backup, the procedure takes quite a bit longer (and backing up can take a while anyway), but it can be more than worth the extra time.

Use data compression   So that you can fit as much data on your tapes or disks as possible, you should have Backup compress the data as you back up. If you don't want the data compressed, deselect this option.

Format when needed on tape backups Before you can use a tape, it must be formatted. You can have Backup format the tape on-the-fly as you do the backup by checking this check box.

Always erase on tape backups   You can choose to erase the tape when backing up.

Always erase on floppy disk backups   You can choose to erase the floppy disk backups.

> To exit the Backup program after making the backup, check the **Quit Backup after operation is finished** check box on the Backup tab of the Settings-Options dialog box.

Restore and Compare Backups

When something goes wrong with your hard disk, you can turn to your backup set and restore the files. Restoring a backup is a lot like creating it: you select the drive from which to restore, and you select the files to restore.

In some cases, you may want to compare the backup sets with the original files to see whether the originals have been modified and therefore, whether the backup is up-to-date. You can use the **Compare** tab to compare a backup set with the original files. The *Guided Tour* covers restoring and comparing backups.

Begin Guided Tour   Do a Full Backup

1 Double-click the **My Computer** icon to display the contents of your computer.

2 Right-click on the disk you want to back up, then select **Properties** from the shortcut menu that appears. In the drive Properties dialog box, click the **Tools** tab.

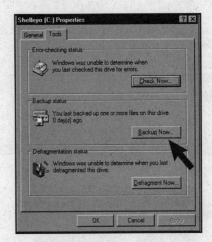

3 The Tools tab contains programs you can use to manage and optimize your disk drives. Click on the **Backup Now** button.

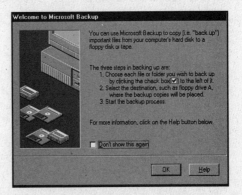

4 The first time you run Backup, you see the Welcome to Microsoft Backup dialog box, which explains the backup process. (If you don't want this displayed each time you use Backup, click the **Don't show this again** check box.) Click **OK**. You also may be reminded that Microsoft Backup did not find a tape backup unit. If you have one, you can have Microsoft detect it. If you don't, click **OK** to skip this message.

(continues)

Guided Tour Do a Full Backup *(continued)*

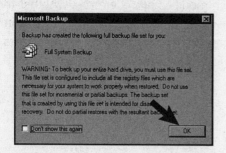

5 If you haven't made a complete backup of your system, Backup recommends this type of backup and creates a full backup file set. (If you don't want this reminder displayed, check the **Don't show this again** check box.) Click **OK**.

> If you cannot get Windows to detect the backup tape unit, you can manually install it. Refer to "Add New Hardware" on page 338.

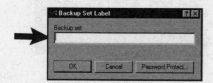

6 Backup prompts you to enter a name for the backup set. Type the name and click **OK**. (This name can help you keep track of the various backup sets you may keep.)

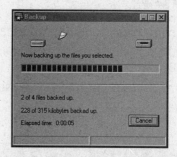

7 Backup backs up the system, and a dialog box appears, displaying the progress of the backup. You may be prompted to insert additional disks if you are backing up to floppy disks. When the backup is complete, you see a message saying so. Click **OK**.

> You also can click on the **Start** button, select **Programs**, select **Accessories**, select **System Tools**, and select **Backup** to start the Backup program.

Begin Guided Tour   Back Up Only Selected Folders Or Files

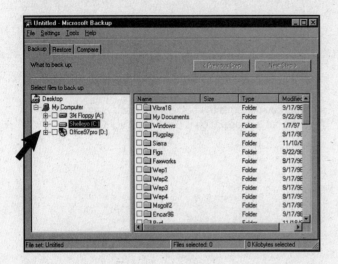

1 Start Backup. In the Select files to back up list, click the plus sign (+) next to the drive that contains the folders or files you want to back up.

2 The list expands to display the folders on that drive. Expand the list to see folders within folders by clicking on the plus sign next to the folder you want to see. When you locate the folder you want, click on the check box next to its name.

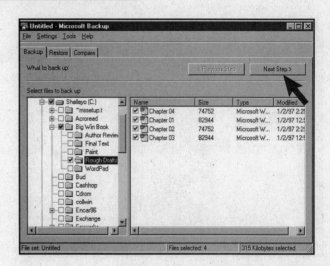

3 Backup selects the files for backup. When Backup finishes selecting those files, they appear listed on the right side of the window. You can uncheck any files you don't want to include in the backup. When you have selected the folders and files you want, click the **Next Step** button.

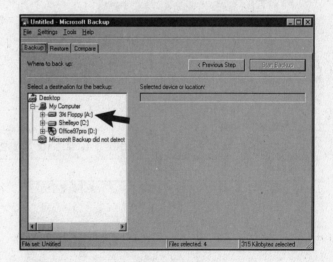

4 To select a destination for the backup, click on the drive to which you want to back up.

(continues)

Guided Tour   Back Up Only Selected Folders or Files   *(continued)*

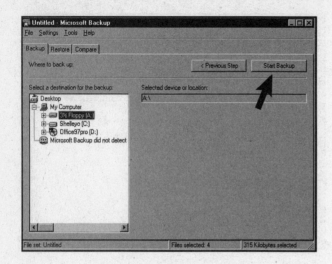

7 Backup performs the backup and displays a message when the backup operation is complete. Click **OK**.

5 Click the **Start Backup** button.

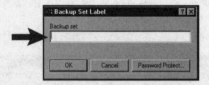

6 In the Backup Set Label dialog box, enter a name for the backup set and then click **OK**.

Begin Guided Tour   Select a Backup Type and Set Backup Options

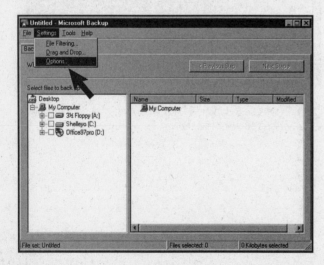

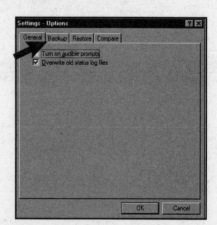

2 In the Settings-Options dialog box, click on the **Backup** tab.

1 Start Backup. Then open the **Settings** menu and select **Options**.

Guided Tour   Select a Backup Type and Set Backup Options

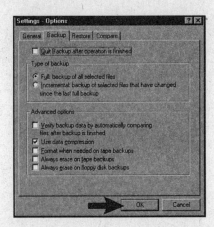

3 If you want to do a full backup, select **Full backup of all selected files**. To back up only files that have changed, select the **Differential backup of selected files that have changed since the last full backup** option. Make any changes to the advanced options, and then click **OK**.

Begin Guided Tour   Exclude Files from a Backup

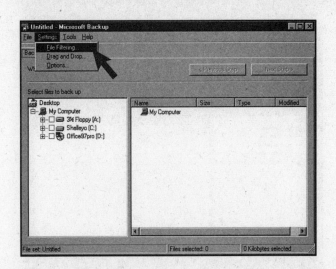

1 Start Backup and then open the **Settings** menu and select **File Filtering**.

2 The File Filtering - File Types dialog box appears. The File types list contains all the files that will be backed up. To exclude a file from the backup, select it in the list and click on **Exclude**. You can select more than one file type by clicking on each of the ones you want to select.

(continues)

Guided Tour   Restore Files

(continued)

4 Click on **OK**. Then make your backup as described in the previous set of steps.

3 (Optional) To exclude all files, click the **Select All** button. (All files are listed in the Exclude file list and the File type list). To add back the files you do want to back up, select the file types in the Exclude file types list and click on **Delete**.

Begin Guided Tour   Restore Files

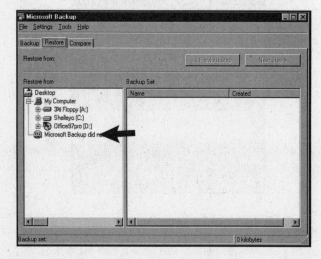

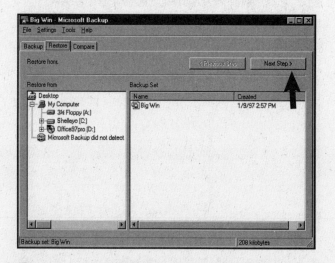

1 Start Backup. Then click on the **Restore** tab. In the Restore from list, click on the drive that contains the backup files.

2 If you backed up to floppy disks, insert the last disk of the set in the correct drive.

3 When you select the drive, Backup displays a list of the backup sets on that drive. If there is more than one set, select the one you want. Then click on the **Next Step** button.

Guided Tour   Restore Files

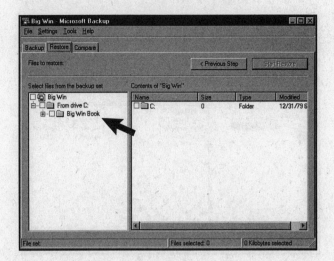

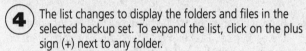

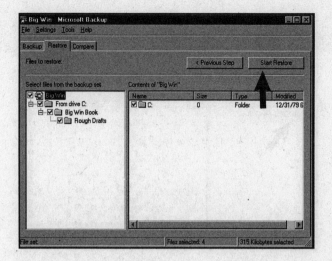

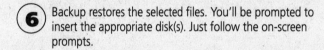

4 The list changes to display the folders and files in the selected backup set. To expand the list, click on the plus sign (+) next to any folder.

5 When the list is expanded, you see all the files included in the backup set. Files that are checked will be restored. If you don't want to restore one of the files, click in the check box next to its name. Then click the **Start Restore** button.

6 Backup restores the selected files. You'll be prompted to insert the appropriate disk(s). Just follow the on-screen prompts.

Begin Guided Tour   Compare a Backup Set

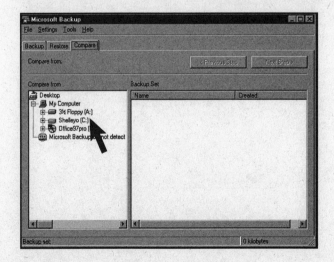

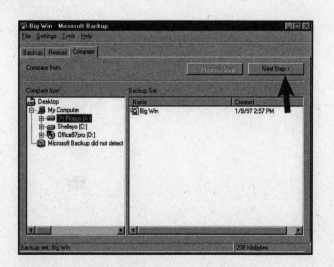

1 Start Backup, and then click on the **Compare** tab. In the Compare from list, click on the drive that contains the backup files.

2 Backup displays a list of the backup sets on that drive. If there is more than one set, select the one you want. Then click on the **Next Step** button.

(continues)

Guided Tour   Compare a Backup Set

(continued)

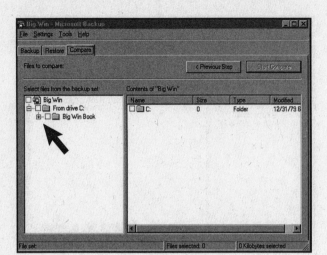

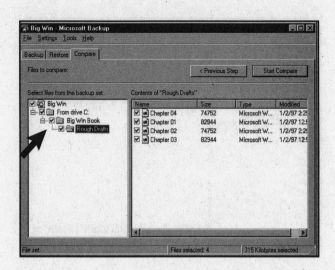

3 The list changes to display the folders and files in the selected backup set. To expand the list, click on the plus sign **(+)** next to any folder.

4 Backup expands the list, displaying all the files included in the backup set. Files that are checked will be compared. Click in the check box to deselect the file name of any files you don't want compared. After you select the files and insert disk 1 of the backup set (if necessary), click on the **Start Compare** button.

5 Backup compares the backup. If there are any errors (files that are different), you'll see a message asking whether you want to review the errors. Click the **Yes** button. You can then check the error log to review the compare findings. For example, if one of the original files is different than the backup, the log will contain a message to this effect.

Improve the Performance of Your Hard Drive

If you read the task on checking a disk for errors, you have some understanding of how a file is stored on disk. Basically, the disk is divided into individual cubbyholes called clusters. When you save a file, Windows goes to the first available cluster and stores as much of the file as will fit, then Windows goes to the next available cluster and stores the next part of the file there. This process continues until all of the file has been stored in clusters.

The first time you use a brand new disk, all the clusters are available, so Windows stores the file in contiguous clusters. As you use the disk more and more, the available clusters fill up. When you delete files, their clusters become available, and Windows may use these clusters to store other files or parts of files. The result of this process is that your files eventually become scattered throughout the clusters all over the disk. When this happens, we say the disk is *fragmented*; you may find that it takes longer to open a file for editing.

You can straighten up the disk and put the files back in order (and hopefully improve the performance of your drive) by defragmenting the disk. Therefore, Windows 95 includes Disk Defragmenter, a defragmentation program that reads the clusters on the drive and then rearranges them so that they are in a better order. As much as possible, Disk Defragmenter rearranges the files so they are stored in contiguous clusters.

If your disk drive seems slow, try running Disk Defragmenter as described in the *Guided Tour*.

> It's a good idea to back up your system before you make a major change such as defragmenting your hard disk.

Begin Guided Tour   Defragment Your Computer

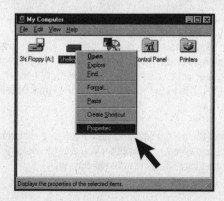

1 Double-click the **My Computer** icon to display the contents of your computer and then right-click on the disk you want to check, and select **Properties**.

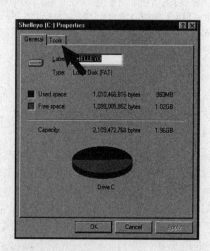

2 In the drive Properties dialog box, click the **Tools** tab.

(continues)

Guided Tour Defragment Your Computer *(continued)*

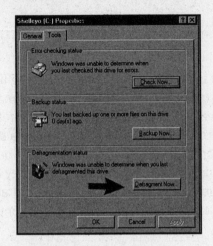

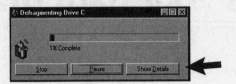

6 Windows displays the progress of the defragmentation process on-screen. To see a detailed map of the changes, click on the **Show Details** button and then click on the **Legend** button.

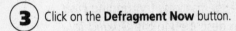

3 Click on the **Defragment Now** button.

4 Defrag analyzes the drive and displays the Disk Defragmenter dialog box. The drive you selected in step 1 is selected. (To choose another drive, click on the **Select Drive** button and then select the drive.)

5 The Disk Defragmenter also makes a recommendation on whether defragmenting is needed. If it is and you want to do so, click the **Start** button to start defragmenting the drive. (If defragmentation isn't recommended, click on the **Exit** button and skip the remaining steps.)

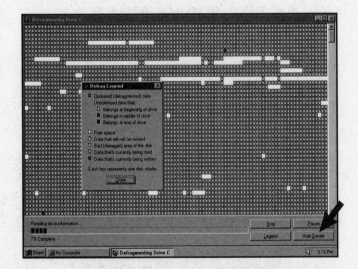

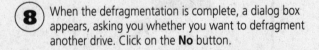

7 You see a map of the clusters on the system as they are being read and written. (You can see in the map, which clusters are free, which clusters are being moved, and which clusters are bad.) To hide the details, click the **Hide Details** button.

8 When the defragmentation is complete, a dialog box appears, asking you whether you want to defragment another drive. Click on the **No** button.

Display System Information

Want to know the nitty-gritty details of each of the components on your system? Want to find out how well your system performs? You can display this and other system information from Windows.

For most beginning users, this information is for review only. For example, you may forget how much memory you have on your system, or you may not know the type of processor you have. If so, you can display the system information to find out. You won't

usually need or want to make changes to any of the settings.

Expert users, on the other hand, might use this system information to make changes. For example, you might want to set up different hardware profiles. For complete information on such advanced features, check the online Help system or your Windows manual.

Begin Guided Tour   Look at the System Information on Your Computer

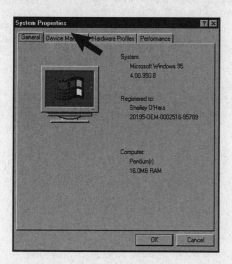

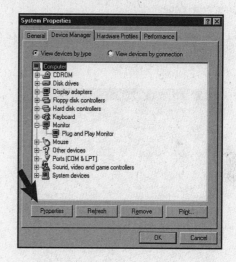

1 Right-click on the **My Computer** icon and select **Properties**.

2 The General tab of the System Properties dialog box displays information about the processor, memory, and Windows version. To see information about the devices installed on your system, click the **Device Manager** tab.

3 The Device Manager tab appears. To expand the list, click on the plus sign (+) next to any item.

4 Windows lists the installed devices for the selected category (monitors, in this case). If you want to display additional information, select the item and then click on the **Properties** button.

(continues)

Guided Tour Look at the System Information on Your Computer *(continued)*

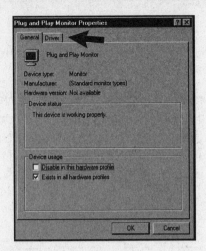

5 The device Properties dialog box appears with the General tab selected. This tab displays the device type, manufacturer, and usage.

6 To see information about the driver for this device, click the **Driver** tab.

7 You see information about the installed driver. Click **OK** to return to the System Properties dialog box.

8 To review hardware profiles, click on the **Hardware Profiles** tab.

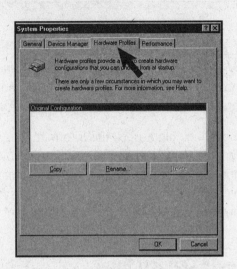

9 Use the options on the Hardware Profiles tab to create more than one hardware setup. This feature is commonly used for laptops with docking stations. (This topic is beyond the scope of this book.) Click on the **Performance** tab.

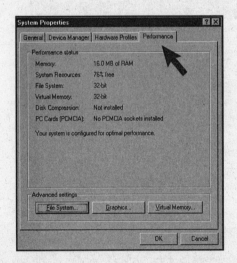

10 The Performance tab displays information about your PC's amount of memory, system resources, and other system information. When you finish reviewing the information, click **OK**.

HOW TO...

Use Windows 95 on a Network

A *network* is a group of interconnected computers, linked for the purpose of sharing files, programs, and peripherals. Through your office network, you can run programs, use printers, and edit files from other computers as if they were located on your own. You also can share your resources (your documents, programs, and printer) with others on the network.

A *server* is the computer on the network that manages the network's resources, such as the shared files, programs, and printers. A *workstation* is a computer (such as yours) that uses these resources. You can share some of your own files and programs and your printer if you want.

This section includes the following tasks, which will teach you the basics of using Windows 95 on a network:

What You Will Find in This Section

Log On and Off the Network

To connect your computer to the network so you can use its resources, you must log on. When you log on, you identify yourself to the network and establish a connection through which the network can direct the resources you request. During the logon process, you enter a unique password; this password protects both you and the network from unauthorized access. Your network administrator assigns your first password, but you can usually change it to something else if you want.

After logging on, you connect to the particular server that contains the resources you want to use. For example, a large company's network might include several servers: the Marketing server, the Human Resources server, and the Administration server. To connect to some of the servers in such a network, you might have to have an additional password; this makes certain information available only on a need-to-know basis. And just as you are allowed to log onto multiple servers, you can log off of a particular server without logging off of the network (which prevents you from tying up the server's resources when you're not using them). In the *Guided Tour*, you'll learn how to log off of a server and/or the entire network.

Most people log onto the network at the beginning of the day, when they start Windows 95. This method is considered the "primary" logon. However, if you use the network infrequently, you may prefer to log on only if needed, after starting Windows 95. To do this, you simply change what Windows 95 considers the primary logon method.

Occasionally, the system administrator must shut down the network for maintenance. Usually the

Keep in mind that during the process of logging on or off the network, your system reboots. Therefore, it can be inconvenient to log on after you've started Windows 95 and several programs because you'd have to close those programs before you restart the PC and log on (or off). If you decide to log off of a single server and not the entire network, you won't have to worry about restarting the PC.

system administrator sends everyone a notice letting them know that this is about to happen. If that's the case, you can quickly log off the network and continue working within Windows 95. However, you won't be able to continue using any network files or programs until you log back onto the network. If your network has several servers (such as Marketing, Personnel, and Sales servers), and one of the servers you're using is going down, you can log off of that one server without having to log off of the entire network. When you're notified that the network and/or server is back up, you can log back on. However, if you're logging back onto the network and not just a server, you need to exit out of your active programs first, because the logon process restarts Windows 95. If you're logging back onto a server, you won't have to worry about your computer restarting.

If you share your computer with someone else, you can easily log off the network so that he or she can log on and use your computer.

After you log onto the network, you can browse its resources with something called the Network Neighborhood. You'll see the Network Neighborhood briefly in the task "Log Off a Server," but you'll really learn how to use it later in "Use Files, Programs, and Printers on the Network" (page 375).

Begin Guided Tour Log On When You Start Windows 95

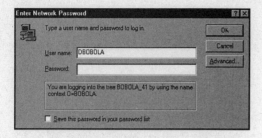

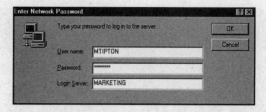

1 When you start (or restart) Windows 95, you see this logon screen.

3 On some networks, you also may be required to type the name of the desired file server. Then click on **OK**.

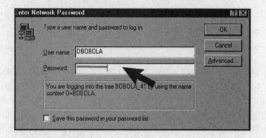

2 Type your password and click on **OK**. Windows 95 completes the startup process.

Begin Guided Tour Log On After Starting Windows 95

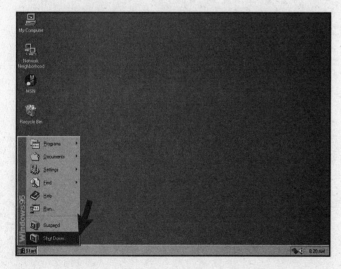

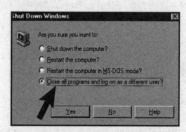

3 In the Shut Down Windows dialog box, select **Close all programs and log on as a different user?** and click on **Yes**.

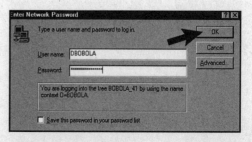

1 First shut down your active programs because this process will restart Windows 95.

2 Click on the **Start** button and select **Shut Down**.

4 After the system restarts, it presents you with the network logon screen. Type your password and click on **OK**.

Begin Guided Tour Change the Primary Logon Method

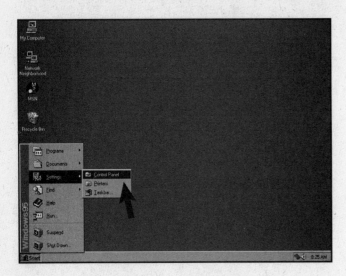

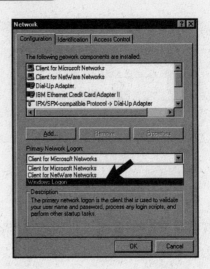

1 Click on the **Start** button, select **Settings**, and select **Control Panel**.

2 In the Control Panel window, double-click on the **Network** icon.

3 Open the **Primary Network Logon** list and select the type of logon you prefer. If you select Windows Logon, you aren't prompted with the network logon dialog box when you start Windows 95, but you can log onto the network at any time via the Start menu (see "Log On After Starting Windows 95" on page 369).

4 Click on **OK**.

Begin Guided Tour   Log Off the Network

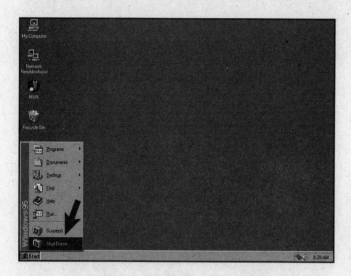

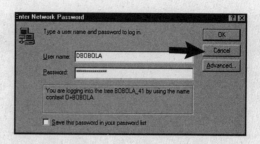

1 First, exit all programs. This is important because when you log off the network, your system will restart.

2 Click on the **Start** button and select **Shut Down**.

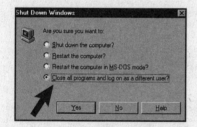

3 In the Shut Down Windows dialog box, select **Close all programs and log on as a different user?** and click on **Yes**.

4 When the system restarts, it presents you with the network logon screen. Do not type a password; just click on **Cancel**. Windows 95 restarts, and you are no longer connected to the network.

Although it seems strange, you must choose the "log on" option to log off.

Begin Guided Tour Log Off So Someone Else Can Log On

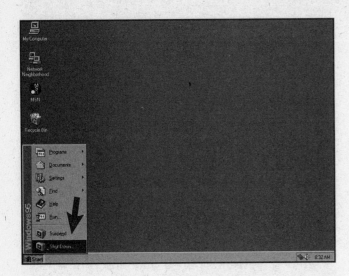

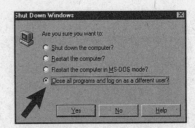

3 In the Shut Down Windows dialog box, select **Close all programs and log on as a different user?** and click on **Yes**.

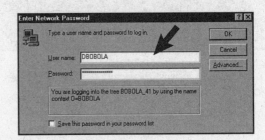

1 Exit all programs.

2 Click on the **Start** button and select **Shut Down**.

4 After the system restarts, someone else can log on.

Begin Guided Tour Change Your Password on a Novell Network

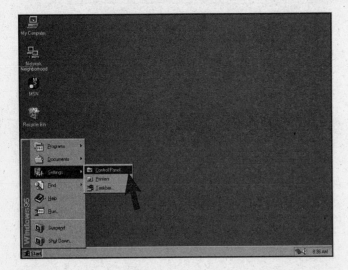

1 Click on the **Settings** button and select **Control Panel**.

2 Double-click on the **Passwords** icon.

Guided Tour   Change Your Password on a Novell Network

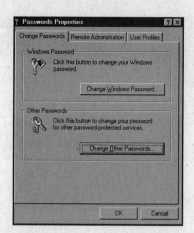

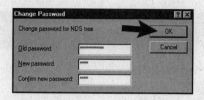

6 Type the desired new password, then press the **Tab** key. Type the new password again in the **Confirm New Password**. Click on **OK**.

3 Click the **Change Other Passwords** button.

7 If successful, click on **OK**. If something wasn't entered correctly, you will be returned to step 5 to try again.

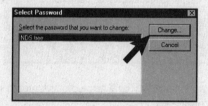

To change your password on earlier versions of a Novell network, click the **Start** button, select **Programs**, and select **MS-DOS Prompt**. Type **SETPASS** and press the **spacebar**. Type your old password, press the **spacebar**, and type your new password. Press **Enter**. Type **EXIT** and press **Enter** to return to Windows.

4 Select either the network tree or a specific file server. Click on the **Change** button.

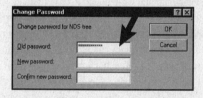

5 Type your current password in the **Old Password** text box. Press **Tab** to move to the **New Password** text box.

Begin Guided Tour Log Off a Server

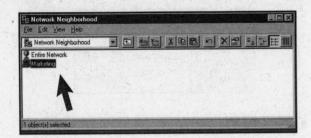

1 If necessary, double-click on the **Network Neighborhood** icon to open its window. Then, from the Network Neighborhood, select the server from which you want to log off.

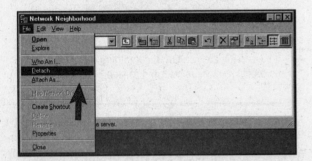

2 Open the **File** menu and select **Log Out**. On a Novell NDS (NetWare Directory Services) network, choose **Detach**.

3 Windows displays a dialog box prompting you to confirm that you want to log out. Click on **Yes**.

4 Click on **OK**.

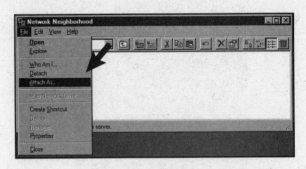

5 When you want to log back onto the server at a later time, open the **File** menu and select **Attach As**.

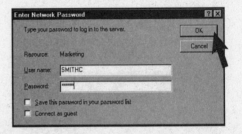

6 You might need to type a password to log onto this particular server. If so, type your password and click on **OK**.

You log onto a particular server by opening the Network Neighborhood window and double-clicking on the icon of the computer (server) to which you want to connect. You'll learn more about this process and how to use a server's resources (such as files, programs, and printers) in "Use Files, Programs, and Printers on the Network" (page 375). After you log onto a server, you can log off of the server (but not the entire network) by following the steps in this task.

Use Files, Programs, and Printers on the Network

The purpose of being connected to a network is so you can share its resources. So what does the network have that you can use? Well, you can use any file, application, or printer on the network that has been designated "shareable." Generally, the network administrator sets up an area on the server where shared programs and documents reside, and he designates the entire area as "shared," which means that anyone with access to the network can use these resources. In addition, you may have multiple servers (such as the Sales server, the Accounting server, and so on) across the network that are set up to share their various resources.

There may be some areas of the network to which you will not have access. For example, there might be a Personnel folder on the main server or there may be an entire server that is shared among the employees in the Personnel department, but that is not open for use by everyone. You won't get into trouble if you accidentally try to access a restricted area; there really is no way to tell if an area is accessible until you try. However, the system will prevent you from getting into anything you shouldn't.

To access network resources, you first open the Network Neighborhood icon on the desktop. The Network Neighborhood window shows the resources available on the network. The following icons appear in the resources list to indicate the type of resource:

 A server on the network

 A separate network attached to the main network

 A printer on the network

The Network Neighborhood window has a toolbar with buttons for commonly used commands. (If necessary, open the **View** menu and select **Toolbar** to display the Network Neighborhood toolbar.) To identify a particular button, move the mouse pointer over it, and a description appears.

If you prefer a more hierarchical view of the network (similar to that of Windows Explorer), right-click on a folder or the **Entire Network** icon and select **Explore**. In some cases, there are things you can only do from an Explorer-type window (use the **Find** command to search for a folder or file, for example). When this is true, I'll remind you to open an Explorer-type window as we go along.

> Keep in mind that programs you access through the network run more slowly than programs that are located on your own hard disk.

Besides using other network resources, you can share your own resources (the folders and files on your system and your printer). You learn how in "Share Folders and Printers with Others on the Network" on page 387.

Begin Guided Tour Use a File on the Network

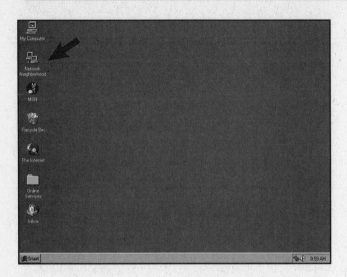

1 Double-click on the **Network Neighborhood** icon. (If you prefer an Explorer-type window, right-click on the icon and select **Explore**.)

2 Double-click on the **Entire Network** icon.

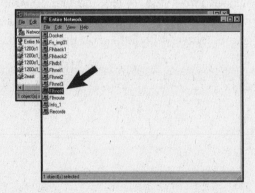

3 To see the contents of a particular computer (server), double-click on it.

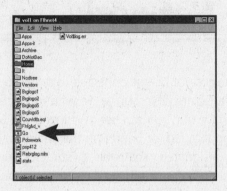

4 When you find a folder you want to open, double-click on it.

5 Continue opening folders as necessary to find the file you want.

Guided Tour Use a File on the Network

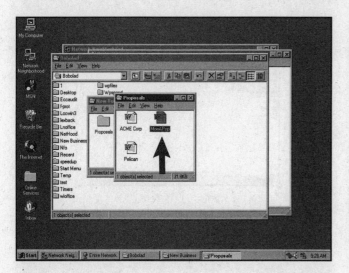

6 When you find the file you want, double-click on it.

7 If the file is associated with a particular program, Windows starts the program in which the file was created.

If you open an Explorer-type window, you can use the **Tools Find** command to locate your file if necessary. See "Locate Network Resources" on page 382.

8 If you plan to use this file often, you can create a shortcut icon for it in your Network Neighborhood by dragging the server icon to your desktop. When asked if you want to create a shortcut, click on **Yes**.

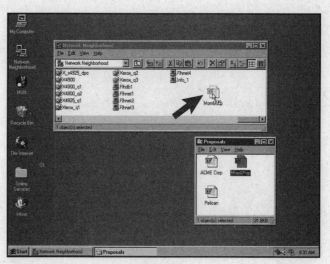

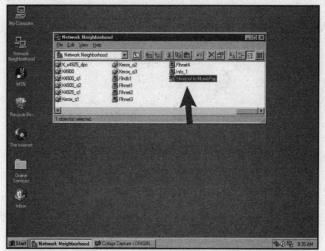

9 In the future, if you want to use the file again, just open the Network Neighborhood and double-click on the shortcut icon. It's much faster than searching for the file again.

If you can't see a particular computer (server), or have difficulty connecting to it, you probably do not have access to it. See your network administrator for help.

Begin Guided Tour Use a Program on the Network

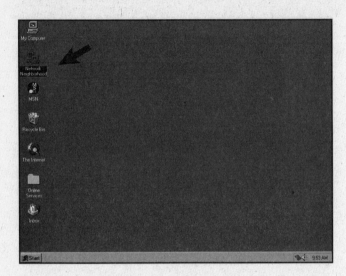

1 Double-click on the **Network Neighborhood** icon. If you prefer an Explorer-type window, right-click on the icon and select **Explore**. With an Explorer-type window, you can use the Tools Find command to locate a particular printer.

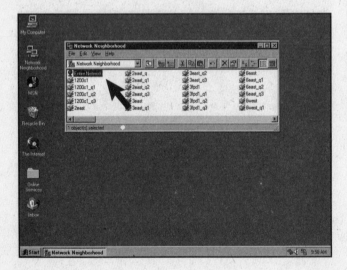

2 Double-click on the **Entire Network** icon.

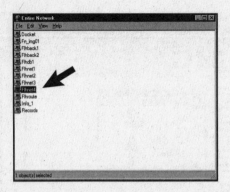

3 To see the contents of a particular computer (server), double-click on it.

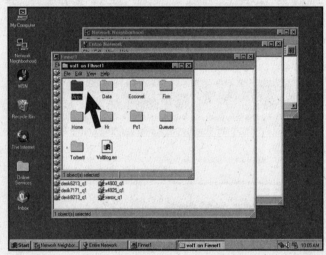

4 When you find a folder you want to open, double-click on it.

Guided Tour Use a Program on the Network

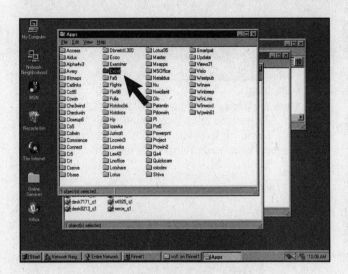

5 Continue opening folders as necessary to find your program.

6 Double-click on the program's icon.

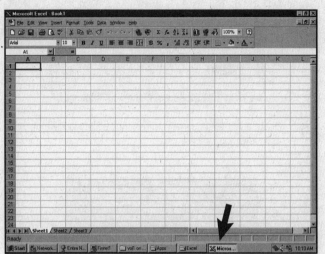

7 The program starts. Use it as you would a program on your own computer. However, keep in mind that the program runs slower than it might if it was actually located on your computer and not on the network.

8 If you plan to use this program often, you can create a shortcut icon for it within your Network Neighborhood by dragging its icon there. When asked if you want to create a shortcut, click on **Yes**. Then double-click this icon at a later time to restart the program.

Begin Guided Tour Use a Network Printer You've Never Used Before

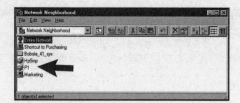

1 Locate a printer you want to use in the Network Neighborhood and double-click on it.

2 You need to know the brand of the printer you want to set up, and you need your Windows 95 installation disks for this task. Click on **Yes**. (If you don't have any, click on **No** and see your network administrator for help.)

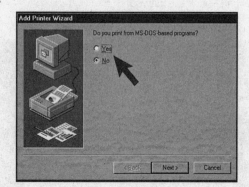

3 If you want to use this printer with your DOS programs, click on **Yes**. Click on **Next**. (If you choose No, you can capture a port later on so that printer will work with a DOS program. To do that, right-click on the printer in the Network Neighborhood and select Capture a Port.)

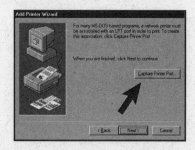

4 If you selected **Yes** in step 3 (to use this printer with DOS programs), click on **Capture Printer Port**.

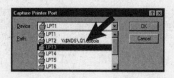

5 Open the **Device** list and select an available port. Click on **OK**. (The port you select here may need to match the port to which the printer has been assigned through the network. Again, see your network administrator for help.)

6 Click on **Next**.

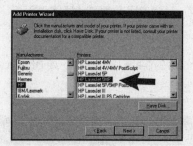

7 Select the network printer from the list and click on **Next**.

8 Type a new name for the printer if you want.

9 If you want to use the network printer as the default printer for your Windows programs, click on **Yes**. Click on **Next**.

Guided Tour Use a Network Printer You've Never Used Before

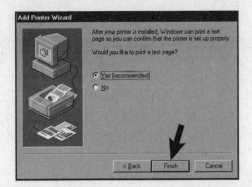

10 If you want to test the network connection, click on **Yes (recommended)** to print a test page.

11 Click on **Finish**.

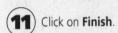

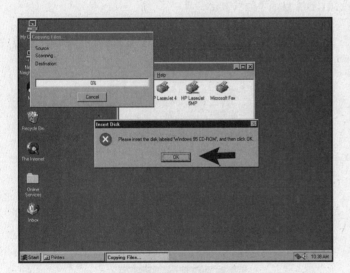

12 Insert the Windows 95 disk as instructed and click **OK**. Repeat for additional disks. If you have the CD-ROM version of Windows 95, place it in your CD-ROM drive now and click on **OK**.

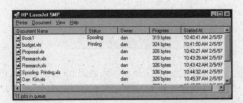

13 Windows 95 displays the status of the network printer. Now that you've set up this printer, when you double-click on its icon in the Network Neighborhood, you see this status screen. (It's a good way to see how busy a printer is before you send a document to it to print.)

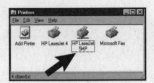

14 The network printer now appears in your Printers folder.

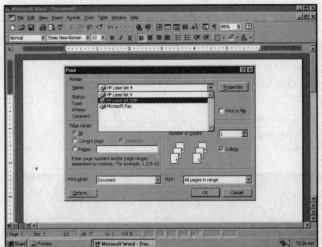

15 The network printer also appears in the list of available printers when you print from any application. So to use it, select the network printer from the list before you print your document.

For the network to print the output of a DOS program, it has to pick it up through one of your computer's ports. DOS programs can only print to an actual output port, not just some network connection. However, Windows programs don't work this way, so step 4 is only necessary for DOS programs.

Locate Network Resources

A resource is a shared file, program, or printer. To use a network resource, you must first find it. If your office network is large, finding the resource you need might take a long time.

To locate a particular file, folder, or computer on the network, you use the Find command. You can use the Find command from the Start menu as explained in the *Guided Tour*. Alternatively, if you open an Explorer-type window in the Network Neighborhood, you can use its Find command instead. (This command is located on the Tools menu.)

If you find a particular folder or computer that you'll probably use often, you can create a drive letter for it. This is called *mapping a drive*. After a folder or a computer on the network is mapped, you can access it by its drive letter just as you would any other drive. For example, you can view the contents of a mapped folder by clicking on its drive letter in Explorer or My Computer. You can disconnect or "unmap" the drive anytime you want.

Begin Guided Tour Locate a File or a Folder on the Network

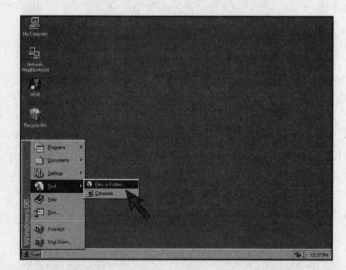

1 Click on the **Start** button, select **Find**, and select **Files or Folders**.

> You need to be logged onto the network in order to search it for a particular file or folder; if you've logged out temporarily, log back in before attempting this task.

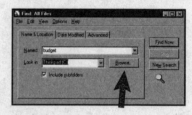

2 In the **Named** text box, type the name of the file or folder you want to find.

3 To indicate that you want Find to search over the network, click on **Browse**.

4 Expand the Network Neighborhood by clicking on its plus (+) sign. (Its plus sign changes to a minus (–) sign, as you see in the figure.)

Guided Tour Locate a File or a Folder on the Network

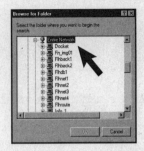

5 From the expanded list under Network Neighborhood, select a shortcut to a folder or a computer.

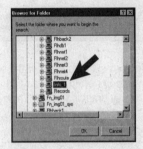

6 Select the folder or computer you want to search and click on **OK**.

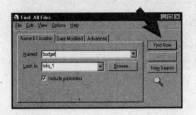

7 Click on **Find Now**.

8 After you find what you're looking for, click on **Stop** to prevent the search from tying up the network. If you use this file or folder often, add it to your Network Neighborhood by dragging it there. When asked if you want to create a shortcut, click on **Yes**.

Begin Guided Tour Locate a Computer on the Network

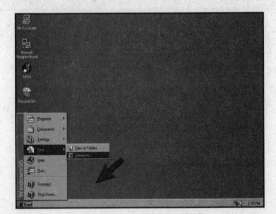

1 Click on the **Start** button, select **Find**, and select **Computer**.

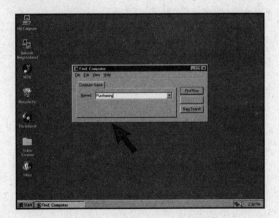

2 Type the name of the computer you want to find, such as **Purchasing**. If you've searched for this computer before, you can just select it from the **Named** list.

(continues)

Guided Tour Locate a Computer on the Network   *(continued)*

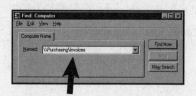

3 (Optional) If you want to look for a particular shared folder on that computer, type either the share name (ask the owner) or the shared folder's complete path, as in **\\PURCHASING\INVOICES**. (Note that you use two backslashes before the name of the computer, and one backslash before the name of the folder you're trying to find.)

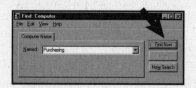

4 Click on **Find Now.**

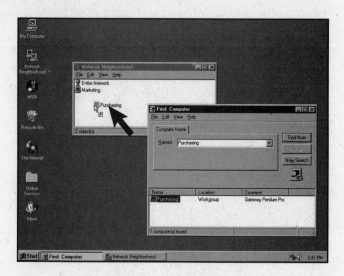

5 The Find dialog box expands to show the search results. If you use this computer often, you can add it to your Network Neighborhood by dragging its icon there. When asked if you want to create a shortcut, click on **Yes**.

If you're already in the Network Neighborhood, you can right-click on a folder you want to search (or the Entire Network) and select **Explore**. In the Explorer window, open the **Tools** menu and select the **Find** command to run the search from there.

Begin Guided Tour Connect to a Drive (Map a Drive)

1 Select the resource (the folder or computer) to which you want to assign a drive letter.

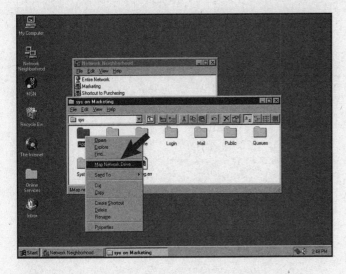

2 Right-click on the resource and select **Map Network Drive** (or click on the **Map Network Drive** icon).

3 Select **Reconnect at Logon** if you want this resource mapped to a drive each time you start Windows. Click on **OK**.

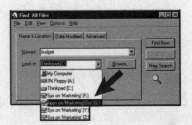

4 You can access the folder or the computer as you would any other drive. (For example, you can quickly search the folder by selecting it as you would a drive within the Find dialog.)

Begin Guided Tour Disconnect from a Drive (Unmap a Drive)

1 Click on the **Disconnect Network Drive** icon.

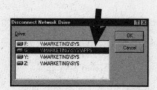

2 In the **Drive** list, select the letter for the drive you want to disconnect (unmap). Click on **OK**.

If you have problems with the network tasks, check out the Network Quick Fixes in Part 3 of this book. Use the Quick-Finder table to find your answers quickly.

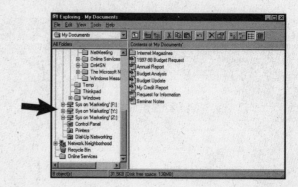

3 You can still use the resource, but there is no longer a drive assignment shortcut. In this figure, the drive letter shortcut no longer appears in Explorer. To view the contents of the folder, you have to use the Network Neighborhood.

Share Folders and Printers with Others on the Network

If you often create documents that others use, you can share them through the network. In addition, you might be able to share your printer. However, before you can share anything over the network, file and/or printer sharing must be enabled. If you attempt to complete the steps in the *Guided Tour*, and you find that sharing has not been enabled, see your network administrator.

After sharing is enabled, you mark which folders or printers you want to share. You can control who accesses your shared folders and the access level they have. You can assign one of three levels of access:

Read Only User can read the contents of files but can't make changes to them.

Full Access User can read and make changes to files.

Custom User's access level depends on his password.

How you control access depends on the type of sharing the network administrator set up for you through the Network icon in the Control folder. If the administrator set up user level access control, you assign access levels by user. This type of access is best if you only have a few specific people with whom you want to share a particular resource. If the administrator set up share level access control, you assign access levels by password. This type of access is best if you want to allow a larger, more diverse group access to the resource. All you'd have to do is give them the password. (If a new person joins the team, you don't have to specifically add her to an access list, you just give her the password.) Be sure to follow the correct task for the type of control access for which you've been set up: user level or share level. After you make an object available for sharing, its icon shows an open hand (a "shared" icon).

Begin Guided Tour Use User Level Access to Share a Folder

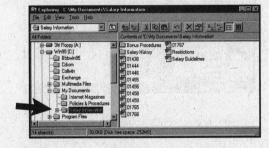

1 In Explorer or My Computer, select the folder you want to share.

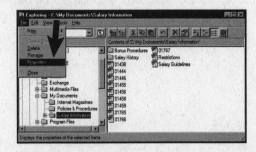

2 Open the **File** menu and select **Properties**.

(continues)

Guided Tour Use User Level Access to Share a Folder   *(continued)*

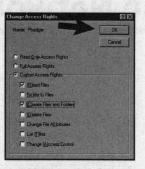

3 In the Properties dialog box, click on the **Sharing** tab. Click on **Shared As** to enable sharing for this folder and add a comment if you want. Click on **Add**.

6 If you choose Custom access for someone, this dialog box appears. Select the access level you want to assign. Click on **OK**.

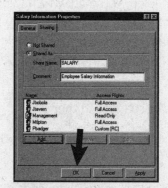

4 Select a user (or group) from the list and then click on the button that describes the type of access you want to assign. In the example, I selected **Mtipton** and clicked on **Full Access**.

7 Click on **OK**.

5 Repeat for additional users, and then click on **OK**.

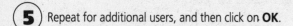

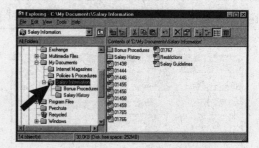

8 The folder appears with a shared icon.

Begin Guided Tour Use Share Level Access to Share a Folder

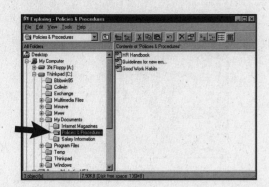

1 In Explorer or My Computer, select the folder you want to share.

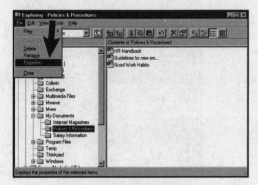

2 Open the **File** menu and select **Properties**.

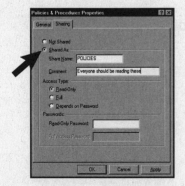

3 In the Properties dialog box, click on the **Sharing** tab. Click on **Shared As** and add a comment if you want.

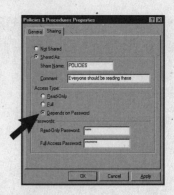

4 Select the level of access you want to give. If you choose **Depends on Password**, enter the password for each level: Read-Only or Full Access. Click on **OK**.

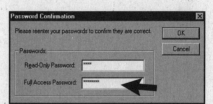

5 If you're using password protection, re-enter the passwords to confirm them, and then click **OK**.

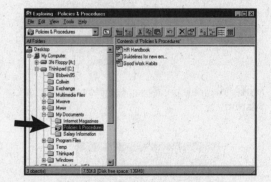

6 The folder appears with a shared icon.

Begin Guided Tour Use User Level Access to Share a Printer

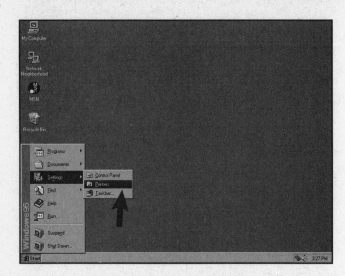

1 Click on the **Start** button, select **Settings**, and select **Printers**.

2 Right-click on the printer you want to share and select **Sharing**.

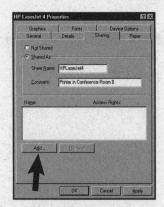

3 Click on the **Sharing** tab if necessary. Click on **Shared As** and add a comment if you want. Click on **Add**.

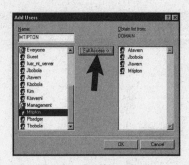

4 Select a user (or group) from the list and click on **Full Access**. (You either have access to a printer or you don't; unlike sharing a folder, there's only one level of access from which to choose.)

5 Repeat for additional users, and then click on **OK**.

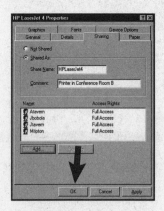

6 Click on **OK**.

7 The printer appears with a shared icon.

Begin Guided Tour Use Share Level Access to Share a Printer

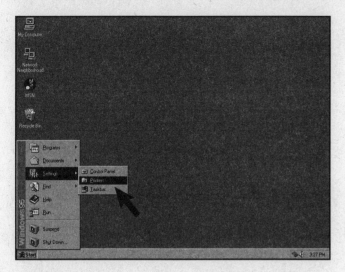

1 Click on the **Start** button, select **Settings**, and select **Printers**.

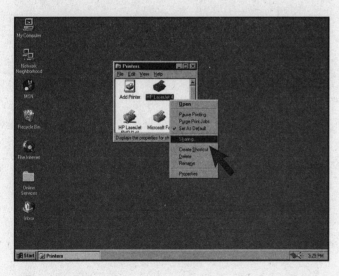

2 Right-click on the printer you want to share and select **Sharing**.

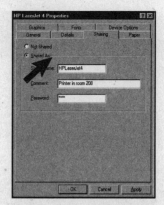

3 Click on the **Sharing** tab if necessary. Click on **Shared As** and add a comment if you want. Enter the access password and click on **OK**.

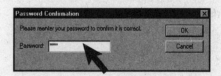

4 Re-enter the password to confirm it, and click on **OK**.

5 The printer appears with a shared icon.

Begin Guided Tour   Cancel Shared Access

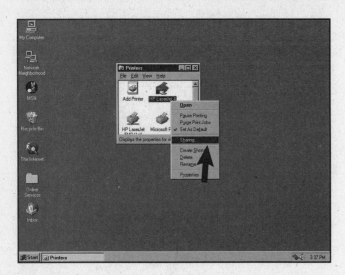

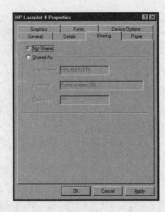

1 Right-click on the shared folder or printer and select **Sharing**.

2 In the Properties dialog box, select **Not Shared** and click **OK**.

3 The folder or printer's icon appears normal again (without the shared icon).

PART 2

Do It Yourself...

n the first part of this book, you learned how to use Windows 95 to copy, move, and delete files and folders, manipulate windows, and run programs. You also learned how to use DOS programs, how to send and receive e-mail and faxes, and how to use your network's resources.

Now that you are feeling comfortable using Windows 95, you're probably at a point where you're ready to try your news skills by creating some useful projects or by customizing Windows 95 so that it works more like you do. That's what this part is all about. Through simple projects, you'll learn how to get the most out of Windows accessories. You'll also learn how to create the perfect Windows 95 environment for your needs. Along the way, you'll learn the simplest and fastest ways to get things done.

This part is broken down into the following sections:

What You Will Find in This Part

DO IT YOURSELF

Get It Done with the Accessories

Windows 95 comes with several small but useful programs called accessories. In this section, you'll learn how to use these accessories to create several practical items, including a customized fax cover sheet, a résumé, and party invitations. The uses for these "freebie" programs are limited only by your imagination.

Let the following tasks be your guide to creating many useful projects with the Windows accessories.

What You Wili Find in This Section

Create a Custom Fax Cover Page

Although Microsoft Fax comes with several fax pages, none of them may suit your exact needs. However, with just a little effort, you can customize one of those pages to make it reflect your own style. For example, you can add a logo (if you have a scanned image stored in a file), or you can create a simple logo with the Paint accessory.

Of course, you can always create a fax cover page completely from scratch. But before you do, you might want to try this project, which makes simple modifications to the generic fax cover page.

Whether you decide to create a new fax cover page or customize an existing one, you use the Cover Page Editor. When you finish creating your new fax cover page, you save it in the same folder that holds all the other fax pages. Then, anytime you use Microsoft Fax to send a facsimile, you can find your customized fax page quickly.

In this project, you edit an existing cover page to customize it to your needs. You can also use the Cover Page Editor to create a fax cover page from scratch.

You'll find that using the Cover Page Editor is similar to using any other drawing or painting program (such as the ones that come with most word processors and spreadsheet programs). Each item in the cover page is called an object. When you click on an object, small black "handles" appear around it to indicate that the item is selected. After you select an item, you can do anything you want to it:

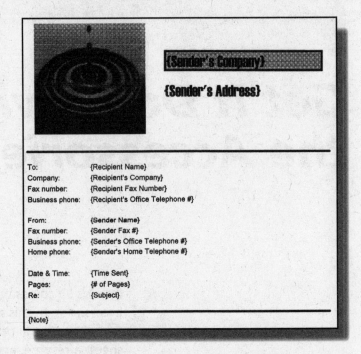

- You can delete the object by pressing **Delete**.

- You can move the object by dragging it somewhere.

- You can resize the object by dragging one of the handles inward (to make the object smaller) or outward (to make it bigger). To resize the object proportionately, press and hold the **Shift** key while you drag.

- You can change the object's characteristics (such as line width and color) by selecting **Line, Fill and Color** from the **Format** menu.

- You can change the characteristics of a text object; for example, you can change its font and add other attributes such as bold and underline.

Begin Do It Yourself Customize the General Purpose Fax Cover

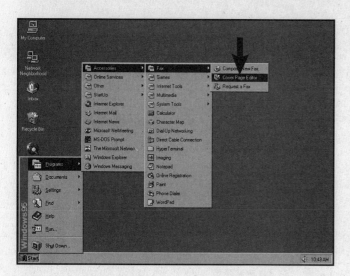

1 Click on the **Start** button, select **Programs**, select **Accessories**, select **Fax**, and select **Cover Page Editor.**

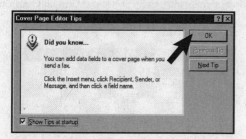

2 The first time you use the Cover Page Editor, you'll see a Cover Page Editor Tips screen. Click **OK** to move past it.

3 The Cover Page Editor window appears. Open the **File** menu and select **Open**.

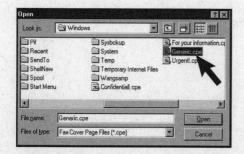

4 In the Open dialog box, change to the folder where you installed Windows (for instance, **Windows** or **Win95**) and select the **General purpose** fax cover from the list. Click on **Open**.

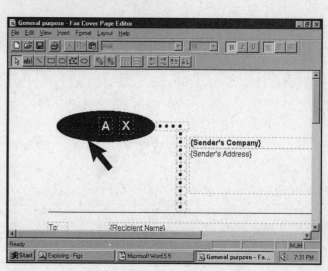

5 Click on the "**F**" text object and press **Delete**.

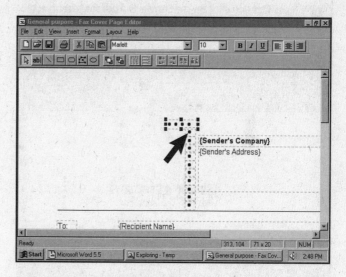

6 Repeat step 5 to delete the other objects that make up the Fax logo. (This includes the letters "A" and "X," the black oval, and the "dots.")

(continues)

Do It Yourself Customize the General Purpose Fax Cover *(continued)*

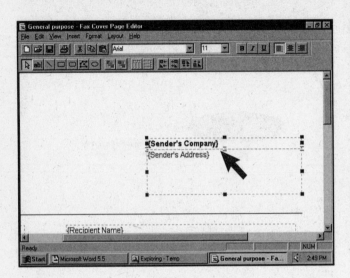

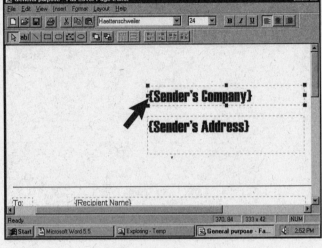

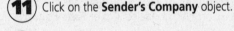

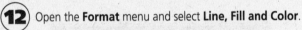

7 Click on the **Sender's Company** text object. Black handles appear around the selected object.

8 Press **Ctrl** and click on the **Sender's Address** text object as well. Both objects are now selected.

11 Click on the **Sender's Company** object.

12 Open the **Format** menu and select **Line, Fill and Color**.

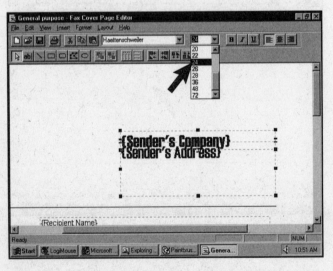

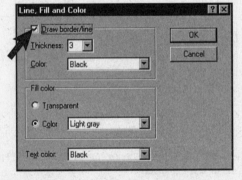

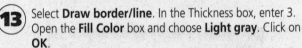

13 Select **Draw border/line**. In the Thickness box, enter 3. Open the **Fill Color** box and choose **Light gray**. Click on **OK**.

9 Open the **Font Size** list on the Style toolbar and select **24**. (You can also change the font style from the Style toolbar if you want.)

10 Move the two objects apart if they overlap. First click in the document to deselect the two objects. Then click on the Sender's Company object and drag it upward (away from the Sender's Address object).

Do It Yourself Customize the General Purpose Fax Cover

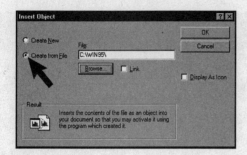

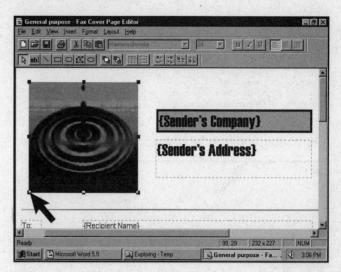

14 To add your logo, first click in the document to deselect the Sender's Company object. Then open the **Insert** menu and select **Object**.

15 Select **Create from File**, and then click on **Browse**.

16 In the Browse dialog box, change to the folder in which your logo file is stored and select it from the list. Click on **Insert**. Click on **OK**.

17 Click on your logo and drag it into position. Resize it by pressing and holding **Shift** and then dragging from a corner, as necessary.

18 Click on the line just above the Recipient's Name text object.

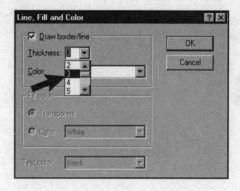

If you want to keep the original version of the General Purpose cover page in addition to your customized version, select the Save As command instead of Save, and give your version a unique name such as General Purpose with Logo or My Version of General Purpose.

19 Open the **Format** menu and select **Line, Fill and Color**. In the Thickness box, enter **3**. Click **OK**.

(continues)

Do It Yourself   Customize the General Purpose Fax Cover   *(continued)*

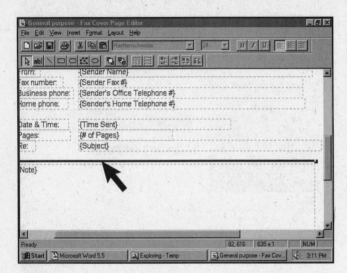

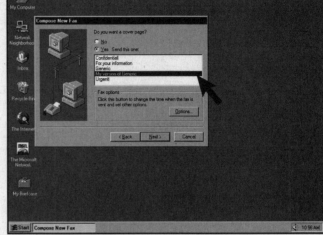

20 Repeat steps 18 and 19 on the second line, which appears just above the Note text object.

21 Open the **File** menu and select **Save**. Windows displays a message asking if it's okay to replace the old version of the General purpose cover page with your new one. Click on **Yes**.

22 Open the **File** menu and select **Exit**.

23 To use your fax cover page, select it in the Compose New Fax dialog box when you create a new fax. For example, select **General Purpose** from the list, or if you saved the customized page under another name, select that name instead.

See "Send or Receive a Fax" on page [10TBD] for more on sending faxes.

Record Your Own Voice

Windows 95 comes with many sounds; there's the "Ahhhhh" sound it makes when it starts up, and there's the "ding" sound it makes when it doesn't like what you're doing. There are even sounds that tell you when you receive new mail, when important information is displayed, and when the Recycle Bin is being emptied.

But with a standard sound card and an inexpensive microphone, you can add your own "voice" to these events. For example, you could record the message "Time to go home!" and save it in a file. Then you could have Windows 95 play that sound file when you exit. You could record other sounds and sayings as well and connect them to other events. You could record a "Happy Birthday," "We've missed you," or a "Congratulations on a job well done!" message and copy it to a colleague's computer.

Voice recordings aren't only for fun and games. For example, you can follow these same steps to record a comment on a report, and then you can embed the recording of your comments into the report document. The recorded comment appears in the file in the form of an icon. When you give the document file back to its owner, he or she can play back the comment file by double-clicking on the embedded icon. Of course, the recipient must have a sound card installed on his PC to hear the sound file.

You can also include your "Happy Birthday" or other special message in an e-mail to a coworker using the same embedding technique. Or, as another example of a business use for sound, you could design a spreadsheet with several charts illustrating your department's expenditures and sales over the past year. Then to make the chart easier to understand, you can embed a voice file in which you include a detailed explanation of each chart. Embedded sound files can also prove to be a valuable aid for training a new employee.

To record your voice, you need a sound card (such as SoundBlaster) and a microphone. See "Add New Hardware" on page 338 for details on installing your sound card. The microphone does not have to be fancy (as a matter of fact, you can get one at Radio Shack for about six dollars). The microphone is connected to your PC through a jack at the back of the sound card itself. After you've installed your sound card and connected the microphone, follow these steps to record your voice in a file.

Begin Do It Yourself Use the Sound Recorder

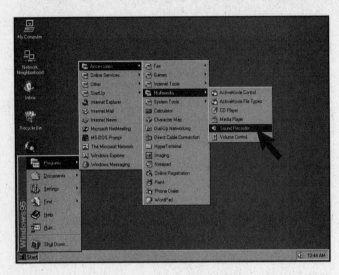

1 Click on the **Start** button, select **Programs**, select **Accessories**, select **Multimedia**, and select **Sound Recorder**.

2 In the Sound Recorder window, open the **Edit** menu and select **Audio Properties**.

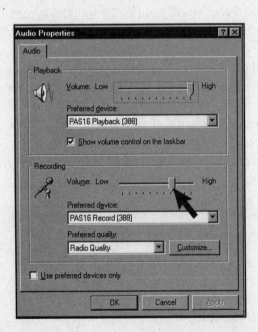

3 The Audio Properties dialog box appears. Adjust the recording volume level by dragging the level left (toward Low) or right (toward High). Then click **OK**.

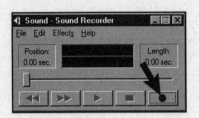

4 Click on the **Record** button and record your message.

5 When you finish, click on the **Stop** button.

6 To review your recording, click on the **Seek To Start** button.

7 Click on **Play**, and Sound Recorder plays back the message.

Do It Yourself   Use the Sound Recorder

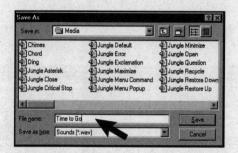

8 Open the **File** menu and select **Save**. Change to the **MEDIA** folder in the folder where Windows is installed, type a name for your sound file, and click **Save**.

9 To record another file, open the **File** menu and select **New**.

Connect to an Internet Server with Dial-Up Networking

As you learn in "Dial Up Your Network at Work" (page 500), Dial-Up Networking enables you to connect to your network at work from a remote location (such as your home) or through a laptop while you're away on a business trip. As you learn in this task, the Dial-Up Networking program can also function as an Internet connector. With Dial-Up Networking and a modem, you can connect to the Internet through an Internet service provider (a company that provides access to the Internet for a fee). Or using Dial-Up Networking and your network card, you can access the Internet through a direct connection (a connection to the Internet through your office network).

If your office doesn't have a direct connection to the Internet and you don't already have an Internet account with a service provider, remember to check out all your alternatives. You can connect to the Internet through the Microsoft Network, as well as many other popular online services such as America Online and PRODIGY. So if you use one of these services, you might not want to pay extra to connect to the Internet through an Internet service provider.

If you do sign up with an Internet service provider, be sure that it gives you the following information, which you need to configure Dial-Up Networking. You need to obtain much of this same information from your system administrator to connect to the Internet through a direct network connection:

- Your username and password
- The phone number you need to call to connect to the service
- Your host and domain name

- DNS server address

- A gateway address. (If you've been using Winsock under Windows 3.1, this is listed as the Default Gateway on the Setup screen.)

- IP address and subnet mask (if necessary). Many Internet providers assign you an address at the time you connect "dynamically," which enables them to service more users with a smaller number of actual Internet connections. But it's possible that your provider might assign you a permanent or dedicated address. An IP address consists of a series of numbers such as 198.70.144.66. Most subnet masks are 255.255.255.0, but yours might be different.

- Compression. If you have a SLIP Internet account (as opposed to a PPP account), you need to know whether the provider uses compression (known as CSLIP).

- Terminal window. You need to know whether you'll need a terminal window displayed after you connect.

You must have the Dial-Up Networking component installed to complete this project. If you need to install it, see "Add and Remove Windows 95 Components" on page 476.

The steps to set up Dial-Up Networking to connect to the Internet are pretty complex. Here's a breakdown of what you're going to do to set up your connection:

1. Add the TCP/IP protocol.

2. Enter your specific Internet account information.

3. Configure the Dial-Up Networking program.

4. Test your connection.

(**Begin Do It Yourself**   Perform the Setup for the Internet Connection)

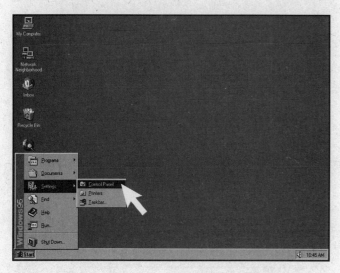

1 Click on the **Start** button, select **Settings**, and select **Control Panel**.

2 In the Control Panel window, double-click on the **Network** icon.

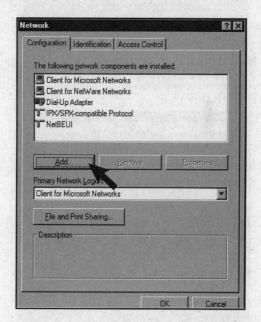

The Network dialog box appears. Click on the **Add** button. (If you have already installed the TCP/IP protocol, skip to step 6.)

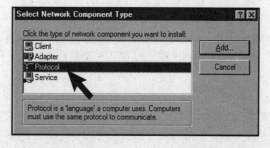

4 Select **Protocol** from the list and click on **Add**.

(continues)

Do It Yourself Perform the Setup for the Internet Connection *(continued)*

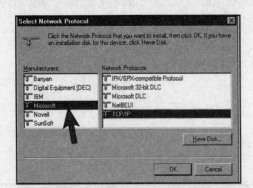

5 In the Select Network Protocol dialog box, select **Microsoft** from the Manufacturers list. Under Network Protocols, select **TCP/IP**. Click **OK**.

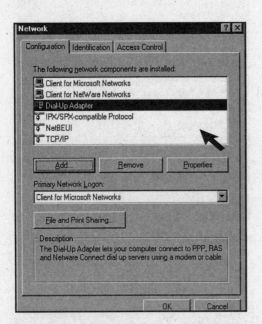

6 If you plan to use a dial-up connection, select **Dial-Up Adapter** from the network components list. To use a direct network connection, select your **network adapter** instead. Click on **Properties**.

If you have a network card installed, and you are not connecting through your network but through a service provider, you should change the Properties settings of the network card so that TCP/IP is not selected on the Bindings tab.

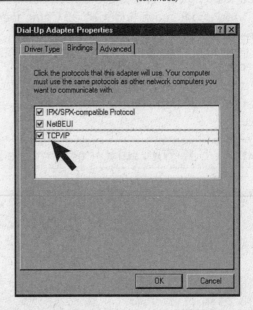

7 The Dial-Up Adapter Properties dialog box appears. Click on the **Bindings** tab and make sure the **TCP/IP** option is selected. Click **OK**.

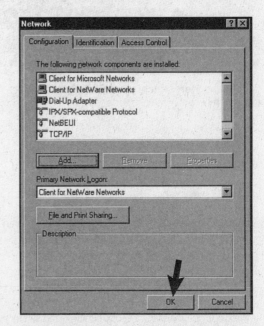

8 Click on **OK** to close the Network dialog box. You'll need to restart your PC to put your changes into effect.

9 Still in the Control Panel, double-click on the **Network** icon.

Do It Yourself Perform the Setup for the Internet Connection

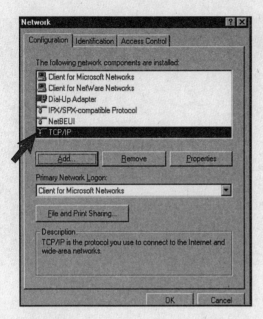

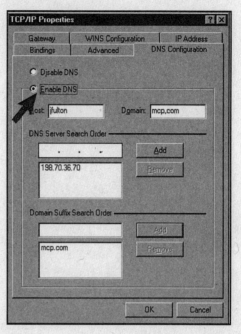

10 Select **TCP/IP** from the network components list and click on **Properties**.

11 In the TCP/IP Properties dialog box, click on the **IP Address** tab.

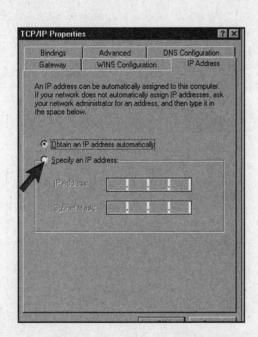

12 Click on **Obtain an IP address automatically**. Or if your service provider for your network connection provided an actual address, click on **Specify an IP address** and enter the IP address and subnet mask.

13 Click on the **DNS Configuration** tab and select **Enable DNS**.

14 Enter the **Host** and **Domain** names you were given. This is probably your Internet address. For example, the Host might be jfulton and the Domain might be mcp.com.

15 Under DNS Server Search Order, enter the DNS server address. If you're not sure, you could try 128.95.1.4, which is common. Click on **Add** to add it. Repeat for additional DNS servers.

16 Under Domain Suffix Search Order, enter the Domain name again, as in mcp.com. Click on **Add** to add it. Repeat for additional domains.

If you are connecting through your network, you may not need to configure DNS. Check with your system administrator.

(continues)

Do It Yourself Perform the Setup for the Internet Connection *(continued)*

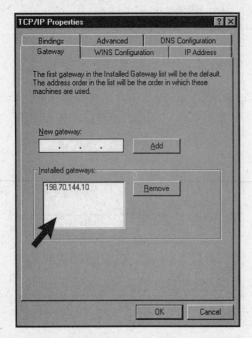

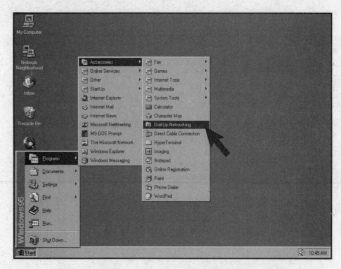

18 Click on the **Gateway** tab.

19 In the **Installed gateways** box, enter the gateway address.

20 Click on **OK**.

22 Click on the **Start** button, select **Programs**, select **Accessories**, and select **Dial-Up Networking**.

23 The Welcome to Dial-Up Networking screen should appear. If necessary, double-click on the **Make New Connection** icon.

If you have a SLIP account, you need to install support for SLIP before continuing. Skip to "Add SLIP Support" on page [14TBD], and then return here to set up Dial-Up Networking.

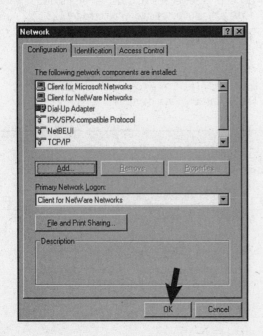

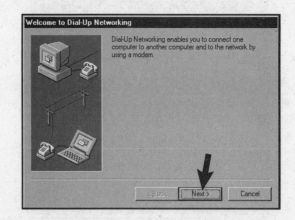
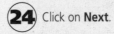

24 Click on **Next**.

21 Click on **OK**.

Do It Yourself Perform the Setup for the Internet Connection

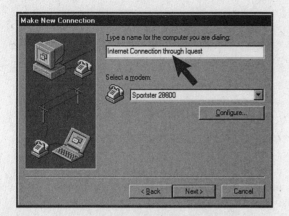

25 Enter a name for your new connection, such as "Internet Connection." Click on **Next**.

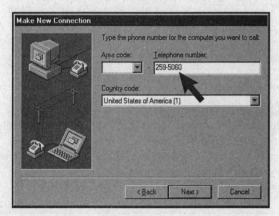

26 Enter the phone number of your service provider. If you're connecting through your network, just enter any number—it will be ignored. Click on **Next**.

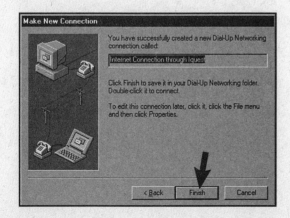

27 Click on **Finish**. Windows adds an icon for the new connection to the Dial-Up Networking folder.

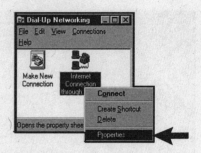

28 Right-click on your new icon and select **Properties** from the shortcut menu that appears.

You can also access Dial-Up Networking by double-clicking on the **Dial-Up Networking** icon in the My Computer folder.

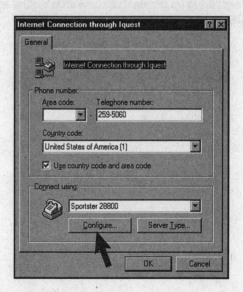

29 If your service provider told you that you would need a terminal window displayed after you connect, click on **Configure**.

(continues)

Do It Yourself Perform the Setup for the Internet Connection *(continued)*

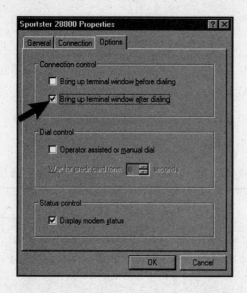

 In the Properties dialog box, click on the **Options** tab. Select **Bring up terminal window after dialing** and click **OK**.

31 Click on **Server Type**, and the Server Types dialog box appears. In the **Type of Dial-Up Server** list, select **PPP**, **SLIP**, or **CSLIP** (if your service provider told you to use SLIP compression). If you're connecting through your network, select **Netware Connect**. Click on **OK**.

Be sure to ask for a PPP account (which Windows 95 supports) from your service provider. If you want to use a SLIP account instead, you must install the SLIP support from the Windows 95 CD-ROM. See "Add SLIP Support" on page 429.

Begin Do It Yourself   Add SLIP Support

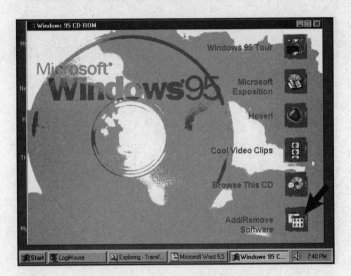

1 Insert the Windows 95 CD. The Windows 95 CD-ROM dialog box appears.

2 Click on **Add/Remove Software**.

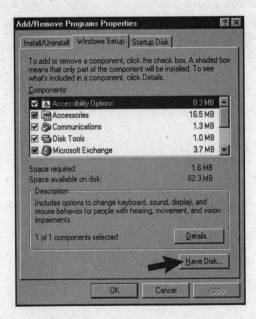

3 In the Add/Remove Program Properties dialog box, click on **Have Disk**.

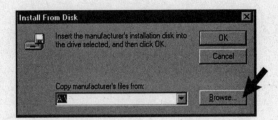

4 Click on **Browse**.

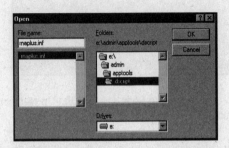

5 Change to the **Admin\Apptools\Dscript** folder.

6 Select the **RNAPLUS.INF** file and click on **OK**.

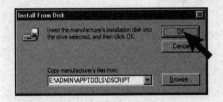

7 Click on **OK**.

(continues)

Do It Yourself Add SLIP Support *(continued)*

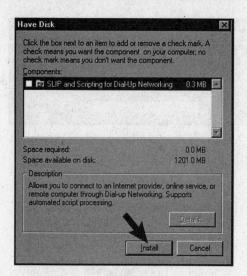

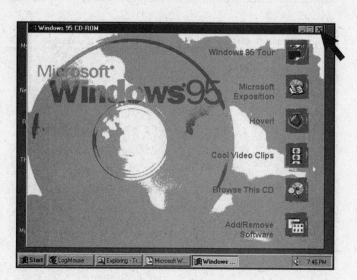

8 Select the **SLIP and Scripting for Dial-Up Networking** option and click on **Install**.

10 Close the Windows 95 CD-ROM dialog box.

If you have any problems connecting to the Internet, check out the *Quick Fixes* in Part 3 of this book. Use the Quick-Finder table to find your solutions fast.

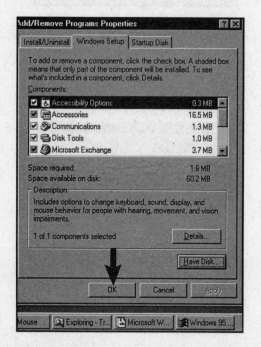

9 Click on **OK**.

Do It Yourself   Connect to the Internet with Dial-Up Networking

1 To connect to the Internet, double-click on your new icon in the Dial Up Networking folder.

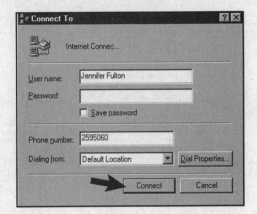

2 If you selected to display a terminal window, do not enter your login name and password; you'll enter them through the window itself. Otherwise, enter them now and click on **Connect**.

3 If a terminal window appears, enter your Username and Password. (The password will not appear on-screen.)
If you are using a SLIP or CSLIP connection, continue to step 4. Otherwise, click on Continue and skip to step 6.

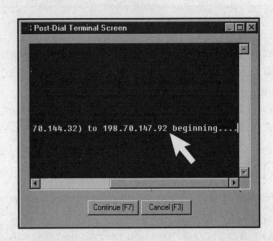

4 Use the scroll bars if necessary to see the IP address to which you've been assigned. Write this number down and click on **Continue**.

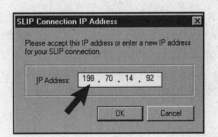

5 Enter the IP address you wrote down and click **OK**.

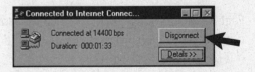

6 You should now have a working connection. At this point, you can use any Internet programs you have (such as Netscape, Mosaic, FTP, or Gopher). When you finish, click on **Disconnect**.

Create an Attractive Résumé

Because a résumé is your most important means of communicating with a prospective employer, you should make yours the best it can be. With Windows 95's WordPad program and a laser printer, you're off to a good start. And because your résumé is on your computer, you'll be able to make quick changes to target different employers.

> If you want to review the basic procedures for using WordPad before you begin your résumé, see "Create a Document in WordPad" on page 161.

The format presented here produces a résumé that is both attractive and easy to read. You can follow these steps to complete a similar résumé. If, on the other hand, you decide to create your own résumé style, follow these simple guidelines to produce the best possible results:

- Limit your résumé to one page. At most, an employer spends only ten seconds glancing over its contents. He or she would probably never look at the second page.

- Feel free to leave out extra information (such as personal activities, organizations, and references) if it doesn't fit.

- Focus on specific, *measurable* accomplishments. Emphasize numbers such as dollars saved, revenues gained, number of personnel managed, or increases in production.

- Use active words when describing what you've done, such as "managed," "demonstrated," or "created."

- In terms of design, keep it simple. Stick to one or two fonts at most.

- Use bold formatting effectively to draw the eye toward important information.

- Proofread your résumé! Nothing leaves a worse impression than a misspelled word.

- Print your résumé on a laser printer using high-quality paper stock.

Meghan Ryan

3286 North Strater Avenue ● Little Town, Ohio 56780 ● (513) 455-6721

Objective

A challenging position in the communications field which will utilize my skill as an effective manager with a thorough knowledge of marketing technique.

Education

Miami University
Miami, Ohio
Bachelor of Science, Telecommunications, 1982

Indiana University
Bloomington, Indiana
Doctorate, 1984

Experience

Bowton Industrials
Director of Communications
October 1992 to Present
Managed a team of 30. Introduced several successful campaigns which resulted in a 20% increase in market share. Decreased department budget by 5%.

Debbington Communications, Inc.
Marketing Manager
July 1989 to October 1992
Managed a team of 15. Reorganized department, resulting in a 25% increase in response to internal needs. Expanded the responsiblities of the department to cover all areas of marketing, including packaging, advertising, and marketing surveys.

Bradford Advertising Agency
Marketing Assistant
February 1987 to July 1989
As marketing assistant, I initiated a successful campaign for a major computer reseller which resulted in a 35% increase in sales. Handled several large accounts totalling over $125,000 in business annually.

Direct Marketing, Inc.
Manager of Client Relations
March 1985 to February 1987
Managed a team of 35 free-lance assistants. Coordinated an average of 50 direct marketing campaigns a month.

Begin Do It Yourself   Use WordPad to Create a Résumé

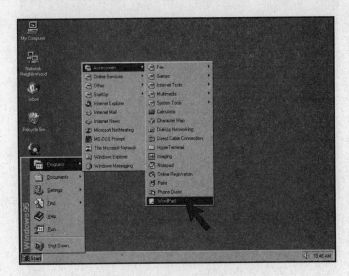

1 Click on the **Start** button, select **Programs**, select **Accessories**, and select **WordPad**.

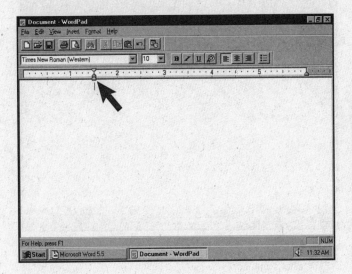

2 Drag the left indent marker on the ruler to the 1 1/2-inch mark.

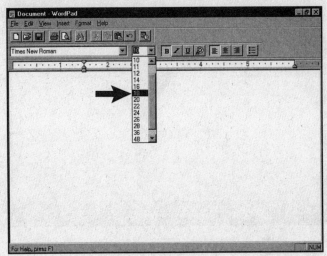

3 Open the **Font Size** list on the formatting toolbar and change the font size to **18**. Click on the **Bold** button.

4 Type your name and press **Enter**.

5 Change the point size to **9**. Click on the **Bold** button to turn it off.

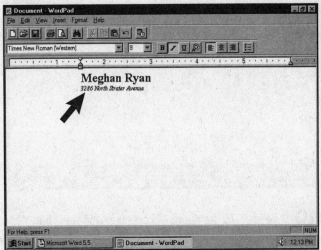

6 Click on the **Italics** button, type your address, and press the **spacebar**.

7 Open the Font list on the formatting toolbar and select the **Wingdings** font.

(continues)

Do It Yourself Use WordPad to Create a Résumé *(continued)*

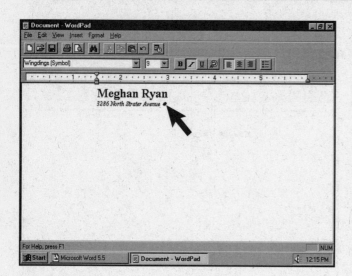

8 Type l (a small L). A small black dot appears. Press the **spacebar**.

9 Open the **Font** list and select **Times New Roman** font.

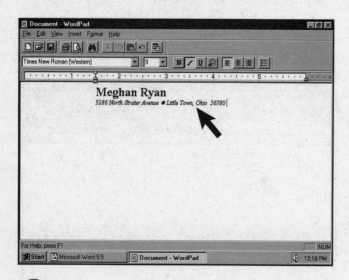

10 Type your city, state, and ZIP code. Press the **spacebar**.

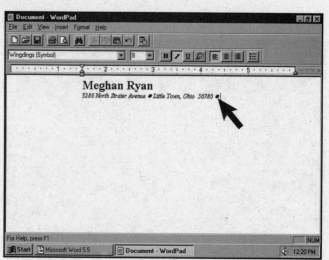

11 Change back to **Wingdings** font. Press **l** again, and another dot appears.

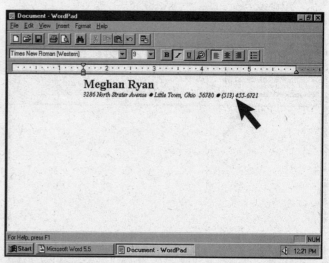

12 Change back to **Times New Roman** font and type your phone number.

Do It Yourself   Use WordPad to Create a Résumé

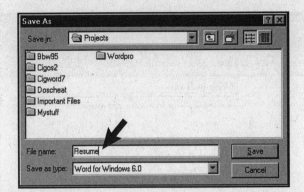

13 Before you lose any work, save your file. Open the **File** menu and select **Save**. Type a name for your document and click on **Save**.

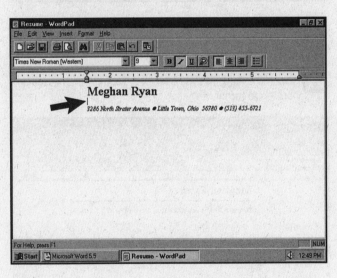

14 Click at the beginning of the address line and press **Enter**. Press the up arrow key to move back up to the empty line.

15 Open the **Insert** menu and select **Object**.

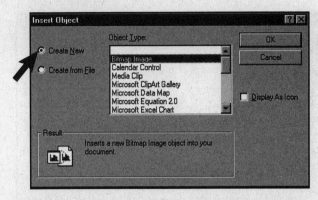

16 In the Insert Object dialog box, select **Create New** and select **Bitmap Image** from the list. Click on **OK**. The tools from the Paint program appear.

17 Open the **Image** menu and select **Attributes**.

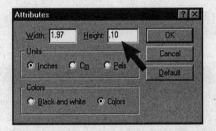

18 The Attributes dialog box appears. Click the **Inches** button. In the Height box, enter **.20** inches. Click on **OK**.

(continues)

Do It Yourself Use WordPad to Create a Résumé *(continued)*

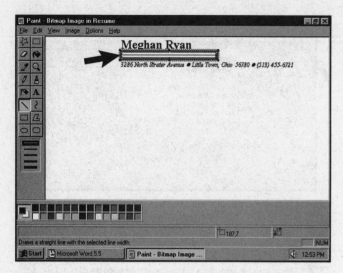

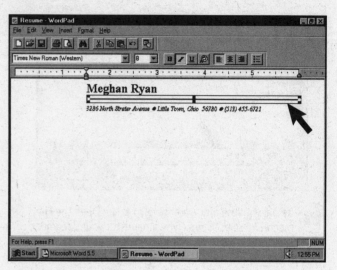

19 Click on the **Line** tool and draw a straight line the length of the work area.

20 Click inside the résumé document. The Paint tools disappear, and you return to WordPad.

22 Click on a side handle and drag the line so it reaches the right-hand margin. Click at the end of the address line and press **Enter** five times.

23 Open the **Font Size** list and select **14**. Click on the **Italics** button to turn it off.

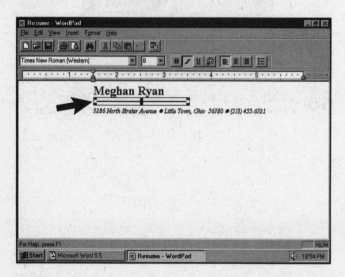

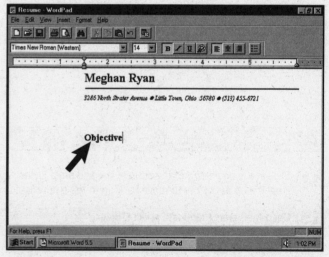

21 Click on the line. Black handles appear to indicate that the line is selected.

24 Click on the **Bold** button and type **Objective**. Press **Enter** twice. Open the **Font Size** list and select **9**.

Do It Yourself   Use WordPad to Create a Résumé

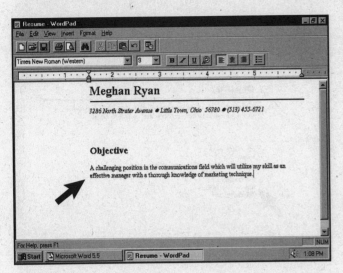

25 Click on the **Bold** button to turn it off and then type your objective.

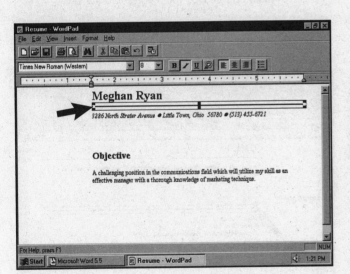

26 Click on the line object. Handles appear to indicate that it's selected.

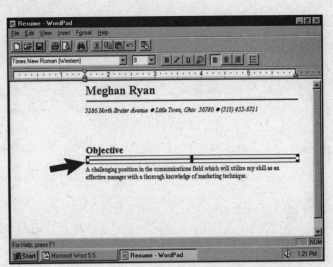

27 Press **Ctrl** and drag the line below the word "Objective." WordPad makes a copy of the original line and places it where you indicated. Drag the side handle as before so that it reaches the right-hand margin.

28 Click at the end of the objective text and press **Enter** three times.

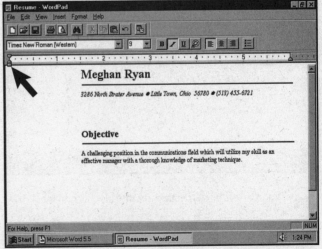

29 Drag the left indent marker on the ruler back to the 0 mark. Open the **Font** list and select **14**.

(continues)

Do It Yourself Use WordPad to Create a Résumé

(continued)

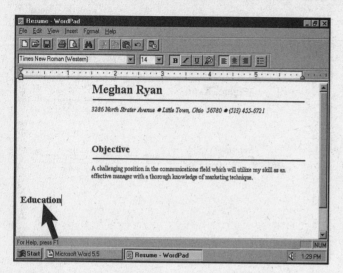

30 Click on the **Bold** button, type **Education**, and press **Enter**.

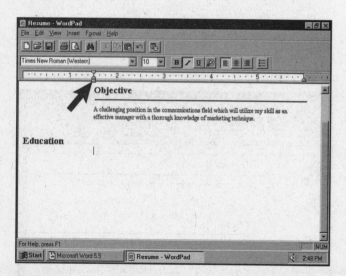

31 Drag the left margin marker on the ruler back to the 1 1/2-inch mark.

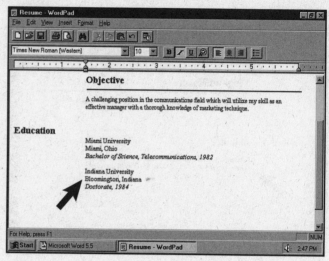

32 Open the **Font** list and select **10**. Click on the **Bold** button to turn it off. Type your education information. Click on the **Italics** button. Type your degree information.

33 Repeat steps 31 and 32 for additional education information.

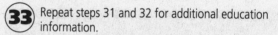

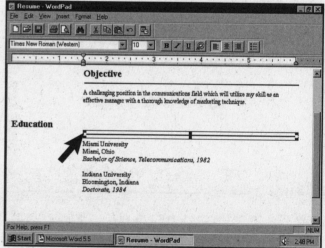

34 Click on the line object below the word "Objective." Handles appear to indicate it's selected.

35 Press **Ctrl** and drag the line below the word "Education." WordPad makes a copy of the original line and places it where you indicated.

Do It Yourself   Use WordPad to Create a Résumé

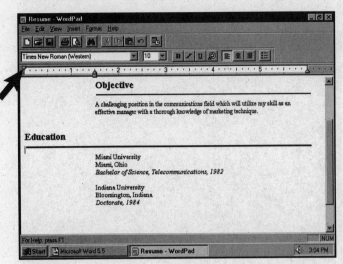

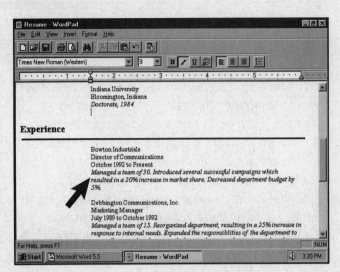

36 Drag the first line marker on the ruler to the 0 mark so the line stretches to touch the left-hand margin.

37 Repeat steps 31 through 36 to add the Experience section to your resumè.

Create Your Own Windows Wallpaper

Windows 95 enables you to customize your desktop by selecting from several patterns it calls *wallpaper*. The wallpaper you select replaces the teal color that normally covers the Windows 95 backdrop. If you don't find a wallpaper pattern you like, you can create one yourself with the Windows 95 Paint program. In this project, you create an abstract bitmap image that looks like a series of bubbles. However, you can easily adapt this project to reflect your own tastes. For example you can type your name, save it as a bitmap, and then display it on-screen. If you have a company logo, you could re-create it with the Paint program.

The wallpaper patterns that come with Windows 95 are formed from graphics files called bitmaps. A *bitmap* is a series of bits stored in memory that form an image when displayed on-screen. A bitmap is sort of like the image on your television, which is made up of small dots. But when you view the television bitmap from a distance, it forms a complete image.

When you use a bitmap image as wallpaper, you can have Windows display it centered on the screen or in a tiled pattern. A tiled pattern repeats the bitmap image in several rows across the screen. After you've created your bitmap (as described here), turn to "Change the Background to Wallpaper" on page 429 to learn how to display it as wallpaper.

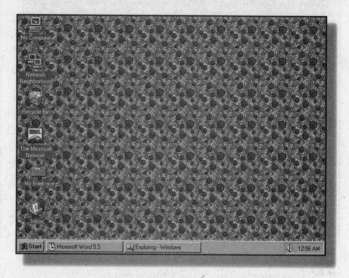

The bitmaps Windows 95 uses are usually pretty small, so you'll be working with Paint's Zoom feature through most of this project. If you need to familiarize yourself with the Paint program before you start this project, see "Use Paint to Create Pictures and Graphics" on page 197.

> If you find a wallpaper pattern you like but you wish it was a little different, you can simply open the file in Paint and make changes to it. For example, you could change the color of an image.

Begin Do It Yourself   Design Windows Wallpaper with Paint

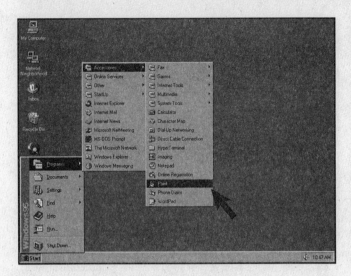

1 Click on the **Start** button, select **Programs**, select **Accessories**, and select **Paint**. The Paint program window appears.

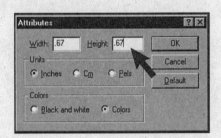

2 Open the **Image** menu and select **Attributes**. In the Attributes dialog box, enter **.67** in the Height and Width boxes. If it's not selected, click on **Inches**. Click **OK**.

A .67 inch square bitmap is the standard for most Windows wallpaper bitmaps. You can make yours larger or smaller to fit your own preferences.

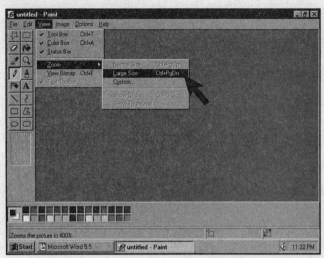

3 Open the **View** menu, select **Zoom**, and select **Large size**.

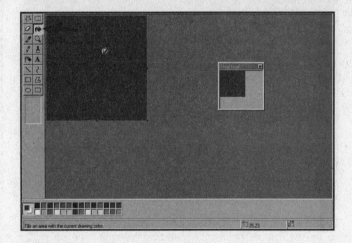

4 Click on the **Paint Can** tool, and then click on your favorite color.

5 Click in the work area to change the background to your favorite color.

(continues)

Begin Do It Yourself Design Windows Wallpaper with Paint *(continued)*

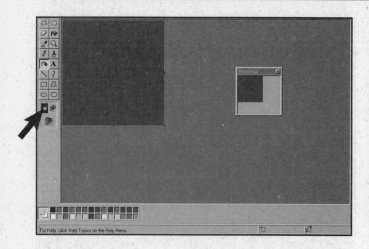

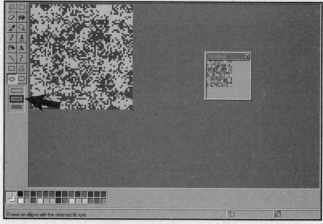

6 Click on the **Spray Can** tool and select the small spray style.

8 Click on the **Ellipse** tool and select the **Filled Ellipse** style.

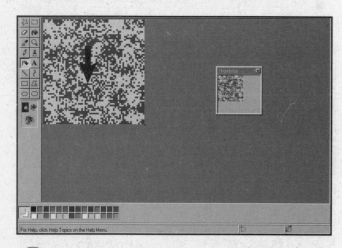

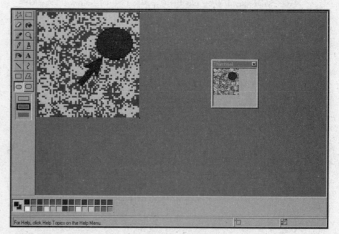

7 Click on a complementary color and spray lightly over the background to create a pleasing pattern.

9 Click on the black color with the left mouse button, and then click with the right mouse button on the color you want to use for your "bubbles." Choose a dark color.

10 Click inside the work area and drag downward and to the right to create a large "bubble."

Do It Yourself Design Windows Wallpaper with Paint

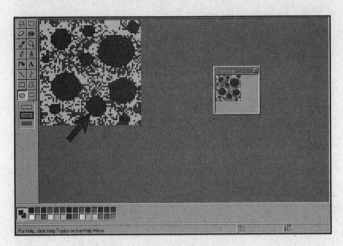

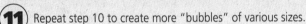

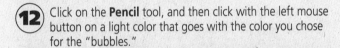

11 Repeat step 10 to create more "bubbles" of various sizes.

12 Click on the **Pencil** tool, and then click with the left mouse button on a light color that goes with the color you chose for the "bubbles."

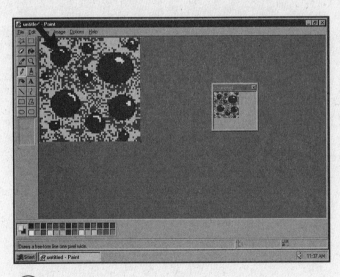

13 With the Pencil tool, click several times within each "bubble" to create some shading.

14 Open the **File** menu and select **Save**. Change to the folder where Windows is installed (probably WINDOWS or WIN95), type a name for your pattern, and click **Save**.

15 Open the **File** menu and select **Exit**.

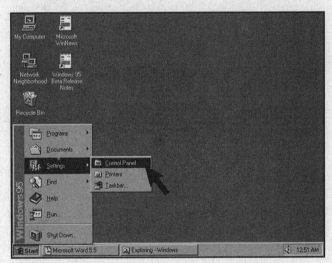

16 To use your new wallpaper, click on the **Start** button, select **Settings**, and select **Control Panel**.

17 Double-click on the **Display** icon.

(continues)

Do It Yourself Design Windows Wallpaper with Paint

(continued)

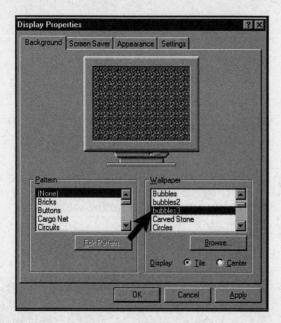

18 In the Display Properties dialog box, click on the **Background** tab if necessary.

19 Select your wallpaper file from the **Wallpaper** list, click on **Tile**, and click **OK**.

DO IT YOURSELF

Use the Control Panel to Customize Windows 95

The Windows 95 desktop is a "workspace" for your computer. Therefore, just as it's important for you to know where your stapler, pens, and sticky notes are located on your desk, it's important for you to know where certain programs, tools, and features are located on your desktop. In addition, you need to know how to access and use those features.

With all due respect to Microsoft, they can't know exactly what you intend to do with Windows 95 because they don't live the life you live and they don't work where you work. However, they provided the tools you need to make your work environment convenient for you.

This section gives you a few ideas for how you can use the tools in the Control Panel folder to start making Windows 95 adapt to the way you work.

What You Will Find in This Section

Change the Background to Wallpaper

If you look around at your coworkers or think about the people you know, you see that each person has his or her own style. Perhaps one person always wears a solid color shirt and a striped tie—plain and simple. Maybe someone else is an explosion of design and color—flowered skirt, bright top, colorful scarf. When you consider how someone dresses, do you ever think that one person is more usefully dressed? No, the matter is purely aesthetic. Well, for the same reason—aesthetic appeal—you can change how the background of your desktop appears by adding wallpaper to it.

When you apply wallpaper, Windows places it on the desktop. Windows comes with several wallpaper designs that it installs in the \WINDOWS folder on your hard drive when you set up Windows. A bitmap (BMP) file holds each design. Using this project, you can select a wallpaper design such as argyle, cars, bricks, pinstripe, or zigzag.

After you're comfortable with selecting a wallpaper, you can adjust it or adapt it in any of the following ways:

- You can choose to repeat (or tile) smaller designs to fill the desktop with many copies of the wallpaper pattern.

- You can *center* a wallpaper design so a single copy of the image appears centered on the desktop. This is great for larger wallpaper designs.

- You can use a bitmap image of your favorite celebrity as wallpaper! You can copy any BMP file to your \WINDOWS folder and select it as wallpaper. Sources of BMP files include online services (like CompuServe), the Internet, graphics programs, and other computer users.

- You can create your own Windows wallpaper with Paint or any other graphics paint program

that can save BMP files. Simply create and save the file, copy it to your \WINDOWS folder, and select it as wallpaper.

> For tips on how to decide whether to use wallpaper or a pattern, see "Change the Background to a Pattern" on page 430.

You can select a pattern or wallpaper, but not both. If you select both, the wallpaper takes precedence. For additional information on using patterns for your background see "Change the Background to a Pattern" on page 430. Besides changing the wallpaper or using a pattern, you also can change the colors used for other elements on the desktop (such as window borders, menus, and buttons). See "Change the Windows Color Scheme" on page 437.

Follow the steps in this project to learn how you can express your style and personality by changing your desktop wallpaper.

Begin Do It Yourself Choose a Wallpaper Design for Your Background

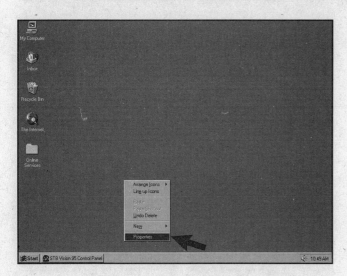

1 Right-click on the desktop and select **Properties** from the shortcut menu that appears.

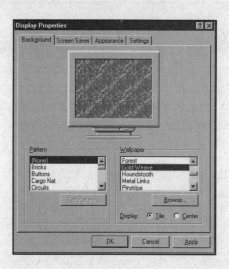

3 On the computer screen at the top of the dialog box, Windows displays a sample of what the desktop will look like. Select **Tile** and click on **OK**.

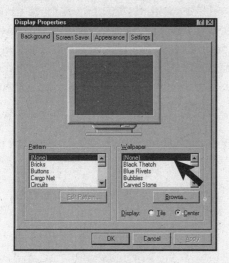

2 The Display Properties dialog box appears, with the Background tab selected. In the **Wallpaper** list, select the wallpaper you want to use. If the wallpaper file is in another folder, you can use the **Browse** button to select the folder and file.

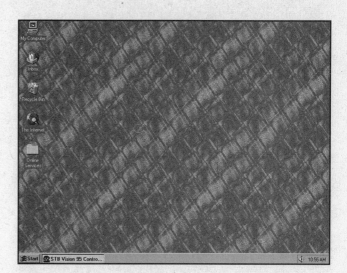

4 The wallpaper is used for the desktop background.

Change the Background to a Pattern

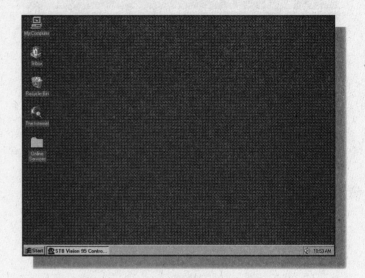

Windows creates a pattern using the currently selected color scheme so the pattern fits right in. Although Windows comes with approximately 20 patterns, you can modify existing patterns or create new ones. You can select the (None) pattern choice to revert to the default desktop background.

Here is the difference between patterns and wallpaper:

- A pattern consists of black plus one other color that's part of or that complements the currently selected color scheme. A wallpaper doesn't adapt to complement the color scheme.

- The patterns are much smaller than the wallpaper designs (which generally create a more subtle effect that's easier on the eyes). You can't adjust the size of the repeat effect with patterns. However, you can use graphics of almost any size—even full-screen images—as wallpaper.

- To edit or create wallpaper, you have to use Paint, be familiar with its tools, and know a few other tricks. In contrast, you can edit patterns in the Control Panel by simply typing a name and clicking on pixels (the small dots that compose on-screen images).

Begin Do It Yourself Use a Pattern

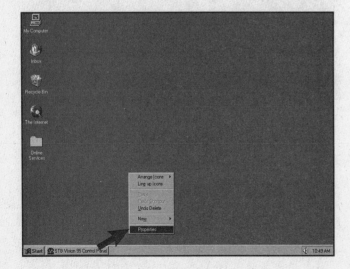

1 Right-click on the desktop and select **Properties** from the shortcut menu that appears.

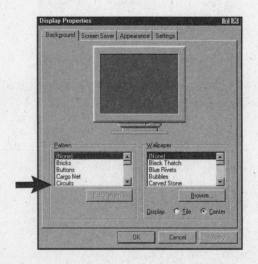

2 The Display Properties dialog box appears, with the Background tab selected. In the Pattern list, select the pattern you want to use.

Do It Yourself Use a Pattern

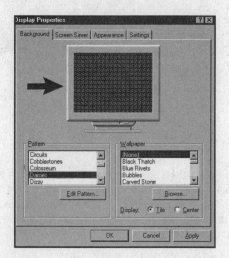

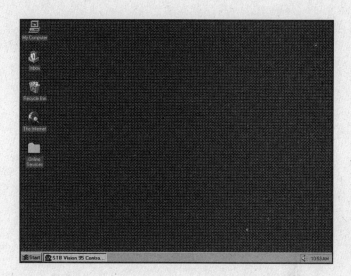

3 At the top of the dialog box, Windows displays a sample of what the desktop will look like. If you like this pattern, click on **OK**. If you don't, select another pattern and click on **OK**.

4 Windows uses the pattern for the desktop background.

You also can click **Apply** to apply the pattern and leave the dialog box open so that you can make other changes.

Begin Do It Yourself Edit a Pattern

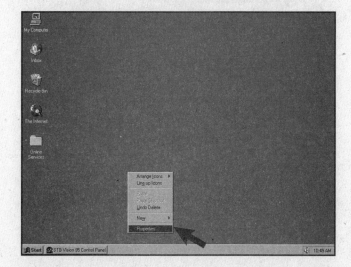

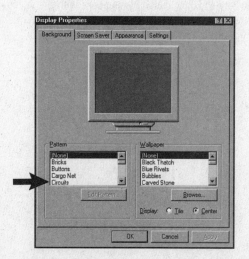

1 Right-click on the desktop and select **Properties** from the shortcut menu that appears.

2 In the Display Properties dialog box, select the pattern that most closely matches what you want.

(continues)

Do It Yourself   Edit a Pattern

(continued)

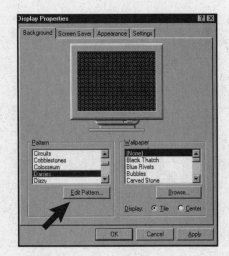

3 With the pattern you want selected, click on the **Edit Pattern** button.

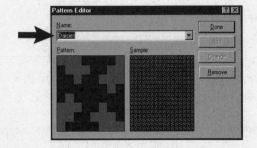

4 The Pattern Editor dialog box appears, with the selected pattern displayed. In the **Name** text box, type a name for this pattern.

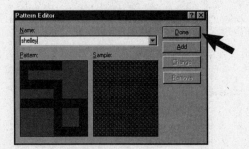

5 Edit the pattern by clicking on the squares in the **Pattern** area. When you click a square, it is reversed (that is, if the squares are green and black and you click a black square, it becomes green). Watch the **Sample** area to see how the pattern will look on the desktop.

6 When you finish editing the pattern, click the **Add** button. Then click the **Done** button to close the Pattern Editor dialog box.

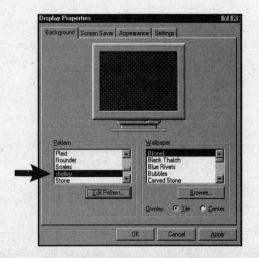

7 The new pattern appears in the **Pattern** list. To use this pattern, select it and click on **OK**.

Use a Screen Saver

If you left an image on-screen for a long time on older PC monitors, that image could become burned in. No matter what you had on-screen, you'd still see a faint outline of the burned-in image. (You can sometimes see a burned-in image on ATM machines.) To prevent burn-in, someone came up with the idea of a screen saver. If you didn't use your computer for a certain period of time, the computer would automatically display an animated graphic, which would prevent burn-in.

Today's monitors don't have burn-in problems, but some users still use a screen saver, mostly for show. If you don't use your PC for a certain amount of time, Windows displays a moving graphics image. (You select the amount of time, and you select the graphic.) Windows 95 includes the screen savers listed in the following table. In addition, you can purchase screen saver programs such as AfterDark (the most popular screen saver program).

Each screen saver has its own set of options that you can change. For example, you can change how fast or slow the graphic or message moves across your screen or the number of minutes before the screen saver appears. Some screen savers have more options than others. As you'll see when you work through

this pro-ject, the 3D Text screen saver has quite a few options that enable you to create some interesting messages.

You can test the results of your changes by clicking the **Preview** button; if you don't like what you see, just change it again.

To stop the screen saver and return to your program, you press any key or move the mouse. The program you were using is not affected in any way by the screen saver.

Windows 95 Screen Savers

Name	Description
Blank Screen	Displays a blank screen
3D Flower Box	Displays a box that turns into a flower
3D Flying Objects	Displays a 3D Windows logo flying around
3D Maze	Moves you through a 3D maze
3D Pipes	Builds a 3D pipe construction
3D Text	Displays 3D text moving on screen
Flying Windows	Displays flying windows that change shape and color

A screen saver also can provide a little bit of security for sensitive material. If you assign a password to your screen saver, you can prevent others from stopping the screen saver and seeing your current work.

You can type as many as 20 characters for the password, including punctuation. The password is not case-sensitive; if your password is Jelly, you can type **Jelly**, **jelly**, or **JELLY**. Don't forget your password! Write it down in a safe place.

Begin Do It Yourself Choose a Screen Saver

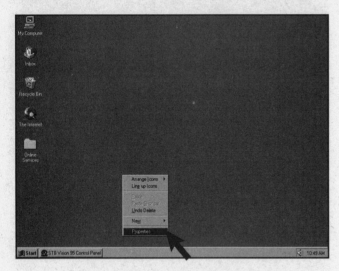

1 Right-click on the desktop and select **Properties** from the shortcut menu that appears.

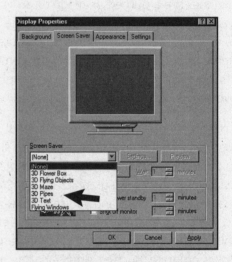

3 Click on the **Screen Saver** drop-down list.

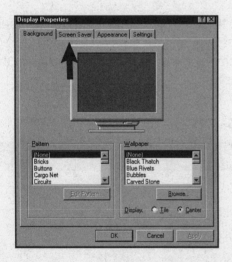

2 The Display Properties dialog box appears, with the Background tab displayed. Click on the **Screen Saver** tab.

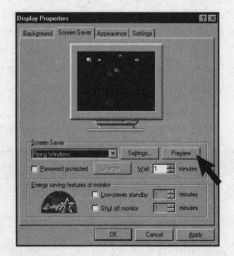

4 Click on the screen saver you want. To see a preview, click the **Preview** button.

Do It Yourself Choose a Screen Saver

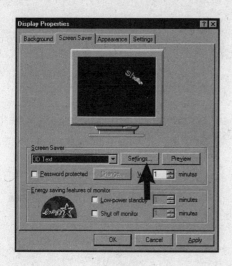

5 In the Wait text box, enter the number of minutes you want Windows to wait before displaying the image.

6 To change any of the screen saver's options, click the **Settings** button.

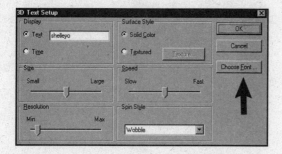

8 In the Font dialog box, you can change the font, style, size, and color of your message. View your changes in the Sample box and click on **OK** when you are satisfied.

9 When you finish making changes, click on **OK** twice.

7 Windows displays the options for the selected screen saver. In this case, you can drag the Speed bar to control how fast the text moves across your screen. You also can enter different text in the Text text box. Also, you can change the size, resolution, surface style, and spin style. To format the text, click on **Choose Font**.

Begin Do It Yourself   Add a Password

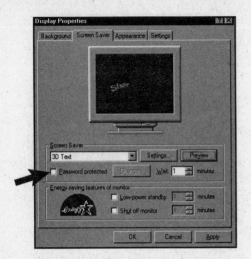

3 In the **Confirm new password** text box, retype the password to confirm it.

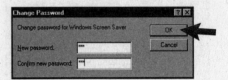

4 Click on **OK**.

1 Follow steps 1 through 8 of the previous section to select and set up a screen saver. With the screen saver you want selected, check the **Password protected** check box and then click the **Change** button.

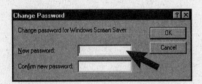

2 Windows displays the Change Password dialog box. In the **New password** text box, type the password you want to assign. As you type, Windows displays asterisks.

Change the Windows Color Scheme

With Windows 95, you can customize the colors used for on-screen elements. You can change the color of almost any on-screen item, such as the active title bar, the desktop, the application background, or the menus. You can choose from a predefined set of colors as you do in this project, or you can create your own color scheme (see "Create a Custom Color Scheme" on page 439).

To start, try using a predefined color scheme. The ones provided by Windows use a complementary palette of colors. Some are designed specifically for certain types of monitors; some change not only the colors used, but the font and font size used for text as well.

When you select a color scheme, Windows displays a sample in the Appearance dialog box so you can see how the screen will look. Experiment a little. As you choose various color schemes, you'll notice right away

that some color combinations are more restful for the eyes than others. If you pick a vibrant scheme, you may find that after using the computer for a while your eyes begin to burn and tire. To return to the default, select **Windows Standard**.

Begin Do It Yourself   Change the Colors of Your Windows

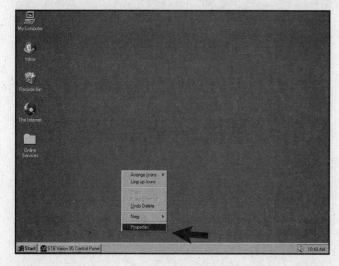

1 Right-click on the desktop and select **Properties** from the shortcut menu that appears.

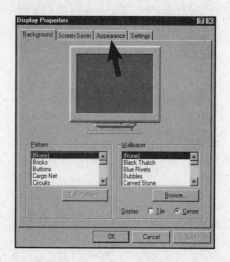

2 The Display Properties dialog box appears. Click on the **Appearance** tab.

Do It Yourself Change the Colors of Your Windows *(continues)*

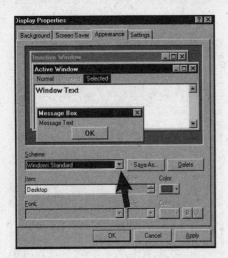

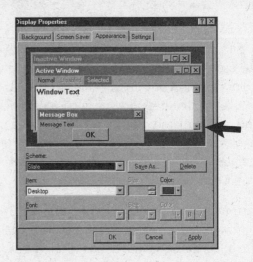

3 The Appearance tab displays a sample of how the desktop looks using the current colors. Open the **Scheme** drop-down list box.

5 You see a preview of how the desktop will look using this new scheme. If you like the colors, click on **OK**. If you don't, select another color scheme and then click on **OK**.

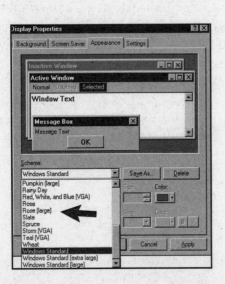

4 In the list of predefined color schemes, select the one you want to use.

6 Windows uses the selected scheme for all on-screen elements.

Create a Custom Color Scheme

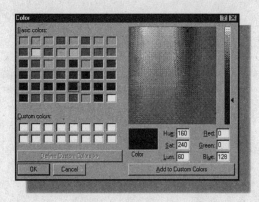

Many users tend to think of color in computing more in the decorative sense than in the functional sense. What color you give your backgrounds, your title bar, and your dialog boxes seems as inconsequential a detail as what color you give your walls and your carpet.

However, color has a function in our everyday environment. The colors you choose for your Windows 95 environment affect the way you work just as the colors in your everyday work environment do. For example, green is often used in LED displays because it is very easy to read when used on a black background. The default Windows 95 colors provide a nice easy-on-the-eyes combination. But maybe you've grown tired of this scheme and are looking for something more exciting.

Although many of the alternative color schemes Windows provides look interesting, over time you might find them monotone. Your eyes are an important work tool in computing. To keep them in shape, you don't want to bombard them with too much of the same color. Windows 95's "Plum" and "Pumpkin" schemes, for example, may have character in the test diagram, but try bombarding your eyes with those basic colors for days on end, and you'll probably find yourself readjusting the color scheme soon.

If you're having trouble finding a Windows color scheme you can work with, you can personalize an existing Windows color scheme by changing only certain colors, such as the color of the title bars. To change a single element of a Windows color scheme, you select it from a list, click on the **Color** button, and select the color you want.

If you don't find a color you like, or if you're feeling adventurous, you can create custom colors. You create custom colors in Windows 95 by changing the values of two sets of numbers, the first of which is called the RGB register. The RGB register enables you to mix the colors red, green, and blue in various amounts. Red, green, and blue are the optical primary colors; all colors on your screen are made up of combinations of these three primary colors.

The second trio of numbers is the Hue/Saturation/Luminance register. In the VGA system, there are 256 "pure" colors, or hues. *Saturation* is a measurement of how much of that pure hue appears in the final color mixture (it's what artists call "brightness"). Gray is a low-saturation color compared to a bright blue. *Luminance* is the measure of how much light is in the color. The variance between light grey and dark grey is the same as the variance between light bright blue and dark bright blue.

If you spend a lot of time getting the colors just right, you should save the scheme so you can use it again. For example, if you create one scheme and then switch to another scheme without saving the first, your custom scheme is lost. To use it again, you'd have to re-create it. Therefore, you should save the scheme so it is always available.

Begin Do It Yourself Choose Your Own Windows Colors

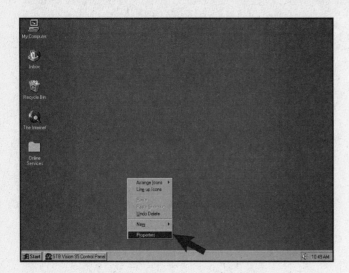

1 Right-click on the desktop and select **Properties** from the shortcut menu that appears.

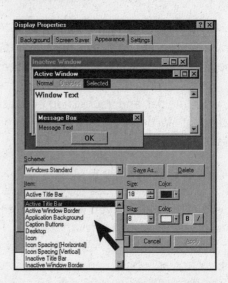

3 To change the color of one of the Windows 95 elements, select it in the **Item** list, or click on it in the sample at the top of the dialog box.

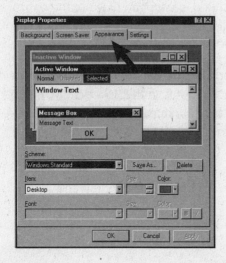

2 The Display Properties dialog box appears. Click on the **Appearance** tab.

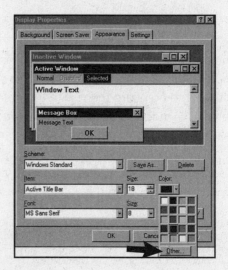

4 To change the color of the item you selected, click on the Color button and click on a color. To create a custom color for your item, click on **Other** instead.

Do It Yourself Choose Your Own Windows Colors

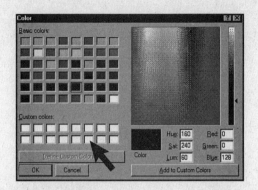

5 Click on an available box in the **Custom colors** area.

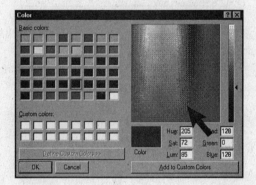

6 The large block in the upper-right corner displays the entire color range of your current resolution setting. Brighter colors are toward the top; more diffuse colors are toward the bottom. Click on the color you want.

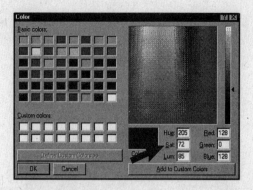

7 Adjust the values in the Hue/Sat/Lum and the Red/Green/Blue text boxes to fine-tune the color you've selected. You also can drag the scroll bar up or down to select a different color range.

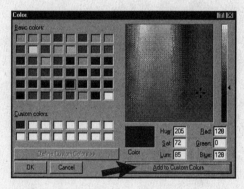

8 When you've got the color you want, click on the **Add to Custom Colors** button.

9 Click on **OK**. Windows 95 applies this color to the chosen item in the Display Properties diagram.

10 Follow steps 3 through 9 for each of the colors you want to set. When the colors are just as you want them, click on **OK**.

Begin Do It Yourself   Save a Color Scheme

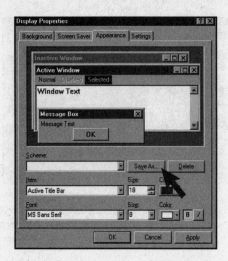

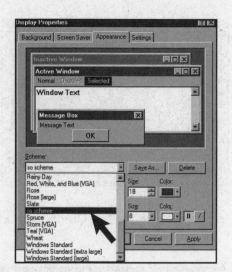

1 After you follow the preceding steps and create the new color scheme, click the **Save As** button.

2 You see the Save Scheme dialog box. Type a name for this scheme and click the **OK** button.

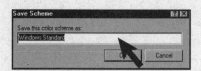

3 The name is listed in the dialog box.

Set the Date and Time

Inside your computer there's a clock that keeps track of the current date and time. This clock's date and time are used when files are saved, modified, and printed. This can be useful if you happen to have two copies of a file, for example, and you don't know which is the more current. A quick look at the date and time of each file quickly tells you which was updated more recently.

If for some reason your computer clock is wrong, you can use Windows to adjust the date and time. For example, if you move from one time zone to another, you need to adjust the time. Likewise, if the date is off for some reason, you can set the correct date.

The Date and Time Properties dialog box contains two tabs. You use the Date & Time tab to change the day, month, or year and local time in hours, minutes, and seconds. You use the Time Zone tab to change your time zone and adjust for daylight savings time.

To display the Date/Time Properties dialog box quickly, right-click on the **clock** in the taskbar and select **Adjust Date/Time** from the shortcut menu that appears.

Begin Do It Yourself Change Your Computer's Date and Time

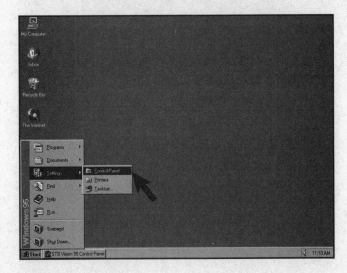

1 Click on the **Start** button, select **Settings**, and select **Control Panel**.

2 In the Control Panel window, double-click on the **Date/Time** icon.

(continues)

Do It Yourself Change Your Computer's Date and Time

(continued)

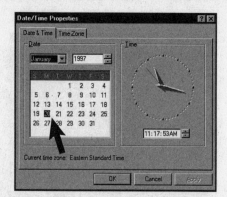

3 The Date/Time Properties dialog box appears, with the Date & Time tab selected. To change the month, display the **Date** drop-down list and select the month. To change the date, click on the date in the calendar to highlight it. To change the year, enter the correct year in the year spin box or use the spin arrows to select the correct value.

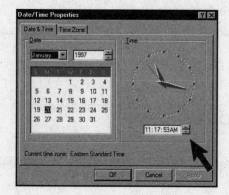

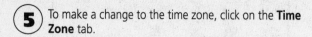

4 To make a change to the time, select the part of the time you want to change (hour, minutes, seconds, or AM/PM), then enter the correct time or use the spin arrows to select the correct time.

5 To make a change to the time zone, click on the **Time Zone** tab.

6 Windows displays a map of the world, with the current time zone highlighted. Click on your area of the world to select a different time zone.

7 (Optional) Check the **Automatically adjust clock for daylight savings changes** check box if you want Windows to take care of this.

8 When you finish making changes, click on **OK**.

You also can double-click on the time in the taskbar to display the Date/Time Properties dialog box.

Change the Mouse Movement and Pointer

Using the mouse is often one of the hardest things for a new computer user to get the hang of. The two most common problems new mouse users encounter are double-clicking and the fact that the mouse is designed to be used in the right hand. Users who have trouble with double-clicking usually don't click fast enough, and left-handed users have a hard time adapting to the mouse buttons.

Because the mouse can be so troublesome, the Mouse Properties dialog box gives you control of the following options:

- **Double-click speed**   If you select a slower speed, you have more time between clicks. A faster speed requires you to click more quickly.

- **Button configuration**   You can choose between Left-handed and Right-handed (the default). If you select Left-handed, the left button does what the right did and vice versa so you can use the mouse with your left hand.

- **Pointer speed**   You can adjust how fast the pointer moves in relation to how far and fast you move the mouse.

- **Pointer trail**   You can add a "trail" that follows behind the mouse pointer if you have trouble finding it on-screen.

Depending on the type of Windows 95 installation you chose, you also might be able to change the appearance of the mouse pointers used for various operations.

If you purchase a new mouse, you must install it in Windows via the General tab in the Mouse Properties dialog box. See "Add New Hardware" on page 338 for information on changing the mouse type.

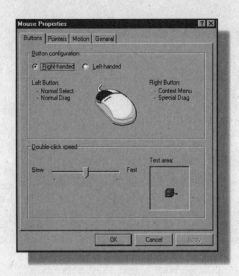

Change the Appearance of Pointers

To clue you in on what the computer is doing and where the mouse cursor is, Windows uses different pointers. For example, when the mouse pointer is in the menu bar, it appears as an arrow. When the computer is busy doing something, the pointer appears as an hourglass. And when the pointer rests on a window border, it becomes a double-headed arrow.

You can change the appearance of these pointers to make them more visible or visually appealing. To change your mouse pointer's appearance, you must have the appropriate pointer image files (cursor or *.cur files) installed on your computer. If you did a typical installation, Windows did not install the cursor files. You can add them as covered in "Add and Remove Windows 95 Components" on page 476.

Begin Do It Yourself   Adjust Buttons, Motion, or General Settings

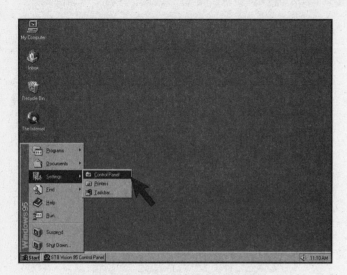

1 Click on the **Start** button, select **Settings**, and select **Control Panel**.

2 In the Control Panel window, double-click on the **Mouse** icon.

If you make a change to a pointer and then change your mind, you can go back to the default. To do so, select the pointer type you changed, and then click the **Use Default** button.

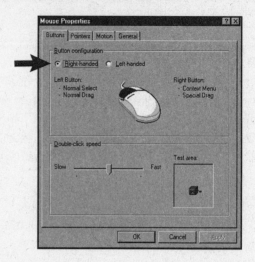

3 The Mouse Properties dialog box appears, with the Buttons tab selected. To change the functions of the left and right buttons, select **Left-handed** or **Right-handed**.

4 To make a change to the double-click speed, drag the control bar left (slower) or right (faster).

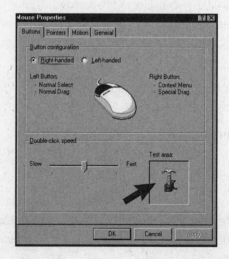

5 To test the double-click speed, double-click in the Test area. When you click within the interval, the jack-in-the-box pops up. If you are finished making changes, skip to step 9.

6 To make changes to the motion of the mouse, click on the **Motion** tab.

Do It Yourself Adjust Buttons, Motion, or General Settings

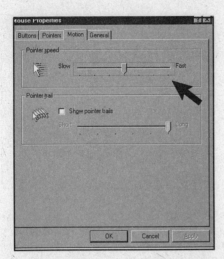

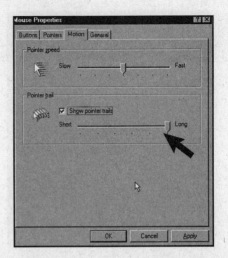

7 The Motion tab appears. To adjust the pointer speed, drag the control bar left (slower) or right (faster).

8 If you want to display a trail behind the pointer, check the **Show pointer trails** check box and drag the control bar to select the length of the trail. You can try moving the mouse around in the dialog box to see what the trail looks like.

9 When you finish making changes, click on **OK**.

Begin Do It Yourself Customize the Pointers

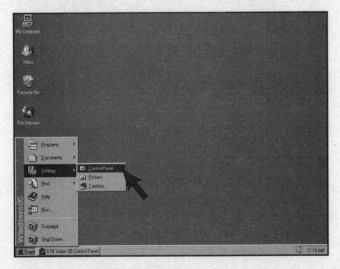

1 Click on the **Start** button, select **Settings**, and select **Control Panel**.

2 In the Control Panel window, double-click on the **Mouse** icon.

(continues)

Do It Yourself Customize the Pointers

(continued)

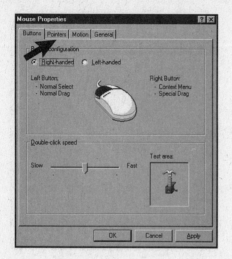

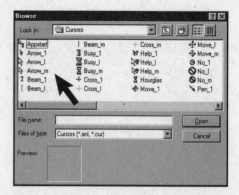

5 You see a list of different pointers you can use. Select the pointer and check the preview. Click the **Open** button. (If you need to change to a different folder, Cursors for example, you can do so and then select the file.)

3 The Mouse Properties dialog box appears, with the Buttons tab selected. Select the **Pointers** tab.

4 You see a list of actions in which a pointer appears, as well as the default pointer that is used. To change the pointer, click on the action in the list and then click on the **Browse** button.

6 Windows uses the new pointer, which is displayed in the Mouse Properties dialog box. Repeat steps 4 and 5 for each action whose pointer you want to change. When you finish making changes, click on **OK**.

Begin Do It Yourself Choose a Scheme for the Mouse Pointer

1 Click on the **Start** button, select **Settings**, and select **Control Panel**.

2 In the Control Panel window, double-click on the **Mouse** icon.

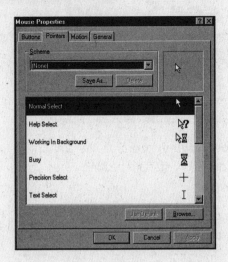

4 Click on the **Scheme** drop-down list.

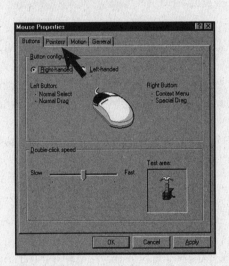

3 The Mouse Properties dialog box appears, with the Buttons tab selected. Select the **Pointers** tab.

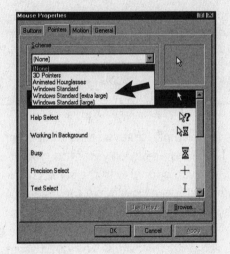

5 Select the scheme you want to use, and Windows displays a preview of each pointer icon for the selected scheme. Click on **OK**.

Change the Keyboard Sensitivity and Cursor Speed

Just as you can change how the mouse operates, you have some control over how the keyboard works. You can set the following options:

Repeat delay Controls the amount of time before a key starts repeating when you hold it down.

Repeat rate Controls the speed at which a key repeats when you hold it down.

Cursor blink rate Controls the rate at which the cursor blinks.

Note that you also can change the language used for the keyboard. To do so, you must install additional language keyboard layouts. For more information on this type of change, see your Windows manual.

Suppose, for example, that you tend to press on a key for a long time. You really only want to type one character, but you end up with the same character several times. You can slow down the repeat delay so Windows waits a little longer before repeating the character. Or, suppose you want to insert a line of asterisks. You press the asterisk key, but it seems to take forever for the character to repeat. In this case, your repeat rate is too slow. You can speed up the rate.

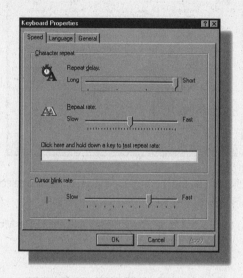

Finally, you can control the cursor blink rate. When you are working in some programs—for example, word processing programs—a flashing vertical line (the cursor) blinks to indicate your position in the file. If the blink annoys you for some reason, you can change the blink rate. If the cursor blinks too fast and makes you nervous, for example, you can slow it down. Windows enables you to select a rate that suits you.

If you want to see the type of keyboard you have installed, click on the **General** tab in the Keyboard Properties dialog box. You also can use this tab if you change to a different type of keyboard.

Begin Do It Yourself Change Keyboard Properties

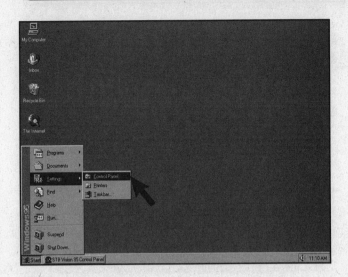

1 Click on the **Start** button, select **Settings**, and select **Control Panel**.

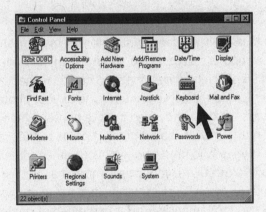

2 In the Control Panel window, double-click on the **Keyboard** icon.

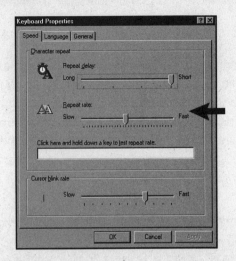

3 The Keyboard Properties dialog box appears, with the Speed tab selected. To change the repeat delay, drag the control bar left (slower) or right (faster). To change the repeat rate, drag the control bar left (slower) or right (faster).

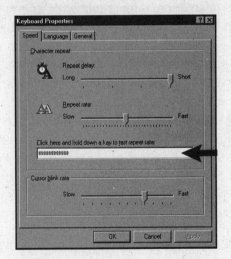

4 To test the repeat rate, click in the text box in the middle of the dialog box and press and hold down a key. To change the cursor blink rate, drag the control bar left (slower) or right (faster).

5 When you finish making changes, click **OK**. Windows makes the changes.

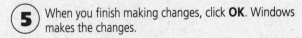

Use Multiple Printers

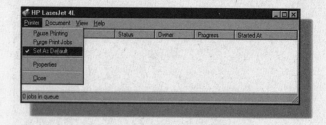

If you own more than one printer or have more than one printer attached to your network, you have a few more considerations to make when printing with Windows 95 than merely choosing the right printer for the right job. Windows 95 handles all printing done by your applications—even DOS and Windows 3.1 applications. Therefore, your printer is controlled by settings in the Control Panel, not by settings in the application doing the printing.

> If you need to add a new printer to your system, see "Set Up a New Printer" on page 150.

One other consequence of this Windows 95/printer/application relationship is more subtle. Whenever your application brings up a what-you-see-is-what-you-get display, the relative positions of text and graphics are to some degree determined by your active printer driver (a special program that controls a particular printer). If your application has a so-called Print Preview mode, what you see on-screen is based on information the program is getting from the current printer driver. If you want to print your document on a different printer, you should change drivers (by changing the active printer) so that what you see on-screen and what is printed will be the same.

Another strange consequence of the way Windows 95 relates to drivers is that certain devices that aren't

even printers are considered to be printers. If you installed Microsoft Exchange with Windows 95, one of your "printers" is Microsoft Fax, a generic driver for a fax machine. The benefit of having your fax driver work like a printer driver is that any Windows 95 application that prints can send a fax. However, when your active printer driver actually drives a fax machine, the appearance of your on-screen documents may be ever-so-slightly different.

Regardless of how many printers (or fax machines) your computer has access to, at any one time Windows 95 only recognizes one such device as the printer (called the active printer). One of your printers is always the default device or active printer. When you print from within a program, it prints to the default printer. To print to one of your other printers (or to Microsoft Fax), you usually must change this default. As you will see in this project, some programs enable you to temporarily print to a different printer (other than the default). You also can create printer shortcuts on your desktop, which enable you to print a document with any printer at any time.

Begin Do It Yourself Change the Default Printer

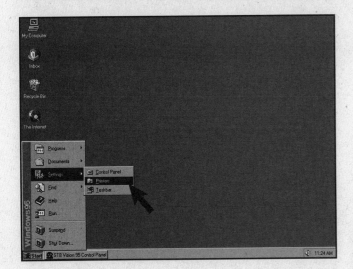

① Click on the **Start** button, select **Settings**, and select **Printers**.

② Double-click on the icon for the printer you want to set as the default printer.

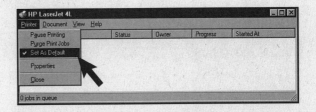

③ Open the **Printer** menu and select **Set As Default**. The next application you bring into the Windows 95 workspace should recognize this printer as the active printer, by default.

You might be able to change active printers from within your application, but you cannot change default printers without opening the Printers window.

Also, you can perform this procedure quickly by right-clicking on the printer icon and selecting Set As Default from the shortcut menu.

Begin Do It Yourself Select a Different Printer from Within an Application

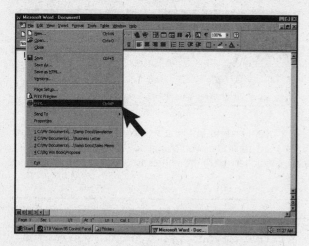

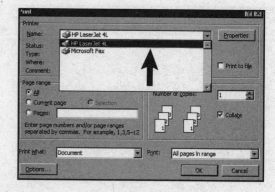

3 Click the printer you want to use. Click the on **OK**.

1 Open your application's **File** menu and select **Print**.

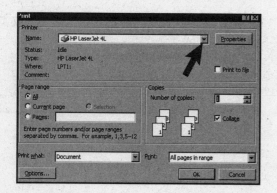

2 In the Print dialog box, display the **Name** drop-down list.

Begin Do It Yourself Create Printer Icons for Your Desktop

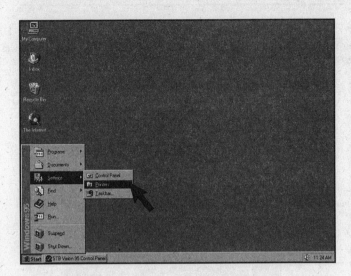

1 Click on the **Start** button, select **Settings**, and select **Printers**.

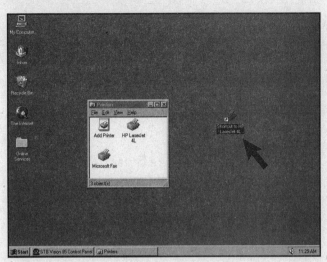

3 Windows adds a shortcut to the printer to your desktop. Repeat steps 2 and 3 for any other printer or fax icons for which you want to create shortcuts.

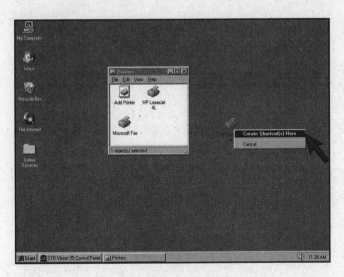

2 With the right mouse button, drag the printer icon onto the desktop. Select **Create Shortcut(s) Here**.

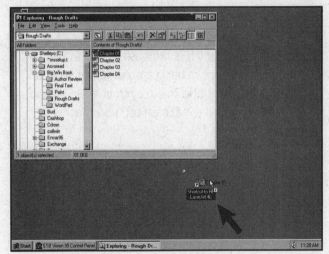

4 To print a document on a particular printer, select that document in the Explorer, drag its icon over to the printer icon on the desktop, and let go. The application that originated the document may start itself (if it hasn't been started already). If so, it automatically closes down when it completes the print job.

Change Regional Settings

If you use Windows in an international setting, you may want to make some changes to the regional settings. These settings control the way numbers, currency, measurements, dates, and times appear.

In the United States, we use a certain format for currency, such as $1,000.99. This number looks right to most Americans. In other countries, though, they use a different format for numbers. For example, $1,000.99 would be represented as 1 000,99F in France. Instead of a dollar sign, the French use F for "franc" and place the indicator after the number. Instead of a comma, the French use a space to separate digit groupings. And finally, instead of a period for a decimal separator, they use a comma.

You can select the country of your choice from a list on the Regional Settings tab and make several changes at once (which is the easiest and most common method for making a change), or you can go through the tabs and make each change individually. For the changes to take effect, you must restart Windows.

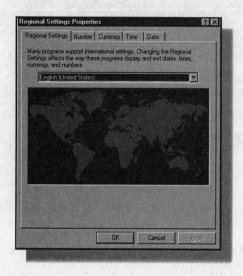

Note that the changes you make to these settings affect all Windows programs. For example, when you format numbers in Excel, Excel uses the appropriate settings from the Regional Settings Properties dialog box.

Begin Do It Yourself   Change Regional Settings When You Change Your Residence

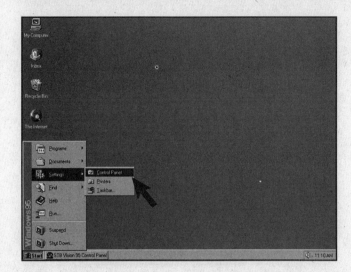

1 Click on the **Start** button, select **Settings**, and select **Control Panel**.

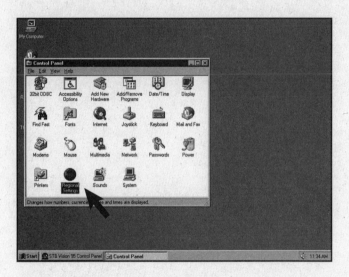

2 In the Control Panel window, double-click on the **Regional Settings** icon.

3 The Regional Settings Properties dialog box appears. To change how numbers appear, click on the **Number** tab.

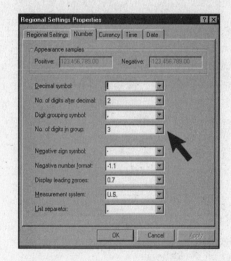

4 Enter the decimal symbol, digit separator, measurement, and other numeric settings you want to use. Click on **OK**. Click the **Currency** tab.

(continues)

Begin Do It Yourself Change Regional Settings When You Change Your Residence

(continued)

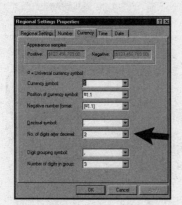

5 Select the currency symbol, decimal indicator, digit separator, and other currency options. Click on **OK**. Click on the **Time** tab.

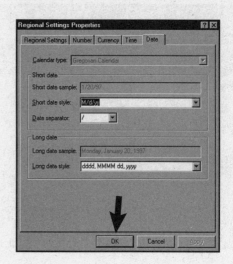

7 Make changes to how short and long dates appear and click on **OK**.

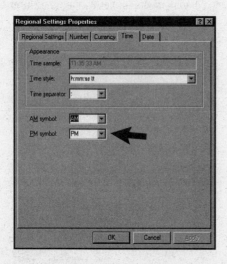

6 Select the format you want to use for times and click **OK**. Click on the **Date** tab.

Set Up Passwords

If several people use the same PC, each person may want to customize Windows to his or her liking. For example, one user may prefer a certain wallpaper pattern and screen saver. When another user uses the computer, she may want to change back to the custom options she prefers. Instead of wasting time continually switching from one set of options to another, you can set up customization options for different users. Each user can have his or her own password and can select whether to change the custom settings he or she has made.

Setting Windows up for multiple users to customize individually is simple: you turn on the option as explained in the *Do It Yourself*. Then you set the options for each user and include the customization options with the user profile. You can choose to include desktop icons and Network Neighborhood contents in the user settings and/or Start Menu and Program groups in user settings.

After you turn on the option, you are prompted to restart Windows. When you do so, you are asked to type in your user name and password (optional). If you type a password, you are prompted to confirm it. You are also given the choice of whether you want to save your customization preferences and desktop settings. Each time you start Windows, you must log on with your user name and password.

You add additional users by typing a new user name and password when you start Windows. Alternatively, you can log on as a different user by selecting the Shut Down command.

To go back to just one set of desktop settings, follow the *Do It Yourself* and select the first option (All users of this PC use the same preferences and desktop settings).

Begin Do It Yourself   Set Up Passwords for Multiple Users

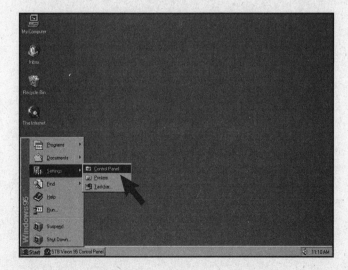

1 Click on the **Start** button, select **Settings**, and select **Control Panel**.

2 In the Control Panel window, double-click on the **Passwords** icon.

(continues)

Do It Yourself Set Up Passwords for Multiple Users *(continued)*

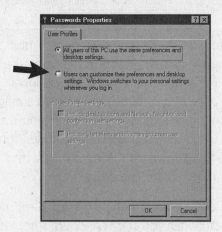

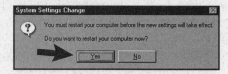

5 When you are prompted to restart Windows, with the System Settings Change message box, click **Yes**.

When you are prompted to restart Windows with the System Settings Change message box, click yes.

3 The Passwords Properties dialog box appears. Select the option **Users can customize their preferences and desktop settings. Windows switches to your personal settings whenever you log in**.

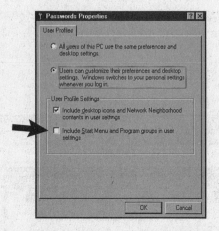

4 When you select this option, the User Profile Settings become available. Select which settings you want to include and click **OK**.

Play a Sound File When a Particular Event Happens

The role of sound in the functionality of a computer is not always obvious at first. Perhaps this is why it took computer software manufacturers so long to recognize sound as an asset, and that the folks at Apple and Amiga were on to something. Sound is part of our everyday sense environment: our minds can make better sense of things by assessing not only how they look, but also how they feel and sound. Obviously, you can't really simulate the texture of an object in Windows 95; if an object has sound, however, you can easily convey its importance.

In Windows 95, sound is used in response to an action or event. Windows 95 makes it possible for you to attach sound files to events so the sound will play when that event happens. For example, you can play various sounds when you start particular Windows 95 programs and when you exit, when a dialog box is displayed, and when you minimize a window (among other things). Windows 95 recognizes a limited set of events and can respond to each event with a sound that can be played through your PC's speaker if you do not have a sound card installed in your computer.

It's easy to make this feature somewhat annoying by attaching too many "cartoon" sounds to ordinary events. For example, telling the computer to make a "boing" sound when you maximize a window may seem cute when you're setting up event sounds for the first time; but after about a week of hearing "boing, boing, boing, boing," you may find that you've got a whopper of a headache. On the other hand, tiny "pings" may be just enough to let you know that Windows has carried out your command.

Think for a moment: have you ever grown tired of hearing the sound of your computer keyboard? Or your mouse? Natural sounds (sounds that seem to fit the objects that make them) can actually be pleasant.

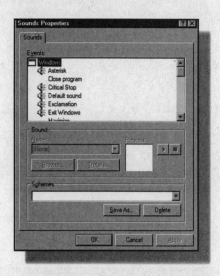

As a result, they may become psychological aides to your work. By using this feature to create natural sounds, you can make the feature work for you.

If you want the sounds that you associate with events to have a "related theme," you can select from a sound scheme. This is a set of related sounds with a theme (such as jungle or robot). You must have installed the sound schemes for this option to be available. If you want to install them now, see "Add and Remove Windows 95 Components" on page 476. If you don't have the sound schemes (or even if you do), you can select the sounds you like best and save them as a scheme of sounds yourself.

Windows 95 sound files are all in "wave" format, which means they all have .WAV file extensions. If you have other sound files with the .WAV extension that you'd like to add to Windows 95's repertoire, copy them to the \WINDOWS\MEDIA folder and select them when you work through the steps in the *Do It Yourself*.

Begin Do It Yourself Assign a Sound to an Event

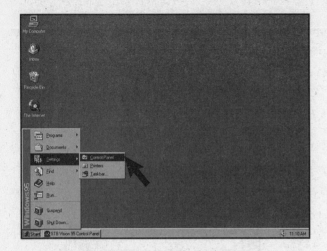

1 Open the **Start** menu, select **Settings**, and select **Control Panel**.

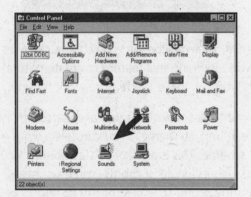

2 Double-click on the **Sounds** icon. Windows 95 displays the Sounds Properties dialog box.

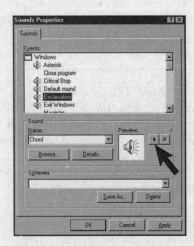

3 In the **Events** list, events that already have sounds attached to them are marked with a "blaring speaker" icon. Click on a marked event and click on the **Play** button to hear the sound.

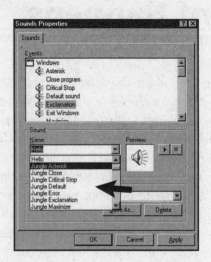

4 To attach a sound to an event or to change the sound currently attached to an event, click on that event in the Events list.

5 Select a sound file from the Name list. (This is a list of the WAV files in the \MEDIA subfolder of the Windows 95 folder.)

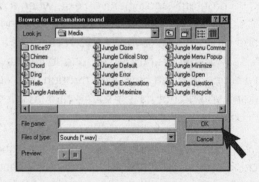

6 If you have a WAV file in some other folder that you want to use, click on the Browse button.

7 Change to the folder in which the sound file is kept, select it from the list, and click on **OK**.

Do It Yourself Assign a Sound to an Event

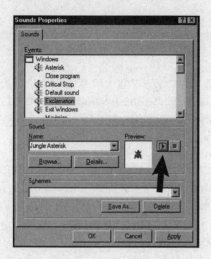

If you want to select a sound scheme instead of changing the sounds for individual events, select a scheme from the **Schemes** list. To switch back to the default sounds, select **Windows Default** from the Schemes list.

8 To test your sound file, click on the **Play** button. (There's a similar button in the Browse dialog box.)

9 Repeat steps 4–8 for additional events. Click on **OK** when you're finished.

Begin Do It Yourself Save Your Selections as a Sound Scheme

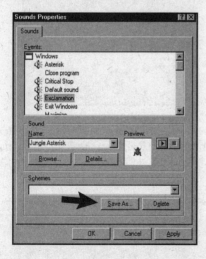

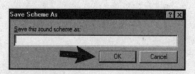

3 In the Save Scheme As dialog box, type a name for your scheme and click **OK**.

1 To save a set of sounds as a scheme you can select and deselect, you first assign whatever sounds you want to the appropriate events (as explained in the previous steps).

2 When you're ready to save your set of sounds, click on the **Save As** button.

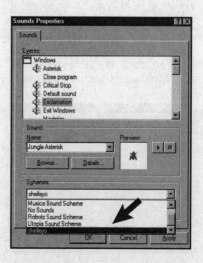

4 Your new scheme is listed in the dialog box.

Record a Sound File from Your Favorite CD

In the project "Play a Sound File When a Particular Event Happens" (page 461), you learned how to associate a sound file with a particular Windows event, and in "Play a CD" on page 240, you learned how to play a music CD on your computer's CD-ROM drive. So if you have a favorite song on CD, why not combine these two tasks? Save a key phrase from your favorite song and use it when a particular sound event happens, such as when you start Windows.

Of course, you won't want to record an entire song in a sound file because the resulting file would be huge, would waste disk space, and would take a long time to play back.

In this project, you'll record only a small segment of a song, such as a favorite riff or a key phrase. To do this, you'll need both CD Player and Sound Recorder active. In addition, you also should adjust the recording volume for the CD player (how to do this also is covered in this project).

Begin Do It Yourself Set the Recording Volume for the CD

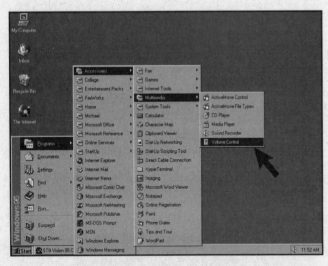

1 Open the **Start** menu, select **Programs**, select **Accessories**, select **Multimedia**, and select **Volume Control**.

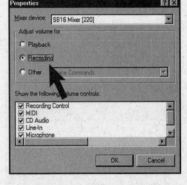

3 The Properties dialog box appears. Select the **Recording** option button. In the **Show the following volume controls** list, make sure **CD Audio** is checked and click **OK**.

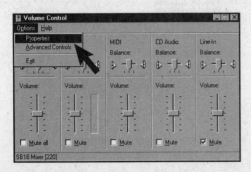

2 In the Volume Control window, open the **Options** menu and select **Properties**.

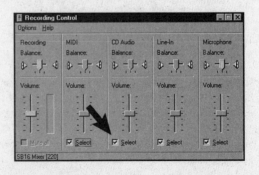

4 Check the **Select** box under the CD Audio volume bar. This turns the input "on." Set the recording volume relatively high and close the window.

Begin Do It Yourself Record Your Sound File

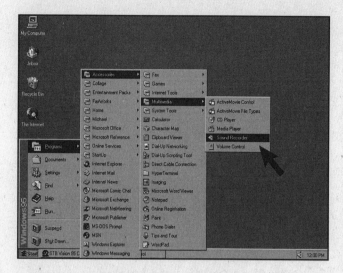

1 Open the **Start** menu, select **Programs**, select **Accessories**, select **Multimedia**, and select **Sound Recorder**.

2 The Sound Recorder program is started. Insert the CD you want to record. The CD Player should start automatically and then minimize itself to the taskbar.

3 Click on the **CD Player** taskbar button to restore the CD Player window.

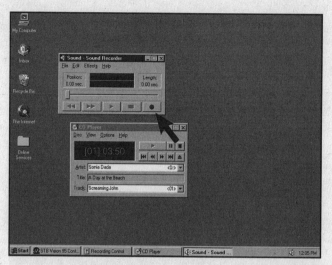

4 When you hear something you want to record, click on the **Record** button in the Sound Recorder window.

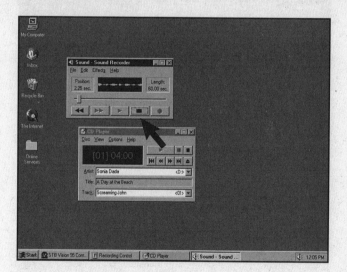

5 Record what you want, and then click on the **Stop** button in the Sound Recorder window.

6 In the Sound Recorder window, open the **File** menu and select **Save**.

(continues)

Do It Yourself Record Your Sound File *(continued)*

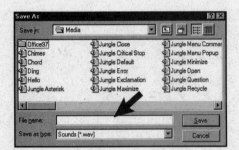

7 In the Save As dialog box, change to the \WINDOWS\MEDIA folder, type a name for your file, and click on **Save**. You can then exit the Sound Recorder and CD Player programs.

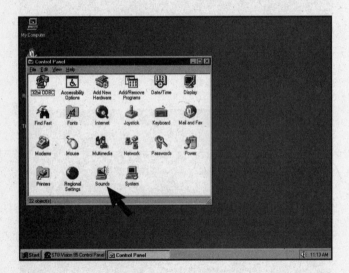

8 Open the **Control Panel** by clicking on the Start button, selecting **Settings**, and selecting **Control Panel**. Double-click on the **Sounds** icon.

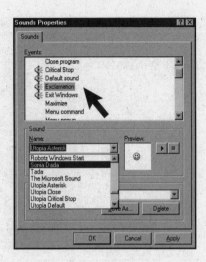

9 In the Sounds Properties dialog box, select the event to which you want to attach the new sound from the Events list.

10 Select your sound file from the Name list, and then click on **OK**. Your recording is set to play whenever the specified event happens. In this example, the sound file will play when you exit Windows 95.

Customize the Taskbar

When you first start using Windows 95, the taskbar seems like a great thing. Within easy reach at the bottom of your screen, the taskbar is the quickest way to switch between programs. Just click a button, and you're there.

As is true of many elements in Windows, you can control certain aspects of the taskbar's appearance. For example, by default, the taskbar always displays the time in a little clock at the right end; however, you can turn off this clock display if you want. If you use your sound card a lot to play CDs or to record music, you can place the volume controls within easy reach by adding a Volume icon to the taskbar, beside the clock. You also can add an icon to monitor your laptop's battery life. In addition, if you've added commands with long descriptions to your Start menu, you can have Windows display smaller icons on the Start menu so that more of the descriptions show (which produces the same result on the taskbar button).

By default, the taskbar doesn't disappear when you're using a program (such as Word for Windows 95). Because it remains at the bottom of the program window, you can easily switch to another application without having to switch back to the desktop first. Most programs today, though, include their own toolbars, status bars, and so on in various areas of the program window. So you may find that having the taskbar displayed in addition to all these other tools leaves you very little room to work. In some cases, the taskbar may even cover up important information within a program running full screen. Windows 95 provides an easy way for you to hide the taskbar yet keep it easily accessible so you can redisplay it when you need it.

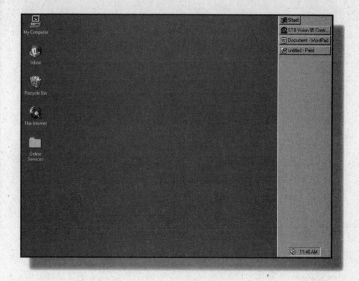

Finally, if you decide you want Windows to display the taskbar all the time, you can move it to a side of the screen where it doesn't conflict with your work (to the right side of the screen, for example). Although you can't move the taskbar into the middle of the screen (as you can an application's toolbar), you can make it wider or narrower to make it easier to see or less obvious, whichever is more convenient. You also can change the size of the text on the taskbar by changing the size of the text used on the title bars. You also can change the color of the taskbar by changing the color of "3D objects." For more information on that subject, see "Change the Windows Color Scheme" on page 437.

The clock on the taskbar also gives you access to the current date. To see the current date, point to the clock display on the taskbar. The date pops up. You can change the current date and time by double-clicking on the clock button in the taskbar.

Begin Do It Yourself Hide the Taskbar

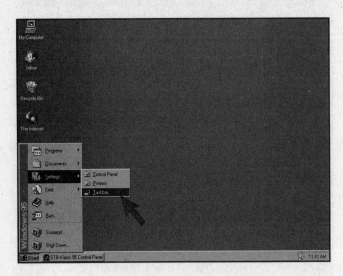

(**1**) Open the **Start** menu, select **Settings**, and select **Taskbar**.

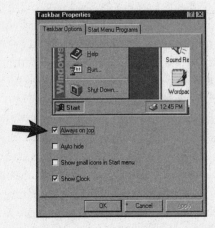

(**2**) Select the **Always on top** option, and whenever the taskbar is visible, it appears on top of any other window on the screen. This makes it easy to find and use the taskbar. If you turn this option off, you'll need to click on a visible part of the taskbar to bring it to the front of the other windows so you can use it.

(**3**) (Optional) Select the **Auto hide** option to have Windows hide the taskbar from view all the time until you "recall" it to the screen (which you'll see how to do in a moment).

(**4**) Click on **OK**.

(**5**) If you selected the Auto hide option, Windows hides the taskbar from view, except for a small sliver that's visible at the bottom of the screen. (If you've moved the taskbar to some other edge of the screen, the sliver appears there, not at the bottom.)

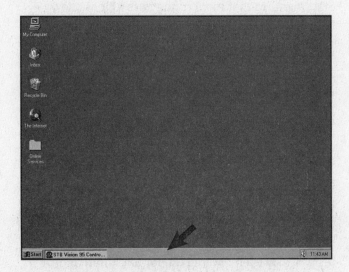

(**6**) To redisplay the taskbar, drag the mouse pointer to the bottom of the screen (or the side on which it was displayed). To hide the taskbar again, move the mouse away from the bottom of the screen.

Begin Do It Yourself Hide the Clock or Use Small Icons on the Taskbar

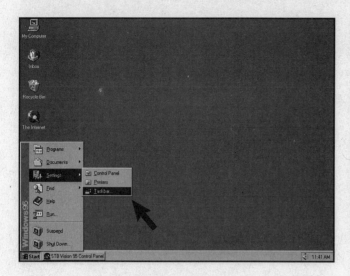

1 Open the **Start** menu, select **Settings**, and select **Taskbar**.

4 Windows displays the taskbar according to your settings (in this case, without the clock, and using small icons).

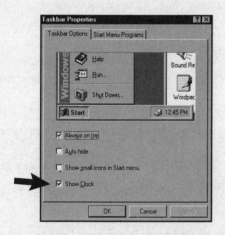

If moving the mouse pointer away from the bottom of the screen fails to hide the taskbar again, just click once on the desktop.

To hide the taskbar temporarily, you can resize it so that it's barely visible.

2 In the Taskbar Properties dialog box, click on the **Taskbar Options** tab (if necessary). To remove the clock display from the taskbar, click on **Show Clock** to deselect it.

3 To have Windows display small icons on the Start menu (and thus the taskbar buttons), click on **Show small icons in Start menu**. Click the on **OK**.

Begin Do It Yourself   Move the Taskbar

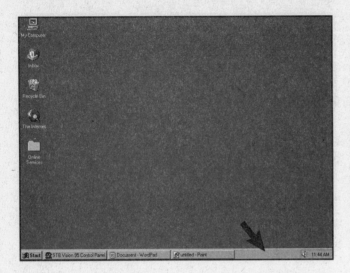

1 Click on a blank area of the taskbar and hold down the mouse button.

2 Drag the taskbar to another edge of the screen. (Again, you can move the taskbar only to a screen edge, and not into the middle of the screen.)

3 When you release the mouse button, the taskbar appears in the new location.

Begin Do It Yourself   Resize the Taskbar

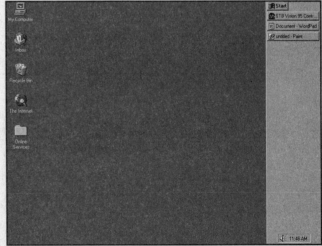

1 Position the mouse pointer on the taskbar edge that borders the desktop. The pointer becomes a two-headed arrow. Drag the border to the size you want.

2 The taskbar is resized.

DO IT YOURSELF

Perform Common Housekeeping Chores

Unfortunately, computers are not self-maintaining machines. From time to time, you need to perform some basic housekeeping to keep them running their best. You see, computers (like desk drawers, closets, and garages) tend to become collectors of things: from the umpteen fonts that every program adds to your master list, to the utilities you once thought were useful but can't remember why. So every once in a while, you need to do some "spring cleaning."

"Spring cleaning" your computer usually involves adding new features as your system grows, and removing old ones as they grow outdated. Sometimes it's as simple as getting windows out of your way so you can work more efficiently, and sometimes it's as important as maintaining an up-to-date address book. The following tasks teach you how to perform the most common housekeeping chores:

What You Will Find in This Section

Maintain Your Address Book

In "Use Microsoft Exchange to Send and Receive E-Mail" (page 286), you learned how to use Microsoft Exchange to send electronic messages (e-mail) and faxes. An important part of sending e-mail (or faxes for that matter) is addressing them correctly, and the best way to make sure you do that is to maintain an accurate address book. So Microsoft Exchange includes an Address Book program that makes it easy to do just that.

Microsoft Exchange comes configured for sending and receiving e-mail through the Microsoft Network, and Microsoft Mail (provided that you installed these options). So you already have separate address books for each of these services. In addition, you have a personal address book in which you can store information such as company name and department, and you can ignore the other address books and keep all your entries in the personal address book.

If you added additional services (such as CompuServe, PRODIGY, or America Online), Windows 95 created additional address books for them as well. In any case, this project shows you how to maintain your e-mail addresses in any of the address books.

An e-mail address consists of a unique name or number that identifies the receiver. Each e-mail service has some method by which it assigns addresses to each member. Here's a sample of some of the address types you might encounter:

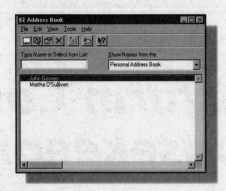

Besides storing e-mail addresses, the Personal Address Book is capable of storing other information such as a person's home and work phone numbers. You can use these numbers to have the Phone Dialer dial the phone for you.

When you add an entry to the personal address book, you must identify its type (such as Microsoft Fax). If you want to add a CompuServe address and a Microsoft Fax address to the Personal Address Book for the same person, you must make two entries. For that reason, you might want to keep all your CompuServe addresses in the CompuServe address book, all your Microsoft Network addresses in the MSN address book, and so on.

Internet	jfulton@iquest.com
CompuServe	70690,3122
America Online	wordlady
GEnie	jl.fulton12
PRODIGY	rtpc69c
Delphi	j_fulton

Begin Do It Yourself   Add a New Entry to the Address Book

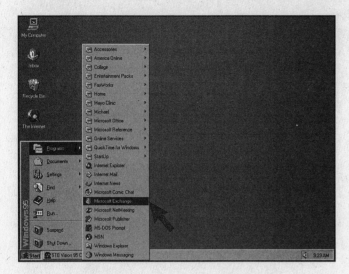

1 Click on the **Start** button, select **Programs**, and select **Microsoft Exchange**.

2 Click on the **Address Book** icon.

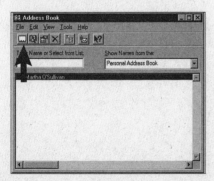

3 The Address Book window appears. Click on the **New Entry** icon.

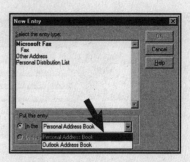

4 In the New Entry dialog box, open the **Put this entry In the** list box and select the address book to which you want to add the entry.

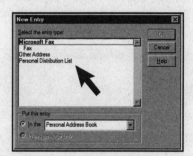

5 In the **Select the entry type** list box, select the type of entry you want to make. Click on **OK**.

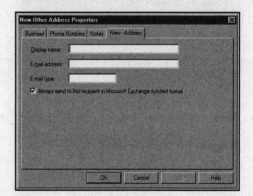

6 Depending on what you selected in step 5, the dialog box will vary. Enter the address information. To complete other tabs, click on the tab and then complete that information.

(continues)

Do It Yourself Add a New Entry to the Address Book *(continued)*

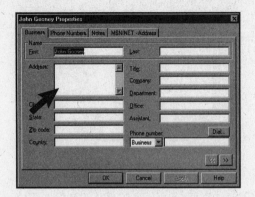

The entry type determines which program can use the entry. For example, if you select cc:Mail, only cc:Mail can use the information you place in the entry. So if you need to enter a CompuServe and an Internet address for the same person, you must make two entries. The Phone Dialer is the only exception to this; it can use any phone number you place in the entry, regardless of which type you select.

7 Use the Business tab to enter business information such as company name, address, title, and phone numbers. Complete this information and then click on the next tab.

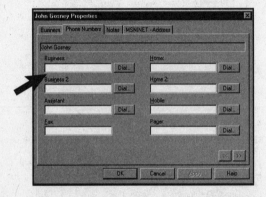

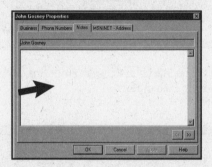

9 Click on the **Notes** tab.

10 Enter any additional information and then click **OK**.

8 Use the Phone Numbers tab to enter phone numbers (business, home, fax, and so on) for this contact. Complete this information.

Begin Do It Yourself Delete an Entry from the Address Book

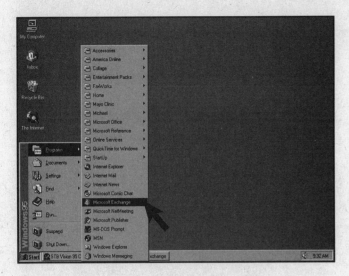

1 Click on the **Start** button, select **Programs**, and select **Microsoft Exchange**.

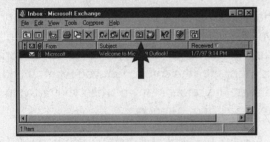

2 Click on the **Address Book** icon.

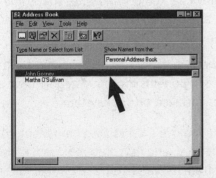

3 In the **Show Names from the** list, select the address book that contains the entry you want to remove.

4 Click on the entry you want to delete.

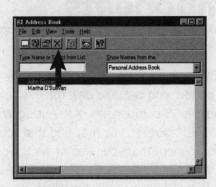

5 Click on the **Delete** icon.

6 Microsoft Exchange prompts you to confirm the deletion. Click on **Yes**.

Add and Remove Windows 95 Components

If you chose to install Windows 95 using the Typical option, you installed only the most often used Windows 95 components. After using Windows 95 for a while, however, you may find that you didn't install a component that you need or want. For example, you might want to use one of these useful programs that are not normally installed:

Backup

Microsoft Mail

Sound Schemes

Microsoft Network

Microsoft Fax

Networking Support

Accessibility Options

This task shows you step-by-step how to add any of these components or any other component you want. However, if you start to add a Windows 95 component and find that your hard disk is too crowded to hold the new component, you may need to remove one first. Therefore, this task also shows you how to remove a component if necessary. You also can choose to remove a component you no longer use.

> This task describes how to add and remove Windows components—not applications. If you have a Windows program (such as Excel) that you want to remove because you no longer use it, see "Remove an Old Program" on page 481.

Windows components are organized by category. So when you want to add a Windows component, you must select the category (such as Accessories or Disk Tools) for the component you want to add. Keep these indicators in mind when you're trying to locate the correct category:

- A blank box indicates that no components from that category have been installed on your system.

- A gray checked box indicates that some—but not all—of the components in that category have been installed.

- A check mark in a white box indicates that all the components for that category have already been installed on your system.

When you remove a Windows component, its program is deleted, and its icon is removed. It also is removed from its standard place on the Start menu. Any additional icons (shortcuts) or extra menu commands are not removed, however; you must delete them manually.

Begin Do It Yourself   Add New Components

1 Click on the **Start** button, select **Settings**, and select **Control Panel**.

2 Double-click on the **Add/Remove Programs** icon.

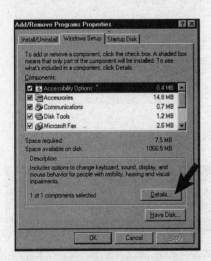

3 In the Add/Remove Programs Properties dialog box, click on the **Windows Setup** tab.

4 In the Components list, select the category of the component you want to install, and click on **Details**.

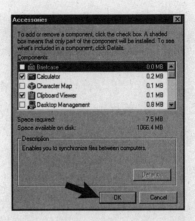

5 The dialog box changes to display the individual components in the selected category. Select the individual components you want to install. (A check mark indicates that the component is already installed.) Click **OK**.

6 You're returned to the Add/Remove Properties dialog box. Click **OK**.

7 A message appears telling you to insert the proper disk (or CD-ROM). Insert the disk or CD and click **OK**. You see a progress window as the appropriate files are copied.

Begin Do It Yourself   Remove a Component

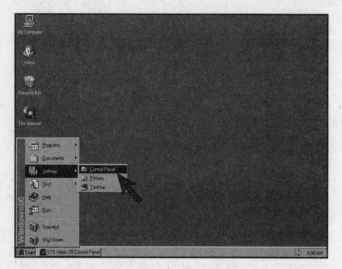

1 Click on the **Start** button, select **Settings**, and select **Control Panel**.

2 Double-click on the **Add/Remove Programs** icon.

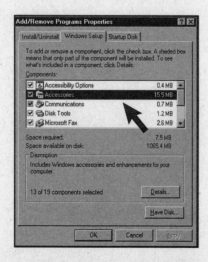

3 Click on the **Windows Setup** tab, and then double-click on the category that contains a component you want to remove.

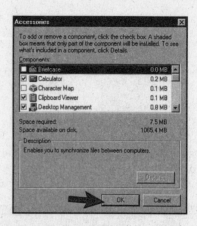

4 The dialog box changes to display the individual components in the selected category. Click to deselect the components you want to remove. (No check mark indicates that you want the component removed.) Then click **OK**.

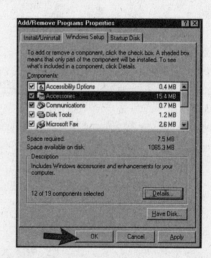

5 Click on **OK**.

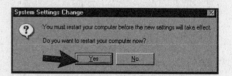

6 Click on **Yes**. Windows 95 removes the components you selected.

Clear the Document Menu

When you create or open a document within most Windows programs (such as Microsoft Word), that program remembers the name of the document. The next time you start the program, you can reopen that document by selecting it from a list at the bottom of the program's File menu. Having your most-often-used documents listed on a menu saves you the time and trouble of searching through files and folders to find them. However, most programs keep track of only the last four documents you created or changed. Some, but not all, allow you to slightly increase the number of tracked documents.

Windows 95 has expanded this idea on a global scale. When you create or open a document, Windows makes a note of it and adds the name of that document to the Document menu. The Document menu gives you easy access to documents you've used recently. To open a recently used document, click on the **Start** button, select **Documents**, and select the document from the list that appears (the documents appear in alphabetical order). If you select an Excel worksheet, for example, Windows 95 starts Excel and opens that document for you.

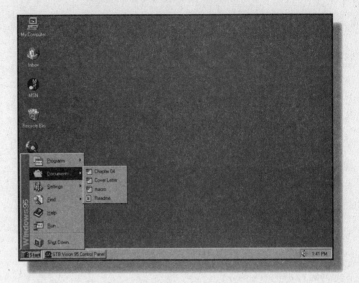

As you open more documents, the Document menu grows until it holds the maximum 15 documents. After that, the next document replaces the oldest document on the menu. And if, after a while, you find that your Document menu is cluttered with documents from an old project, you can clear it out and start over with recently used documents.

Begin Do It Yourself Remove Documents from the Document Menu

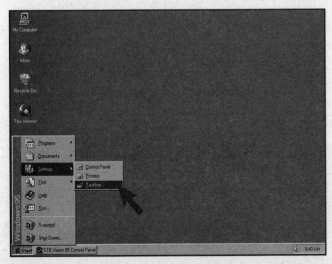

1 Click on the **Start** button, select **Settings**, and select **Taskbar**.

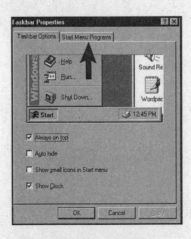

2 Click on the **Start Menu Programs** tab.

(continues)

Do It Yourself Remove Documents from the Document Menu *(continued)*

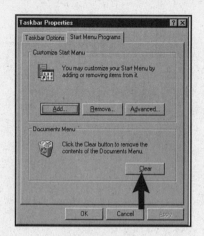

Not all programs are capable of adding their documents to the Document menu. For example, you'll find that documents you open in DOS programs do not appear on the Document menu. This is not restricted to DOS program documents, though; some Windows 3.1 programs are not capable of adding their documents to the Document list either.

3 In the Documents Menu section, click on the **Clear** button.

4 Click on **OK**.

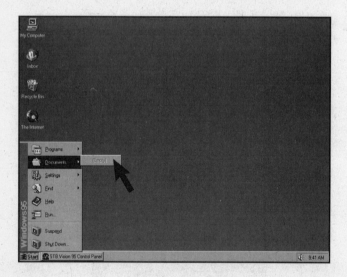

5 If you access the Document menu now, you see that it is empty.

Remove an Old Program

Suppose you have a program you haven't used in a while, and you decide you don't really need it anymore. Naturally, you want to remove the program from your hard disk to make room for more important things.

If you've installed DOS programs or programs compatible with earlier versions of Windows, you may remember that removing a program was always a difficult process because Windows programs, as a rule, place their files in several folders, including the Windows folder itself. In addition, Windows programs usually make undocumented changes to your system files, and trying to find those changes (and subsequently remove them) can be a pain.

With Windows 95, the process has changed somewhat. Windows 95 provides a method that makes removing a program (a Windows 95 program, that is) a simple task. The Windows 95 Uninstall process eliminates all of the program's files, its icons, and any changes the program might have made to shared system files.

A Word About Removing Windows 3.1 Programs

Windows 3.1 programs are difficult to remove because they make changes all over your system. You easily can remove just the program files, but other files and changes to shared files still exist. For example, there is one file in the Windows 95 folder called WIN.INI. Almost all Windows 3.1 programs make changes to this file. Eliminating those changes requires you to open the file and delete the commands associated with the program you're removing. Luckily, this is not difficult because programs identify their sections within the WIN.INI with a header like this:

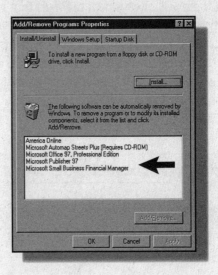

```
[Collage Capture]
Save on Exit=1
Prompt on Entry=0
Collage Capture Settings
File=C:\COLLAGE9\ORIGINAL.SET
```

To eliminate the changes made by Collage (a screen capture program), you need to open the capture win.ini file by double-clicking on it in Explorer. Notepad opens the file. Then you select the section, press **Delete**, save the file, and exit.

Windows 3.1 programs often create subfolders within the Windows 95 folder, so be sure to delete those, too. For example, Lotus programs create a central folder called \LOTUSAPPS for their shared files, and Microsoft programs have a folder called \MSAPPS. Be careful when deleting such folders: if you have several Lotus programs, you may remove some files that a remaining Lotus program needs.

Also, you might want to make a careful search of the Windows 95 folder for any remaining files associated with your Windows 3.1 program, and then delete them. Such files are usually easy to identify because they include some part of the program's name (such as LOTUS.INI). To eliminate the difficulty that comes with correctly identifying which files to delete (and because there will always be a few files that escape your notice no matter how careful you are), you might consider investing in a good uninstall program, such as MicroHelp UNINSTALLER to help you get rid of them. Just be sure that the uninstaller program is compatible with Windows 95.

To recap, here are the basic steps for removing a Windows 3.1 program from your system:

1. Delete the program's main folder and its icon.

2. Search the Windows 95 folder and eliminate any additional folders or files that belonged to the program.

3. Open the WIN.INI file and delete the changes made by the program.

Begin Do It Yourself Remove a Windows 95 Program

1 Click on the **Start** button, select **Settings**, and select **Control Panel**.

2 Double-click on the **Add/Remove Programs** icon.

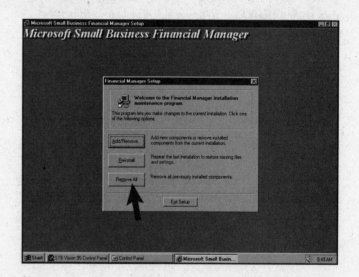

5 The install program for that particular application is started. You are prompted to select what changes you want to make. Click the **Remove All** button and then follow the on-screen instructions. These instructions may vary from program to program.

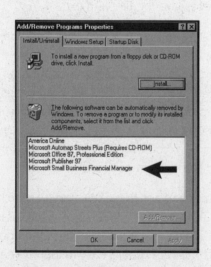

3 In the Add/Remove Programs Properties dialog box, click on the **Install/Uninstall** tab if necessary.

4 Select the program you want to uninstall from the list, and click on **Remove**.

Add and View Fonts

After you get the basics down for creating documents, you'll want to give your documents a more professional, creative finish. Changing fonts is one of the most dramatic ways to add power and poise to the printed word. And one of the benefits of Windows technology is how fonts are handled.

A *font* is a collection of characters in a certain typeface, size, and style. For example, Arial 12-point is one type of font. The font styles make text bold, italic, or bold and italic.

By changing fonts for various documents, you can create a different tone for each document. For example, for an invitation, you may want to use a script font like this one:

Wedding Invitation

For a party, you may want to use a more fun font, like this one:

MONSTER BASH

The fonts you can use depend on the fonts you have installed on your computer. You can get fonts from the following sources:

- **Printer** Your printer will come with some fonts. In font lists, these fonts have printer icons next to them.

- **Windows** Windows uses a font technology called TrueType fonts. These fonts are actually files stored on your hard disk. When you want to print using one of these fonts, Windows sends the information on how to print the font to the printer. Windows comes with some TrueType fonts; you can buy additional TrueType font collections and install them. TrueType fonts have a TT next to their names in font lists.

- **Font cartridge** Your printer may be able to use font cartridges. You can purchase cartridges, insert them in the printer, and use the fonts on the cartridge.

- **Soft fonts** Your application may be able to use other types of downloadable fonts (software files).

When you first start using Windows, you can use any of the installed fonts without making any changes. To view the available fonts, open the Fonts folder as described in this task. If you purchase a font collection, you will need to install these new fonts to let Windows know they are available. This task also shows you how to install new fonts.

When you are looking through a font list, the entire list may seem unbelievably long. You can limit the list by hiding variations of the font (bold, italic, and so on). To do so, select **My Computer**, select **Control Panel**, and select the **Fonts** folder. Then open the **View** menu and select **Hide Variations**. You can have Windows display the fonts in a font list by similarities by opening the **View** menu and selecting **List Fonts by Similarity**.

Begin Do It Yourself   View the Installed Fonts

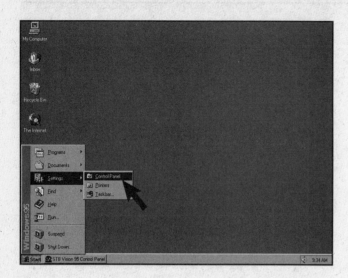

3 Windows displays the fonts installed on your system. To see an example of a font, double-click on the font file icon.

1 Click on the **Start** button, select **Settings**, and select **Control Panel**.

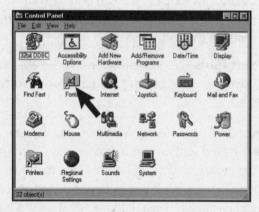

2 In the Control Panel window, double-click on the **Fonts** folder.

4 Windows displays a sample of the selected font.

To print a page using the sample font, click the **Print** button. You also can print a font directly from the Font folder by selecting it, selecting the **File Print** command, and clicking **OK**.

Begin Do It Yourself   Install New Fonts

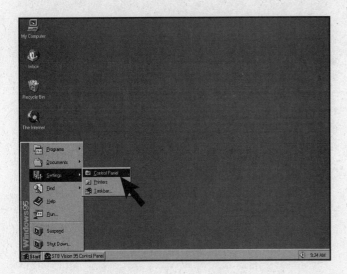

1 Click on the **Start** button, select **Settings**, and select **Control Panel**.

2 In the Control Panel window, double-click on the **Fonts** folder.

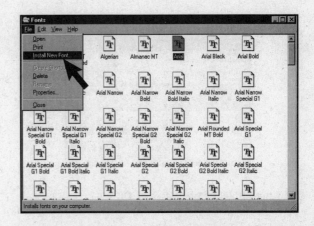

3 Windows displays the fonts installed on your system. Open the **File** menu and select **Install New Font**.

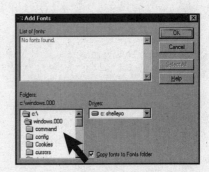

4 The Add Fonts dialog box appears. If the font you want to add is in a different drive, display the **Drives** drop-down list and select the drive. In the Folders list, select the folder that contains the font(s) you want to add.

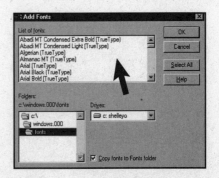

5 In the List of fonts box, select the fonts you want to install. To select all fonts, click the **Select All** button.

(continues)

Do It Yourself Install New Fonts

(continued)

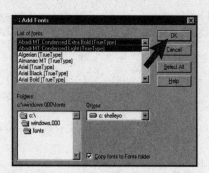

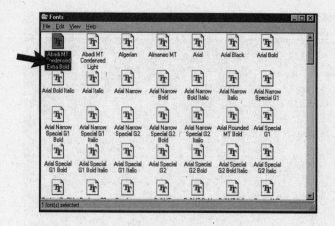

6 After you select the fonts, click **OK**.

7 Windows adds the new fonts.

Remove Fonts

Technically, the word "font" describes the combination of a typeface and a point size, as in Times New Roman 10-point. In reality, each *variation* of the font, such as bold or bold italic, is stored in its own file that contains the point size variations. As a result, a single typeface, such as Book Antiqua, may take up a lot of room on the hard disk.

If you find that you have fonts you don't use, you might want to remove them. Removing them gives

you several immediate benefits: more room on the hard disk, and a smaller, simpler font list. A smaller font list, by the way, speeds up the amount of time it takes to load a program and to display its font list.

To completely remove a font that you no longer want to use, you need to locate all of its variations. Windows 95 provides a method by which you can do just that, as you'll see in this project.

Begin Do It Yourself Remove Similar Fonts

1 Click on the **Start** button, select **Settings**, and select **Control Panel**.

2 In the Control Panel window, double-click on the **Fonts** icon.

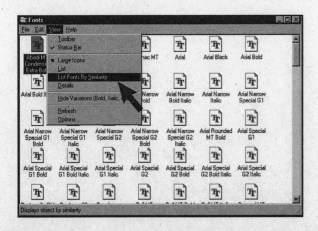

3 The Fonts window appears. Open the **View** menu and select **List Fonts by Similarity**.

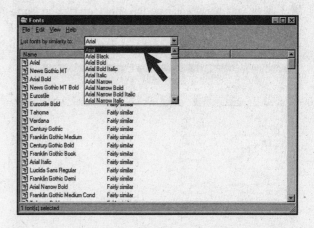

4 The fonts are listed by similarity. Open the **List fonts by similarity to** list and select the font you want to delete.

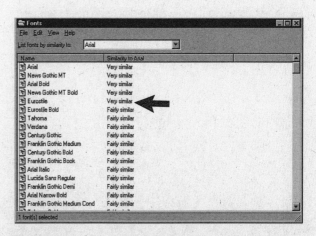

5 Fonts that are similar to (and probably variations of) the font you want to delete appear with the notation "Very Similar." You probably want to get rid of these fonts, too.

(continues)

Do It Yourself Remove Similar Fonts   *(continued)*

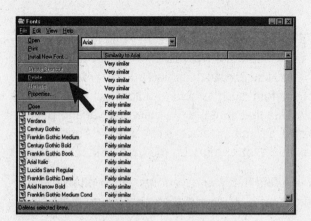

6 To be sure that you have the correct font, double-click on it. A window opens to show you what the font looks like.

7 When you're sure you have the right font, click on **Done**.

9 Open the **File** menu and select **Delete**.

10 Windows prompts you to confirm the deletion. Click on **Yes**.

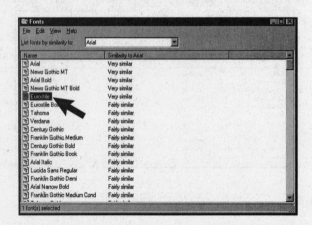

8 Click on the font you want to delete. To delete several fonts, press **Ctrl** and click on each font you want to delete.

DO IT YOURSELF

Get the Most from Your Laptop with Windows 95

Windows 95 provides many useful tools that make living with a laptop much more enjoyable. For example, if you generally use a desktop PC, but often use a laptop when you travel, you will want to read this section to find out about the many tools that help you transfer files, print your documents, and keep your files in synch.

In addition, you'll find several tools for maximizing your laptop's power so you don't run out just when you're in the middle of finishing a big project. There's even a simple way for you to make the mouse easier to see on the laptop's darker screen. The following projects will help you make the most of working with your laptop:

What You Will Find in This Section

Keep Your Desktop and Laptop Files in Synch with Briefcase

Windows 95 provides several ways to transfer files between your desktop and your laptop PC. In the most common method, you use a program called Briefcase and a disk to transfer files back and forth and to keep them synchronized.

The other method, called Direct Cable Connection, involves physically connecting the two PCs with a special cable. After you connect the computers, you can use the files, programs, and even the printer on your desktop when you type commands on your laptop. You also can copy files back and forth through the connection, using the Briefcase as described here. You'll learn more about Direct Cable Connection in "Link Your Laptop PC to Your Desktop" (page 493).

Most of the tasks in this section use programs (such as Briefcase and Direct Cable Connect) that Windows did not install unless you chose the Portable option during Setup. You can still install these programs via the Add/Remove Programs icon in the Control Panel. See "Add and Remove Windows 95 Components" on page 476 for more details.

More About Briefcase and How it Works

This task concentrates on using the Briefcase program to transfer files between your desktop and laptop PCs and to keep them in synch. Basically, you double-click on the **Briefcase** icon, and it opens into a window. Drag the files you want to take with you for use on your laptop into this window. Then close the window and drag the Briefcase icon onto a disk. This copies the files to the disk. You can drag the Briefcase from the disk onto the laptop, open its window, and use the files.

Although so far this method seems similar to the process of copying files, it's actually more than that.

The Briefcase keeps track of the changes you make to any of its files so that when you copy the Briefcase back onto the disk and return to your desktop PC, the Briefcase knows which files have been changed. It then helps you update the corresponding files on the desktop PC so the two sets of files (the ones on your laptop PC and the ones on the desktop PC) remain in synch. In the unlikely case that you want some of the files to not be updated, you can actually choose which files to update. If you used the usual copy method, you'd have to figure out for yourself which files had been changed (and thus, which files should be updated).

The Briefcase can only hold as many files as will fit onto a disk. If you plan to take more files than will fit on a disk with you, you need to create a second briefcase on your desktop and place it on a separate disk. To create a brief-case, open **Explorer** and select the folder on the desktop PC in which you want to create a briefcase. Open the **File** menu, select **New**, and select **Briefcase**.

Begin Do It Yourself   Transfer Files from Desktop to Laptop

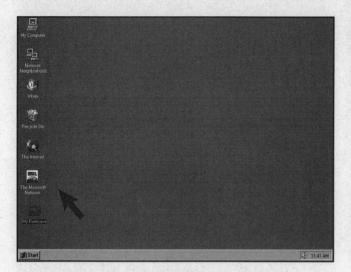

1 Double-click on the **My Briefcase** icon located on the desktop. (If this is your first time to use Briefcase, a welcome box appears. Click on **Finish** to close it.)

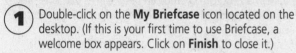

2 The My Briefcase window opens.

3 Click on the **Start** button, select **Programs**, and select **Windows Explorer**.

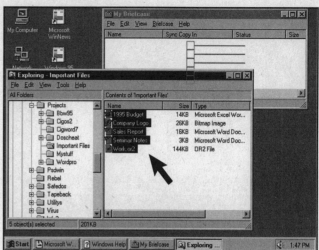

4 Drag the files you want from the Explorer window to the Briefcase window. Close Briefcase by clicking on its **Close** button.

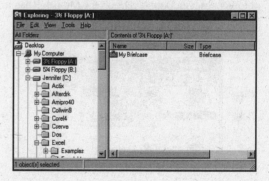

5 Drag the Briefcase icon off of the desktop and onto the disk.

6 Remove the disk and take it with you on your trip. Use the files as needed. You can open the Briefcase folder on the disk and use the files from there, or you can drag the Briefcase off the disk and onto the laptop's hard drive to use the files. (Just be sure to drag the Briefcase back onto the disk when you finish.)

(continues)

Do It Yourself Transfer Files from Desktop to Laptop *(continued)*

7 When you return from your trip, insert the Briefcase disk into your desktop PC's floppy drive.

8 Open **Explorer** and drag the My Briefcase folder back onto the desktop. Double-click on the **My Briefcase** icon to open it.

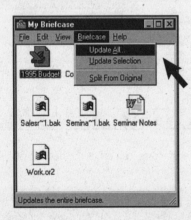

9 In the My Briefcase window, open the **Briefcase** menu and select **Update All**.

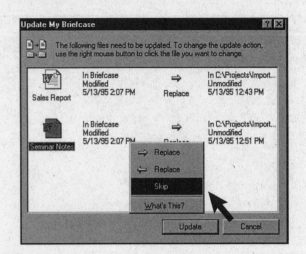

10 (Optional) You can override an update on a particular file by right-clicking on it and selecting **Skip** from the shortcut menu.

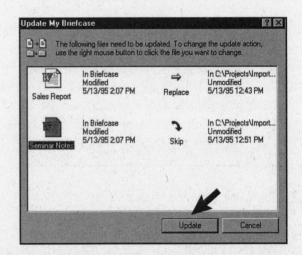

11 When you're ready, click on **Update**.

After Windows updates the files on the desktop PC, use them as you would normally. When you leave on another trip, open the Briefcase and repeat steps 11 through 13 to update the files in the Briefcase. Drag the Briefcase onto a disk, and you're ready to go.

Link Your Laptop PC to Your Desktop

With Direct Cable Connection, you can connect two computers via a cable so that each computer gains access to the other computer's resources (its programs, its files, and its printer). And if one PC is connected to a network, the other computer gains access to the network as well.

Almost all PCs have at least one parallel and at least one serial port. These ports can be used to link the two PCs together by using the appropriate cable. To connect the two PCs, you'll need either:

- Parallel to parallel cable, to use the parallel ports

- Serial to serial cable (must be a null modem cable), to use the serial ports

Although you can use Direct Cable Connection with any two PCs, it comes in handy when dealing with a desktop PC and a portable laptop. Through the connection, you can run your desktop PC's programs without having to install them on a laptop, which might have limited disk space. In addition, you can use the desktop PC's data files without having to copy them to the laptop's hard disk.

If you have room on the laptop's hard drive, however, you might want to drag them to the Briefcase and then drag the Briefcase over to the laptop instead of using the files through the connection. When Windows can locate the files on the laptop, your program can access them more quickly. When you finish with the files, simply drag the Briefcase back to the desktop and update the files.

When two PCs are connected in this manner, one acts as the Host, and the other acts as the Guest. The Host computer is the one that shares its files, programs, or printer. The Guest computer is the one that uses these resources. In the most common scenario, the Host computer is your desktop PC, and the Guest computer is your laptop PC.

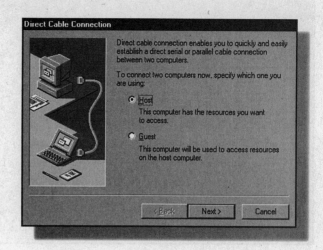

You follow four steps to set up this connection:

1. Connect the two computers with a cable.

2. Prepare the Host computer and select the resources you want to share. (Specifically, select individual folders, complete drives, or your printer to share.)

3. Set up the Guest computer and activate the connection.

4. Break the connection and disconnect the two computers.

After the laptop is connected to the desktop, you can use its printer to print your files. You can even "print" documents to a storage queue while you're away from the office, and then print them for real once you make the connection to your desktop PC. See "Defer Printing on Your Laptop Documents" on page 498 for the details.

Begin Do It Yourself Set Up the Host Computer

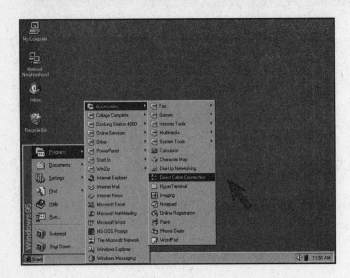

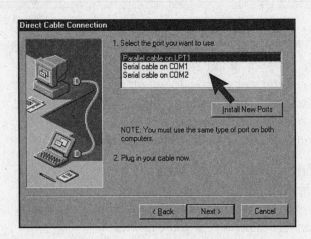

1 Connect the two PCs using a cable.

2 On the Host computer, click on the **Start** button, select **Programs**, select Accessories, and select **Direct Cable Connection**.

4 Select the port to which you connected the cable and click on **Next**.

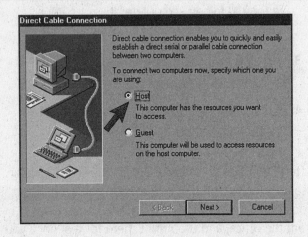

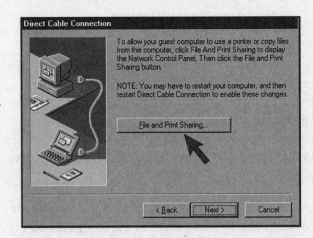

3 Select **Host** and click on **Next**.

5 Click on **File and Print Sharing**. (If you've already enabled file and/or print sharing on your PC, you won't see this screen. Skip to step 11.)

6 In the Network dialog box, click on the **File and Print Sharing** button again.

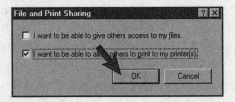

7 The File and Print Sharing dialog box appears. Select what you want to share and click **OK**. You can choose to share your files, your printer, or both. If you're not sure what you might want to share, choose both options just in case.

Do It Yourself Set Up the Host Computer

8 Click **OK** again. If Windows 95 wants to restart your PC, click on **Yes**. (It wants to restart if you have enabled file/print sharing.)

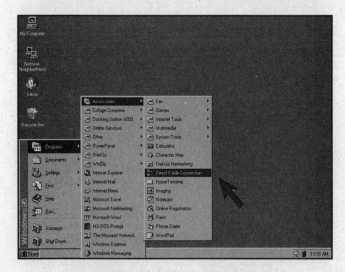

9 Click on the **Start** button, select **Programs**, select **Accessories**, and select **Direct Cable Connection**.

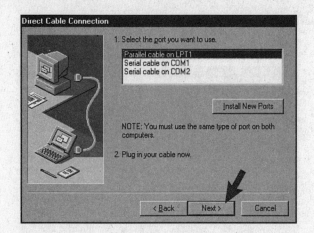

10 The Direct Cable Connection dialog box appears again. Make sure it still says Host, and then click on **Next** to move to the next screen. The next screen asks you to select a port, which you've already done. Click on **Next** again.

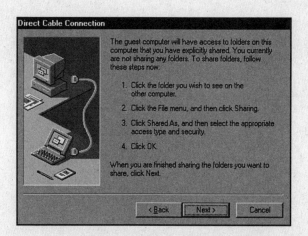

11 A message appears, telling you to select the folders (or drives) whose files you want to share. (Don't click **Next** yet!)

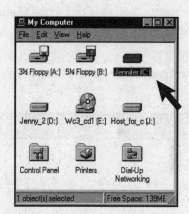

12 Double-click on the **My Computer** icon to open the My Computer window.

13 Double-click on the drive whose folders you want to share. To share an entire drive, click on it to select it, and then skip step 14. (To share a printer, open the **Printer** folder and select the printer to share.)

14 Select the folder whose files you want to share.

15 Open the **File** menu and select **Sharing**.

(continues)

Do It Yourself Set Up the Host Computer *(continued)*

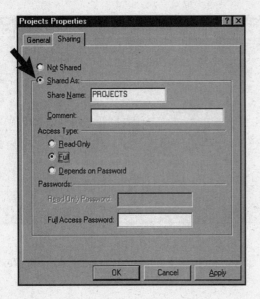

16 In the Properties dialog box, click on the **Sharing** tab and select the **Shared As** option.

17 Select the type of access you want to provide, and add password protection if you want. Click on **OK**.

18 The Sharing icon (an open hand) appears to mark the folder or drive you selected. Repeat steps 13 through 17 for additional folders or drives you want to share.

19 After you've set up your file sharing options, switch back to the Direct Cable Connection window and click on **Next**.

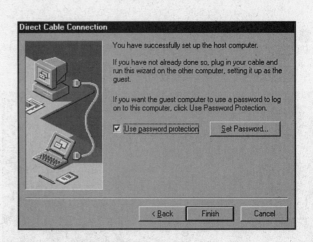

20 To set up password access to the connection, click on **Use password protection** and click on **Set Password**.

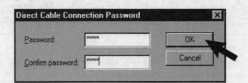

21 Type a password, type it again to confirm it, and click on **OK**.

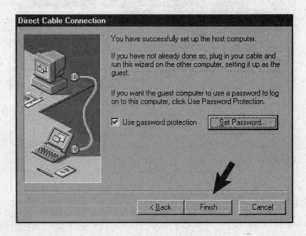

22 Complete the steps to configure the guest computer, then come back to the host and click on **Finish**.

Begin Do It Yourself   Set Up the Guest Computer

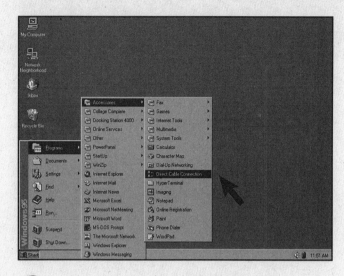

1 Click on the **Start** button, select **Programs**, select **Accessories**, and select **Direct Cable Connection**.

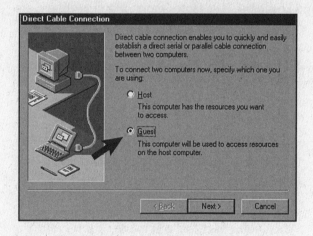

2 Select **Guest** and click on **Next**.

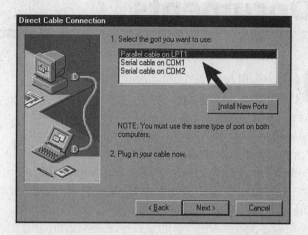

3 Select the connection to which you connected the cable and click on **Next**.

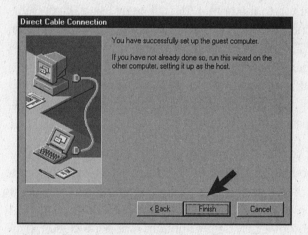

4 Click on **Finish**. The connection is now active, and you can use the Host computer's resources.

When you finish with the connection, close the Direct Cable Connection box. To reconnect at a later time, connect the cable and restart Direct Cable Connection on each PC. On the Host computer, click on **Listen** to start the connection. On the Guest computer, click on **Connect**.

Defer Printing on Your Laptop Documents

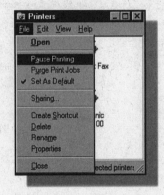

If you want, you can defer printing your laptop documents temporarily. This is handy when you're using your laptop on the road, far away from the nearest printer. When you defer printing, you still "print" your documents—that is, you still use the File Print command within a program to send a document to the printer—but Windows 95 doesn't actually print the document at that time. Instead, it holds all your "printed documents" until you give the command to send them on to the printer.

When you get back to your office, connect your laptop to the printer (directly or by using Direct Cable Connection, as explained in "Link Your Laptop PC to Your Desktop," page 493) and "release" your documents by turning off the Pause Printing or Work Offline option. Windows 95 immediately places the printer back into active mode and starts printing the files in the queue.

If you have a laptop and a docking station combo, you won't really have to do anything to get the pause printing option to work because when you're working on your laptop and it's not docked, Windows 95 automatically defers printing. A docking station, by the way, contains a slot in the front into which you place or "dock" the laptop (like a piece of bread in a toaster). When the docking station and the laptop are

connected in this manner, the laptop becomes a kind of desktop computer, with a regular-sized monitor and keyboard. (The larger monitor and keyboard are connected to the docking station in the same way that your monitor and keyboard are connected to the system unit of your PC.) The docking station might also provide a link to a network, a printer, or a modem.

If you use a docking station, you may see an extra command at the bottom of the Start menu: Eject PC. This enables you to undock your PC without shutting it down completely. When you select this command, it puts your laptop into Suspend mode and undocks it. Only docking stations with power docking/undocking support this feature.

Begin Do It Yourself Defer Printing on Your Laptop Documents

1 Double-click on the **My Computer** icon, and then double-click on the **Printers** folder.

2 Select the printer on which you want to print your documents later.

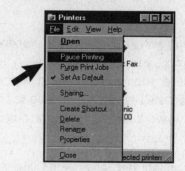

3 Open the **File** menu and select **Work Offline** or **Pause Printing**.

4 Continue to work, using the **File Print** command as usual to print your documents. Windows stores the files in the print queue but doesn't actually print them.

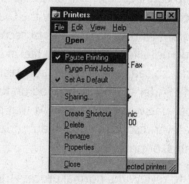

5 When you're ready to print the documents, open the **File** menu in the Printers folder window and select **Work Offline** or **Pause Printing** again. Windows begins printing.

Depending on the type of laptop computer you're using (and whether it has a docking station), you might see the Print queue at this point, or you might see a message telling you that there are documents waiting to print. Follow additional on-screen instructions to begin printing.

Dial Up Your Network at Work

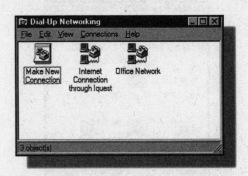

When you're away from the office working with your laptop, you don't have to feel "disconnected." Whenever you need something on the network, you can use Dial-Up Networking to connect to the network at work and access the resources you need.

In "Connect to an Internet Server with Dial-Up Networking" (page 422), you learn how to use Dial-Up Networking to connect to the Internet. Here you learn a similar method that enables you to use Dial-Up Networking to connect to your network at work.

You connect to the network through a network server that allows dial-up connections. (You don't dial into your own work computer; that's not how the Dial-Up Networking program works.) For reasons of security, a lot of networks do not allow outsiders to dial in; however, some do, so see your network administrator before you try this. After dialing in, you log on to the network with your password as normal. At that point, you can use whatever resources you are authorized to use: files, programs, or printers.

You might want to review the normal process for logging in and locating and using network resources before you continue; see "Use Windows on a Network" on page 367. Also, if you want to use a network printer from your laptop at home, you need to set it up on the laptop first. To do so, you have to work through a series of steps to add a printer icon for the network printer to the desktop. After that, you simply print whatever you want to that printer, and it goes to the network to be printed.

You must have the Dial-Up Networking option installed in order to complete this project. If you need to install it, flip to "Add and Remove Windows 95 Components" on page 476. (The Dial-Up Networking option is one of the Accessories programs.) In addition, you need to verify that the following things are true of your system:

- Your laptop and the computer to which you're connecting (network server) must have modems.

- Your laptop must have networking support installed. You do this through the Network icon in the Control Panel. Ask your network administrator for help because the support you install must work with the type of network you have.

- The server on your office network must allow a dial-up connection.

Begin Do It Yourself Connect to Your Network at Work

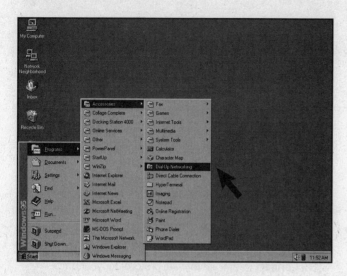

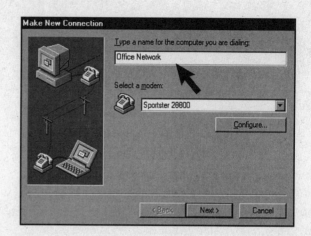

1 Click on the **Start** button, select **Programs**, select **Accessories**, and select **Dial-Up Networking**.

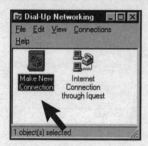

2 If you've used Dial-Up Networking before, double-click on the **Make New Connection** icon. Click on **Next**.

If you normally dial a 9 or some other access code to get an outside or a long distance phone line, enter that access code in the Dialing Properties dialog box. You can display the Dialing Properties dialog box by opening the Control Panel, double-clicking on the **Modems** icon, and clicking on **Dialing Properties**.

3 In the Make New Connection dialog box, enter a name for your new connection. Click on **Next**.

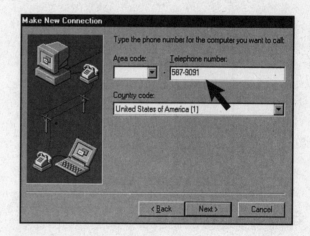

4 Enter the phone number of the dial-up network connection and click on **Next**.

(continues)

Do It Yourself Connect to Your Network at Work *(continued)*

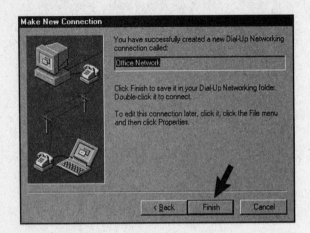

5 Click on **Finish**, and you return to the Dial-up Networking window.

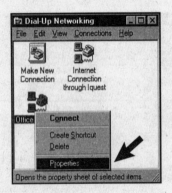

6 Right-click on your new icon and select **Properties** from the shortcut menu that appears.

7 Click on the **Server Types** tab.

The exact information to enter on the Server Types tab depends on the type of LAN and the way it is set up. Contact your administrator for more information if you are not sure what to enter at any point.

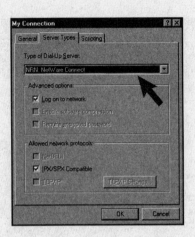

8 Under Type of Dial-Up Server, select **NRN: Netware Connect** (or the appropriate protocol for your office network) and click on **OK**.

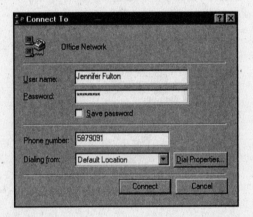

9 Double-click on your new icon. Then enter your user name and password and click on **Connect**. After you log onto your network at work, you can access the network through the Network Neighborhood icon as usual. When you finish, return to the Connect To dialog box and click on **Disconnect**.

Suspend Your Laptop's Activity Temporarily

If you plan to leave your laptop computer for a short time, you can conserve battery life by suspending activity temporarily (which is like putting it to sleep). Note, however, that if you turn off the computer instead, you use much more energy when you turn it back on than you do if you simply put the laptop to sleep for a short time.

Before you suspend activity, do the following:

- Save your documents.

- If you're connected to a network, log off. Although suspending activity on your laptop will probably knock you off the network, it won't log you off properly.

Note that most laptops suspend activity automatically after a period of time; however, by following these steps, you can suspend it immediately and save even more battery life.

You also can conserve energy by putting just the monitor to sleep when you haven't used the

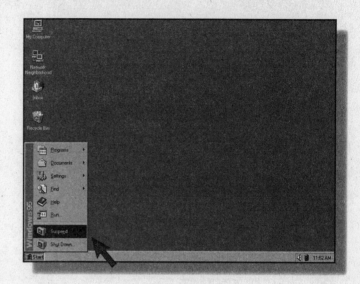

computer for a short time. You set up your system so that the monitor goes into low power standby mode after, say, one minute of inactivity. Then you can put it to sleep after five minutes. (The *Do It Yourself* steps outline this procedure.)

Begin Do It Yourself Configure Your Monitor to Suspend Activity

To suspend activity immediately, click on the **Start** button and select **Suspend**. To reactivate your laptop later, consult your owner's manual for specific instructions.

(continues)

 Click on the **Start** button, select **Settings**, and select **Control Panel**. In the Control Panel window, double-click on the **Display** icon.

Do It Yourself Configure Your Monitor to Suspend Activity *(continued)*

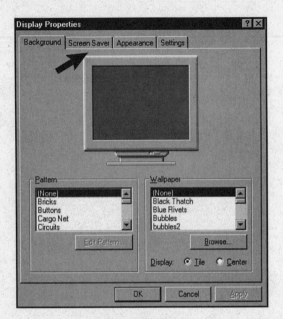

2 Click on the **Screen Saver** tab.

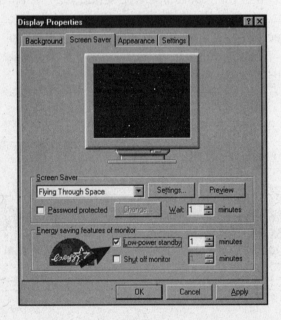

3 Click on **Low-power standby** and enter the number of minutes of inactivity you want Windows to wait before it reduces the power to the monitor.

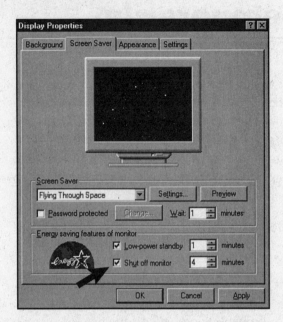

4 Click on **Shut off monitor** and enter the number of additional minutes of inactivity you want Windows to wait before it shuts down power to the monitor.

5 Click **OK**.

6 Close the Control Panel window by clicking on its **Close** button. When your monitor suspends activity, you can simply move the mouse to reactivate the screen.

PART 3

Quick Fixes...

This is the part of the book that no one really wants to read because if you have to turn to this part, you must be having a problem. But don't despair! This part lists 101 of the most common problems along with their solutions. You won't have to fumble through the entire book saying to yourself "I know I've seen the solution in here somewhere." The solutions are all right here for easy reference.

To use this section, look for your problem in the Quick-Finder tables. This part is broken down into sections such as installation problems, MS-DOS problems, modem problems, and so on. When you find your problem in the table turn to the Quick Fix to find the solution.

This part is broken down into the following sections:

What You Will Find in This Part

101 QUICK FIXES

Questions and Answers

Installation and Startup Problems

1 Setup freezes and tells me there are errors with my hard drive.

You may have some bad sectors on your disk. To fix the problem, exit Setup, exit Windows, and follow these steps:

1. If you are installing from floppy disk, insert disk 1 into your floppy drive. From the command prompt, type the following:

   A:SCANDISK /ALL

   where **A:** is the drive the disk is in. If you are installing from CD-ROM, insert the Windows 95 CD and type the following:

   D:\WIN95\SCANDISK /ALL

   where **D:** is the letter of your CD-ROM drive.

2. ScanDisk runs and tells you if there are any errors with your disk. If ScanDisk finds an error, click the **Fix** button to allow ScanDisk to fix the problem. When ScanDisk asks you if you want to do a surface test, click **Yes**. It may take awhile, but you need to make sure your disk is good before you can set up Windows 95.

> If ScanDisk finds an error, it asks you if you want to repair the error. Click **OK** to repair the error and continue with the scan.

3. When you are sure that your hard drives do not have any errors, start Windows.

4. In Program Manager, open the **File** menu and choose **Run**. Type **A:SETUP/IS** (or **D:\WIN95\SETUP/IS** if you are installing from CD-ROM) and click **OK**. This setup tells Windows to bypass running ScanDisk when Setup starts.

> If you get a message saying there is not enough memory to run ScanDisk try freeing up some conventional memory (see your DOS manual for details) and running ScanDisk again. If all else fails, you can run Setup using the command in step 5 and bypass running ScanDisk.

2   Setup stopped responding during hardware detection. What do I do now?

First, make sure that Setup has really stopped responding. Sometimes, hardware detection can take several minutes. If you have waited 10 minutes or so and nothing is happening, do not press Ctrl+Alt+Del to restart the computer. Instead, do the following:

1. Turn off your computer, wait 10 seconds, and turn the computer back on.

2. After your computer boots up, open **Windows** and run **Setup** again.

3. When Setup starts, it asks you if you want to begin a new installation or use Smart Recovery. Choose **Smart Recovery** to run Setup in Smart Recovery mode. In Smart Recovery mode, Setup skips the section that caused a problem.

If Setup stops responding again, there is a different problem than the first time. Repeat steps 1 through 3 as many times as necessary until Setup is complete.

3   I chose not to create a startup disk during installation. How can I create one now?

A startup disk is a good thing to have around in case you ever have problems starting Windows 95. (If the system Registry becomes corrupted, for example, a startup file can be a lifesaver.) Follow these steps to create a startup disk:

1. Click on the **Start** button, choose **Settings**, **Control Panel**.

2. Double-click **Add/Remove Programs**.

3. Click the **Startup Disk** tab.

4. Click the **Create Disk** button.

5. Windows prompts you to insert the Windows 95 installation disk 1 into your floppy drive (or the Windows 95 CD in your CD-ROM). Insert the disk and click **OK**.

6. If your copy of Windows 95 was installed from floppy disk, Windows will prompt you to insert disk 2. Insert disk 2 and click **OK**.

7. Windows prompts you to insert a disk in your A: drive. Use at least a 1.2MB disk and make sure the disk doesn't have anything important on it because when you create the startup disk, the data is erased. Click **OK**.

8. After Windows finishes creating your startup disk, click **OK** to close the dialog box. Remove the disk from the drive and label it "Windows 95 Startup Disk."

4   There was a power failure during Setup. Now I can't even start Windows to run Setup again.

If Windows 95 was in the middle of installation when the power failed, your old Windows files may have been upgraded before enough new files were installed to run Windows 95. You can still run Setup from the MS-DOS prompt. To do this, insert the Windows 95 installation disk 1 into your floppy drive (or the Windows 95 CD in your CD-ROM drive) and type:

A:SETUP

or

D:\WIN95\SETUP (for CD-ROM installation)

A: is the letter of the installation drive. Setup asks you if you want to begin a new installation or use Smart Recovery. Click the **Smart Recovery** button to continue Setup.

5   When I start my computer, I get an error message that says "Invalid system disk, replace the disk, and then press any key."

This error occurs when you have a floppy disk in your A: drive that is not a bootable disk. A bootable disk is a disk from which you can boot the computer (like the Windows 95 Startup Disk you created during installation). Ordinarily, you would not want to boot from a floppy disk unless you are having major problems. More than likely, you just forgot to take the disk out of your A: drive the last time you used the computer. Eject the disk and press any key to continue.

6   Setup freezes after it restarts the computer.

A video driver conflict or a damaged Windows 3.x group file can cause this problem. To see if you have a video driver conflict, follow these steps to start Windows 95 in safe mode:

1. Turn off your computer. Wait a few seconds and turn it back on.

2. When you hear a beep, press the **F8** key.

3. Choose **Safe Mode** from the Startup menu.

If Windows 95 starts in safe mode, there is a conflict with your video driver. Follow these steps to change the video driver to the standard VGA driver:

1. Click on the **Start** button, select **Settings**, and select **Control Panel**.

2. Double-click the **Display** icon.

3. Choose the **Settings** tab and click the **Change Display Type** button.

4. In the Adapter type section, click the **Change** button.

> If you recently bought a computer with Windows 95 preinstalled, step 4 will be slightly different. Click the **Advanced Properties** button. In the Advanced Display Properties dialog box, click the **Change** button.

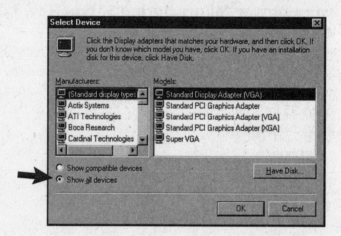

5. Click the **Show all devices** option button.

6. In the Manufacturers box, choose (**Standard display types**).

7. In the Models box, choose **Standard Display Adapter (VGA)**.

8. Click **OK**.

9. A dialog box appears, telling you to restart your computer for the settings to take effect. Click the **Yes** button.

If Windows 95 wouldn't start in safe mode, there could be a problem with one of your group files. Follow these steps to fix the problem:

1. Turn off your computer. Wait a few seconds and turn it back on.

2. When you hear a beep, press the **F8** key.

3. Choose **Command Prompt Only** from the Startup menu.

4. Switch to your Windows directory by typing:

CD\WINDOWS

5. Type the following command to repair your group files:

   GRPCONV

6. Press **Ctrl+Alt+Del** to restart your computer. Windows 95 should now start normally.

7 I can't uninstall a program because it doesn't show up in the Add/ Remove Programs dialog box.

Windows 95 makes it easy to uninstall programs using Add/Remove Programs. Unfortunately, some programs were not written to take advantage of this feature. If you no longer need a program and want to free up some disk space, do the following:

1. Check the documentation that came with your software to see if there is an uninstall program for the software. If there is, follow the instructions to uninstall the program.

2. If there isn't an uninstall program available, locate the folder that contains the program in My Computer or the Explorer.

3. Browse through the folder to ensure there are no files you created that you want to keep. If there are data files that you need, move them to another directory or copy them to a floppy disk.

4. Delete the folder containing the program.

If the program was an old Windows 3.x application, there are probably other files scattered in various folders on your hard drive that you don't need. Unfortunately, there is no easy way to identify which files went with the application you removed. It's probably safer to leave the other files on the disk because you may accidentally delete a file that another program needs. Also, if you had a shortcut for this program in another folder or on the desktop, it is not deleted. See "Delete a Shortcut from the Desktop" (page 66) for instructions on deleting the shortcut.

System Problems

Problem	Quick Fix Number	Page
Applications take too long to load	24	520
Can't find the **buttons** in Windows Explorer	13	514
Can't **compress hard drive**	23	520
Context menu pops up on left mouse button	19	517
Delay too short in screen saver	10	513

(continues)

Problem	Quick Fix Number	Page
Too long to **switch between applications**	21	518
Can't find the **taskbar** in a DOS application	12	514
Can't find the **toolbar**	13	514
Toolbar is missing in Windows Explorer	13	514
Can't find the **volume control**	8	513

8 I can't find the volume control on the taskbar.

The volume control is not available if you do not have a sound card installed in your computer. If you do have a sound card but the volume control is not shown on the taskbar, do the following:

1. Click on the **Start** button, select **Settings**, and select **Control Panel**.

2. Double-click the **Multimedia** icon.

3. Click the **Audio** tab.

4. Click the check box next to **Show volume control on the taskbar**.

5. Click **OK** to close the dialog box.

9 When I open a folder in My Computer, it opens in the same window instead of creating a new one.

In My Computer, you can control whether a new window opens when you open a folder, or whether the folder opens in the same window and replaces what was there before. It's a matter of personal preference on how you would like this to work. To change it, follow these steps:

1. Double-click **My Computer** on the desktop, open the **View** menu, and choose **Options**.

2. Choose the **Folder** tab.

3. Click the radio button next to the browsing option you prefer.

4. Click **OK** to close the dialog box.

10 I selected a screen saver, but nothing happened.

The screen saver does not come up until after a period of time in which there is no activity. That means you can't move the mouse, click any buttons, or press any of the keys on the keyboard. If it takes too long for your screen saver to come up, follow these steps to change the delay time:

1. Move your mouse to an empty area on the screen (desktop) and click the right button.

2. Choose **Properties** from the shortcut menu that appears.

3. Choose the **Screen Saver** tab. In the box next to Wait, enter the time in minutes that you want to wait before the screen saver appears.

4. Click **OK** to close the dialog box.

11 I reduced the size of one of the folder windows in My Computer. Now I can't see all of the files. Are they gone?

Your files are still there, you just can't see them all because the window is no longer large enough to display all of your files at once. You may have noticed that there is now a horizontal and/or a vertical scroll bar on the bottom and/or right of the window. To view the rest of your files, click the arrows on the scroll bars until the files come into view.

12 I am running a DOS application full screen, and I can't see the taskbar to switch to one of my other applications.

To switch from your DOS application back into Windows 95, hold down the **Alt** key and press **Esc**. This brings up the Windows 95 interface and moves your DOS application to a button on the taskbar. To switch back to your DOS application, simply click its button on the taskbar.

13 The toolbar is missing in Windows Explorer.

By default, Windows Explorer opens without a toolbar. If you want to use a toolbar with the Explorer, follow these steps:

1. Click on the **Start** button, select **Programs**, and select **Windows Explorer**.

2. Open the **View** menu and click on **Toolbar**.

The toolbar is now available.

14 The icons on my desktop are scattered all over the place. Is there an easy way to line them up?

Follow these steps to arrange the icons on your desktop:

1. Move the mouse pointer to an empty place on the desktop and click the right button.

2. From the shortcut menu that appears, choose either **Arrange Icons** or **Line up Icons**.

If you choose Arrange Icons, another menu appears. All of the choices in the menu arrange the icons along the left edge of the desktop. Here are the choices:

- **by Name**   Sorts the icons by name.

- **by Type**   Sorts the icons by file type.

- **by Size**   Sorts the icons by file size.

- **by Date**   Sorts the icons by the date the file was created.

- **Auto Arrange**   Automatically arranges the icons whenever you add a new icon to the desktop. Note that this is a toggle option. Click it the first time to turn it on; click it again to turn it off.

- **Line up Icons**   Allows you to straighten out your columns and rows of icons. This is useful if you like to have icons on the desktop at other places than just the left side. To effectively use this option you have to move your icons into rows or columns (they don't have to be lined up perfectly, just in a general line). When you use the Line up Icons option, Windows neatly straightens up the rows and columns.

15   When I try to use the numbers on the numeric keypad, they don't work.

The numeric keypad on your keyboard serves a dual purpose. You can use it to type in numbers or to move the cursor around. To make the numbers work on the keypad, you need to press the **NumLock** key (on most keyboards it's the key directly above the 7). Many keyboards also have a light that comes on when the keypad is in NumLock mode. When the light is on, the numbers on the keypad will be typed as numbers when you press them. If you want your computer to always start with NumLock on, there is usually a setting in your system setup. Consult your computer documentation for details.

16   When I hold a key too long, the letter repeats twenty times.

Either the repeat rate or the repeat delay is set too high on your keyboard. The repeat rate is the speed that the characters repeat when you hold down a key. The repeat delay is how long you have to hold down a key before it repeats. To change these settings, follow these steps:

1. Click on the **Start** button, select **Settings**, and select **Control Panel**.

2. Double-click the **Keyboard** icon and click the **Speed** tab.

3. Change the Repeat rate and Repeat delay using the sliding arrows.

4. Click in the box labeled **Click here and hold down a key to test repeat rate** to check your settings. Hold down a key and see what happens. If you don't like it, change the settings and test it again.

5. When you are happy with the repeat rate and repeat delay you have set, click the **OK** button.

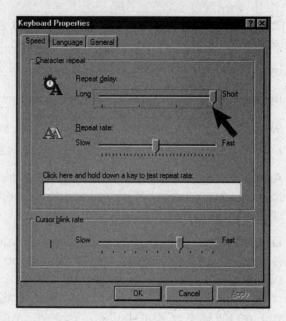

17 The mouse pointer moves too quickly across the screen.

You can change the speed of your mouse pointer to make it easier to use. Follow these steps:

1. Click on the **Start** button, select **Settings**, and select **Control Panel**.

2. Double-click the **Mouse** icon and click the **Motion** tab.

3. Move the slider under Pointer speed to the left to slow down the speed of the pointer or to the right to speed it up.

4. After you move the slider, click the **Apply** button.

5. Try moving the mouse across the screen. Repeat steps 3 and 4 until you are comfortable with the speed you selected.

6. Click **OK** to close the dialog box.

18 I can't ever find the mouse pointer.

Sometimes the mouse pointer does a great job of hiding. It is especially hard to see on the black-and-white LCD screen on some older notebook computers. If you are always searching for the pointer, you might want to try a feature called pointer trails. A *pointer trail* is a trail of pointers that follows the mouse pointer when you move it. Follow these steps to enable pointer trails:

1. Click on the **Start** button, select **Settings**, and select **Control Panel**.

2. Double-click the **Mouse** icon.

3. Click the **Motion** tab. In the Pointer Trail section, click the **Show pointer trails** check box. You also can vary the length of the pointer trail by moving the slider below the check box.

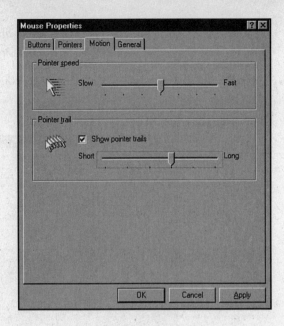

4. Now, move your mouse pointer around to see the pointer trails. If you like the way they look, click **OK** to close the dialog box. If you don't like them, click the check box again to uncheck it; then click **OK**.

19 When I try to select something using the left mouse button, a menu pops up next to the mouse pointer.

When this book refers to the left mouse button, it really means the primary button. If you have your mouse set up left-handed, the right button is the primary button. Therefore, whenever this book tells you to click the left button, click the right button. If you want your mouse set up right-handed, follow these steps to change it:

1. Click on the **Start** button, select **Settings**, and select **Control Panel**.

2. Double-click the **Mouse** icon.

3. Click the **Buttons** tab and click the **Right-handed** option button.

4. Click **OK**, and your mouse is set up right-handed.

20 When I try to double-click something, it takes three or four times to get it.

The double-click speed is not set correctly for you. The double-click speed controls how much time can pass between clicks when you double-click. If it is set to Fast, you must click very rapidly. To change it, do the following:

1. Click on the **Start** button, select **Settings**, and select **Control Panel**.

2. Double-click the **Mouse** icon.

3. Click the **Buttons** tab. In the Double-click speed area at the bottom of the dialog box, there is a sliding bar that controls the speed of your double-click. Click on the

slider and drag it to change the speed. Move the pointer left for a slower speed or right for a faster speed. Double-click the jack-in-the-box to test the configuration.

4. Once you get the double-click speed set to your liking, click **OK** to close the dialog box.

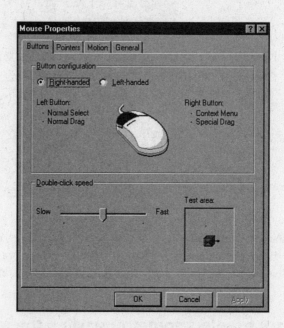

21   It takes forever to switch between applications.

Your computer is low on physical memory. Physical memory is the amount of RAM you have installed in your system. When Windows 95 runs out of RAM, it swaps the information that is in RAM to your hard drive. Because it takes longer to access memory from the hard drive than it does to access it from RAM, your computer seems sluggish when you switch between applications. The best way to fix the problem is to install more RAM in your computer. Windows 95 runs best with 16MB or more of RAM (luckily RAM prices have dropped significantly). If you are not ready to run out and buy more computer hardware, remember to close any applications that you don't need. Also, remove any unnecessary applications from the Startup folder. If you open a lot of applications in the Startup folder, you may not have enough memory left to open more applications. Follow these steps to delete applications from the Startup folder:

1. Click on the **Start** button, select **Settings**, and select **Taskbar**.

2. Choose the **Start Menu Programs** tab and click the **Remove** button.

3. Double-click the **Startup** icon to display the contents of the Startup folder.

4. Highlight any programs that you don't need and click the **Remove** button. Remember, when you remove a program from the Start menu, you are not removing the program from the hard drive; you are only deleting the shortcut.

5. Click the **Close** button and then the **OK** button.

22   When I try to start an application, I get a message that says there is insufficient memory.

More than likely the problem is caused by a lack of free disk space on your hard drive. Windows 95 can use *virtual memory* to fool your computer into thinking it has more memory available. Virtual memory is actually just hard drive space. When you are not using an open application, Windows 95 can move the memory to your hard drive which frees up your computer's memory to work in another application. If your hard drive is almost full, you may not have enough space left to effectively use virtual memory. Try the following to free up disk space:

- Use My Computer or Windows Explorer to copy files that you don't use anymore to floppy disks (or if you have a tape backup, use it). After you have copied the files, delete them.

- When the Recycle Bin is full, it can take a lot of disk space. Follow these steps to empty it:

  1. Double-click the **Recycle Bin** icon.

  2. Check the list of files to be sure there aren't any you want to recover.

  3. Open the **File** menu and choose **Empty Recycle Bin**.

  4. A dialog box appears, asking if you're sure you want to delete the files. Click **Yes** if you're sure.

  5. Close the Recycle Bin by clicking on the **Close** button.

If you still don't have enough disk space, you may want to consider buying a new hard drive (the prices are pretty reasonable these days). If that's not in your budget right now, you might want to try using DriveSpace. DriveSpace is a program that compresses all the data on your hard drive and then uncompresses it as you need it. Depending on the type of data on your drive, you could almost double the space on your hard drive. In other words, if you had a 200 megabyte hard drive, you could put 400 megabytes of data on it. The penalty for this is that it may slow down your computer a little bit. If you have a pretty fast computer (Pentium 75 or faster), you probably won't notice the difference. Follow these steps if you're willing to try DriveSpace:

1. Click on the **Start** button, select **Programs**, select **Accessories**, select **System Tools**, and select **DriveSpace**.

2. Select the drive that you want to compress and choose **Compress** from the **Drive** menu.

3. The Compress a Drive dialog box appears, giving you the specifics of the compression. Click **Start** to begin compressing the drive.

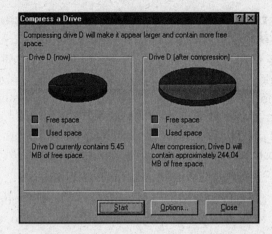

4. A dialog box will open asking you if you have created a Startup disk. If you didn't create one during installation (or you've lost it), click **Yes** to create one now. You will need a blank floppy and the Windows 95 installation disk. If you know where your Startup disk is, click **No** to continue.

5. Another dialog box appears, asking if you're sure you want to compress the drive. Click **Compress Now** if you are ready.

Windows 95 has to devote all of its time to compressing your drive, so you won't be able to use it for a while. Depending on your system, it could take several hours to finish.

23 When I tried to use DriveSpace to compress my drive, I got an error message telling me it couldn't compress the drive because it is a FAT32 drive.

Sounds like your hard drive needs to go on a diet! Actually, your hard drive was format-ted with the new FAT32 file system (FAT stands for File Allocation Table, 32 means 32 bit). FAT32 does a much better job with large hard drives (greater than 500MB) than the old FAT16 system. Unfortunately, FAT32 does not work with many drive utilities (including DriveSpace). The only way you will be able to use DriveSpace is to reformat your hard drive to the FAT16 system. Doing this will also wipe out everything on the drive, and you will have to reload all your programs. You are probably better off either deleting some seldom used programs or buying a new hard drive to gain more space.

24 My applications seem to take longer to open files than they used to.

Your hard disk is probably *fragmented*, which means that parts of your files are scat-tered all over your hard disk. Don't worry, fragmented disks are not a real problem; in fact, it is a natural occurrence. When you create a file, the information is stored on your hard disk. If you create another file later, its information is stored right next to the information from the first file. If you edit the first file and add information, there isn't enough room in the original space to save all of the file, so part of the file is stored at a different location on the disk.

Windows 95 remembers where it stores all the parts of your file, so you won't have any trouble using your file. The problem is that it is very inefficient when your disk is fragmented because it takes longer to open files. Fortunately, Windows 95 includes a utility to defragment your disk. Follow these steps:

1. Click on the **Start** button, select **Programs**, select **Accessories**, select **System Tools**, and select **Disk Defragmenter**.

2. A dialog box appears, asking which drive you want to defragment. If you have more than one drive you can choose **All Hard Drives** from the drop-down list, or you can select only one. Click **OK**.

3. In the dialog box, click the **Start** button to begin defragmenting. Depending on the speed of your system and how much of the disk was fragmented, it could take a couple of hours to defragment the disk. You can continue working on other things while it is defragmenting.

4. When Disk Defragmenter finishes, a dialog box appears, asking if you want to defragment another drive. Click **Yes** if you want to, or click **No** if you don't.

Your disk is no longer fragmented, and it won't take Windows as long to load your files. You should defragment your disk on a regular basis to keep performance at an optimum level.

25 When I open a certain MS-DOS program, the mouse won't work in Windows.

The mouse properties for the MS-DOS application are set to Exclusive mode. This allows the mouse to be totally dedicated to your MS-DOS application. On some stubborn DOS applications, you may need to turn Exclusive mode on to get the mouse to work correctly with that application. To return mouse control to Windows, exit your MS-DOS application. If you don't like Exclusive mode, follow these steps to turn it off:

1. From My Computer or the Explorer, click the program that you want to change.

2. Open the **File** menu and choose **Properties**.

3. Select the **Misc** tab.

4. In the Mouse section of the dialog box, select the **Exclusive Mode** check box to remove the X.

5. Click **OK** to close the dialog box.

26 When I click on a folder in Windows Explorer, I get an error message telling me that the folder cannot be moved.

This error occurs when you inadvertently move the mouse while you click on the folder. Windows 95 thinks that you are trying to move the folder to a new location. Since you haven't moved very far, it thinks you are moving the folder onto itself. Of course, you can't do that, so you get an error message. No problem! Just click **OK** and continue what you were doing. Try to hold the mouse still the next time you click on the folder.

Accessories Problems

27 **When I print with the Notepad, it always prints the file name at the top. How can I make it stop?**

Follow these steps to keep the file name from printing at the top of the page:

1. In Notepad, open the **File** menu and choose **Page Setup**.

2. In the Header box, you see **&f**. This is the code to print the current file name. Click in the **Header** box and delete the **&f** or enter another header.

3. Click **OK** to close the dialog box.

4. Print the document. The file name no longer appears at the top of the page.

Notepad stores the page setup information with the document, so you have to follow this procedure for every document that you print.

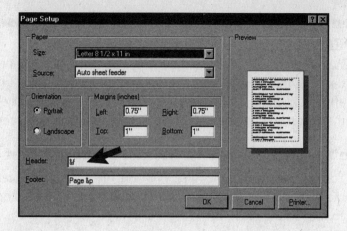

28 When I type past the edge of the window in Notepad, the text scrolls to the left.

Notepad is not like a normal word processor with set margins. You have to hit a Return at the end of each line where you want the margin to be. If you want to see all of a line that is wider than the width of the screen, you can turn on word wrap. With word wrap on, the text wraps to the next line automatically when you reach the edge of the window. To enable word wrap, just choose **Word Wrap** from the **Edit** menu in Notepad.

29 I want to copy some text between two WordPad documents, but WordPad only lets me open one document at a time.

Unfortunately, WordPad only supports opening one document at a time. There are two ways you can handle this problem. The first is as follows:

1. From WordPad, open the document you want to copy from.

2. Highlight the text you want to copy, open the **Edit** menu, and choose Copy to copy the text to the Clipboard.

3. Open the **File** menu, select **Open**, and select the document to which you want to copy the text. If you made changes to the document you were copying from, WordPad asks you if you want to save the changes. Click **Yes** to save the changes or **No** to close the file without saving the changes.

4. Position the mouse pointer where you want to copy the text, open the **Edit** menu, and choose **Paste**.

The above method would be rather tedious if you had several different sections to copy text from. An easier way is to open WordPad twice. Open the first document in WordPad. Then click on the **Start** button, select **Programs**, select **Accessories**, and select **WordPad** to open another copy of WordPad. From the File menu, choose **Open** to open the document you want to copy to. You can now copy the text from one document, switch to the other document, and paste the text.

30 When I highlighted text in WordPad and pressed a key, the text disappeared.

When you highlight text and begin typing, the text you type replaces the highlighted text. This makes it easier to replace text because you don't have to press the Delete key after highlighting it. To bring back the text you accidentally deleted, immediately open the **Edit** menu and choose **Undo** before doing anything else.

31 I can't remember where the tab stops are that I set in WordPad.

You need to turn on the ruler. With the ruler on, you can tell at a glance where the margins and tab stops are. It is also easier to set the tab stops and margins in the ruler. To turn on the ruler:

1. Open the **View** menu and choose **Ruler**.

2. A ruler appears, showing you where your margins are and the location of your tab stops. A bold L-shaped character marks each tab location.

3. If you want to add more tab stops, simply click in the ruler where you want the tab stop to go. If you want to delete a tab stop, click it and drag it past the left margin.

32 The ruler in WordPad shows the units in inches. I would rather work in picas.

It is easy to change the units on your ruler. You can choose from inches, centimeters, points, or picas. Follow these steps to change the units:

1. In WordPad, open the **View** menu and choose **Options**.

2. Click the **Options** tab.

3. Click on the option button beside the measurement unit you want to use.

4. Click **OK** to close the dialog box. The ruler now displays the units you chose.

33 When I drag my cursor across text in WordPad, it highlights whole words. How can I get it to highlight only the characters I want it to?

By default, WordPad highlights whole words when you drag the cursor across text. You can still highlight only part of one word, but as soon as you try to highlight more than one word, whole words are highlighted. If you don't like this feature, follow these steps to turn it off:

1. From WordPad, open the **View** menu and choose **Options**.

2. Click the **Options** tab.

3. Click the **Automatic word selection** check box to deselect it.

4. Click **OK** to close the dialog box. Now you can select any part of a word that you choose.

34 I used the Fill With Color tool to fill in an area in Paint, but the whole screen filled in.

The first thing you need to do is open the **Edit** menu and choose **Undo**. This erases the color you just filled your entire screen with. If you've done other things and Undo won't reverse the action you want to reverse, simply exit Paint. When Paint asks if you want to save changes, click on **No**. Changes you made since the last save are not incorporated into your picture.

In Paint, when you use the Fill With Color tool, the color fills the enclosed area that you point to. The key word here is enclosed. If you try to fill in an area that is not completely enclosed with a line, it fills in everywhere until it finds an enclosed area (which may end up being the entire screen). If you think you are filling in an enclosed area, make sure that there are no gaps in the lines enclosing the area. You may need to use the Zoom command in the View menu to help you find gaps in your enclosure.

35 I want to use a certain color in Paint, but I can't find it in the color palette.

Paint enables you to define a custom color. Follow these steps:

1. In Paint, open the **Options** menu and choose **Edit Colors**.

2. Click the **Define Custom Colors** button.

3. In the large box with a color spectrum in it, click in the area where your desired color seems to be. For example, if you want a color that is generally red, click in a red area of the box.

4. There is a vertical color bar on the right edge of the dialog box with an arrow next to it. Drag the arrow up or down to refine the color. You can see what the color looks like in the Color|Solid box.

5. When you get the color the way you want it, click the **Add to Custom Colors** button.

6. You can repeat steps 3 through 5 to define more custom colors.

7. When you finish, click the **OK** button. Your new colors are available for use.

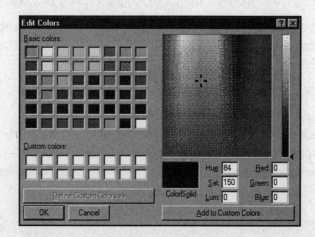

Windows Application Problems

Problem	Quick Fix Number	Page
My Windows 95 **application is frozen**	36	526
Application will not run	39	527
I want to open the **Close Program dialog box**	36	526
Accidentally **deleted shortcut**	40	527
My file was saved with **double extensions**	38	527
Error message opening file	37	527
Error message trying to run old application	39	527
Cannot add **file extension**	38	527
General Protection Fault in windows application	39	527
Can't find **icon** to start application	40	527
My Windows 95 application is **locked up**	36	526
Can't **open** file	37	527
Can't find **shortcut** to application	40	527
I want to **view file extensions**	38	527

36   My Windows 95 application has frozen.

Every once in a while you will get a program that just locks up. Usually, it is just a random occurrence. All the right things (or wrong things) have come together to cause your application to crash. Luckily, Windows 95 is a pretty robust operating system. That means one program can crash without bringing down the whole operating system. This can be a lifesaver if you happened to be working on something important in another application. Unfortunately, whatever you were working on in the frozen application is probably lost. The best thing you can do now is to close the frozen application. Follow these steps:

1. Press **Ctrl+Alt+Del**. The Close Program dialog box opens.

2. You will see a list of all the applications currently running. The application that is frozen will probably have (not responding) next to it. Use the up or down arrows to highlight the frozen application.

3. Click on the **End Task** button.

The frozen application closes and you can save information you were working on in other applications. After you do that, it is usually a good idea to restart your computer. Windows 95 may have become unstable when the application crashed.

37 When I tried to open a previously saved file from the File menu of my Windows application, I get an error message telling me it can't open the file.

You have probably moved the file to a different folder. Your windows application cannot tell when you move a file, so it just tells you that it can't open it. If you remember where you moved the file, open the **File** menu and choose **Open** to open the file. If you don't remember which folder to which you moved the file, Windows 95 can search for it. To Come.

38 I named a file 12229.txt in the Save As dialog box, but when it placed the name in the title bar, it was "12229.txt.txt".

By default, Windows 95 hides the extension of files it knows what to do with. In other words, if you have a file named 12229.txt, Windows 95 displays the file as 12229. Since Windows 95 knows that your file is a text file, it doesn't show you the extension. This can create some confusion, however, if you try to add the extension yourself. The best way to handle this problem is to let the program you are using assign the extension for you. That way, there won't be any confusion. If you prefer, Windows 95 will allow you to always display the file extensions. Just follow these steps:

1. From My Computer or Windows Explorer, open the the **View** menu and choose **Options**.

2. Click on the **View** tab.

3. Uncheck the box next to Hide MS-DOS file extensions for file types that are registered.

Your file extensions will now be visible in all file dialog boxes.

39 My Windows 3.x application won't run after I installed Windows 95; instead, it tells me there is a General Protection Fault.

Microsoft has gone through great pains to ensure that all your old Windows 3.x programs will run in Windows 95. Unfortunately, there are a few programs out there that still won't run. The first thing to try is reinstalling the Windows program that you can't get to run. Follow the documentation that came with your program to reinstall it. If the program still won't run, contact the manufacturer to see if there is an upgrade available that will run under Windows 95.

40 I accidentally deleted the icon to start the application. How can I get it back?

More than likely, you just deleted the shortcut to start the application. First, double-click the **Recycle Bin** to see if the shortcut is there. If it is, click it, open the **File** menu, and choose **Restore**. If it's not in the Recycle Bin, follow these steps to re-create it:

1. Click on the **Start** button, select **Settings**, and select **Taskbar**.

2. Choose the **Start Menu Programs** tab and click the **Add** button.

3. In the Command line box, type the path and file name of the program you just deleted. If you don't know the path, click the **Browse** button. Browse through your folders until you find the program and click it. Then click the **Open** button. The correct path and file name should show up in the Command line box. Click the **Next** button.

4. Choose the folder to which you want to add the program and click it to highlight it. Click **Next**.

5. A dialog box appears, asking you to choose a name for the shortcut. This is the title of the program that appears next to its icon. Type in the name you want and click the **Finish** button.

6. Click **OK** to close the Taskbar Properties dialog box.

DOS Application Problems

Problem	Quick Fix Number	Page
Alt+Enter does not work correctly	44	530
DOS **Application is locked up**	42	529
Full screen application will not return to window	44	530
Can't **edit PIF file**	41	528
Can't find the **PIF editor**	41	528
Can't **switch back to Windows** from DOS application	44	530

41 I want to create a PIF file to run my MS-DOS application, but I can't find the PIF editor.

The old PIF editor from Windows 3.x doesn't exist anymore. Windows 95 has a much better way of dealing with these files. Whenever you create a shortcut to an MS-DOS program, it is really a PIF file. To create a shortcut, do the following:

1. In My Computer or the Explorer, locate the DOS program you want to create a shortcut for. Right-click on the file name and choose **Create Shortcut** from the shortcut menu that appears.

2. A new icon appears titled **Shortcut to _program name_** (where _program name_ is the name of the original program). It has the MS-DOS icon with a little arrow in the lower-left corner of the icon, which indicates that it is a shortcut.

3. You can set all of the properties that you used to set in the PIF editor (and more) in the properties of the shortcut. To view or edit these properties, click the newly created shortcut, open the **File** menu, and choose **Properties**.

4. When you finish setting the properties, click **OK** to close the dialog box.

5. To run the program using the settings you have created in the shortcut, double-click the shortcut icon in My Computer or the Explorer.

42 My DOS application is locked up. What do I do now?

Sometimes, errors occur in DOS applications that cause them to lock up. This is generally a random occurrence, but sometimes it happens every time you run the program. If so, first try to optimize the program using the steps in "Optimize How a DOS Program Runs" (page [9TBD]). If all else fails, try to remember what you were doing when the program locked up. Call the software manufacturer and tell them about it. Maybe they have an update to the program. For now, to close the DOS application that is locked up, press **Ctrl+Alt+Del**. The Close Program dialog box appears. From the list, choose the program that is locked up and click the **End Task** button. This closes the program and returns you to Windows.

43 The characters in my DOS window are too small to see.

You need to change the font in your DOS window to make it easier to see. Windows 95 makes it easy to accomplish this task. Follow these steps:

1. From My Computer or the Explorer, click the program in which you want to change the font size.

2. Open the **File** menu and choose **Properties**.

3. Choose the **Font** tab.

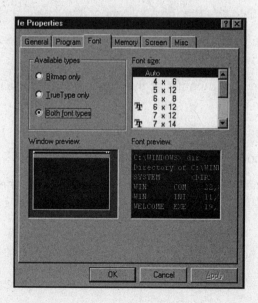

If the DOS window is open, you can skip steps 1–3 and click the **Font** button on the toolbar instead.

4. In the **Font size** box, choose a larger font size. The Font preview box gives you an idea of what the font will look like.

5. Click the **OK** button to close the dialog box.

The next time you run the program, the font size will be the one you selected.

44 I'm running a DOS application full screen, but Alt+Enter won't return me to Windows.

The Alt+Enter shortcut has been disabled in the properties of your DOS program, because that key combination is used by the program. You can return to Windows by pressing **Alt+Tab** or **Alt+Esc** instead. You may want to run this application in a window instead of full screen, so you don't have to worry about switching to Wwindowed mode. Follow these steps to open this application in a window:

1. From My Computer or the Explorer, click the DOS application you were just running.

2. Open the **File** menu and choose **Properties**.

3. Choose the **Screen** tab and click on the **Window** option button.

4. Click **OK** to close the dialog box.

The next time you run the application, it will be in a window.

If you don't need the Alt+Enter shortcut in your DOS application, you can re-enable it for Windows use. Follow these steps:

1. From My Computer or the Explorer, click the DOS application you were just running.

2. Open the **File** menu and choose **Properties**.

3. Choose the **Misc** tab.

4. In the Windows shortcut keys section, check the **Alt+Enter** check box.

5. Click **OK** to close the dialog box.

The next time you run the application, Alt+Enter will function normally.

File Problems

Problem	Quick Fix Number	Page
Association does not exist for file type	53	535
Confirmation dialog when deleting a file	52	535
Can't **copy a file to floppy disk**	49	533
Copy file **instead of moving**	50	533
Can't **create new folder**	48	532
Accidentally **deleted a file**	47	532
Can't **delete a file without asking**	52	535
Drag-and-drop moves instead of copies	50	533
Error message copying file to floppy	49	533
Error message creating new folder	48	532
File name has weird character in it	45	531
File not listed in Explorer	46	532
File type not registered	53	535
Need to use **File Finder**	51	534
Can't **find file**	51	534
Can't **find file in old application**	45	531
Can't **find new file in Explorer**	46	532
Floppy disk is write-protected	49	533
Floppy is compressed with DriveSpace	54	536
Folder already exists error message	48	532
Long file names not supported	45	531
Need to **mount a floppy disk**	54	536
Can't **move file**	50	533
New file does not show up in My Computer	46	532
Can't **open file from Windows Explorer**	53	535
READTHIS only file on floppy	54	536
Need to **recover a file**	47	532
Can't remember **which folder file is in**	51	534

45 I renamed one of my files to My Windows File, but when I try to open the file in an old Windows application, I can't find it.

While it's great that Windows 95 enables you to name your files with more than eight characters, your old Windows 3.x and MS-DOS applications cannot use these long file names. So although you are still able to open your file, it is not called what you expect it to be called. Windows 95 automatically assigns an eight-character name to the files you name with long file names. For example, if your file My Windows File is a Word document, it may be shortened to MYWIND~1.DOC. If you want to see what the eight-character abbreviation for your long file name is, right-click on the file in My Computer or Explorer and select **Properties** from the shortcut menu. The eight-character file name appears next to **MS-DOS name** in the Properties dialog box. Eventually, if you decide to upgrade your old applications to Windows 95 versions, you will be able to use the long file names in your applications.

46 I created a file in one of my applications, but when I switched to the folder that I put it in, it wasn't there.

Don't worry; your file is safely in the folder that you saved it to, it just isn't displayed right now. When you have a folder open in My Computer or the Explorer, and you save a new file to that open folder, it is not displayed right away. To view the file, switch to the open folder and click **Refresh** from the **View** menu.

To refresh your screen quickly, press **F5**.

47 I accidentally deleted a file. Is it gone forever?

Fortunately, all is not lost. Windows 95 has included a wonderful utility called the Recycle Bin. When you delete a file, your computer doesn't erase the file; it moves the file to the Recycle Bin. If you just deleted the file from My Computer or Explorer, open the **Edit** menu and choose **Undo Delete**. If you have already closed My Computer or Explorer, or you have deleted some other files after the one you want to recover, do the following:

1. Double-click the **Recycle Bin** icon on the desktop.

2. Scroll through the list of files until you find the one you want to recover. Click the file to highlight it. Remember, you can select multiple files by holding down the **Ctrl** key as you select files.

3. Open the **File** menu and select **Restore**.

4. When you finish restoring files, click the **Close** button. Windows restores your files to their original locations.

48 I tried to create a new folder, but I got an error message telling me that a folder with the name I specified already exists.

When you created your new folder, you tried to name it the same as a folder that already existed. You cannot have two subfolders with the same name under the same folder. To fix the problem, type in a different name for your folder and press **Enter**.

49 I tried to copy a file to a floppy disk, but got an error message telling me that the disk is write-protected.

All floppy disks can be write-protected. When a disk is write-protected, you cannot delete or change the files on that disk. It is a good idea to write-protect floppies when you have important data on them. If the data on the disk is not that important, or if you just want to add a file to the disk, you remove the write protection. How you write-protect a disk differs depending on the type of floppy disk.

- For a 3 1/2-inch floppy disk, turn the disk to the back side. There is a square piece of plastic in the upper-left corner of the disk that you can move to cover or un-cover a square hole. If the square hole is visible, the disk is write-protected. If the hole is covered by the plastic piece, the disk is not write-protected. Use your fingernail or the end of a pen to move the piece of plastic to the desired location.

- For a 5 1/4-inch floppy disk, there is a notch on the right edge of the disk about an inch from the top. To write-protect a 5 1/4-inch disk, get a piece of tape and cover the notch (packages of disks come with pieces of tape for this purpose). To unprotect the disk, simply remove the tape.

50 I tried to copy a file to a different folder using drag-and-drop, but it moved instead.

By default, when you drag a file from one folder to another on the same drive, Windows 95 moves the file. If you drag the file to another drive, Windows 95 copies the file. You can change the way these defaults work by holding down a key as you drag the file.

Hold down the **Shift** key while dragging the file to move it. Hold down the **Ctrl** key while dragging the file to copy it. Another way to force Windows 95 to move or copy is by dragging the file using the right mouse button instead of the left. This accesses a menu after you drag the file. Click **Copy Here** to copy the file or **Move Here** to move the file.

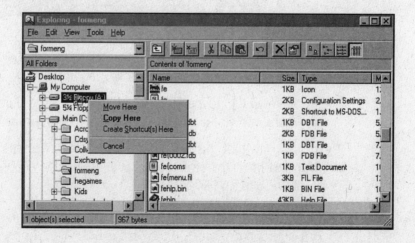

51 I can't remember which folder I put my file in.

Windows 95 includes a powerful search utility to find files when you forget where you put them. Follow these steps to find your file:

1. Click on the **Start** button, select **Find**, and select **Files or Folders**.

2. If you remember the name (or part of the name) of the file, click the **Name & Location** tab and type the name in the Named box. You can use wild cards if you like. (Use the asterisk wild card to represent a whole word or group of characters; use the question mark wild card to represent a single character.)

3. If you can't remember the name, but you remember when you worked on it last, click the **Date Modified** tab. Click the **Find all files created or modified** option button, and click one of the following options:

   - **between**   If you know that you last modified your file between two dates, select this option and type in the dates.

   - **during the previous month(s)**   Select this option if you want to find files that you modified within a certain number of months. Type in the number of months you want to look back.

   - **during the previous day(s)**   Select this option if you want to find files that you modified within a certain number of days. Type in the number of days you want to look back.

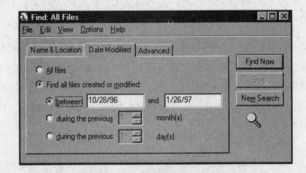

4. If you don't remember when you last worked on the file, click the **Advanced** tab. Choose one or a combination of the following options:

   - If you know what type of file it was (such as a Word document), select the **Of type** drop-down list and choose the file type from the list.

   - If you know that the file contains certain text, type the text in the **Containing text** box. (This search takes awhile because Windows has to search the contents of each file on the drive.)

   - If you know that the file is greater than (or less than) a certain size, choose the appropriate entries in the **Size is** box. First, choose **At least** or **At most** from the drop-down list, and then type the size in KB (kilobytes).

You also can choose combinations of steps 2–5, for example, if you know the date you modified the file, and you know that it contains a certain text phrase.

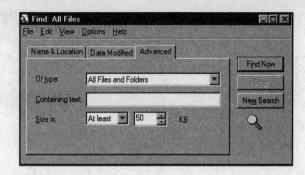

5. Click the **Find Now** button to begin your search. A window appears below the Find dialog box with a list of files that it finds. The window shows which folder the file is in. If you want to edit the file now, double-click it. The application in which it was created opens so you can edit the file.

52 Every time I delete a file, Windows asks me if I'm sure I want to delete it.

By default, Windows 95 warns you when you are deleting a file. If you don't feel like you need to be warned, follow these steps:

1. Right-click on the **Recycle Bin** icon.

2. Choose **Properties** from the shortcut menu that appears.

3. Choose the **Global** tab.

4. Uncheck the **Display delete confirmation dialog** check box.

5. Click **OK** to close the dialog box.

53 When I double-click a certain file in My Computer or Windows Explorer, a dialog box appears, asking me what I want to open the file with.

This dialog box appears if you double-click a file that Windows 95 doesn't know what to do with. For most files, Windows 95 knows which application to start when you double-click on the file. Sometimes, however, Windows 95 can't tell which application you used to create the file. Maybe you saved a file with an extension that Windows didn't recognize. Whatever the reason, if you know which application you used to create the file, you can tell Windows 95 which one it was.

Follow these steps when you get the Open With dialog box:

1. In the list of programs, click the one you want to use to open this file. If the program is not on the list, click the **Other** button and navigate through the folders until you find your program.

2. Check the **Always use this program to open this file** check box, and Windows 95 remembers to use this program the next time you double-click the file.

3. Click **OK** to open the file using the program you chose in step 1.

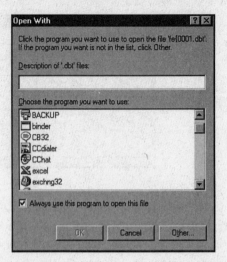

54 A friend gave me a floppy disk with several files on it. When I used My Computer to look at the disk, there was only one file called READTHIS.

Your friend has given you a floppy disk that has been compressed using DriveSpace. This allowed her to fit more files on the disk before she gave it to you. To use the disk, you need to tell Windows 95 that this is a compressed disk. Follow these steps:

1. Click on the **Start** button, select **Programs**, select **Accessories**, select **System Tools**, and select **DriveSpace**.

2. Select the drive that contains the compressed floppy disk.

3. Open the **Advanced** menu and choose **Mount**.

4. A dialog box appears, telling you the drive has been mounted. Click **OK**.

When you use My Computer or Windows Explorer, you can see the files. You can see this will be inconvenient if you are using a lot of compressed floppies. Fortunately, you can tell DriveSpace to automatically mount compressed floppy disks when you insert them in the drive. To do so, follow these steps:

1. Click on the **Start** button, select **Programs**, select **Accessories**, select **System Tools**, and select **DriveSpace**.

2. Open the **Advanced** menu and choose **Settings**.

3. Check the **Automatically mount new compressed devices** check box.

4. Click **OK**.

The next time you insert a compressed floppy into the drive, it is mounted automatically.

Printing Problems

Problem	Quick Fix Number	Page
Prints **8 x 11 instead of 8 by 14**	59	539
Will not print on **bottom of page**	59	539
Characters do print like the screen	56	538
Printer **cuts off end of line**	60	540
Edges do not print	60	540
Error message when trying to print	55	537
Error writing to LPT1	62	541
Fonts print incorrectly	56	538
Graphics are jagged	57	539
Only **half of page prints**	58	539
Printer not **installed**	55	537
Laser printer has too little memory	58	539
Legal paper does not print correctly	59	539
Can't **print**	55	537
Printer does not support font	56	538
Printer not installed	55	537
Printer setup incorrect	55	537
Need to set **Print Spooler**	61	541
Resolution is too high	58	539
Resolution is too low	57	537
Separator page always printed	63	542
Printing **takes too long**	61	541
Unprintable area too big	60	540

55 **When I tried to print a document, I got an error message that said Windows could not print due to a problem with the printer setup.**

You probably do not have a printer installed or it is installed incorrectly. To install your printer, do the following:

1. Click on the **Start** button, select **Settings**, and double-click the **Printers** folder.

2. Double-click the **Add Printer** folder.

3. The Add Printer Wizard opens to help you add your printer. Click **Next** to begin installing your printer.

4. If you are connected to a network, the Wizard will ask you if you want to add a local printer (one attached directly to your computer) or a network printer. Click the option button next to the correct choice and click **Next**.

5. If you are connecting a network printer the Wizard will ask you to choose a network path for the printer. You can click the **Browse** button to help you locate the correct path. If you're not sure about the network path, ask your network administrator. Under **Do you print from MS-DOS programs?**, click **Yes** if you do, **No** if you don't. Click **Next** to continue with the installation.

6. Choose your printer from the list of Manufacturers and Printers. If you have a disk from your printer manufacturer, click the **Have Disk** button. After choosing your printer, click the **Next** button.

7. Choose the port you want to use with this printer. Most printers are connected to the parallel port (LPT1). Click the **Next** button.

8. Type a name for the printer and click **Yes** if you want to use this printer as the default printer or if this is your only printer. Click the **Next** button.

9. Click **Yes** to print a test page and click the **Finish** button. It is a good idea to print the test page to see if your printer works correctly.

10. A dialog box appears, asking if your test page printed correctly. If it did, click the **Yes** button and you are finished setting up your printer. If it didn't print correctly, click the **No** button. Windows brings up the Help menu to aid in troubleshooting the problem. Make sure the cable is attached to the computer and the printer, and make sure the printer is on, is online, and is loaded with paper.

56 When I print my document, the fonts don't look the same as they do on the screen.

Your printer probably doesn't support the font you have chosen. Check the printer documentation to see what fonts are supported with your printer and use one of those. Another alternative is to use a TrueType font (they are the ones labelled TT in the font list). These fonts print well on virtually all printers. If you want to check which TrueType fonts are available for use, do the following:

1. Click on the **Start** button, select **Settings**, and select **Control Panel**.

2. Double-click the **Fonts** icon. A folder opens showing all of the fonts that are installed. The TrueType fonts have TT in the icon; standard fonts have A in the icon.

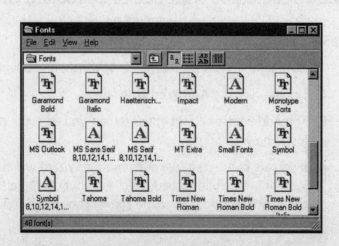

3. Double-click one of the font icons, and Windows displays some information about the font and a sample of what the font looks like.

4. Click the **Print** button if you want to print the sample.

5. When you're finished, click the **Close** button.

57 When I print graphics, the lines are all jagged, and it doesn't look good.

You may have the resolution set too low. The resolution is how many dots per inch the printer uses to print your graphics. The higher the resolution, the better your work looks, but it also takes longer to print. To change the resolution, follow these steps:

1. Click on the **Start** button, select **Settings**, and select **Printers**.

2. Select the printer you are using to print your graphics, open the **File** menu, and choose **Properties**.

3. Choose the **Graphics** tab and open the **Resolution** drop-down list. The list shows all of the resolutions your printer supports. Click the highest one.

4. Click **OK** to close the dialog box.

58 When I try to print a graphic on my laser printer, only half of it prints.

Your laser printer doesn't have enough memory to print the entire graphic. Unlike a dot-matrix or inkjet printer, a laser printer has to load the entire page into its memory before it can print. The best way to fix the problem is to add more memory to your printer. Consult your printer documentation for information on what type of memory to buy. If you can't afford an upgrade right now, try printing with a lower resolution. Follow these steps to change the printer resolution:

1. Click on the **Start** button, select **Settings**, and select **Printers**.

2. Select the printer you are using, open the **File** menu, and choose **Properties**.

3. Click the **Graphics** tab, open the **Resolution** drop-down list, and choose a lower resolution from the list.

4. Click **OK** to close the dialog box.

More of your graphics image should print. If the full page still doesn't print, you may have to choose a lower resolution than you did in step 3. Another option is to use your graphics program to make the image smaller. This may enable the full image to print, but it covers only part of the page.

59 I loaded 8 1/2-by-14-inch paper in my printer, but it only prints on the top 10 inches.

Windows 95 is usually not smart enough to know when you have changed the size of the paper in your printer. You have to tell it when you change paper sizes. Follow these steps to let Windows 95 know there is different paper in your printer:

1. Click on the **Start** button, select **Settings**, and select **Printers**.

2. Click the printer you are using to highlight it. Then open the **File** menu and choose **Properties**.

3. Click the **Paper** tab and click the appropriate paper size in the Paper size box. In this case, choose **Legal**.

4. Click **OK** to close the dialog box. Remember to change the paper size back to **Letter** when you finish.

5. You may also have to set your printer to use the larger paper. Check the printer documentation for information on how to do this.

> You also can set the paper size directly in the application. Look for a Page Setup command or a Print Setup command in the File menu.

60   The edges of my document do not print.

You are probably trying to print on too much of the paper. Most printers require you to have at least a 1/2-inch margin on all edges of the paper. Consult your printer manual for specifics. To fix this problem, the first thing you need to do is find out if your print driver has the correct settings for the unprintable area. Follow these steps to check:

1. Click on the **Start** button, select **Settings**, and select **Printers**.

2. Select the printer you are using to highlight it, then open the **File** menu and choose **Properties**.

3. Click the **Paper** tab and click the **Unprintable Area** button.

4. Check your printer documentation to ensure the values in Left, Right, Top, and Bottom are correct. The units are in .001 inches, so a value of 250 is .25 inches (1/4-inch). You also can select the units in .01 millimeters by selecting it in the Units box.

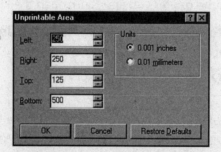

After you configure the unprintable area correctly, you must change the margins in your document to match these settings. Each application is different. In WordPad, the program automatically adjusts your margins to be at least as big as the unprintable area you have set. WordPad does not let you set your margins smaller than the unprintable area.

61 It takes too long to print my document.

There isn't much you can do to speed up the actual printing of your document. If you do a lot of printing, you may want to consider buying a faster printer. While you can't really speed up the printing process, you can use the print spooler to allow you to work on something else as your document is printing. You can print your entire document to the spooler quickly. Then you can return to your work and let Windows 95 worry about your slow printer. Follow these steps to enable print spooling:

1. Click on the **Start** button, select **Settings**, and select **Printers**.

2. Select the printer you want to use, open the **File** menu, and choose **Properties**.

3. Click the **Details** tab and click the **Spool Settings** button.

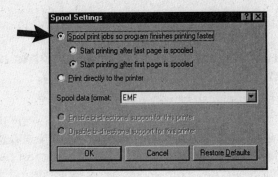

4. Click the **Spool print jobs so program finishes printing faster** option button.

5. Choose one of the following options:

   - **Start printing after last page is spooled** Sends your whole document to the spooler before it starts printing. This is the fastest way to allow your program to work on other tasks, but it takes more disk space because the entire file must be stored on disk while it is waiting to print.

   - **Start printing after first page is spooled** Starts printing immediately while the rest of your document is being spooled. If you are short on disk space, you should use this option.

6. Click **OK**; then click **OK** again to close the dialog boxes.

62 When I tried to print a document, I got a message telling me that there was an error writing to LPT1.

There is a problem with the communication to your printer. Work through this checklist to correct the problem:

- Make sure the printer is turned on and is online. Most printers have a light that comes on to indicate when the printer is online.

- Make sure that the printer cable is securely connected to the printer and your computer.

- Make sure the paper in your printer is not jammed and that there isn't a problem with your print cartridge or ribbon.

If you didn't find a problem with any of the above, your computer may have trouble printing in Enhanced Metafile (EMF) format. Follow these steps to disable EMF:

1. Click on the **Start** button, select **Settings**, and select **Printers**.

2. Select the printer you are using, open the **File** menu, and choose **Properties**.

3. Click the **Details** tab and click the **Spool Settings** button.

4. Click on the **Spool data format** drop-down list. Click **RAW**.

5. Click **OK**; then **OK** again to close the dialog boxes.

Try printing your document again. It should print normally.

63   When I print a document, it always prints a separator page after the document. How can I make it stop?

A separator page can be very useful if you are on a network and several people print to your printer. You can choose a simple separator page that includes the name of the file being printed, who printed the file, and the date and time it was printed. If you want a more impressive look, you can use the full separator page, which includes the same information but uses more impressive graphics. If you are the only one that uses the printer, however, it may just be a waste of paper. Follow these steps to tell Windows 95 not to print a separator page:

1. Click on the **Start** button, select **Settings**, and select **Printers**.

2. Select the printer you are using, open the **File** menu, and choose **Properties**.

3. Click the **General** tab.

4. In the **Separator page** box, choose (**none**) from the drop-down list.

Modem and Connection Problems

Problem	Quick Fix Number	Page
Call preferences not set correctly	67	547
Can't use **calling card**	69	548
Can't **connect to another computer**	67	547
Connection is lost	66	546
Need to **dial 9** to get an outside line	65	545
Modem does not **dial correctly**	68	548
Can't **dial from remote location**	69	548
Need to set **dialing properties**	65	545

Problem	Quick Fix Number	Page
Need to use **manual dialing**	68	548
Need a special number to get an **outside line**	65	545
Modem not **set up correctly**	64	543
Can't change **volume**	64	543
Volume control not available	64	543

64   When I try to change the volume of my modem, the volume control is unavailable.

Windows 95 probably installed the Standard Modem configuration for your modem. It uses this configuration if it doesn't have a configuration file for your brand of modem. To check it, do the following:

1. Click on the **Start** button, select **Settings**, and select **Control Panel**.

2. Double-click the **Modems** icon. The Modems Properties dialog box appears.

3. Click the **General** tab and see which modem is listed in the dialog box.

If it is **Standard xxxx bps Modem** (where *xxxx* is the speed of your modem, for example, 9600), Windows 95 has used the standard configuration for your modem. Unfortunately, many of the user-defined options (such as volume control) are not available with the standard modem configuration.

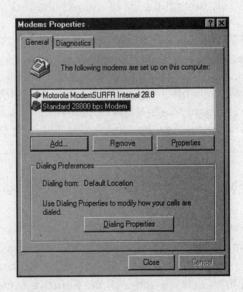

If you know the manufacturer and model of your modem, it is probably worthwhile to try to manually install your modem. To do so, follow these steps:

1. In the Modems Properties dialog box, click the **Add** button.

2. The Install New Modem Wizard appears. If your modem is external, make sure it is turned on and connected to the computer and that you don't have any applications open that use the modem. Click the **Next** button.

3. Windows 95 attempts to determine what type of modem you have. If it tells you that it found your make and model of modem, click the **Next** button and skip to step 7. More than likely, the Wizard tells you that it found a standard modem because that's what it found in your original installation. If that is the case, click the **Change** button.

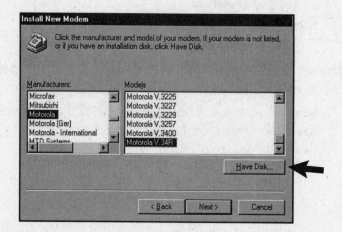

4. If you have a disk from your modem manufacturer, click the **Have Disk** button. Enter the drive letter for the disk and click **OK**. Skip to step 7.

5. Scroll through the list of manufacturers and click the one that matches your modem.

6. Scroll through the list of models and click the correct model.

> If you're unable to find the manufacturer and model of your modem in these lists, Windows 95 probably doesn't include a driver for your modem. Contact your modem manufacturer to see if it has a Windows 95 driver available. For now, click the **Standard Modem Types** option in the Manufacturers box, and choose the speed of your modem in the Models box. Click the **OK** button.

7. Click the **Next** button; click the **Finish** button.

You now have two modems listed in the Modems Properties box. If you have the correct modem installed, click the **Standard xxxx bps Modem** and click the **Remove** button. If you install the standard modem again, it appears as **Standard xxxx bps Modem #2**. Highlight this choice and click the **Remove** button.

If you were able to install the correct configuration for your modem, follow these steps to change the speaker volume.

1. Highlight the modem description and click the **Properties** button.

2. Click and drag the arrow on the sliding bar in the Speaker volume section. The choices range from off to high.

3. Click **OK** and click **Close**. The modem responds with the volume you selected.

Even if you are not able to install the correct configuration for your modem and are forced to use the Standard Modem configuration, there may still be hope. Most modems respond to the standard Hayes commands. You can manually enter the Hayes command for speaker volume into the modem configuration. Follow these steps:

1. Highlight **Standard xxxx bps Modem** in the Modems Properties dialog box and click the **Properties** button.

2. Click the **Connection** tab and click the **Advanced** button.

3. In the Extra settings box, type one of the following:

    M0 To turn the speaker off

    M1 For low volume

    M2 For medium volume

    M3 For high volume

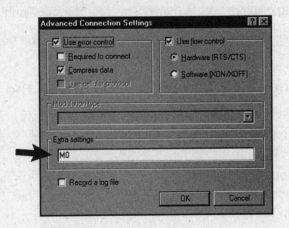

4. Click **OK**; click **OK** again and click **Close**.

65 I need to dial a 9 to get an outside line. How can I get my application to do it?

Many businesses require you to dial an access number to get an outside line. You can tell your application to do this for you using the following steps:

1. Click on the **Start** button, select **Settings**, and select **Control Panel**.

2. Double-click the **Modems** icon.

3. Click the **General** tab and click the **Dialing Properties** button.

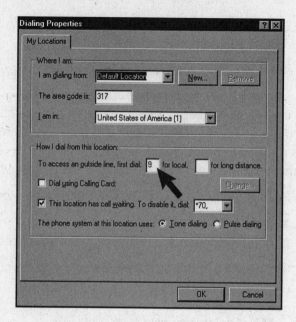

4. In the box next to **To access an outside line, first dial**, type the number(s) you must dial to get an outside line.

5. In the box next to **for long distance**, type the number(s) you must dial to get a long distance line. In many cases, it is the same number(s) you entered in step 4.

6. Click **OK**; then click **OK** again to close the dialog boxes.

66   I keep losing the connection when I'm in the middle of something.

This problem can be very annoying, especially if you're in the middle of downloading a file or chatting with someone over the Internet. It could be caused by a number of things. Check the following:

- If you have an external modem, make sure the connections to the computer and modem are tight. You could also have a bad cable. Try a new cable. If it doesn't help the problem, take the modem back.

- Check the connections of the phone line. Make sure they are securely inserted in your modem and the phone jack.

- If you have access to a different phone line, try using it. If you don't have the same problems on the other line, contact your phone company and have them check the line.

- If you have call waiting, be sure to disable it when you use the modem. Call waiting can cause problems with your modem if someone calls while you're online with your computer. Follow these steps to disable call waiting:

  1. Click on the **Start** button, select **Settings**, and select **Control Panel**.

  2. Double-click the **Modems** icon.

3. Click the **General** tab and click the **Dialing Properties** button.

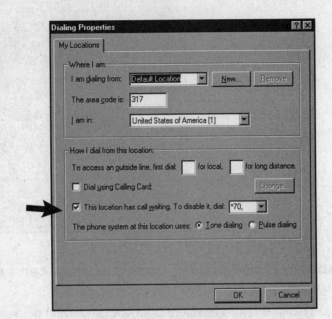

4. Check the **This location has call waiting** check box.

5. In the box next to **To disable it, dial**, type the sequence that disables call waiting in your area (in most areas it is ***70**). If you click the arrow in the box, a list appears showing the common commands to disable call waiting. Contact your phone company if you are unsure what you need to type here. The last thing in the box should be a comma. This tells your modem to pause after dialing the sequence.

6. Click **OK**; then click **OK** again to close the dialog boxes.

67   When I try to call another computer with my modem, time runs out before I get connected.

Sometimes it can take longer than you expect to dial a number and make a connection. Follow these steps to increase the time your modem waits for a connection:

1. Click on the **Start** button, select **Settings**, and select **Control Panel**.

2. Double-click the **Modems** icon.

3. Select the modem you are using and click the **Properties** button.

4. Click the **Connection** tab.

5. In the box next to **Cancel the call if not connected within**, type in a higher number. Click **OK**, then **Close**, to close the dialog boxes.

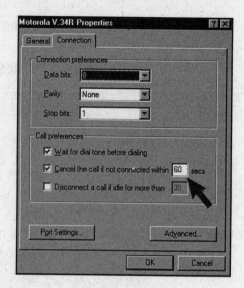

68 My modem is not dialing correctly. How can I use my phone to dial the number?

If you need to talk to an operator or you are having problems making a connection, dialing the phone number using your telephone may solve the problem. Follow these steps to manually control the dialing in HyperTerminal:

1. From HyperTerminal, click the session you want to use, open the **File** menu, and choose **Properties**.

2. Choose the **Phone Number** tab and click the **Configure** button.

3. Choose the **Options** tab. In the Dial control section, check the **Operator assisted or manual dial** check box.

4. Click **OK**; then click **OK** again to close the dialog box.

5. Double-click the connection icon and click **Connect**.

6. A dialog box appears telling you to dial the number. Pick up your phone and dial.

7. When you hear the computer answer, click the **Connect** button and hang up your phone.

69 I can't use my calling card to dial from my laptop.

You're stuck in a hotel room on business and you want to use your company calling card to check your e-mail (or surf the Internet), but it just isn't working for you. Luckily, Windows 95 has a feature that makes it easy to use your calling card to make a connection. Follow these steps:

1. From the **Start** menu, select **Settings**, and select on **Control Panel**.

2. Double-click the **Modems** icon.

3. From the Modems Properties dialog box, click the **Dialing Properties** button.

4. At the top of the dialog box, click the **New** button. Type in where you are now located and click **OK.**

5. Toward the bottom of the **Dialing Properties** dialog box, check the box next to **Dial using Calling Card**.

6. The Change Calling Card dialog box opens. In the **Calling Card to use** drop-down list, select your calling card. If your long distance company is not listed, click the **New** button and enter a name for the calling card.

7. Type in your calling card number in the **Calling Card number** box.

8. Click **OK** to close the dialog box. Click **OK** again twice to close the dialog boxes.

9. You are now ready to make your connection. Open the Dial-Up networking folder and double-click on the connection you wish to make.

10. In the Connect To dialog box, drop down the list in the **Dialing from** box and select the location you are in.

11. Your connection will be made using your calling card.

Windows Messaging (Microsoft Exchange) Problems

Problem	Quick Fix Number	Page
Address Book does not open correctly	76	552
Won't **check Internet Mail**	75	552
Accidentally **deleted a message**	72	550
Deleted Items folder emptied on exit	73	551
Need to **import messages**	71	550
Can't find **MS Mail messages**	71	550
MSN address book opens instead of local address	76	552
Need Windows messaging to **navigate like MS Mail**	74	551
Next message not displayed after reading	74	551
Other people are reading my e-mail	77	553
Need to **password protect** my e-mail	77	553
Need **privacy** for my e-mail	77	553
Need to **recover a deleted message**	72	550
Remote mail options set incorrectly	75	552
I want to **upgrade Exchange to Windows Messaging**	70	550
Can't find **Windows Messaging**	70	550

70   I am using Microsoft Exchange, but my friend is using Windows Messaging. What's the difference.

Microsoft Exchange is the e-mail client that shipped with earlier versions of Windows 95. In more recent versions, Microsoft Exchange was replaced with Windows Messaging. Windows Messaging is very similar to Exchange, but has a few new features. Not to worry, you don't have to go out and buy another copy of Windows 95 to upgrade to Windows Messaging. You can call Microsoft and have them send you the upgrade. Or, if you want to save a little time and money, you can download the upgrade from Microsoft's web site. Follow these steps:

1. Open your web browser and go to the site at **http://www.microsoft.com/ windows/common/aa2719.htm**

2. Click on the **Microsoft Exchange Update for Windows 95** link.

3. Choose a location for the file and click **Save**.

4. After the file is downloaded, open the file using the Windows 95 Run command.

5. Follow the instructions to upgrade to Windows Messaging.

71   After I installed Windows Messaging, all of my old MS Mail messages were gone.

Windows Messaging does not automatically import your old MS Mail messages. You must do that manually. Before you do it, you need to talk to your MS Mail system administrator to find out the name and location of your MS Mail message file. This is the file that contains all of your old messages. It is probably located somewhere on your network, or it could be right on your own hard drive. Once you know where your message file is, follow these steps:

1. Click on the **Start** button, select **Programs**, and select **Windows Messaging**.

2. Open the **File** menu and choose **Import**.

3. In the File name box, type the full path and file name of your message file. Click the **Open** button.

4. A dialog box appears asking you to enter your password. Type the same password that you use to log in to MS Mail. Be sure to check the **Import messages** check box. Check the **Import personal address book entries** check box if you want to import your old personal address book. Click **OK**.

5. A dialog box appears asking you where you want to put the messages. Click the **Put messages into existing personal folders** option button. Click **OK**.

6. A message box appears, notifying you that the import is complete. Click **OK**. All of your old MS Mail messages are now available.

72   I accidentally deleted a message. Is there any way to get it back?

Luckily, Windows Messaging doesn't actually delete your messages until you exit the program (it moves the messages to the Deleted Items folder). So if you haven't exited yet, you can follow these steps to get your message back:

1. Click the **Deleted Items** folder to show its contents.

2. Click the message that you just deleted and drag it to the Inbox folder.

3. Click the **Inbox** folder, and you will see that your deleted message is now safely in your Inbox.

You must retrieve any accidentally deleted message from the wastebasket before you exit Windows Messaging because Windows Messaging empties the wastebasket whenever you exit.

73 Windows Messaging empties my Deleted Items folder whenever I exit. How can I get it to leave them there?

You can change the way Windows Messaging handles messages in the Deleted Items folder. Some people like Windows Messaging to empty the folder whenever they exit (this is the way MS Mail works); others would rather keep the deleted messages in the folder until they delete them manually. To change how Windows Messaging handles the Deleted Items folder, follow these steps:

1. Open Windows Messaging by clicking the Start button, choosing Programs, and choosing **Windows Messaging**.

2. Open the **Tools** menu and select **Options.**

3. Click the **General** tab.

4. Check the **Empty the 'Deleted Items' folder upon exiting** check box to permanently delete the messages in the Deleted Items folder every time you exit Windows Messaging. If you uncheck the check box, Windows Messaging will leave them in the folder. You will have to delete the messages from the Deleted Items folder yourself to erase them permanently.

5. Click **OK** to close the dialog box.

74 After I read a message in Microsoft Mail and deleted it, the next message came up. In Windows Messaging it just goes back to the Inbox.

In Windows Messaging, if you delete a message after reading it, it goes back to your Inbox by default. If you prefer the way Microsoft Mail does it, it is easy to change. Follow these steps:

1. In Windows Messaging, open the View menu and choose **Options**.

2. Click the **Read** tab.

3. In the **After moving or deleting an open item** box, choose **Open the item below it** to open the message below the one you were reading.

4. Click **OK** to close the dialog box.

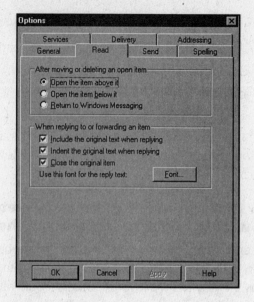

75   When I open Windows Messaging, it doesn't check Internet Mail for messages.

You can configure the Windows Messaging to download your Internet messages at a specified interval. Follow these steps to change the download options:

1. Click on the **Start** button, select **Programs**, and select **Windows Messaging**.

2. Open the **Tools** menu and choose **Options**.

3. Click the **Services** tab.

4. Click **Internet Mail** and click the **Properties** button.

5. Be sure that the **Work off-line and use Remote Mail** check box is unselected. Click the **Connection** tab and click the **Schedule** button in the **Transferring Internet Mail** section.

6. In the dialog box that appears, type in the desired time interval to check for new messages. Click **OK**.

7. Click **OK** then **OK** again to close the Options dialog box.

8. Click the **Close** button to close Windows Messaging. Open Windows Messaging again by repeating step 1. The options you chose in step 5 take effect.

76   When I click the Address Book button in Windows Messaging, the Microsoft Network sign-on screen appears.

The Microsoft Network address book is set up as the default address book. When you access that address book, Windows Messaging logs onto MSN to get the most recent update.

1. From Windows Messaging open the **Tools** menu and select **Address Book**.

2. When the MSN sign-in screen appears, click **Cancel**. The Address Book appears.

3. Open the Address Book's **Tools** menu and select **Options**.

4. Open the **Show this address list first** drop-down list and select **Personal Address Book**.

5. Click **OK** to close the dialog box. From now on, when you click the Address Book button, your personal address book will appear.

77 Other people who use my computer are reading my e-mail. Is there any way to protect it?

You can password-protect your Personal Information Store folder. Other people will still be able to use Windows Messaging, but they won't be able to read the e-mail you've sent and received. Follow these steps:

1. From within Windows Messaging, choose **Tools**, **Services**.

2. From the Services list, choose **Personal Folders**.

3. Click **Properties**.

4. Click the **Change Password** button.

5. Type a password in the **New Password** text box, then type it again in the **Verify Password** text box.

6. Click **OK**, then **OK** again to return to the Services window. Finally, click **OK** to return to Windows Messaging.

The next time you (or someone) open Windows Messaging, you'll be prompted for the password. If you don't enter it, the folders and messages in your personal folders will be hidden, even though Windows Messaging will open.

Internet and Microsoft Network Problems

Problem	Quick Fix Number	Page
File is **compressed** from MSN	87	558
Connection settings incorrect in Internet Mail	82	556
Need to switch to **conversation view** in BBS on MSN	86	557
Need to automatically **decompress files** from MSN	87	558
Internet Explorer not **default browser**	78	554
Need to change **default e-mail**	81	555
Can't get **e-mail from new MSN**	84	557
Need to change **home page**	80	555
Internet Mail cannot find mail server	82	556

(continues)

Problem	Quick Fix Number	Page
Internet Mail will not read MSN messages	84	557
Can't find **Internet Connection Wizard**	79	554
Need to change **Internet settings**	79	554
Need to change **mail server** in Internet Mail	82	556
MSN prompts for upgrade	85	557
File **takes forever to download**	88	558
MSN Today does not work correctly	85	557
Can't find **original message** in BBS on MSN	86	557
Need to change **security level**	83	556
Security warning appears when filling out forms	83	556
Need to **set up the Internet**	79	554
Start page incorrect	80	555
Download **stops in the middle**	88	558
Need to change **view** in BBS on MSN	86	557
Windows Messaging starts instead of Internet Mail	81	555
Can't use **ZIP** file from MSN	87	558

78 When I open Internet Explorer, I get a message that it is not the default browser. What do I do now?

Internet Explorer is no longer your default web browser. The default browser is the one that opens when you click on internet links inside a document, mail message, or any other place you find links to the internet. The reason Internet Explorer is not the default browser is because you have installed another web browser that is now the default. Now, when you click a link in a document, the other web browser will launch. If you would rather Internet Explorer be your default browser, click **Yes** in the dialog box. If you want your other browser to remain the default, click **No** in the dialog box. If you don't want to get this message the next time you start Internet Explorer, uncheck the box next to **Always perform this check when starting Internet Explorer**.

79 I messed up setting up my Internet connection, now I can't find the Internet Connection Wizard.

When you first click the **Internet** icon on your desktop, the Internet Connection Wizard starts automatically. After you have set it up the first time, clicking on the **Internet** icon simply starts Internet Explorer. If your Internet connection is not working properly, or if you need to set it up for a different Internet service provider, you can still use the Connection Wizard. From the **Start** menu, select **Programs**, select **Accessories**, select **Internet Tools**, and click on **Get on the Internet**. This launches the Internet Connection Wizard.

80 Whenever I start Internet Explorer, the wrong page opens.

The page that opens when you start Internet Explorer is called the start page (some people refer to it as home page). By default, Internet Explorer uses the Microsoft start page. If you would rather use another start page follow these steps:

1. Open Internet Explorer and connect to the Internet.

2. Type the address of the site you would like to make your home page in the **Address** box.

3. After the site opens, select **Options** from the **View** menu.

4. Click the **Navigation** tab in the Options dialog box.

5. In the Customize section, open the drop-down list in the **Page** box and select **Start Page**.

6. Click the **Use Current** button and click **OK**. Your new start page will open the next time you run Internet Explorer.

81 When I try to send e-mail from a web page in Internet Explorer, Windows Messaging (Microsoft Exchange) opens instead of Internet Mail.

If you would rather use Internet Mail to handle your mail messages while you're on the Internet, follow these steps:

1. From Internet Explorer, select **Options** from the **View** menu.

2. In the Options dialog box, click on the **Programs** tab.

3. In the Mail and news section, click on the drop-down arrow in the **Mail** box.

4. Select **Internet Mail** from the list, and click **OK** to close the dialog box.

82 **When I try to send a message with Internet Mail, I get an error message that says it cannot find the mail server.**

You probably do not have the correct mail server configured in Internet Mail. Follow these steps to fix the problem:

1. From Internet Mail, choose **Options** from the **Mail** menu.

2. Click the **Server** tab.

3. Enter the correct servers in the **Outgoing Mail** and **Incoming Mail** boxes. Check with your Internet provider for the correct information.

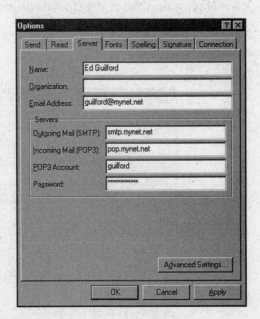

4. Click **OK** to close the dialog box. Now, you should be able to send and receive your e-mail.

83 **Whenever I fill out forms on the Internet, I get a message warning me about security.**

When you send information over the Internet, it passes from computer to computer until if finally gets to the intended site. What this means is any computer in the line could gain access to the information you have sent. Therefore, whenever you send any information that you might not want others to see (e.g. for example, a credit card number, your social security number, etc.), you need to be careful. You can avoid this problem by only sending crucial information to a secure web site. When you are at a secure web site there will be a lock displayed on the status bar in Internet Explorer. At a secure web site, the information is encrypted, so even if it fell in the wrong hands, they wouldn't be able to tell what the information was.

Now that you have a good idea about security, you may not want to see this warning message every time you send information. To disable the message, click the check box next to **Do not show this warning** and click the **Yes** button. If you decide you would rather not send the data, click the **No** button. The information will not be sent over the Internet.

84 The new MSN tells me that I have new e-mail messages, but when I click on the link and Internet Mail opens, there are no new messages.

If you are connecting to MSN through a third-party Internet provider, Internet Mail will not handle mail from the Microsoft Network. Internet Mail is only designed to send and receive mail from one service, and you probably have it set up for your Internet provider. Follow these steps to view your MSN e-mail using Windows Messaging:

1. Double-click the **Inbox** icon on the desktop to start Windows Messaging.

2. Open the **Tools** menu, select **Deliver Now using**, and select **The Microsoft Network** (if the menu item only says **Deliver Now**, you only have to select it).

You can now read your MSN messages from Windows Messaging.

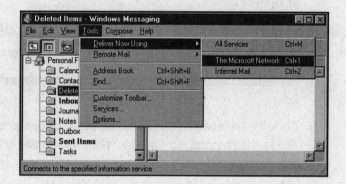

85 When I started the Microsoft Network and clicked on MSN Today, all I got was a message about upgrading to the new MSN.

Microsoft has recently upgraded MSN to have a whole new look. Since you must be a registered user to get to this screen, Microsoft has your address. You will probably receive an upgrade CD. When you get it, pop it in your CD drive and follow the instructions.

86 I'm reading a reply to a message in a BBS, but I can't find the original message.

It can often be confusing to try to read messages in a BBS when the replies to messages are scattered throughout the other messages. The Microsoft Network enables you to choose from three views for arranging the messages in a BBS:

- **List view**   Lists messages in chronological order.

- **Conversation view**   Lists all original messages with their replies beneath them.

- **File view**   Lists only messages with attached files.

If you switch to Conversation view you can easily find the original message to the reply you just read. To switch to Conversation view, follow these steps:

1. In the Microsoft Network, go to the BBS in which you want to work.

2. Open the **View** menu and choose **Conversation**.

An even easier way to switch to Conversation view is to click the **Conversation View** button in the toolbar of the BBS.

87 I just downloaded a file with a ZIP extension. How can I see what's in it?

Some files on the Microsoft Network are compressed using PKZIP to make the files smaller so they can be downloaded faster. Of course, if you can't use the file after you download it, it doesn't do you much good. The Microsoft Network includes a utility to automatically uncompress these files after you download them. Follow these steps to automatically uncompress your files:

1. Open the **Microsoft Network** and go to the file library from which you want to download a file.

2. Open the **Tools** menu and choose **File Transfer Status**.

3. In the File Transfer Status window, open the **Tools** menu and choose **Options**.

4. In the Compressed files section, click the **Automatically decompress files** check box.

5. Click the **Delete compressed file after decompressing** check box if you want to delete the compressed file. You really don't need the compressed file after you have uncompressed it; so you can save some disk space by using this option.

6. Click **OK** to close the dialog box. The next time you download a compressed file, it automatically decompresses after it is downloaded.

88 This file is taking forever to download.

You must be downloading a popular file. When the Internet gets busy, or there are a lot of people trying to download the same file, it can take a very long time to download. Sometimes it may seem like the download has completely stopped. The best thing to do is click the **Cancel** button in the File Download dialog box to end the download. Try to download the file at another time. Late at night or early in the morning is a good time to try.

Network Problems

Problem	Quick Fix Number	Page
Dial-Up Networking does not work correctly	93	561
Error message logging on to network	91	560
Remote computer **hangs up** after answering	93	561
NetWare **login script** does not run at logon	90	560
Only one computer visible in **Network Neighborhood**	92	561
Can't see **other computers** from Network Neighborhood	92	561
Server not available error message	91	560
Sharing option not available	89	559

89 I want to share a folder, but the Sharing tab is not available in the Properties dialog box.

Your network settings are not configured properly to allow you to share files. Follow these steps to change the settings to enable file sharing:

1. Click on the **Start** button, select **Settings**, and select **Control Panel**.

2. Double-click the **Network** icon.

3. Click the **File and Print Sharing** button.

4. Click the **I want to give others access to my files** check box.

5. Click **OK** to close the dialog box.

6. Click **OK** again. A dialog box appears, telling you that you must restart your computer before the new settings will take effect. Click the **Yes** button to restart.

After Windows 95 restarts, use My Computer or the Explorer to display the folder you want to share and do the following:

1. Click the folder you want to share to highlight it.

2. Open the **File** menu and select **Sharing**.

3. Click **Shared As** and type a name for the share in the **Share Name** box.

If you are using a Novell Netware network, go to step 7.

For a Microsoft network:

4. Click the appropriate Access Type.

> **Read-Only**   Allows users to copy or open files, but not change, add, or delete files.

> **Full**   Allows users to copy, open, change, add, or delete files.

> **Depends on Password**   Allows the security to be determined by which password they use.

5. Type a password in the appropriate box. If you chose **Depends on Password** in step 5, you need to enter two passwords. Click **OK**.

6. A dialog box appears asking you to retype the password(s). This makes sure you didn't inadvertently mistype your password the first time. Click **OK**. You can skip steps 7 and 8.

For Novell NetWare networks follow these steps:

7. Click the **Add** button to select the users you want to share with. If you choose The World, everyone in your group has access to your folder. Click the desired user and click the appropriate button to give the user the required rights to your folder. Read-Only and Full Access are discussed in step 4. If you add the user to the Custom access group, you are asked to choose which file operations the user can perform.

8. When you finish adding users, click **OK**. If you added any users to the Custom group, a dialog box appears, allowing you to choose the access rights. Click the check boxes next to the desired rights and click **OK**.

The dialog box closes, and the shared icon appears (a hand holding the folder).

90   My login script doesn't run when I log on to my Novell NetWare network.

A *login script* is a list of commands that are supposed to run when you log on to the network. The login scripts are usually created by your network administrator. You might need the login script to log on to several different servers or to connect to a network printer. Follow these steps to enable login scripts:

1. Click on the **Start** button, select **Settings**, and select **Control Panel**.

2. Double-click the **Network** icon.

3. Click **Client for NetWare Networks** and click the **Properties** button.

4. Check the **Enable logon script processing** check box.

5. Click **OK**; then click **OK** again to close the dialog boxes. You have to restart Windows to log on to the network again.

91   When I tried to log on to my Novell NetWare network, I got an error message that said server name is not valid or server is not available.

If you normally do not have any problems logging on to the network, your server could be down. Contact your network administrator to see when he expects the server to be available. If you've never logged on before, follow these steps to check your configuration:

1. Click on the **Start** button, select **Settings**, and select **Control Panel**.

2. Double-click the **Network** icon.

3. Click **Client for NetWare Networks** and click the **Properties** button.

4. Make sure the correct preferred server is listed in the Preferred Server box. If you're not sure what your preferred server is, contact your network administrator. If the correct server is not listed in the box, type in the correct one.

5. Click **OK**; then click **OK** again to close the dialog box.

If the server was not correct and you corrected it, try restarting Windows to see if you can log on. If you still can't log on or the server listed in the Preferred Server box was correct, contact your network administrator for assistance.

92 I can only see my computer in the Network Neighborhood.

When you open Network Neighborhood, you only see computers that are in your *workgroup* (a group of computers you are likely to share information with). If you are unsure which workgroup you should be in, contact your network administrator. Follow these steps to tell Windows which workgroup you should be in:

1. Click on the **Start** button, select **Settings**, and select **Control Panel**.

2. Double-click the **Network** icon.

3. Click the **Identification** tab.

4. Type a name for your computer in the Computer name box.

5. Type your workgroup name in the Workgroup box.

6. If you want to, you can type a description in the Computer description box.

7. Click **OK** to close the dialog box.

93 When I try to connect to a computer using Dial-Up Networking, the remote computer hangs up right after it answers.

There could be a problem with your configuration. Follow these steps to check it out:

1. From the **Start** menu, select **Programs**, select **Accessories**, and select **Dial-Up Networking**.

2. Select the computer you are trying to make a connection to, open the **File** menu, and choose **Properties**.

3. Click the **Configure** button and click the **Options** tab.

4. Check the **Bring up terminal window after dialing** check box.

If the check box in step 4 was not checked, click **OK** to close the dialog box and try to make the connection again. If you have the same problem, or if the check box in step 4 was already checked, make sure you are typing the correct password. If you still cannot connect, contact the operator of the remote computer and make sure you have the appropriate access and your password has not expired.

Miscellaneous Problems

Problem	Quick Fix Number	Page
Application will not run from shortcut	100	565
Auto hide needs to be turned off	97	564
Bar at bottom of screen is missing	97	564
Date is incorrect	96	563
Desktop settings cannot be set for multiple users	98	564
Application needs to be **maximized**	94	562
Need **Military time** format	95	563
Need to **move taskbar**	94	562
Forgot windows **password**	99	565
Need to reset **password**	99	565
Need to use **Quick View**	101	566
Shortcut can't find application	100	565
Shortcut does not work	100	565
Can't find the **taskbar**	97	564
Taskbar covers application	94	562
Taskbar keeps disappearing	97	564
Time is in incorrect format	95	563
Time is incorrect	96	563
User profiles not set correctly	98	564
Need to **view contents of file**	101	566

94   The taskbar is covering up part of my application.

The taskbar is a great addition to your desktop, but it doesn't do you much good if it covers up key information. It's easy to remedy this situation. You can simply click the **Maximize** button in the application in which you are working so the bottom edge of the application is just above the top of the taskbar, or you can move the taskbar to a different position.

Windows 95 lets you place the taskbar on any of the four edges of the screen. To move the taskbar, just click anywhere on it and, while you are holding down the left mouse button, drag it to the desired edge. When you release the mouse button, the taskbar moves to its new location. Another option is to Auto hide the taskbar. When you turn on Auto hide, Windows reduces the taskbar to a thin line when you are not using it. Just point to the thin line to bring back the taskbar. Follow these steps to enable Auto hide:

1. Click on the **Start** button, select **Settings**, and select **Taskbar**.

2. In the Taskbar Properties dialog box, click the **Taskbar Options** tab.

3. Click on the **Auto hide** check box.

4. Click **OK** to close the dialog box.

95 The time on the taskbar is in standard format. How can I change it to military format?

The procedure used here will change the time format in all your Windows applications. To change the time format, follow these steps:

1. Click on the **Start** button, select **Settings**, and select **Control Panel**.

2. Double-click the **Regional Settings** icon.

3. Click the **Time** tab.

4. Open the **Time style** drop-down list to see your choices.

5. Choose the style you prefer. A style with a capital "H" is in military format. Choose a style with a lowercase "h" to display the time in regular format.

6. Click **OK** to close the dialog box.

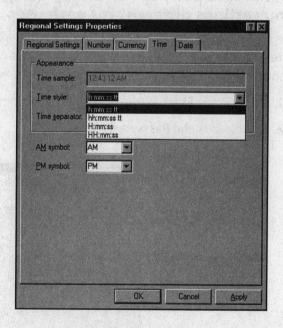

96 The date and time on the taskbar are incorrect. How can I change them?

It is easy to change the date and time if the time appears on the taskbar. Simply double-click the time on the taskbar to bring up the Date/Time Properties dialog box. If the time does not appear on the taskbar, follow these steps to change the date and time:

1. Click on the **Start** button, select **Settings**, and select **Control Panel**.

2. Double-click the **Date/Time** icon.

3. Click the **Date & Time** tab and change the date and the time as necessary. You also can change the time zone by clicking on the **Time Zone** tab.

4. Click **OK** to close the dialog box.

97 The taskbar keeps disappearing.

Your taskbar is set to Auto hide. This reduces the taskbar to a thin line when you are not using it and gives you more room on your desktop. When you need to use the taskbar, point to the thin line at the bottom of the screen. The taskbar reappears. If you don't like the Auto hide feature, follow these steps to turn it off:

1. Click on the **Start** button, select **Settings**, and select **Taskbar**.

2. Click the **Taskbar Options** tab.

3. Uncheck the **Auto hide** check box.

4. Click the **OK** button to close the dialog box.

98 I have multiple users set up on my computer, but I can't make the desktop settings different for each user.

The multiple user option is a great thing when more than one person uses your computer. It enables each user to customize his or her own desktop and even have different menus on the Start menu. To make these options available, follow these steps:

1. Click on the **Start** button, select **Settings**, and select **Control Panel**.

2. Double-click the **Passwords** icon.

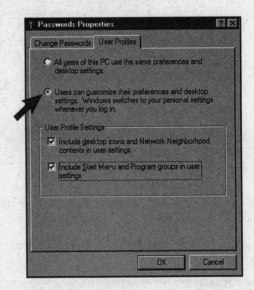

3. Click the **User Profiles** tab.

4. Click the **Users can customize their preferences** option button.

5. Under **User Profile Settings**, check the check boxes that you want to enable.

- **Include desktop icons**   Includes the desktop icons and Network Neighborhood contents in each user's profile.

- **Include Start menu and Program groups**   Allows each user to set his own start menu and program groups.

If you leave both of these unchecked, only the desktop preferences (desktop colors, mouse settings, and so on) are different.

99 I forgot my password to log in to Windows. What do I do now?

If you are on a network and you use your network password to log on to Windows 95, you need to have your network administrator reset your password. If you use a Windows 95 password instead of a network password to log on, you can reset your password, but you lose all of the custom desktop settings you had under the other account. To reset your password, follow these steps:

1. At the Welcome to Windows login screen, press **Esc** to bypass the login procedure.

2. Click on the **Start** button, select **Find**, and select **Files or Folders**.

3. In the Named box, type ***.pwl**.

4. Click the **Find Now** button.

5. In the Find window, a list of files appears corresponding to the user accounts you have set up. For example, if your username is MYNAME, there is a file called MYNAME.PWL. Click this file and press the **Delete** key to delete the password list for this username.

The next time you log on to Windows, type your username in the **Username** box and type in a password in the **Password** box. You are logged on as a new user.

100 I tried to run a program from a shortcut I created, but Windows told me that it couldn't find the program.

You have probably moved the program to a different folder or renamed the folder that contains the program. Check your shortcut to see which folder Windows expects the program to be in by following these steps:

1. From My Computer or Windows Explorer, click the shortcut icon that you are trying to run.

2. Open the **File** menu and choose **Properties**.

The next steps are different depending on whether the shortcut is to a Windows program or a DOS program.

For a DOS shortcut:

3. Select the **Program** tab.

4. Check the contents of the **Cmd** line box.

For a Windows shortcut:

3. Select the **Shortcut** tab.

4. Check the contents of the **Target** box.

The contents of the boxes show you the path and file name of the program that the shortcut expects to run. Use My Computer or Explorer to see if the program actually exists in the folder that is shown in step 4. If the program does not exist in that location, type in the correct path and file name in the box. If you can't find the correct, folder, try clicking the **Find Target** button. Windows will attempt to find the program.

5. Click **OK**.

101 I only want to look at the contents of a file. Is there any way to view it without opening the application?

Windows 95 includes an application called Quick View that shows you the contents of a file without taking the time to open the application that created the file. For example, maybe you want to check a couple of numbers on an Excel spreadsheet, but you don't want to take the time to open Excel. With Quick View, you can view several different file types.

Follow these steps to view a file with Quick View:

1. In My Computer or Explorer, click the file you want to view.

2. Open the **File** menu and choose **Quick View** (or right-click the file and select **Quick View** from the shortcut menu).

3. Quick View opens, displaying the contents of your file. If you decide that you want to edit the file, open the **File** menu in Quick View and choose **Open File for Editing**.

PART 4

Handy References...

n this part, you will find everything you need to be able to use Windows 95 without stopping every five minutes to check something in Help. And instead of confusing technical talk, you'll find easy-to-understand lists, tables, and other handy references for such topics as how to use the keyboard instead of the mouse and what those icons in Explorer are trying to tell you. You even get a road map for finding where most common items in Windows 95 are located, and you'll find some things that aren't in the Help system.

This part covers the following topics:

What You Will Find in This Part

Handy References

Windows 95 Reference Tables

Keyboard Commands Used Only at Startup

Action	Keypress
Start the computer with your old DOS, if you have dual boot	F4
Bypass all startup commands and start at a DOS prompt	F5
Display a menu of startup options	F8

General Keyboard Alternatives

Action	Keypress
Get help	F1
Display the Start menu	Ctrl+Esc
Switch to the next open window	Alt+Esc
Switch the active window on the taskbar	Alt+Tab
Close a program	Alt+F4
Browse the menu bar	Ctrl+F10
Open the Control menu	Alt+Spacebar
Stop the CD from playing	Shift (while inserting an audio CD)
Capture screen to Clipboard	Print Screen
Capture window to Clipboard	Ctrl+Print Screen

(continues)

General Keyboard Alternatives   Continued

Action	Keypress
Copy an object	Ctrl+drag the object
Move an object	Shift+drag the object
Create a shortcut	Ctrl+Shift+drag the object
Rename an object	F2
Find an object	F3
Change an object's properties	Alt+Enter
Move forward from tab to tab in a dialog box	Ctrl+Tab
Move backward from tab to tab in a dialog box	Ctrl+Shift+Tab
Move forward through options in a dialog box	Tab
Move backward through options in a dialog box	Shift+Tab
Display shortcut menu for object	Shift+F10

Keyboard Alternatives to Use in Programs

Action	Keypress
Open a menu	Alt+underlined letter
Select a command	Underlined letter
Select text	Shift+arrow keys
Copy text	Ctrl+C
Cut text	Ctrl+X
Paste text	Ctrl+V
Undo a change	Ctrl+Z
Switch between DOS windowed and full-screen sessions	Alt+Enter
Close a program	Alt+F4
Open the active drop-down list in Save or Open dialog box	F4
Refresh the Look in list in Save or Open dialog box	F5
Move one folder up in Save or Open dialog box	Backspace
Move to beginning of a line	Home
Move to end of a line	End

Action	Keypress
Move up one line	Up arrow
Move down one line	Down arrow
Move down one screenful	Page Down
Move up one screenful	Page Up
Move to beginning of document	Ctrl+Home
Move to end of document	Ctrl+End

Keyboard Alternatives to Use in Explorer and My Computer

Action	Keypress
Switch panes	F6
Expand a folder	Right arrow
Collapse a folder	Left arrow
Expand a folder all levels	* on the numeric keypad
Go to a particular folder	Ctrl+G
Move up one folder level in folder list	Backspace
Select all files or folders within this folder	Ctrl+A
Refresh a window	F5

Comparison Between Windows 3.1 and Windows 95

Windows 3.1 Feature	Windows 95 Equivalent
Program Manager	Start menu
Task List	Taskbar
Program groups	Programs menu
File Manager	Explorer or My Computer
Search command	Find command (works throughout Windows 95, not just in Explorer)
Print Manager	Printers Folder/Print Queue
Start Up folder	Start Up menu

(continues)

Comparison Between Windows 3.1 and Windows 95   Continued

Windows 3.1 Feature	Windows 95 Equivalent
Run command	Same command, but it remembers previous Run commands
Write	WordPad
Paintbrush	Paint
PIF Editor	Properties dialog box
Terminal	HyperTerminal
Delete Tracker or Delete Sentry	Recycle Bin
Undelete	Recycle Bin
Exit	Shut Down option
Scroll box shows relative location in document	Scroll box shows relative location, and relative portion of total document that you're currently viewing
Close a window with the Control-menu box	Close a window with the Close button
INTERLNK and INTERSVR	Direct Cable Connection
POWER	Control Panel, System Icon, Device Manager tab
DEFRAG	Disk Defragmenter
Cardfile	Address Book
Clock	Taskbar displays the time

Windows 95 Features with No Windows 3.1 Equivalent

Feature	Description
Long file names	As many as 254 characters, including spaces
Properties	Sets properties for all objects, including files, folders, and programs
Shortcut menus	Menus that pop up to provide convenient access to commands
Drag-and-drop	Drags icons into documents to embed data, on top of printer to print, or on top of Recycle Bin to delete (drag-and-drop may have worked with some programs in Windows 3.1, but now this feature is standardized).

Feature	Description
Right-click-and-drag	Displays shortcut menu for quick copying, moving, and so on
One-click menus	Clicks once to open a menu, then drags to open additional menus
Font Viewer	Previews fonts before you install them
Network Neighborhood	An Explorer-like program for viewing resources (files, programs, and printers) available through your network
Exchange or Windows Messaging (Inbox)	Central clearinghouse for all e-mail and faxes
What's This button	Describes options in dialog box without jumping to Help
Password Keys	Prevents unauthorized access to Windows, your network, and shared resources
User Profiles	Makes it easier to customize Windows for multiple users of the same PC
Documents menu	For quickly opening recently used documents
Send To command	Available in Explorer and My Computer, provides quick copy, e-mail, and fax options
Quick View	Available in Explorer or My Computer, enables you to preview a file before you open it
File Associate	While file association was available in Windows 3.1, with Windows 95, you can associate more than one command with an extension; also provides Open With dialog box for unassociated files.
Plug and Play	Walks you through the process of installing a new device (such as a sound card) under Windows
Briefcase	Enables you to easily keep the files on your laptop and your desktop computers in synch
Shortcut	Icon that provides quick access to a program, file, or folder located somewhere else

(continues)

Windows 95 Features with No Windows 3.1 Equivalent   Continued

Feature	Description
Microsoft Network	Fee-for-use online service similar to CompuServe, PRODIGY, or America Online
Dial Up Networking	Enables you to connect to a network or the Internet through a modem
VDM (Virtual DOS Machine)	DOS programs are run in their own segment of memory
Phone Dialer	Dials your phone for you
Microsoft Fax	Composes and sends a fax
FreeCell	Card game
Hearts	Card game
CD Player	Plays audio CDs
Volume Control	Sets volume control for all inputs and outputs
Inbox Repair Tool	Repairs damaged Exchange folders
NetWatcher	Monitors how your shared folders or printer are being used
System Monitor	Monitors system and network resources
System Resource Meter	Monitors Windows 95 resources
Accessibility Options	Provides easier access for the disabled
NetMeeting (**ac**)	Enables real-time voice and data communication over your intranet or the Internet
Internet Explorer (**abc**)	Browses the World Wide Web
Internet Mail (**ac**)	Manages your Internet mail
Internet News (**ac**)	Reads Internet newsgroups
ActiveMovie Controls (**ac**)	Plays ActiveMovie video files
Compression Agent (**ab**)	Optimizes DriveSpace 3's space usage
Imaging (**ac**)	Enables image manipulation and scanner operation
System Agent (**b**)	Schedules routine tasks to happen automatically at specified times

a Comes with new PCs running Windows 95 OSR2 version.
b Comes with the Windows 95 Plus Pack.
c Can be downloaded for free from Microsoft's Web site if your version of Windows 95 doesn't have it.

Windows 3.1 Features with No Windows 95 Equivalent

Feature or Program	Description
Microsoft Anti-Virus	Protected against computer viruses
Recorder	Recorded macros for automating tasks
Calendar	Simple day planner

Explorer's Icons

Icon	Description
	Generic Application icon
	Generic Windows file icon (used for hidden file, animated cursor, icons, application extensions, .BAK files, screen savers, downloadable files within MSN, and so on)
	Folder (directory)
	Hard disk drive
	Floppy disk drive
	CD-ROM drive
	Backup set for MS Backup
	File set for MS Backup
	Batch file
	Bitmap
	Briefcase file
	CD audio track
	Configuration settings
	Control Panel program or Dynamic Link Library file
	Fax cover page
	Fax
	Bitmap font file

(continues)

Explorer's Icons   Continued

Icon	Description
	Help file
	HyperTerminal file
	Inbox
	Mail message
	MIDI instrument definition file
	MIDI sequence
	MSN phone book
	MSN search
	Program group
	Registration file
	Saved search
	Scrap file
	Shortcut
	Text document
	TrueType font file
	Video clip
	Wave sound
	Write document (for WordPad)

Windows 95 DOS Commands

Follow these guidelines when entering a DOS command:

- Type the command and press **Enter** to execute it.

- Capitalization is not something to worry about. Use caps or don't; it doesn't matter to DOS.

- A DOS command is made up of three parts:

  The command itself   For example, the word DIR.

  Applicable parameters   *Parameters* tell the command which files, directories, or drives to work with. For example, you can type **DIR HARD2FND.DOC** after the search command to have DOS search for and list that specific file. You can type **DIR A:** to have DOS list only the files on drive A.

  Applicable switches   *Switches* are options you can use with a command. Switches are always preceded by a forward slash (/). For example, the DIR command has a switch (/P for pause) that lists enough files to fill a screen, and then pauses until you're ready to see more files.

- Separate the parts of a DOS command with single spaces.

Command	Description
ATTRIB	Sets a file's properties
CD	Changes directory
CHKDSK	Checks hard disk for problems
CLS	Clears the screen
COPY	Copies files
DATE	Changes the system date
DEL	Deletes a file
DELTREE	Deletes a directory
DIR	Displays the contents of a directory
DISKCOPY	Copies a diskette
DOSKEY	Quickly recalls previous DOS commands
DRVSPACE	Compresses a hard disk
EDIT	Edits text files
EXIT	Returns to Windows 95

(continues)

Windows 95 DOS Commands   Continued

Command	Description
EXTRACT	Decompresses Microsoft files from a diskette
FC	Compares two files
FDISK	Configures a hard disk for use
FIND	Searches for text within a file
FORMAT	Prepares a disk for use
HELP	Accesses the DOS Help system
KEYB	Configures the keyboard for a specific language
LABEL	Adds an electronic label to a disk
MD	Makes a directory
MEM	Displays memory usage
MODE	Sets the display mode
MORE	Controls the display of a command result
MOVE	Moves files; renames directories
PROMPT	Changes the DOS prompt
RD	Removes a directory
REN	Renames a file
SCANDISK	Scans hard disk for errors
SHARE	Enables file sharing for a network
SORT	Sorts the contents of a text file
START	Runs a program from the DOS prompt
SYS	Copies the system files to a disk
TIME	Changes the system time
TREE	Displays the directory tree
TYPE	Displays the contents of a file
UNFORMAT	Restores an accidentally formatted disk
XCOPY	Copies entire directories with subdirectories and files
XCOPY32	Copies entire directories with subdirectories and files (32-bit version of XCOPY)
VOL	Displays electronic disk label

Road Map to Common Tasks

Task	Where to Go to Perform the Task
Activate/Deactivate Screen Saver	Start menu > Settings > Control Panel > Display > Screen Saver tab
Add a new printer	Start menu > Settings > Printers > Add Printer
Add other new hardware	Start menu > Settings > Control Panel > Add New Hardware icon
Add folder to desktop	Desktop > Right-click > New > Folder
Add a command to the Start menu	Start menu > Settings > Taskbar > Start Menu Programs tab > Add
Add Windows 95 features	Start menu > Settings > Control Panel > Add/Remove Programs > Windows Setup tab
Adjust the keyboard rate	Start menu > Settings > Control Panel > Keyboard > Speed tab
Adjust mouse tracking	Start menu > Settings > Control Panel > Mouse > Buttons tab
Arrange icons	Right-click > Arrange icons
Associate a sound with an event	Start menu > Settings > Control Panel > Sounds
Change date or time	Double-click date display on taskbar
Change password	Start menu > Settings > Control Panel > Passwords > Change Passwords tab
Change screen resolution	Start menu > Settings > Control Panel > Display > Settings tab
Change the wallpaper	Start menu > Settings > Control Panel > Display > Background tab
Change window colors	Start menu > Settings > Control Panel > Display > Appearance tab
Change the volume	Click on the Volume control on taskbar
Copy, move, or delete a file	My Computer or Explorer
Create or remove a folder	My Computer or Explorer
Create a Windows 95 boot disk	Start menu > Settings > Control Panel > Add/Remove Programs > Startup Disk tab > Create Disk

(continues)

Road Map to Common Tasks   Continued

Task	Where to Go to Perform the Task
Display volume control on taskbar	Start menu > Settings > Control Panel > Multimedia > Audio tab
Enable file and printer sharing	Start menu > Settings > Control Panel > Network > Configuration tab
Exit Windows 95	Start menu > Shut Down
Locate a file or a folder	Start menu > Find > Files or Folders
Locate a computer on a network	Start menu > Find > Computer
Install a font	Start menu > Settings > Control Panel > Fonts icon
Make a mouse pointer visible on a laptop	Start menu > Settings > Control Panel > Mouse > Motion tab
Receive a fax	Double-click Inbox > Double-click fax modem icon on taskbar
Receive e-mail from online service	Double-click Inbox > Tools > Remote Mail
Remove a program	Start menu > Settings > Control Panel > Add/Remove Programs > Install/Uninstall > Add/Remove
Restart the PC	Start menu > Shut Down
Send an e-mail	Double-click Inbox > Compose > New Message > Send
Send a fax Compose New Fax	Start menu > Programs > Accessories > Fax >
Start My Computer	Double-click on the My Computer icon
Start Explorer	Start menu > Programs > Windows Explorer
Start a program	Start menu > Programs

Index